PREVENTIVE DETENTION:
ASKING THE FUNDAMENTAL QUESTIONS

PREVENTIVE DETENTION: ASKING THE FUNDAMENTAL QUESTIONS

Patrick KEYZER (ed.)

intersentia

Cambridge – Antwerp – Portland

Intersentia Publishing Ltd.
Trinity House | Cambridge Business Park | Cowley Road
Cambridge | CB4 0WZ | United Kingdom
tel.: +44 1223 393 753 | email: mail@intersentia.co.uk

Distribution for the UK:
NBN International
Airport Business Centre,
10 Thornbury Road
Plymouth, PL6 7PP
United Kingdom
Tel.: +44 1752 202 301
Fax: + 44 1752 202 331
Email: orders@nbninternational.com

*Distribution for the USA
and Canada:*
International Specialized Book
Services
920 NE 58th Ave Suite 300
Portland, OR 97213
USA
Tel.: +1 800 944 6190 (toll free)
Email: info@isbs.com

Distribution for Austria:
Neuer Wissenschaftlicher Verlag
Argentinierstraße 42/6
1040 Wien
Austria
Tel.: +43 1 535 61 03 24
Email: office@nwv.at

Distribution for other countries:
Intersentia Publishing nv
Groenstraat 31
2640 Mortsel
Belgium
Tel.: +32 3 680 15 50
Email: mail@intersentia.be

Preventive Detention: Asking the Fundamental Questions
Patrick Keyzer (ed.)

© 2013 Intersentia
    Cambridge – Antwerp – Portland
    www.intersentia.com | www.intersentia.co.uk

Cover illustration: Alfred Dreyfus dans sa prison, Royer Lionel (1852-1926)
© BnF, Dist. RMN-Grand Palais / image BnF

ISBN 978-1-78068-117-7
D/2013/7849/40
NUR 824

British Library Cataloguing in Publication Data. A catalogue record for this book
is available from the British Library.

CONTENTS

PREVENTIVE DETENTION: ASKING THE FUNDAMENTAL QUESTIONS

Patrick KEYZER

If a person poses a risk to society, why not lock them up before they do something bad? If they haven't been rehabilitated in prison, why let them out? These questions have vexed governments throughout the world. 'Preventive detention' is now widely used for the management of 'dangerous people', particularly terror suspects and sex offenders. The chapters of this volume examine preventive detention jurisprudence in Australia, Germany, New Zealand, the United Kingdom and the United States and address the fundamental questions that need to be asked and answered when governments consider whether to introduce these regimes:

– Can preventive detention regimes be consistent with human rights?
– Are our risk assessment methodologies sufficiently reliable to justify preventive detention orders?
– Are there policy alternatives to preventive detention?

In their important chapter in this volume, Arlie Loughnan and Sabine Selchow have challenged preventive detention scholars to go further: to go '*beyond* traditional legal concerns and a concern for effectiveness, to ask what preventive detention does to society' (emphasis added). I briefly address that question at the end of this chapter, which defines key concepts and themes used in this collection.

1. WHAT IS 'PREVENTIVE DETENTION'?

At the outset it is important to clear aside some confusion around the terminology of 'preventive detention' (or 'preventative detention' as it is sometimes called). Four varieties of preventive detention are discussed in this volume:

1. preventive detention in prison, ordered as part of a prison sentence;[1]
2. preventive detention in secure facilities that are not prisons;[2]
3. preventive detention that is said to be non-punitive and for therapeutic objectives, but nevertheless takes place in a prison;[3] and
4. control orders and supervision orders that incorporate detention and that have a preventive objective. [4]

Each of these varieties raise distinct human rights issues. They can be dealt with in turn.

2. CAN PREVENTIVE DETENTION REGIMES BE CONSISTENT WITH HUMAN RIGHTS?

2.1. PREVENTIVE DETENTION IN PRISON, ORDERED AS PART OF A PRISON SENTENCE

All prison sentences are preventive, in a sense. While people are in prison they are prevented from committing crimes in the community.[5] Courts have also identified the prevention of risk to the community as a rationale for sentencing, particularly (though not exclusively) in cases involving recidivists.[6]

One variety of sentencing that has a heightened preventive rationale is indefinite or indeterminate sentencing.[7] Indefinite sentences contemplate that after a convicted offender serves a nominal sentence, typically calculated by reference to proportionality principles, they will remain in prison for a further, indefinite period, subject to regular reviews, at which time they will be assessed for suitability for release on the basis of a risk assessment and adjudication.[8] The punitive and

---

[1] These regimes are explored in this volume by Vivien Stern, Kris Gledhill and Warren Brookbanks.
[2] These regimes are explored in this volume by Kris Gledhill.
[3] These regimes are explored in this volume by Chris Slobogin, Warren Brookbanks, and Brendan Gogarty, Benedict Bartl and Patrick Keyzer.
[4] Terrorist 'control orders' are discussed by Vivien Stern and Rebecca Welsh.
[5] People can commit crimes in prison, and are likely to be exposed to criminal activity in prison, but the human rights issues engaged by imprisonment, while important, are outside the scope of this book.
[6] See eg. *Veen v The Queen (No 2)* (1988) 164 CLR 465 (High Court of Australia).
[7] Today, section 65 of the *Sentencing Act 1995* (NT), section 163 of the *Penalties and Sentences Act 1992* (Qld), sections 22 and 23 of the *Criminal Law (Sentencing) Act 1988* (SA), section 19 of the *Sentencing Act 1997* (Tas), section 18A of the *Sentencing Act 1991* (Vic) and section 98 of the *Sentencing Act 1995* (WA) all allow for an order for indefinite detention to be passed at the time of sentence.
[8] These regimes are explored in this volume by Vivien Stern, Kris Gledhill and Warren Brookbanks.

preventive components of the sentence are joined in a single order of the court that is made when an offender is convicted of a crime.

Mandatory sentencing can be argued to have a preventive character. Mandatory sentencing regimes are typically activated by recidivism. 'Three strikes' legislation is the archetypal example. However, any preventive rationale for mandatory sentencing is muted when the offences that trigger the mandatory sentencing are not serious.

If (ordinary, indefinite or mandatory) sentencing regimes authorise sentencing that is prospective and properly administered, they are less likely to offend constitutional or human rights principles.[9] That 'if' is a pregnant 'if'.[10] Vivien Stern draws attention to the decision of the United Kingdom Court of Appeal that indefinite sentencing will offend the principle against arbitrary detention in circumstances where rehabilitation programs said to be a necessary predicate to release are not provided.[11]

2.2. PREVENTIVE DETENTION IN SECURE FACILITIES THAT ARE NOT PRISONS

A second variety of preventive detention regime contemplates detention in a secure facility for a non-punitive purpose. The US regimes for the post-sentence management of sex offenders, considered by Chris Slobogin in this volume, are the archetypal example. Regimes for the management of people with mental health issues or infectious diseases and regimes for the management of enemy combatants and, in Australia, asylum seekers, are other examples. The stated purpose of these varieties of preventive detention is that they minimise risk to the community; they do not have a punitive purpose, per se. The common criticisms of these preventive detention regimes are that:

– They are, in fact, punitive in effect because the detention is prison-like or highly restrictive[12] and/or because people are seldom released;[13]

---

9   Bernadette McSherry, Patrick Keyzer and Arie Freiberg, *Preventive Detention for 'Dangerous' Offenders in Australia: A Critical Analysis and Proposals Policy Development* (Criminology Research Council, 2006).
10   As Vivien Stern points out in her contribution to this volume.
11   *Secretary of State for Justice v Walker* [2008] EWCA Civ 30 [40].
12   H R Willis, 'Creeping by Moonlight: A Look at Civil Commitment Laws for Sexually Violent Predators Through the Lens of the Yellow Wallpaper' (2008) 15 *William and Mary Journal of Women and the Law* 161–88.
13   Bernadette McSherry and Patrick Keyzer, *Sex Offenders and Preventive Detention: Politics, Policy and Practice* (Federation Press, 2009) 56–63 and references there cited.

- They collapse the criminal standard of proof, replacing it with a civil standard that widens the net to cover people who could be released on licence;[14]
- They dilute standards of mental illness by allowing people to be detained for 'mental abnormality' or 'an utter lack of power to control sexual impulses' – standards for which the diagnostic criteria is unclear;[15]
- They are typically accompanied by the de-funding of community-based programs designed to minimise risk, so that the detention option becomes, practically, the only option available;[16]
- Courts have been unwilling to engage in judicial review of the actual conditions of detention; and[17]
- Courts have been unwilling to critically scrutinise the risk assessment tools and techniques used to justify detention orders.[18]

For any or all of these reasons, preventive detentions regimes can breach human rights.

It is conceivable that preventive detention, if ordered prospectively and administered in a non-punitive environment, can be consistent with constitutional or human rights principles. However, this cannot be so when the venue for 'detention' is prison.

2.3.   PREVENTIVE DETENTION IN PRISON

The third variety of preventive detention identified above is said to be non-punitive and directed to therapeutic or treatment objectives, but it is, nevertheless, specifically ordered to take place in a prison. This variety of 'preventive detention' is used to re-incarcerate serious sex offenders in the Australian states of Queensland, Western Australia, New South Wales and Victoria.[19]

The first such regime, Queensland's *Dangerous Prisoners (Sexual Offenders) Act 2003*, was found to be constitutionally valid in 2004.[20] This opened the door for

---

[14]   Ibid 107–8.

[15]   Ibid 27–8.

[16]   Patrick Keyzer and Ian Coyle, 'Reintegrating Sex Offenders into the Community – Queensland's Proposed Reforms' (2009) 34 *Alternative Law Journal* 27–31.

[17]   Patrick Keyzer, 'Preserving Due Process or Warehousing the Undesirables: To What End The Separation of Judicial Power of the Commonwealth?' (2008) 30 *Sydney Law Review* 101–14.

[18]   See the contribution of Ian Coyle and Robert Halon in this volume.

[19]   *Dangerous Prisoners (Sexual Offenders) Act 2003* (Qld); *Dangerous Prisoners Act 2005* (WA); *Crimes (Serious Sex Offenders) Act 2006* (NSW); *Serious Sex Offenders (Detention and Supervision) Act 2009* (Vic).

[20]   *Fardon v A-G (Qld)* (2004) 223 CLR 575; see Patrick Keyzer, Cathy Pereira and Stephen Southwood, 'Pre-emptive Imprisonment for *Dangerousness* in Queensland under the

Western Australia (2005), New South Wales and Victoria (2009) to follow suit.[21] As Rebecca Welsh points out in her analysis of Australia's anti-terror 'control order' system, Australia's capacity to use preventive detention is 'largely unconstrained' because Australia has no bill or charter of rights.

The Queensland and New South Wales regimes were found to have violated the *International Covenant on Civil and Political Rights* in 2010 in the decisions of *Fardon v Australia* and *Tillman v Australia*, respectively.[22] The decisions of the United Nations Human Rights Committee (UNHRC) in *Fardon* and *Tillman* confirmed that post-sentence preventive detention in prison is arbitrary detention contrary to Article 9 of the *Covenant* (because it was not the least restrictive alternative available), contrary to standards of due process under Article 14 (because imprisonment is penal in character and can only be ordered after a person has been convicted of a crime), and contrary to Article 15 (because the effect of the legislation was to retroactively inflict further punishment).[23] An argument that the regimes effected double punishment contrary to Article 14(7) of the *Covenant* was not considered.[24] The UNHRC also pointed to Australia's obligation under Article 10(3) of the *Covenant* to enact policies to ensure the rehabilitation of the prisoners.[25]

Australia has declined to enact legislation overriding the legislation in the four states that now have post-sentence prison-based preventive detention regimes.[26] At the time of writing, the Northern Territory has indicated that it intends to

---

Dangerous Prisoners (Sexual Offenders) Act 2003: The Constitutional Issues' (2004) 11 *Psychiatry, Psychology and Law* 244.

[21]   Bernadette McSherry, 'Indefinite and Preventive Detention Legislation: From Caution to an Open Door' (2005) *Criminal Law Journal* 94–110.

[22]   Human Rights Committee, *Communication No 1629/2007*, UN Doc CCPR/C/98/D/1629/2007 (10 May 2010) ('*Fardon v Australia*') <http://www.unhcr.org/refworld/docid/4c19e97b2.html>; Human Rights Committee, *Communication No 1635/2007*, UN Doc CCPR/C/98/D/1635/2007 (10 May 2010) ('*Tillman v Australia*').

[23]   Patrick Keyzer, 'The "Preventive Detention" of Serious Sex Offenders: Further Consideration of the International Human Rights Dimensions' (2009) 16(2) *Psychology, Psychiatry and Law* 262–70.

[24]   This argument is set out in Patrick Keyzer and Sam Blay, 'Double Punishment? Preventive Detention Schemes under Australian Legislation and Their Consistency with International Law: The Fardon Communication' (2006) 7 *Melbourne Journal of International Law* 407.

[25]   Patrick Keyzer, 'The United Nations Human Rights Committee's Views about the Legitimate Parameters of the Preventive Detention of Serious Sex Offenders' (2010) 34 *Criminal Law Journal* 283–91, 289; see also Patrick Keyzer, 'What Are the Legitimate Parameters for the Preventive Detention of Serious Sex Offenders?' in Bernadette McSherry and Patrick Keyzer (eds), *Dangerous People* (Routledge, 2011).

[26]   On 9 November 2012, the United Nations Human Rights Committee published a 'List of issues prior to the submission of the sixth periodic report of Australia (CCPR/C/AUS/6), adopted by the Committee at its 106th session (15 October–2 November 2012)', question 18 of which was: 'What steps have been taken to review the system of preventive detention of convicted prisoners beyond the length of their sentences, on grounds of predicted dangerousness, in order to repeal it or to reform it in a manner consistent with the Covenant?' The Australian

introduce such a regime.[27] In New South Wales, there are plans to introduce this regime for violent offenders who are not sex offenders.[28]

2.4. CONTROL ORDERS AND SUPERVISION ORDERS THAT INCORPORATE DETENTION AND THAT HAVE A PREVENTIVE OBJECTIVE

A fourth variety of preventive detention that emerged following the terror attacks of a decade ago are 'control orders', considered in this volume by Vivien Stern and Rebecca Welsh. These orders are designed to restrict the movement and freedom of association of people suspected of participating in planning to commit terror attacks. They are putatively preventive: designed to stop people from associating with others with whom they may plan crime.[29] However, while these orders can incorporate curfews, they arguably do not inflict a punitive form of detention.

Another example of control order is the supervision order made under the dangerous prisoner legislation in the Australian states, which, like terror control orders, impose locational restrictions and can impose curfews. These regimes are controversial if they are employed in the post-sentence context, and the 'community supervision' takes place in prison-like conditions.[30]

2.5. ANALYSIS

Detention for what a person might do in the future is, by its very essence, predictive of what may or may not occur in the future.[31] Since there exists the possibility that a predicted offence may never occur, which renders any consideration of the proportionality of the response meaningless, preventive detention is always an extraordinary step to take.[32] Chris Slobogin, in his contribution to this

---

Government had previously indicated, in October 2011, that it rejected the findings of the Committee.

[27] On 11 October 2012, in a press release, Northern Territory Attorney General John Elferink re-affirmed his commitment to reintroduce the *Dangerous Prisoners (Sexual Offenders) Restraint Bill* into the NT Legislative Assembly.

[28] As Arlie Loughnan and Sabine Selchow point out in their contribution to this volume.

[29] A number of the Australian States have also implemented 'criminal organisations' legislation designed to criminalise 'bikie gangs', which are anti-consorting legislation under a different guise: see further Alex Steel, 'Consorting in New South Wales: Substantive Offence or Police Power?' (2003) 26 University of New South *Wales Law Journal* 567–602. For a critical analysis of the Queensland *Criminal Organisations Bill 2009*, along with a response from then Attorney-General Cameron Dick MP, see Scrutiny of Legislation Committee, Queensland Parliament, *Legislation Alert*, No 11 of 2009, 10 November 2009, 11–30.

[30] Keyzer and Coyle, above n 16.

[31] Keyzer and Blay, above n 24.

[32] Ibid.

volume, develops a theory that attempts to account for these extraordinary cases. Analysing the decisions relating to the post-sentence preventive detention of serious sex offenders delivered by the constitutional courts of the United States (*Kansas v Hendricks*), Germany (*M*) and Australia (*Fardon v Attorney-General (Queensland)*), Slobogin settles on the fulcrum of 'undeterrability':

> The better rationale for these types of preventive detention … is that the criminal justice system must be the response to antisocial behavior unless it *cannot work as a preventive mechanism*. Consider the three categories of people just described. Individuals who are so mentally ill that they misperceive reality will not be concerned about criminal punishment … Similarly, assuming no reasonable medical alternative to confinement, people who suffer from highly contagious and deadly diseases cannot prevent infection as they go about their daily lives no matter how hard they try; thus, criminal punishment cannot do so either. Soldiers who are under orders to kill or be killed or terrorists who have no compunction about dying in their efforts to assassinate others are also unaffected by the prospect of criminal penalties, even when serious. In other words, the danger represented by these people is *undeterrable* through the criminal sanction; even if the proverbial cop were standing near their elbow, they would harm others (including, perhaps, the cop).[33] The undeterrability rationale also clarifies that the state's interest in protecting its citizens, while always significant, nonetheless only outweighs the un-convicted individual's liberty interest sufficiently to permit non-criminal confinement when the criminal justice system can have no impact. In short, the undeterrability rationale better explains why many nonautonomous actors may be subject to long-term prevention detention – their undeterrability, not their lack of autonomy or their unconvictability – and also explains why some autonomous actors may be so detained.

Professor Slobogin goes on to say that, subject to strict conditions, post-sentence preventive detention of people who are seriously 'undeterrable' could be justified on similar grounds. The state would 'have to show that the individual is impervious to criminal sanction'. A candidate for this type of preventive detention would be likely to suffer from psychosis or psychopathy, but not necessarily. 'The absence of a psychotic disorder would not necessarily mean that post-sentence preventive detention is impermissible.' A person could be detained if they suffered a 'disorder of desire' or an 'utter lack of power to control their sexual impulses' or, perhaps, antisocial personality disorder.

The difficulty, of course, is this: when *is* a person undeterrable? What constitutes acceptable, cogent evidence of undeterrability (is this a synonym for

---

[33]   (Footnote in original) The 'policeman-at-the-elbow' test is one way in which the irresistible impulse prong of the insanity test has been operationalized in the United States. See Gary B Melton et al, Psychological *Evaluations for the Courts: A Handbook for Mental Health Professionals and Lawyers* (Guilford Press, 3rd ed, 2007) 216.

'dangerousness')? Traditionally, if a person had a serious mental illness and there was a risk that they might harm themself or others, that provided a justification for their involuntary detention and treatment. But there are no diagnostic criteria for undeterrability. Until there is, there is a substantial risk (which Slobogin recognises) that detention will be a disproportionate response to the risk.

3. ARE OUR RISK ASSESSMENT METHODOLOGIES SUFFICIENTLY ROBUST TO JUSTIFY PREVENTIVE DETENTION ORDERS?

Today, psychological or psychiatric expert evidence is pivotal in judicial decision-making in preventive detention regimes. This is so even in those regimes where a mental illness is not required to justify or authorise detention.

The dominant paradigm in the risk assessment field at present is actuarially-adjusted clinical judgment. Astrid Birgden explains:

> *Actuarial assessments* are based on empirical research and theories to develop a list of risk factors, empirically test them on various populations, and create a common set of questions applied to everyone and weighted to produce a score to categorise the person. *Structured clinical judgement* is a more comprehensive analysis of theoretically and empirically determined static and dynamic risk factors linked to re-offending with an overall opinion of re-offence risk provided rather than a probability estimate. It has been argued on the one hand that actuarial methods should completely replace clinical judgement[34] and on the other hand, that clinicians should be able to revise actuarial risk estimates on the basis of clinical judgement.[35]

While there is general consensus that actuarially-adjusted clinical judgment is the best available methodology for assessing risk, the psychometric instruments employed are experimental in nature, and, ironically, fraught with risk of error.[36] The ability to estimate the average risk for a group is not matched by any corresponding ability to predict which individuals are going to commit crimes in the future. Terence Campbell sums up the problem in the following statement:

---

[34] See, eg, Quinsey et al, *Violent Offenders: Assessing and Managing Risk* (American Psychological Association, 1998) (footnote in original).
[35] See, eg, R K Hanson, 'What Do We Know about Sex Offender Risk Assessment?' (1998) 4 Psychology, *Public Policy and Law* 50–72 (footnote in original).
[36] For a telling critique of the 'science' of contemporary approaches to risk prediction in this context see Terence Campbell, 'Sex Offenders and Actuarial Risk Assessments: Ethical Considerations' (2003) 21 *Behavioural Sciences and the Law* 269.

> [A]djusted actuarial assessments rely on (i) methods that are trivially correlated with recidivism (clinical judgment) (ii) to identify factors that bear a small correlation with recidivism, (iii) in order to adjust actuarial estimates that are moderately correlated with recidivism. This procedure obviously creates ample opportunities for error.[37]

In their detailed and erudite contribution to this volume, Ian Coyle and Bob Halon have taken one further step, arguing that actuarially-adjusted risk assessment techniques *cannot* be relied on to enable the assessment of risk to the evidentiary standard required by civil preventive detention regimes:

> The law guarantees that a decision will be made but it does not guarantee outcomes. Yet that is precisely what the law seeks to require of those engaging in the task of risk-analysis of dangerousness. It is time, once and for all, to acknowledge that estimates derived from actuarial tests cannot predict the future behaviour of individuals with anything approaching that implicit in the minimum legal standards of proof. Estimates of 'absolute' and relative accuracy in risk assessments derived from actuarial tests give the impression of scientific accuracy that is simply not warranted. It is arrant nonsense to assert otherwise.

In spite of this problem and in spite of recommendations to the contrary (as Kris Gledhill notes in his analysis of the UK regime), 'risk' remains the pivotal concept in contemporary post-sentence preventive detention regimes. Are we so anxious to respond to our fear of releasing serious offenders that we are prepared to accept experimental science without critical scrutiny? It 'remains worrying', David Cooke and Christine Michie have written,[38]

> that the significance of uncertainty in violence risk assessment based on actuarial risk assessment instruments is not widely understood. The illusion of certainty engendered by the presentation of a single estimate can have profound effects in everyday practice. If a judge is persuaded by such figures it may lead to sub-optimal action.

Imprisonment is, to say the least, a sub-optimal outcome for the prisoner. While it has been argued that many mental health professionals do admit their capacity to predict risk is limited,[39] all stakeholders in preventive detention systems need to be conscious of the limitations and ramifications of risk assessments. This is

---

[37]   Ibid 275.

[38]   David J Cooke and Christine Michie, 'Violence Risk Assessment: Challenging the Illusion of Certainty', in Bernadette McSherry and Patrick Keyzer (eds), *Dangerous People* (Routledge, 2011).

[39]   C C Mercado and J R P Ogloff, 'Risk and the Preventive Detention of Sex Offenders in Australia and the United States' (2006) 20 *International Journal of Law and Psychiatry* 49–59.

particularly important when a person who is subject to an adverse risk assessment is ordered to be detained in a punitive environment. In places where post-sentence preventive detention takes place in a prison, an abuse of human rights has taken place. This highlights the ethical obligation of expert witnesses to point to the limitations of risk prediction techniques in every case. At the very least, judges and counsel have an ethical responsibility to ensure that risk assessment evidence is carefully tested.

Unfortunately, as Kris Gledhill points out in his detailed review of the United Kingdom *Mental Health Act* and other risk-based sentencing options such as Indeterminate Sentences for Public Protection (IPPs), the judiciary have been 'singularly non-interventionist' when it comes to the assessment of the reliability of psychometric assessment tools.[40] This is so even though historical evidence (not to mention study after study) indicates that there is a poor correlation between predictions of future violent offending and violent offending:

> In *Baxstrom v Herold*,[41] detention in a prison hospital after the end of a sentence was found to be unconstitutional because the process followed (certification by a doctor) was not as stringent as that applicable to a person being detained from the community (jury trial); as such, there was differential treatment that breached the equal protection provisions of the Fourteenth Amendment to the United States Constitution.[42] As a result, many patients were transferred to civil mental hospitals and often then released;[43] this allowed research on whether the claims that they were dangerous to be borne out. The recidivism rate for violent offending was found to be 11 per cent (though it is to be noted that about a third of the patients remained detained in civil hospitals).[44] This poor correlation between predictions of future crime and recidivism provides reasons for caution about the ability to predict the future and base action on such predictions.

---

[40] See the contribution of Kris Gledhill in this volume.
[41] (1966) 383 US 107 (footnote in original).
[42] § 1: 'No state shall … deny to any persons within its jurisdiction the equal protection of the laws.' (footnote in original).
[43] (Footnote in original) Tony Maden, *Treating Violence* (Oxford University Press, 2007) 28: 'New York State realized that 966 other detained patients in their hospitals for the criminally insane could petition … on the same grounds and could expect to win. They gave in gracefully and ordered that all 967 patients should be transferred to civil mental hospitals within the space of a few months.' There was another case, *Dixon v A-G (Pennsylvania)* (1971) 325 F Supp 966, which had a similar impact in that state.
[44] (Footnote in original) See Thomas R Litwack et al, 'Violence Risk Assessment: Research, Legal and Clinical Considerations' in Irving Weiner and Allen Hess (eds), *The Handbook of Forensic Psychology* (Wiley and Sons, 3rd ed, 2006) 491: in relation to the *Baxstrom* and *Dixon* patients, 'Follow-up studies determined that only a small percentage had to be returned to secure facilities, and that only a small minority of patients ultimately released to the community were rearrested for violent offenses.' Therefore, 'determinations of dangerousness for the purpose of preventive detention warrant careful judicial scrutiny'.

4.   ARE THERE POLICY ALTERNATIVES?

Leroy Hendricks, the defendant in *Kansas v Hendricks*, the decision of the US Supreme Court that constitutionally validated post-sentence preventive detention regimes in the United States,[45] famously promised that if he was released from prison he would commit sexually predatory acts on children.[46] It would be an abdication of responsibility and a grave breach of public trust for governments to ignore threats like this and fail to take steps to remove them. Preventive detention is warranted when a person has a mental illness that causes them to engage in serious criminal activity.

However, unless we lock up all serious offenders indefinitely, we will continue to be faced with the problem of how to manage these offenders after their criminal sentences have been served. Preventive detention systems that employ re-imprisonment abuse human rights. The United Nations Human Rights Committee has said: 'Imprisonment is penal in character. It can only be imposed on conviction for an offence in the same proceedings in which the offence has been tried.'[47] It cannot be right to say, as the High Court of Australia has done, that prison is not punitive if it is ordered for non-punitive reasons.[48] As Andrew Coyle observes in his contribution to this volume, to 'talk of imprisonment which is not punitive is an oxymoron, a contradiction in terms'.

Preventive detention systems that detain people in environments that are punitive are no different. It is the *effect* of the detention order – not the name assigned to the detention facility – that renders it punitive or non-punitive.[49] Decisions that immunise governments from searching scrutiny of detention facilities are an abdication of the judicial power to protect liberty.[50] As Ian Freckelton SC observes in his analysis of the decision of the United States Supreme Court in *Brown v Plata*,[51]

> [T]he decision constitutes a robust assertion that it is the business of the courts to do what is necessary to protect...rights, even to the extent that such enforcement has fundamental and radical structural injunctions to change the functioning of the custodial system.

---

[45]   Mercado and Ogloff, above n 39.
[46]   Ibid.
[47]   Ibid.
[48]   Ibid.
[49]   In his contribution, Ian Freckelton draws attention to the Canadian and US cases on the writ of habeas corpus that have explored the utility of that device to release people who are unlawfully detained.
[50]   Keyzer, above n 17; contrast the discussion of *Prisoners A to XX Inclusive v New South Wales* (1994) 75 A Crim R 205 (Dunford J) by Ian Freckelton SC in this volume.
[51]   Mercado and Ogloff, above n 39.

Preventive detention in genuinely non-punitive facilities is an option that is open to governments. As the United Nations Human Rights Committee pointed out in *Fardon v Australia* and *Tillman v Australia*, there is a human right to rehabilitation, and in the least restrictive environment.[52] The objectives of reintegration and release into the community, respect for the principles underpinning the criminal justice system and post-sentence 'detention' as a last resort would be more likely to be realised if governments funded a system of community-based programs involving qualified, independent experts for preventive detention, where it is necessary.[53]

Are we paying sufficient attention to rehabilitative studies that illuminate solutions that are consistent with human rights? In her contribution, Astrid Birgden emphasises the need for mental health professionals to respect human rights, avoid involvement in anti-therapeutic approaches and promote ethical rehabilitation. Birgden writes, 'While legislation may or may not support human rights, practitioners ought to regardless.'

5. CONCLUSIONS

Arlie Loughnan and Sabine Selchow have challenged scholars to go '*beyond* traditional legal concerns and a concern for effectiveness, to ask what preventive detention does to society' (emphasis added). So what does preventive detention do to society? Bill Hebenton and Toby Seddon have observed that there is a paradox in that 'the limitless pursuit of security can end up subverting security and justice in deeply damaging ways'.[54] Many authors in this volume point to the dangers associated with preventive detention.

There is a danger that to manage our fear we will abandon fundamental principles of the rule of law and human rights. There is a danger that to achieve a sense of security we will lock people up when we do not need to and that we will lock people up for longer than we need to. There is a danger in some jurisdictions that we will lock people up rather than looking for community-based treatment solutions. There is a danger that we will rely on preventive detention rather than conduct research into the improvement of sex offender treatment programs and other rehabilitative policies. There is a danger that preventive detention will become an 'easy' form of re-imprisonment. There is a danger that our courts will turn a blind eye to the punitive effect of detention orders. There is a danger that

---

[52] Keyzer, above n 25.
[53] McSherry and Keyzer, above n 13, 110–11.
[54] Bill Hebenton and Toby Seddon, 'From Dangerousness to Precaution: Managing Sexual and Violent Offenders in an Insecure and Uncertain Age' (2009) 49 *British Journal of Criminology* 343–62, 358.

fear will drive us to inflict punishment as a solution to problems that we have not tried to understand. There is a danger that preventive detention regimes will expand prison populations in a way that is impractical, unaffordable, and, as Vivien Stern observes, bereft of 'any convincing argument that it had benefitted society'.

As Warren Brookbanks observes in his detailed analysis of contemporary New Zealand proposals to introduce post-sentence preventive detention in that country, it is ironic that a government would introduce a preventive detention regime at precisely the same time that they were being rejected in other countries and found to have violated human rights. The chapters in this volume reinforce these concerns and counsel us to critically and honestly examine our knowledge gaps and public policy failures in this area. We must learn more about what it is we are trying to fix. We must be cautious and we should respect human rights.

PREVENTIVE DETENTION[1]

Vivien STERN

> Article 5 (1) of the European Convention on Human Rights 'gives no free standing
> right to detain a person on the ground that his character or personality is such that
> he poses a danger to his fellow men. Conviction of an offence in respect of which
> such detention is imposed is a prior requirement if the detention is not to infringe
> article 5.'[2]

Governments are often tempted to use preventive detention for those who seem
to present a real danger to society but, for some reason, cannot be held following
a lawful sentence of a court. Such measures have been seen in Australia[3] and
Germany[4] and have been proposed in New Zealand.[5] The idea of preventive
detention, however, has spread more widely, and elements of the preventive
detention approach have infiltrated and changed criminal policy. In this chapter,
two examples of such an infiltration in the United Kingdom are described and the
implications considered.

1. IMPRISONMENT IN A HUMAN RIGHTS FRAMEWORK

In all the 140 countries that have abolished the death penalty in law or in
practice, loss of liberty by imprisonment is the most severe penalty available as
the punishment for breaking the criminal law. Such loss of liberty brings with
it the loss of many of the basic human rights that have been accepted by the 167
countries that have signed the United Nations fundamental human rights treaty,
the International Covenant on Civil and Political Rights.[6] Prisoners, by definition,

---

[1]   I am grateful to Helen Fair, Research Associate at the International Centre for Prison Studies
      for providing research assistance for this chapter.
[2]   *Secretary of State for Justice v Walker and James* [2008] EWCA Civ 30.
[3]   *Fardon v A-G* (Qld) (2004) 210 CLR 50.
[4]   *Jendrowiak v Germany* [2011] ECHR No 30060/04.
[5]   Andrea Vance, *New Orders Could Keep Inmates behind Bars Indefinitely* (18 September 2012) *Stuff.
      co.nz* <http://www.stuff.co.nz/national/politics/7696244/New-orders-could-keep-inmates-
      behind-bars-indefinitely>.
[6]   *International Covenant on Civil and Political Rights*, GA Res 2200A (XXI), 21 UN GAOR Supp
      No 16, UN Doc A/6316/1966, 999 UNTS 171 (entered into force 23 March 1976).

Vivien Stern

lose the right to freedom of movement (Article 12) and the right to enjoy family life (Article 23). Some states permit prisoners to have limited private visits with members of their families, but many others do not grant even that concession. The right to freedom of association is also, by definition, lost, and the right to freedom of expression is severely limited. Few prisoners live in conditions where their privacy is respected, and many factors of imprisonment lead inevitably to a failure to treat detainees with 'humanity and respect for the inherent dignity of the human person'.[7] Many prison experiences assault individuality and destroy self-respect. The stigma of a prison record can last for the rest of a person's life.

Prison, by definition, creates social exclusion. Many ex-prisoners can feel their incarceration has left them to face a lifetime of disadvantage. It has given them an indelible stamp of 'ex-convict' on their foreheads.

Clearly, therefore, imprisoning a human being is an act by the State of extreme seriousness. As such, it makes clear society's abhorrence of terrible crimes and shows victims that the State recognises the harm done to them and will hold a perpetrator accountable; but since so many basic human rights are denied or reduced through imprisonment, there is a requirement that it should be used proportionately. Therefore, it is required by the international human rights framework that the use of imprisonment will be hedged around with many protections such as the need for a fair trial, implying the necessity for an accused person to be adequately defended as well as a framework of law that allows appeal procedures, and often procedures for compassionate early release.

It is very appropriate therefore that the use of imprisonment is the subject of scrutiny by academics, parliamentarians and human rights defenders and, particularly, when such use comes into a category that can be described as preventive detention.

2. THE EXPANSION OF THE PREVENTIVE DETENTION APPROACH

The use of preventive detention has expanded considerably in recent years in a number of Western countries. The trend towards keeping people in detention longer than would be deemed proportionate to the offence they have committed has accelerated. The United States, as in much to do with incarceration, sets the pace on this with the policy colloquially called 'three strikes and you're out'.[8] After

---

[7]   Ibid. Article 10:1. All persons deprived of their liberty shall be treated with humanity and with respect for the inherent dignity of the human person.
[8]   'Three Strikes' Sentencing Laws (2012) FindLaw <http://criminal.findlaw.com/criminal-procedure/three-strikes-sentencing-laws.html >: 'Under the Violent Crime Control and

16

Intersentia

two prison sentences for offences involving violence, a third offence, even if non-violent, would trigger a life sentence. The policy became widely known through the story of a man whose third offence was stealing a pizza and who ended up being given a life sentence for it. The pizza thief, one Jerry Dewayne Williams, eventually appealed and was released after serving five years for the theft of the slice of pizza.[9] After nearly twenty years of this law and huge costs (estimated at around $20 billion), voters in California rejected the policy in 2012 by agreeing to a proposition that a life sentence can no longer be imposed for a third minor or non-violent offence.[10]

The tale of Jerry Dewayne Williams is an illustration of an approach that has become very much a feature of the United States criminal justice system, an approach that sees criminals as enemies of society whose acts must be punished as if there were a war against them and whose incarceration conditions must be harsh. This can be contrasted with the social democratic approach that puts criminal justice into a context of what is most likely to promote an inclusive society and, therefore, emphasises minimum use of incarceration and prison regimes which aim to be rehabilitative.[11]

Therefore, after the terrorist attacks of 2001, when terrorism became more widely perceived as a serious threat, this approach of dealing with fellow-citizens as enemies was already well established in the psyche and the system. Those involved with terrorist organisations claimed that they were indeed enemies of western societies. The development of a socially exclusionary ethos in criminal justice in the United States, so much a feature of the last two decades of the twentieth century,[12] made it easier, once terrorism was perceived as a serious threat, to

---

    Law Enforcement Act of 1994, the "Three Strikes" statute (18 U.S.C. § 3559(c)) provides for mandatory life imprisonment if a convicted felon:
- has been convicted in federal court of a "serious violent felony" and
- has two or more previous convictions in federal or state courts, at least one of which is a "serious violent felony." The other offense may be a serious drug offense.

    The statute goes on to define a serious violent felony as including murder, manslaughter, sex offenses, kidnapping, robbery, and any offense punishable by 10 years or more which includes an element of the use of force or involves a significant risk of force.

    The State of Washington was the first to enact a "Three Strikes" law in 1993. Since then, more than half of the states, in addition to the federal government, have enacted three strikes laws. The primary focus of these laws is the containment of recidivism (repeat offenses by a small number of criminals). California's law is considered the most far-reaching and most often used among the states.'

9   J Leonard, '"Pizza Thief" Walks the Line', *Los Angeles Times* (Los Angeles), 10 February 2010.

10   L Lyman, *California Votes to Reform Draconian 'Three Strikes' Mandatory Minimum Law* (7 November 2012) Huffington Post < http://www.huffingtonpost.com/lynne-lyman/california-votes-to-refor_b_2089469.html>.

11   See V Stern, 'Prisoners as Citizens: A View from Europe' in D Brown and M Wilkie (eds), *Prisoners as Citizens: Human Rights in Australian Prisons* (Federation Press, 2002).

12   See M Mauer and M Chesney-Lind (eds), *Invisible Punishment: The Collateral Consequences of Mass Imprisonment* (New Press, 2003) for an analysis of the growth of social exclusionary measures in criminal justice.

apply preventive detention to terrorism offences and to those deemed to present a terrorist threat. The iconic symbol of preventive detention is the orange-jump-suited inhabitant of Guantanamo Bay where, in October 2012, 166 detainees were still held outside the law and with no access to due process.[13]

As terrorism became more of a shaping feature of the criminal justice systems of many states, a debate arose as to whether there was a conflict between respecting the human rights of suspects and detainees and respecting the right of the public to be protected by the state from violence. As with many (though not all) of the human rights set out in the *Universal Declaration on Human Rights and the International Covenant on Civil and Political Rights*, was there a question of the balancing of rights, the right of a person to be punished only for what he or has done and not to be detained without a fair trial and the entitlement of all to be protected by the state from violent harm?[14] This debate was much to the fore during the time that George W. Bush was the president of the United States and Tony Blair was the Prime Minister of the United Kingdom, but its salience diminished following the election of President Obama who made it clear in his inaugural address:

> As for our common defence, we reject as false the choice between our safety and our ideals. Our founding fathers faced with perils that we can scarcely imagine, drafted a charter to assure the rule of law and the rights of man, a charter expanded by the blood of generations. Those ideals still light the world, and we will not give them up for expedience's sake.[15]

This theme, how to preserve human rights and the rule of law in the face of external dangers (perceived or real), must be the focus of a discussion on preventive detention. To illuminate that theme, two developments in England and Wales to bring in a form of preventive detention will be considered in some detail, along with the parliamentary response and the response of the courts. The hope is that this will suggest ways in which lines can be drawn between what measures are within the limits of justifiable and legitimate, even though they might not be very palatable in human rights terms, and what are not.

The first is the government's introduction of indeterminate sentences for public protection in England and Wales, and the second is an attempt to use a form of preventive detention for those deemed to be associated with terrorism, where the

---

[13] US Government Accountability Committee (2012) *Guantanamo Bay Detainees: Facilities and Factors for Consideration if Detainees Were Brought to the United States.* Washington DC: GAO.
[14] See B Goold and L Lazarus, *Security and Human Rights* (Hart Publishing, 2007).
[15] Barack Obama, 'Inaugural Address' (Speech delivered at the US Capital Building, Washington DC) 20 January 2009.

authorities felt there was no possibility of charging them with an offence in the normal way. This system was called 'control orders'.

3. INDETERMINATE SENTENCES FOR PUBLIC PROTECTION

The first development was the indeterminate sentences for public protection (IPPs) experiment in England and Wales.[16] In 1997, a government that called itself 'New Labour' came in, with some approaches to criminal justice policy that marked a departure from an older, socially inclusive Labour ethos. New Labour policies showed an enthusiasm for long punishments and for weakening the relationship between the seriousness of the crime and the severity of the sentence. This began with a new approach to previous convictions. The Government explained the new criminal justice legislation in 2003:

> Previous convictions, (where they are recent and relevant) should be treated as an aggravating factor when determining the sentence severity. Persistent offenders must know that there will be steady progress towards custody, increasing in length, if they continually offend and fail to respond to previous sentences.[17]

This thinking is very much in the tradition of authoritarian rather than social democratic governments and was very much a feature of the sentencing system of the former Soviet Union. Those who had committed small, low-value thefts frequently were sentenced not just for the crime but also for the repetition of the crime. Refusing or being unable to reform was in itself the aggravating factor.[18] The Labour government picked up that idea, that failing to respond to what the State expects of you renders you liable to punishment in itself, without any qualms about its antecedent, and took it into its philosophy of punishment. The adoption of that philosophy was the beginning of a substantial expansion of the use of imprisonment in England and Wales. When Labour came to power in 1997, the prison population was 61,467. They bequeathed to their successors a population of 85,000, an increase of nearly 40 per cent.[19]

The idea that prison was the place where risky people should spend a long time went deep into political consciousness and led in 2003 to the development of the indeterminate sentence for public protection, brought in through the *Criminal Justice Act 2003*. It required the courts to give all those sentenced for a specified

---

[16]   The United Kingdom is made up of three jurisdictions: England and Wales, Scotland and Northern Ireland.

[17]   United Kingdom, House of Lords, 16 June 2003, vol 649, col 632 (Charles Falconer).

[18]   P Moczydlowski, *The Hidden Life of Polish Prisons* (Indiana University Press, 1992).

[19]   G Berman, *Prison Populations Statistics* (House of Commons Library, 2012).

offence (and 153 offences were so specified, ranging from manslaughter and using nuclear weapons to assisting in female circumcision and affray) a term marking the seriousness of the offence. The courts then further required these convicted persons to remain incarcerated indefinitely until the parole board was satisfied they could be safely released, after which they would be on licence for at least ten years.[20] This system did not produce a pizza thief with a life sentence, but in 2007, it did produce a prisoner given a punishment length of twenty-eight days and, thereafter, to remain in prison until safe to release.[21]

The parole board made its decisions about whether a prisoner was safe to release through a report that the prisoner had reduced his or her risk, and this was established by undertaking and successfully completing appropriate 'offending behaviour programmes'. The fact that these programmes were of dubious predictive value did not cast any cloud over the process. But the provision of such programmes was in short supply and waiting lists were long. This led to the first challenge to the courts. The Divisional Court looked at two cases and decided that the Secretary of State had acted unlawfully by not providing facilities for the prisoners to demonstrate to the parole board that they were safe to release. The judge ordered one of the two complainants to be released but stayed execution of the judgement pending appeal.[22] The Government appealed. The Court of Appeal ruled that the Secretary of State had acted unlawfully by not providing facilities but that the detention was not unlawful.

> This cannot simply be regarded as a discretionary choice about resources, which is pre-eminently a matter for the government rather than the courts. We are satisfied that his conduct has been in breach of his public law duty because its direct and natural consequence is to make it likely that a proportion of IPP prisoners will, avoidably, be kept in prison for longer than necessary either for punishment or for protection of the public, contrary to the intention of Parliament (and the objective of Article 5 of which Parliament must have been mindful).[23]

The court also made it clear that:

> [t]his appeal has demonstrated an unhappy state of affairs. There has been a systemic failure on the part of the Secretary of State to put in place the resources necessary to implement the scheme of rehabilitation necessary to enable the relevant provisions of the 2003 Act to function as intended. So far as the two

---

20   *Criminal Justice Act 2003* (UK) cl 5.
21   United Kingdom, House of Commons, 4 March 2009, vol 488, col 1710 (Hanson).
22   *Wells v the Parole Board and Secretary of State for Justice; Walker v Secretary of State for the Home Department* CO/2480/ 2007& CO/2537/2007.
23   *Secretary of State for Justice v David Walker; Secretary of State for Justice v Brett James* [2008] EWCA Civ 30 [40].

claimants are concerned the appropriate remedy is limited to declaratory relief. For the reasons that we have given, however, the prevailing situation is likely to result in infringement of article 5(4) and may ultimately also result in infringement of article 5(1).[24]

This form of preventive detention had a rapid effect on the size of the prison population in England and Wales. Between 2005 and 2008, the numbers of these prisoners went up from 24 to 4,461 and the total prison population went up from 75,979 in 2005 to 82,572 in 2008.[25] By 2008, it had become clear that the policy was going in an unsustainable direction; in that year, a measure was brought into the *Criminal Justice and Immigration Act*[26] to restrict the eligibility for such sentences to those whose actual offence merited a minimum term of at least two years or those with a previous conviction for a particularly serious violent or sexual offence.

Even so, by 2010, England and Wales led Europe in locking up people on an indeterminate basis with nearly 24 people per 100,000 of the general population serving an indeterminate sentence (either an indeterminate sentence for public protection or a traditional life sentence), compared with 0.81 in France, 2.51 in Germany, 0.15 in the Netherlands and 1.69 in Sweden.[27]

The conservative/liberal coalition government that took power in 2010 brought in legislation in its first session to abolish the indeterminate sentence for public protection.[28] The legislation went through parliament without much difficulty, although with some protest from the Labour party, not any longer very new, and in opposition. 'We believe that there is a continuing role for IPPs,' said the opposition spokesperson.[29] This legislation was not retrospective, however, so there were still more than 6,000 prisoners serving an indeterminate sentence with more than 3,500 of those serving time beyond their tariff and waiting for a parole board hearing.

This was indeed an experiment in preventive detention. It is clear from the original legislation that convicted people sentenced under these provisions were so sentenced because of what they might do but had not yet done. The Act specified that when it said the law applied where:

---

[24]   Ibid [72].
[25]   Berman, above n 19.
[26]   *Criminal Justice and Immigration Act 2008* (UK).
[27]   Marcelo F Aebi and Natalia Delgrande, *Council of Europe Annual Penal Statistics: Space I: Survey 2010* (23 March 2012) Universite de Lausanne (UNIL) < http://www3.unil.ch/wpmu/space/files/2011/02/SPACE-1_2010_English1.pdf>.
[28]   *Legal Aid, Sentencing and Punishment of Offenders Act 2012* (UK).
[29]   United Kingdom, House of Commons, 29 June 2011, col 999 (Khan).

(a) a person aged 18 or over is convicted of a serious offence committed after the commencement of this section, and

(b) the court is of the opinion that there is a significant risk to members of the public of serious harm occasioned by the commission by him of further specified offences.[30]

As such, the measures led to considerable criticism and protest from the beginning. Their introduction was hard fought during the passage of the original legislation through the House of Lords. Their subsequent implementation was questioned frequently in parliament and monitored by a range of bodies. The Chief Inspector of Prisons produced a very critical report saying:

> This report should be required reading for all those within the criminal justice system, but particularly those who propose and put in place new sentences or are responsible for implementing them. It is a worked example of how not to do so.[31]

The Inspector went on to criticise the broad reach of the measure, the failure of planning and resourcing to ensure the system could cope with them, and the control and self-harm problems that were a consequence. The effects on prisoners' mental health were noted. Many reports from the Independent Monitoring Boards (groups of members of the public attached to each prison with a monitoring and oversight role) complained about the damaging effect of the measures on the running of prisons and the injustice of there being no way out, since the way out was through completing programmes and programmes were not available. A distinguished academic, Professor Lucia Zedner, called them 'one of the most pernicious of contemporary penal measures'.[32]

The experiment ended because of its impracticality, unaffordability and absence of any convincing argument that it had benefitted society. In its own consultation paper on the way forward for sentencing and imprisonment, the Ministry of Justice said:

> The limitations in our ability to predict future serious offending also calls into question the whole basis on which many offenders are sentenced to IPPs and,

---

[30] *Criminal Justice Act 2003* (UK) cl 5.
[31] HM Chief Inspector of Prisons, *The Indeterminate Sentence for Public Protection: A Thematic Review* (September 2008) Ministry of Justice Website <http://www.justice.gov.uk/downloads/publications/inspectorate-reports/hmipris/thematic-reports-and-research-publications/ipp_thematic_2008-rps.pdf>.
[32] Lucia Zedner, 'Erring on the Side of Safety: Risk Assessment, Expert Knowledge, and the Criminal Court' in I Dennis and G R Sullivan (eds), *Seeking Security: Pre-empting the Commission of Criminal Harms* (Hart Publishing, 2012).

among those who are already serving these sentences, which of them are suitable for release.[33]

When proposing the reform to the House of Lords, the Minister noted that IPPs were 'poorly understood by the public'. They led to 'inconsistent sentences for similar crimes'. Victims had no idea 'about the length of time an offender will serve'.[34] The measure had not operated even as the previous Government had intended. They had predicted it would lead to an extra 900 prisoners at any one time. In a few years the figure was 6,500.

By 2012, the legislation was no more, but at the end of that year, there was an epilogue to the story. In a unanimous ruling, the European Court of Human Rights declared that the detention of three men held on IPP sentences was 'arbitrary and therefore unlawful within the meaning of Article 5(1) of the Convention'[35] because of the failure to provide 'appropriate rehabilitative courses' the men needed to satisfy the Parole Board that their risk had diminished.[36] The men were awarded compensation. The Government intended to appeal.

What can be learnt from this experiment? It was clear that there are some checks and balances in the system in England and Wales that make it difficult for a government totally to ignore informed criticism of its policies. First, there is always the possible intervention of the domestic courts. The court case in the Divisional

---

[33]   Ministry of Justice, *Breaking the Cycle: Effective Punishment, Rehabilitation and Sentencing of Offenders* (December 2010) Ministry of Justice Website < http://www.justice.gov.uk/downloads/consultations/breaking-the-cycle.pdf> .

[34]   United Kingdom, House of Lords, 21 November 2011, col 825 (McNally).

[35]   *Convention for the Protection of Human Rights and Fundamental Freedoms*, opened for signature 4 November 1950, 213 UNTS 222 (entered into force 3 September 1953), as amended by *Protocol No 11 to Convention for the Protection of Human Rights and Fundamental Freedoms*, opened for signature 11 May 1994, ETS No 155 (entered into force 1 November 1998) ('*ECHR*'): Article 5 (1): Everyone has the right to liberty and security of person.
No one shall be deprived of his liberty save in the following cases and in accordance with a procedure prescribed by law:
(a) the lawful detention of a person after conviction by a competent court;
(b) the lawful arrest or detention of a person for non-compliance with the lawful order of a court or in order to secure the fulfilment of any obligation prescribed by law;
(c) the lawful arrest or detention of a person effected for the purpose of bringing him before the competent legal authority of reasonable suspicion of having committed and offence or when it is reasonably considered necessary to prevent his committing an offence or fleeing after having done so;
(d) the detention of a minor by lawful order for the purpose of educational supervision or his lawful detention for the purpose of bringing him before the competent legal authority;
(e) the lawful detention of persons for the prevention of the spreading of infectious diseases, of persons of unsound mind, alcoholics or drug addicts, or vagrants;
(f) the lawful arrest or detention of a person to prevent his effecting an unauthorized entry into the country or of a person against whom action is being taken with a view to deportation or extradition.

[36]   *James, Wells and Lee v the United Kingdom* (European Court of Human Rights, Application Nos 25119/09, 57715/09 and 57877/09, 2012).

Court[37] that found the Secretary of State to be acting unlawfully by not providing a means for prisoners to reduce their risk was not as decisive as many would have wished, but it put pressure on the government. There was strong criticism from the independent Inspector of Prisons, and that had been picked up in Parliament and used as a basis for questions and debates. The independent monitoring boards produced a constant drip-drip of publicity about the serious consequences of the policy on individual prisoners, prisons and the system at large, and there was no countervailing public pressure to keep the legislation in place. The intervention of the European Court of Human Rights, although belated, was of considerable value in restating that, when the law was passed, there was an understanding that rehabilitation would be provided but the resources were not made available. Therefore, the detention became unlawful because the only route to release was closed to these prisoners. Finally it was clear that there was no public pressure for this form of sentencing and no evidence that it had been effective in ensuring the safety of the public. Politically it had brought problems to the government that introduced it rather than any electoral advantage.

4. CONTROL ORDERS

The second area to be considered is a very different form of preventive detention about which it is debated whether it is detention at all. This is a form of restriction of liberty which has only been tried in two countries, the UK and Australia (and Australia had by 2012 only used this twice),[38] called a control order. A control order imposes restrictions on the movement and living conditions of persons deemed to be involved in terrorism who cannot be taken down the criminal justice route, possibly because the information forming the decision that there is terrorist involvement cannot be used in court because its use might jeopardise the methods of the security agencies.

Control orders in the UK were the government response to a decision by the domestic courts about some foreign nationals being held in prison without charge as suspected terrorists under s 23 of the *Anti-terrorism, Crime and Security Act 2001*.[39] The House of Lords (the highest court, which became the Supreme Court in 2009) held that was unlawful under the *Human Rights Act 1998* in that it discriminated against non-nationals. The question of derogation also arose in that case. Holding people in detention without charge or due process would be in violation of Article 5 of the *European Convention* and, to do so, the Government

---

[37]   *Wells v the Parole Board and Secretary of State for Justice; Walker v Secretary of State for the Home Department* CO/2480/ 2007 & CO/2537/2007.
[38]   D Anderson, *Control Orders in 2011: Final Report of the Independent Reviewer on the Prevention of Terrorism Act 2005* (London: The Stationery Office, 2012).
[39]   *Anti-terrorism, Crime and Security Act 2001* (UK) s 23.

would need to derogate from Article 5. Derogation required the Government to establish that there was a 'public emergency threatening the life of the nation'.[40]

The Government was convinced that these people needed to be held, and therefore legislation was rushed through in March 2005 as part of the *Prevention of Terrorism Act*[41] of that year establishing a new method of detaining that would be lawful because it was not total deprivation of liberty. The legislation went through but with a requirement that it should be renewed by 11 March each year for one year by parliament through a statutory instrument, without which it would fall. An annual debate had therefore to take place in both Houses before renewal. This annual review process was very important in terms of getting information from the Government on exactly what was happening and triggering an up-to-date report from the parliamentary Joint Committee on Human Rights.

For a control order to be imposed, the Home Secretary had to apply to the court for the order to be made. When it was made, it was then referred to a court for judicial review. These court proceedings were very controversial as they were normally required to be held in secret. Neither the person to be subject to the order nor his (they have all been men) legal advisers could go to the hearing, but a security cleared, government-appointed lawyer called a Special Advocate could attend the hearing but was not permitted to tell the controlled person or his lawyers what had taken place.

The requirements of the order were extensive. They could include: an 18-hour curfew; electronic tagging monitored twice a day by a private tagging company; a ban on the use of the garden; limitation on visitors and meetings to persons approved in advance by the Home Office; allowing the police to enter the house at any time to search and remove any item and to allow the installation of monitoring equipment; prohibitions on phones, mobile phones and internet access; restrictions on movement to within a defined area; needing approval to send anything abroad apart from personal letters; not being allowed to go to a port or a railway station; daily reporting to a police station; and having to get prior approval to study. A reviewer's report further shed light on what actually happened to people when the reviewer reported a controlee was:

> No longer required to report by telephone to a police station in the early hours of the morning; nor to obtain prior approval for female visitors to his family at home.[42]

---

[40]   *A and others v Secretary of State for the Home Department* [2004] UKHL 56.
[41]   *Prevention of Terrorism Act 2005* (UK).
[42]   A Carlile, *Fourth Report of the Independent Reviewer Pursuant to Section 14(3) of the Prevention of Terrorism Act 2005* (London: The Stationery Office, 2009).

Another controlee was not allowed to attend advanced level science courses because 'attendance would enable him to acquire skills and information about production of pathogens and explosives'. Also available was what came to be known as relocation, though some opponents called it 'internal exile', whereby the controlee could be sent to live in another town where he had no family or contacts.

The Act came into force on 11 March 2005, and that day the first ten control orders were issued. From the time it was activated, the measure was the focus of discussion and debate and a gradual process of modification began. As a safeguard for its anti-terrorism legislation, the government appointed a Reviewer, a post held for nearly ten years by a lawyer who was also a member of the House of Lords in the Liberal Democrat party. From 2005, he produced annual reports covering the operation of control orders. Following criticism from this Reviewer, in 2006 the Home Office set up a Control Order Review Group which was charged with 'monitoring the impact of the control order on the individual, including on their mental health and physical well-being, as well as the impact on the individual's family' and to 'consider whether the obligations as a whole and/or individually require modification as a result'.[43]

A key question was how preventive this form of control could be before it became deprivation of liberty and therefore in violation of Article 5 of the *European Convention on Human Rights* (the right to liberty and security) and needing a derogation. After a number of court rulings and finally a decision of the House of Lords, it seemed that eighteen-hour curfews constituted deprivation of liberty. Sixteen hours per day was the maximum length of a curfew to ensure deprivation of liberty was not taking place.[44] A second House of Lords ruling concerned how far the process by which orders were imposed satisfied the requirements of due process and were compatible with the right to a fair hearing. In this ruling the House of Lords held that proceedings to impose a control order are not criminal proceedings, and therefore the right to a fair trial under Article 6 does not come into play. But in a middle ranging judgement that disappointed the government presumably and also disappointed the parliamentary Joint Committee on Human Rights and human rights advocates, the House of Lords held that the proceedings must be carried out in such a way that they are, in the words of the late Lord Bingham, 'commensurate with the gravity of the potential consequences' for the person who is to be controlled. The House of Lords, therefore, finally concluded that it would not be acceptable for a case against a controlee to be entirely undisclosed to him, although a summary of the material would suffice.[45] The third

---

[43]   Anderson, above n 38.
[44]   *Secretary of State for the Home Department v JJ* [2007] UKHL 45.
[45]   *Secretary of State for the Home Department v MB (FC) (Appellant)* [2007] UKHL 46.

was concerned with how far efforts had been made to observe the requirement in the Act to keep the possibility of a criminal prosecution instead of a control order under review. The House of Lords found that the Secretary of State must keep the possibility of taking out a prosecution under continuing review. Baroness Hale of the House of Lords said,

> [A] control order must always be seen as 'second best'. From the point of view of the authorities, it leaves at liberty a person whom they reasonably believe to be involved in terrorism. … From the point of view of the controlled person, serious restrictions are imposed upon his freedom of action on the basis of mere suspicion rather than actual guilt.[46]

A disappointing judgement was that of *CD* where the court held that the system whereby a controlee could be ordered to move to a town other than his hometown, where he knew no one and had no family, was acceptable.[47]

During the whole time of their operation control orders were made on 52 people. Ten men were served with deportation notices, and six of these were deported. Twenty had their orders revoked, fifteen of these because the Government felt they were no longer necessary, three because the court's decision about disclosure would be too damaging and two on the direction of the court. Four were not renewed because the Government deemed they were no longer necessary. Three were quashed by the High Court. Five expired after the controlled person absconded and was not found. One absconded after his order had been quashed and before a new one could be served. Nine were continued under a new regime.[48]

The experiences of one controlee are illustrative. Cerie Bullivant was on a control order for two years. He then absconded but gave himself up and was tried for absconding, which is a criminal offence. He was found not guilty, and the judge said that the security services had no grounds for subjecting him to an order. There were 'no reasonable grounds' for suspicion. He was the only controlee who had been available to talk to the press and members of parliament. His view of his experience was that 'his life had been wrecked'. He claimed that the control order meant he had to give up studying for a nursing degree because the requirement to sign in with police every day meant he was always late, and the authorities would not change his signing-in times. His marriage failed because his wife could not put up with the early-morning police checks on them at home. His friends drifted away because associating with him made them suspect also. He developed depression. Once the order had been lifted, he could not get a job teaching English because he

---

[46]   *Secretary of State for the Home Department v E* [2007] UKHL 47.
[47]   *CD v Secretary of State for the Home Department* [2011] EWHC 1273.
[48]   Anderson, above n 38.

could not pass the criminal records check. It took months to be allowed to open a bank account. And, so he told a newspaper, 'Two weeks ago I was walking down my road and someone recognised me and went: "Oi, it's the bomber!"'[49]

These orders, affecting such small numbers of people, gave rise to many reports, hours of parliamentary debate and a substantial number of court cases. So much attention did not succeed in bringing the regime of control orders to an end, but it mitigated its worst features and can be seen as an indication of the level of vigilance civil society and parliament bring to bear on the UK's adherence to its human rights obligations. The coalition government of conservatives and liberal democrats that came into power in 2010 was committed to a rolling back of some of the counter-terrorism measures of the previous government and to ending the control order regime to reach more of a 'correct balance between state powers and the civil liberties of individual citizens'.[50]

Therefore, in December 2011, the *Terrorism Prevention and Investigative Measures Act* came into force, which brought in a similar regime to the control order regime but with some welcome modifications. The measures that could be imposed were not open-ended but were set out in statute. There was an overnight curfew but not a daily one and no power to relocate without the controlee's consent. The controlee could have a landline telephone, a computer with access to the internet and a mobile phone, but there were considerable powers to restrict and control their use. Work and study would be allowed, but the Secretary of State would have to be notified of any work or study and could impose conditions. The Secretary of State would need to have a higher level of suspicion to impose an order, that is, to *reasonably believe* rather than *reasonably suspect*. The length of order could only be for one year, renewed once. Courts would have more involvement in making the order and in reviewing it, taking account of the case law developed in the era of control orders including allowing controlees to, in the words of the Minister introducing the Bill, 'know the key elements of the case against them even if it is not possible for them to see all the underlying intelligence'. The legislation would expire after five years. The Secretary of State was required to make a quarterly report to Parliament.[51] An independent reviewer has been appointed.

5. SOME CONCLUSIONS

Preventive detention is a great temptation for governments. It is easy to see how they end up succumbing to that temptation. Whenever there is a serious

---

[49]   N Morris, 'A Control Order Ruined My Life – and My Respect for Britain', *The Independent* (London), 7 January 2011.
[50]   United Kingdom, House of Lords, 5 October 2011, col 1133 (Henley).
[51]   *Terrorism Prevention and Investigative Measures Act 2011* (UK).

crime perpetrated by someone who has committed a serious crime before, some newspapers will say, '*Why was he or she let out of prison in the first place?*' What a deceptively simple idea it must seem to governments to look for a law that means such people will not be let out at the end of the sentence. When dealing with terrorism, who can argue with the assertion that certain people are very dangerous and intent on terrorist activity but it is all secret and so public debate is not possible? It is not easy to find a counter-argument to these positions. So what should those concerned for the protection of human rights and the preservation of the rule of law do?

Clearly, it would be preferable for governments not to take this path, and widespread debate and public discussion is necessary. If, however, the government is not persuaded to abstain from using the law in this way, other actions are necessary. Checks and balances must be in place. First, there must be recourse to the courts. Credit has to be given to the UK parliament. Whenever the government has tried to seriously restrict access to the courts, Parliament has drawn the line at that. The courts have played an important role in modifying the control order regime and defining the maximum level of restriction that is acceptable. They have also played a lesser but still important role in highlighting the injustice of the indeterminate sentence for public protection.

Second, an active parliament and politicians with the energetic and assiduous input of civil society organisations are needed. Parliament has played a part by ensuring the legislation incorporates regular review and the concomitant provision of information by government. Then Parliament has taken advantage of these provisions to put on the pressure, keep the restrictions to the minimum and discourage any expansion or net-widening. Politicians ask questions and get information into the public domain that the non-governmental organisations and the press can then disseminate more widely.

Third, it is a huge bonus to have an active and well-staffed parliamentary human rights committee,[52] and over the years, that committee, through its many reports, has established how the repressive effect of such measures can be minimised. They have suggested there must be time limits on such legislation to establish that it is exceptional and the need for it should be temporary. The length of time any

---

[52] I spent four years as a member of the Parliamentary Joint Committee on Human Rights, a select committee of both houses of the UK Parliament that was set up after the passing of the *Human Rights Act 1998*, which brought the *European Convention on Human Rights* into British law and had the role of holding the Government to account on meeting its human rights obligations. This it did by scrutinising all proposed legislation for compatibility and by doing thematic reviews on human rights questions. For much of those four years the main issue which dwarfed all others and which led to a substantial body of work was terrorism legislation. Between the date I joined in November 2004 and when my term ended in November 2008, we produced 18 major reports on terrorism issues and projected terrorism legislation.

individual can be subject to detention should be limited and the limits set in law. If any process has to be secret for reasons of national security, the minimum due process rights should be incorporated. That means knowing the gist of the case and being legally represented. Appeal rights are essential.

Fourth, external oversight by an independent person is an essential element. And the post of independent reviewer of terrorism has been filled since it was created by a person of considerable legal standing and independence of mind.

Finally, it is important to point out that the end result of these two unprecedented experiments in preventive detention is not more of it, but less. The idea has not become more acceptable, but with both these measures the outcome has been a more nuanced and questioning approach. We have not been softened up for its extension to other groups of people seen as risky. It has been pulled back. But it is certain there is a need for constant vigilance still.

PREVENTIVE DETENTION IN EUROPE, THE UNITED STATES, AND AUSTRALIA

Christopher SLOBOGIN

1. INTRODUCTION

The protection of citizens from offenders who are perceived to be dangerous has always been a prominent goal of governments. The usual mechanism for protecting society from a convicted individual is, of course, sentencing. But from time to time governments have also experimented with special preventive detention regimes that exist either in lieu of or are triggered subsequent to the completion of a sentence. In the past two decades, these alternative regimes have come under judicial scrutiny in a number of countries. This paper discusses how post-sentence preventive detention has been analyzed by four important tribunals: the European Court of Human Rights, the United States Supreme Court, the Australian High Court and the United Nations Human Rights Committee.

To date, the most far-reaching preventive detention decision from the European Court of Human Rights is *M v Germany*,[1] decided in 2010. The judicial activity in this case – in the lower level German courts, through the Federal Constitutional Court in Germany, and at the European Court – illustrate a range of approaches to this difficult issue. The leading case on post-sentence confinement in the United States is *Kansas v Hendricks*.[2] Finally, the analogous decision from the High Court of Australia is *Fardon v Attorney-General for the State of Queensland*,[3] a case that was subsequently addressed by the UN Human Rights Committee in *Fardon v Australia*.[4] This chapter looks at all of these decisions.

---

[1]   [2010] ECHR No 19359/04 ('*M v Germany*'); descriptions of the lower court opinions in the case, as well as of other European Court opinions, are all taken from the opinion in *M v Germany* rather than the original sources.

[2]   521 US 346 (1997) ('*Hendricks*').

[3]   (2004) 223 CLR 575.

[4]   Human Rights Committee, UN Doc CCPR/C/98/D1629/2007 (10 May 2010) ('*Fardon v Australia*') <www.unhcr.org/refworld/docid/4c19e97b2.html>.

All four tribunals permit preventive detention as part of a criminal sentence. All also appear to permit preventive detention outside the criminal justice system if it is focused on people with mental disorder and is not punitive. But the European Court and the U.N. Committee decisions part ways from the U.S. Supreme Court and the Australia High Court with respect to the all-important definitions of "mental disorder" and "punitive." Finally, all of these decisions leave unanswered a number of questions about the permissibility and scope of preventive detention, whether it occurs within or outside the criminal justice system, and whether it is focused on people with mental disability or some other group, such as soldiers, terrorists or people with infectious diseases.

After describing the import of these decisions with respect to both post-sentence preventive detention and preventive detention as part of a sentence, this chapter tries to make sense out of the various positions they advance. Despite decisions like *M, Hendricks*, and *Fardon,* preventive detention following a criminal conviction remains under-theorized in Europe, the United States and Australia. The article suggests a more coherent approach, based on my work setting out a jurisprudence of dangerousness.

2. THE FACTS AND HOLDINGS OF *M V GERMANY*

M was born in 1957. His criminal history is extensive.[5] Between the ages of 14 and 18 he was 'repeatedly convicted' of theft and burglary. While the record does not reveal how many times he was convicted during this period, it does indicate that he escaped from prison four times in those years. In 1977, at the age of 20, he was convicted of attempted murder, robbery, aggravated battery and blackmail, for a series of acts committed approximately one week after he had been released from his previous incarceration. Although the court found that his responsibility for these crimes was diminished due to a 'pathological mental disorder', it sentenced M to six years confinement. A year and a half later, while in prison, he was convicted of another aggravated assault, this time for throwing a heavy metal box at the head of a prison guard and then stabbing him with a screwdriver after being reprimanded for the initial assault. Less than two years later, in 1979, he assaulted a disabled prisoner over an argument about whether a cell window should remain open. The latter two crimes resulted in a cumulative sentence of two and a half years tacked on to his original six-year sentence; in light of his continued diminished responsibility, the court directed that M be placed in a mental hospital. In 1986, just as these sentences were about to end, he was convicted of attempted murder and robbery of a woman who had volunteered to supervise him on a furlough from the hospital. He received a sentence of five

---

[5]   *M v Germany* [6]–[12],[16].

years, but this time with an additional order that, if necessary due to his continued dangerousness, he could be preventively detained after that sentence terminated.

Under authority of the latter order, in 1991 – the year his five-year sentence for his latest crime ended – a German regional court ordered his continued incarceration, based on an expert report concluding that he 'was likely to commit offences'.[6] Over the next six years he escaped at least once, became involved with a group of skinheads, assaulted and broke the nose of a fellow prisoner, and 'grossly insulted' the warden of the prison. In 2005, he punched a fellow prisoner in the face in a dispute over a baking tin.[7] However, the record suggests that from the mid-1990s through the time his case came before the European Court in 2008 (a time period which saw M reach the age of 51), the number and intensity of his antisocial incidents decreased significantly.

M challenged his prevention detention initially in 1992 as well as at the periodic review hearings, required every two years by statute, that were held in 1994, 1996, 1998 and 2001. The German regional courts consistently rejected his challenges and continued to authorize his detention on prevention grounds. At the 2001 hearing, M argued not only that he was no longer dangerous but also that Article 67 of the German Criminal Code – which at the time he was sentenced in 1986 limited preventive detention to ten years[8] – required that he be released in 2001 (ten years after completion of his last, five-year sentence). However, the regional court noted that Article 67 had been amended in 1998 to allow extension of preventive detention beyond ten years if 'there is . . . danger that the detainee will, owing to his criminal tendencies, commit serious offences resulting in considerable psychological or physical harm to the victims'.[9] The court then expressly authorized preventive detention beyond the ten-year period because such detention 'was not disproportionate' to 'the gravity of the applicant's criminal past and possible future offences'.[10]

The Frankfurt am Main Court of Appeal affirmed the regional court's holding in October 2001 and further held that M could not challenge his detention again until another two-year period elapsed.[11] The latter holding was based in part on the Court of Appeal's conclusion that M no longer suffered from a pathological disorder that might be amenable to treatment that could result in earlier release.[12] The Court of Appeal also held that continued preventive detention under

---

6   Ibid [14].
7   Ibid [44].
8   Ibid [48].
9   Ibid [53] (describing amended provision 67d).
10   Ibid [19].
11   Ibid [21].
12   Ibid [22] (concluding, according to the European Court, that 'it was clear that M no longer suffered from a serious mental disorder which should be qualified as pathological').

the amended 1998 statute did not violate Germany's Basic Law prohibiting 'retrospective criminal provisions' (analogous to ex post facto laws in American jurisprudence) because the 1998 statute only prescribed 'preventive measures', not 'penalties'. In such cases, the Court of Appeal reasoned, retrospective application is permissible if 'weighty public-interest grounds', such as the protection of the public from dangerous offenders, exist.

Although M immediately filed a petition with the German Federal Constitutional Court, that Court did not hand down a decision in his case until 2004.[13] After a hearing in which it not only heard arguments from both sides but also consulted psychiatric experts and prison wardens, a panel of eight judges on the Constitutional Court upheld the Court of Appeal in an 84-page opinion. It considered M's case in light of four guarantees found in Germany's Basic Law – the right to liberty, protection from retrospective criminal laws, respect for the rule of law, and respect for human dignity.[14] The Constitutional Court began by acknowledging the serious deprivation of liberty preventive detention imposes. It stressed that, given the content of Article 67 at the time M was sentenced, extension of preventive detention beyond ten years should be the exception rather than the rule and require significant proof of danger.[15] Further, prison authorities implementing such detention should work to 'relax' detention conditions to facilitate prognosis regarding possible release and should also make sure that detention conditions are 'improved to the full extent compatible with prison requirements'.[16] However, the Court continued, if these requirements are met, M's detention beyond the ten-year period did not violate the right to liberty or the ex post facto prohibition against criminal punishment because the detention was focused on prevention, not punishment.[17] Nor did the detention violate the rule of law guarantee. According to the Court, 'the legislator's duty to protect members of the public against interference with their life, health and sexual integrity outweighs the detainee's reliance on the continued application of the ten-year limit';[18] in any event, the Court implied that the detainee should have known the detention might be prolonged given its preventive nature.[19] Finally, if a detainee continues to pose a high level of danger, the Court held, his dignity is not violated even by long periods of preventive detention as long as the government's goal is to rehabilitate the detainee and programs exist that give him 'real prospects of regaining [his] freedom'.[20]

---

[13] Ibid [27].
[14] *Grundgesetz fur die Bundesrepublik Deutschland* [Basic Law of the Federal Republic of Germany] art 2(2), art 103(2), art 20(3), art 1(1), respectively.
[15] *M v Germany* [29].
[16] Ibid [29], [30].
[17] Ibid [33].
[18] Ibid [37].
[19] Ibid [36].
[20] Ibid [38].

Thus, by the time M's case came before the European Court of Human Rights a number of German courts, including the country's highest, had affirmed his detention on prevention grounds beyond the ten-year period German law originally imposed as a limit on that detention. The European Court nonetheless decided that M had been unlawfully detained since 2001 and was entitled to damages.[21] While not disputing the German courts' interpretation of German law, the Court concluded that the disposition in M's case violated both Article 5 and Article 7 of the European Convention on Human Rights.

> Article 5, section 1 of the Convention provides, *inter alia*, that:
> No one shall be deprived of his liberty save in the following cases and in accordance with a procedure prescribed by law:
> (a) The lawful detention of a person after conviction by a competent court; ...
> (c) The lawful arrest or detention of a person effected for the purpose of bringing him before the competent legal authority ... or when it is reasonably considered necessary to prevent his committing an offence or fleeing after having done so;
> ...
> (e) The lawful detention of persons for the prevention of the spreading of infectious diseases, of persons of unsound mind, alcoholics or drug addicts or vagrants; ... .[22]

The Court quickly ruled out the possibility that either paragraph (c) or (e) applied to M's case. The prevention language in s 1(c), the Court stated, refers not to sentencing but to pretrial detention after prompt arraignment before a judge, based on a finding that the arrested individual would otherwise commit a 'concrete and specific offence'.[23] And the preventive detention of persons with unsound mind referenced in s 1(e) did not apply to M's case, given the German courts' finding that he no longer suffered from serious mental disorder.[24]

That left only s 1(a) of Article 5 – 'detention after conviction by a competent court' – as a possible legitimate ground for M's continued confinement. The European Court found that M's initial preventive detention after his conviction in 1991 was justified under this provision. However, the Court held that his detention beyond the ten-year period violated s 1(a) because 'there was not a sufficient causal connection' between the conviction and the extension of his sentence.[25] More specifically, the Court held 'the courts responsible for the execution of sentences were competent only to fix the duration of the applicant's preventive detention within the framework established by the order of the sentencing court, read in

---

[21]   This was the only relief described in the European Court's opinion [141]. It may be that M had been released at the time the Court's opinion was issued.
[22]   European Convention on Human Rights, Article 5, s 1.
[23]   *M v Germany* [102].
[24]   Ibid [103].
[25]   Ibid [100].

the light of the law applicable at the relevant time'.[26] Since the sentencing court's preventive detention sentence was limited to ten years by the law extant at the time of sentencing, German courts had no jurisdiction to detain M beyond that period. The European Court distinguished M's case both from *Van Droogenbroeck v Belgium*,[27] where it had upheld a preventive sentence enhancement imposed on a habitual offender at the time of sentencing rather than some later point in time,[28] and from *Kafkaris v Cyprus*,[29] where it sanctioned extension of a sentence beyond the twenty-year term authorized by prison regulations because the sentencing court had authorized a sentence of life imprisonment.[30]

The European Court also held that M's disposition violated Article 7's prohibition against imposing a 'heavier penalty . . . than the one that was applicable at the time the criminal offence was committed'.[31] The key question here was whether M's confinement beyond 1991 was a 'penalty'. M emphasized that, with the extension, he had been incarcerated for 'considerably longer' than most offenders who commit *murder* and that the incarceration took place in a prison, without any significant effort to prepare him for release.[32] The government countered that people subjected to preventive detention in Germany received several privileges not accorded those being punished, including the ability to wear their own clothes, receive longer visits, obtain more pocket money and mail and experience more time outside the cell within the prison as well as short periods of leave under escort.[33] The European Court agreed with the government's contention – and indeed called it 'clear' – that as a matter of theory, confinement 'of a purely preventive nature aimed at protecting the public from a dangerous offender' is not a penalty.[34] But it went on to hold that the detention in M's case was not purely preventive in nature.

The Court reached this conclusion relying on several factors, here organized somewhat differently than in the Court's opinion. First, the Court stated, preventive detention is a deprivation of liberty that, given its unlimited nature in cases like M's, 'appears to be among the most severe – if not the most severe – which may be imposed under the German Criminal Code'.[35] Second, the Court noted that preventive detention orders enhance the typical sentence and are issued by criminal courts against persons who have repeatedly been found

---

[26] Ibid [99].
[27] (1982) 4 EHRR 443, 50.
[28] *M v Germany* [94].
[29] [2008] ECHR No 21906/04.
[30] *M v Germany* [101].
[31] European Convention on Human Rights, Article 7, s 1.
[32] *M v Germany* [110]–[111].
[33] Ibid [114], [116].
[34] Ibid [125].
[35] Ibid [132].

guilty of serious offences, all of which suggests that the detention is additional punishment as much as it is preventive in orientation.[36] Finally, the Court found 'striking' the fact that preventive detention in Germany takes place in 'ordinary prisons, albeit in separate wings', and characterized the privileges accorded those who are preventively detained as so 'minor' that 'there is no substantial difference between the execution of a prison sentence and that of a preventive detention order'.[37] More specifically, the Court concluded that, contrary to the government's submissions, those subject to such orders received no special programs designed to reduce the duration of their detention and that 'treatment' staff was often absent and lacked the necessary expertise. Here it referred to part of a report prepared by the European Committee for the Prevention of Torture and Inhuman or Degrading Treatment or Punishment that had found that, while the physical facilities in which people like M are housed are of 'a good or even very good standard', the vast majority of inmates 'were completely demotivated' and their 'psychological care and support appeared to be seriously inadequate'.[38] The Court quoted with approval the conclusion of the Committee's report that achieving the objective of crime prevention requires 'a high level of care involving a team of multi-disciplinary staff, intensive work with inmates on an individual basis, within a coherent framework for progression towards release, which should be a real option'.[39]

Having found that preventive detention as implemented in Germany is a 'penalty', the Court then had to decide whether the extension of M's preventive detention was part of the original penalty applicable at the time of the conviction – and therefore legitimate – or was instead an additional, subsequently imposed penalty – and therefore in violation of Article 7. While the sentencing court had ordered M's preventive detention without stating a time limit, the European Court held that, given the law applicable at the time, the detention could not lawfully exceed ten years.[40] Therefore, any confinement beyond ten years was a retrospectively applied penalty in violation of Article 7.

Germany's reaction to the holding in *M v Germany* has been dramatic. In 2010, the German legislature passed the *Violent Offenders (Custodial Therapy) Act*, which transferred jurisdiction over dangerous offenders who require post-sentence incapacitation from the criminal courts to the civil courts, apparently in the hopes this move would evade *M's* strictures.[41] But in 2011, the German High Court declared all post-sentence incapacitation orders of the German Code

---

36   Ibid [124], [128].
37   Ibid [127].
38   Ibid [77].
39   Ibid [129].
40   Ibid [135].
41   Michael Bohlander, *Principles of German Criminal Procedure* (Hart Publishing, 2012) 235.

unconstitutional, on the ground, highlighted in *M v Germany*, that dispositions under those orders were not sufficiently therapeutic and distinct from prison conditions.[42] Directing the legislature to reform the law accordingly by May 2013, it held that in the interim only those who pose an extreme likelihood of committing serious violent and sexual offences and who suffer from a serious mental disorder may be confined.[43] The German court also reduced the review period from two years to one.[44]

The European Court's decision in *M v Germany* leaves two important aspects of preventive detention law under the European Human Rights Convention unresolved, or at least murky. First, if the government provides the type of individualized treatment described by the Court, does preventive detention lose its punitive nature, or does the fact that such detention takes place after conviction of a serious offence, is unlimited and potentially prolonged, and takes place in prison-like setting still require the conclusion that it is a penalty? Second, assuming preventive detention after conviction is a penalty, if the state has already authorized indeterminate sentencing (thus mooting the retrospective application problem), and the sentencing court explicitly states that the sentence shall be indeterminate with no fixed endpoint, is there a sufficient 'causal connection' between the conviction and the sentence to satisfy Article 5? If these questions are answered in the affirmative, then Germany can avoid the impact of *M v Germany* in future cases either by providing meaningful treatment to those who are preventively detained or by assuring that the 1998 amendment to Article 67 of its Code is applied only prospectively. The answers to these questions are also important for a number of other countries. France, the United Kingdom, Italy, Austria and at least five other European nations permit post-sentence preventive detention, although some limit it to ten years, as Germany did prior to 1998.[45] At this point, a look at how American law and the *Fardon* decisions answer these questions might be fruitful.

3. UNITED STATES LAW ON PREVENTIVE DETENTION

In *Kansas v Hendricks*,[46] the United States Supreme Court upheld a statute that explicitly permitted preventive detention of an individual who has just completed his sentence, if the person is shown to be dangerous as a result of a

---

[42]   Bundesverfassungsgericht [German Constitutional Court], 2 BvR 2365/09, 4 May 2011, cited in Bohlander, ibid 238.
[43]   Ibid.
[44]   Ibid 239.
[45]   The relevant laws are described in [69]–[73].
[46]   *Hendricks*, 521 US 346 (1997).

'mental abnormality'. This aspect of *Hendricks* could be interpreted merely as an application of the traditional rule permitting long-term preventive detention of those with mental disorder, recognized by provisions such as those found in Article 5, s 1(e) of the European Convention on Human Rights. But the Supreme Court made clear that the mental abnormality underlying a post-sentence commitment need not be a psychosis or a similarly serious disorder. Rather, it can consist of a less-serious disorder, so long as it makes the person 'dangerous beyond [his] control'.[47] According to the Court, a 'lack of volitional control, coupled with a prediction of future dangerousness, adequately distinguishes [those who may be preventively detained] from other dangerous persons who are perhaps more properly dealt with exclusively through criminal proceedings'.[48] In a later decision, the Court emphasized that 'lack of control' is not meant to have 'a particularly narrow or technical meaning' but merely requires 'proof of serious difficulty in controlling behavior'.[49] On authority of *Hendricks*, lower courts have routinely permitted post-sentence preventive of sex offenders who merely have personality disorders, including disorders that are primarily manifested through repeated antisocial conduct.[50] Because M, no longer considered 'pathologically' mentally ill but with a history of impulsive acting out, would seem to fit in this latter category, incarceration functionally equivalent to the post-sentence preventive confinement struck down in *M v Germany* appears to be permissible in the US. In the constitutional terms *Hendricks* used, such confinement does not violate the clause in the Fourteenth Amendment to the US Constitution prohibiting deprivations of liberty 'without due process of law'.[51]

The potential conflict between *M v Germany* and *Hendricks* does not end there. As in *M*, the statute under which Hendricks was confined when his sentence expired was passed after his sentence was imposed. Thus, like M, Hendricks argued that even if preventive detention of dangerous and volitionally impaired individuals is generally permissible, his particular preventive confinement occurred under an ex post facto law (which is explicitly prohibited by the American Constitution).[52] Further, like M, Hendricks argued that, since treatment was minimal, the nature of his post-sentence confinement was no different than the imprisonment he had just completed.[53] The US Supreme Court rejected both of these arguments

---

[47]   Ibid 358.
[48]   Ibid 360.
[49]   *Kansas v Crane*, 534 US 407 (2002).
[50]   See W Lawrence Fitch, 'Sex Offender Commitment in the United States: Legislative and Policy Concerns' (2003) 99 *Annals of New York Academy of Science* 489, 494 (stating that only 12% of individuals committed under *Hendricks*-type laws have 'serious mental illness', with the rest diagnosed with paraphilia or antisocial personality.
[51]   *Hendricks*, 521 US 346, 356.
[52]   *United States Constitution* art I § 9, cl 3.
[53]   However, rather than frame this claim in liberty interest terms as M did, he argued that his detention was a second punishment barred under the double jeopardy clause in the Fifth Amendment to the US Constitution.

on the ground that Hendricks' confinement did not constitute punishment, a conclusion that stands in interesting contrast to the holding in *M v Germany*. According to the Supreme Court, the purpose of the statute at issue was not to exact retribution or to implement general deterrence – typical objectives of punishment – but rather to assure incapacitation of a dangerous individual, a 'civil' regulatory goal. Under the statute, evidence of past conduct is proffered not to determine the punishment deserved for them but only to predict future conduct; moreover, no proof of 'scienter' (culpable mens rea) is required.[54] The Court strongly implied that, to ensure the regulatory nature of the detention, the state must try to provide treatment to committed individuals.[55] But it also stated that treatment need only be 'an ancillary purpose' and need not be successful in order for the confinement to avoid the punitive label.[56] The Court ended by saying: '[w]here the State has disavowed any punitive intent; limited confinement to a small segment of particularly dangerous individuals; provided strict procedural safeguards; directed that confined persons be segregated from the general prison population and afforded the same status as others who have been civilly committed; recommended treatment if such is possible; and permitted immediate release upon a showing that the individual is no longer dangerous or mentally impaired, we cannot say that it acted with punitive intent'.[57]

This latter aspect of *Hendricks* could be said to be similar in content to the decision in *M*, in the sense that both decisions require a treatment regimen in order for preventive detention to avoid the punitive label. But the tone of the European Court's decision, as well as of the German Federal Constitutional Court decision that followed it, is decidedly more demanding in this regard. In a later decision, the US Supreme Court repeated the conclusion that, at least where state law provides that one purpose of preventive detention is treatment, it must attempt to provide treatment.[58] But the Court has yet to state that proposition in the strong terms used by the European courts.

Even if a post-conviction disposition is explicitly criminal rather than regulatory or civil, the US Supreme Court has granted the government considerable leeway in fashioning sentences. As far back as 1937, the Supreme Court made clear that sentences may be based largely or entirely on assessments of risk: 'The government may inflict a deserved penalty merely to vindicate the law or to deter or to reform the offender or for all of these purposes . . . [The offender's] past may be taken to indicate his present purposes and tendencies and significantly to suggest the

---

54 *Hendricks*, 521 US 346, 361–3.
55 However, the Court also made clear that an untreatable individual may still be confined preventively: *Hendricks*, 521 US 346, 366.
56 Ibid 367.
57 Ibid 368–9.
58 *Seling v Young*, 541 US 250, 265 (2001).

period of restraint and the kind of discipline that ought to be imposed upon him.'[59] If there were any doubt about the issue, it was removed 40 years later in *Jurek v Texas*,[60] in which the Supreme Court held that even a death sentence can be based solely on a determination of dangerousness.

Indefinite sentences – that is, sentences with no fixed endpoint – also appear to be constitutionally permissible in the United States. Although the trend in recent years has been toward determinate sentencing,[61] the Supreme Court has never held or intimated that indeterminate sentencing, whereby the maximum sentence is either not stated or is quite lengthy, is unconstitutional. Until the 1970s, most state systems imposed open-ended sentences, often ranging from one year to life, with the ultimate release decision made by a parole board.[62] Today, roughly half the states retain similarly indeterminate sentencing systems.[63]

Furthermore, the Supreme Court has refused to find prolonged or indefinite sentences a violation of the ban, found in the Eighth Amendment to the US Constitution, on cruel and unusual punishment, even when the underlying offences are relatively minor. For instance, in *Ewing v California* the Court affirmed over an Eighth Amendment challenge a sentence of 25 years to life, imposed under a 'three-strikes law', for an offender who had three prior lesser felony convictions and whose most recent conviction was for stealing a set of golf clubs.[64] Analogous to the European Court's holding in *Van Droogenbroeck*, the Court stated that 'nothing in the Eighth Amendment prohibits California from choosing to incapacitate criminals who have already been convicted of at least one serious or violent crime. Recidivism has long been recognized as a legitimate basis for increased punishment and is a serious public safety concern.'[65]

Finally, the Court has apparently also rejected the rule of law concern addressed by the German Federal Constitutional Court in *M v Germany*. In *United States v*

---

[59] *Penn ex rel Sullivan v Ashe*, 302 US 51, 61 (1937).
[60] 428 US 262 (1976).
[61] See Douglas A Berman, 'Foreword: Beyond Blakely and Booker: Pondering Modern Sentencing Process' (2005) 95 *Journal of Criminal Law and Criminology* 653, 654–5; see also, *Tapia v US*, 131 US 2382 (2011) (holding that, under the federal determinate sentencing regime sentences may not be lengthened solely for rehabilitative purposes).
[62] For instance, until 1977, in California, courts imposed open-ended sentences (often one year to life) with release dependent on a decision by the parole board. *Cunningham v California*, 549 US 270, 276–7 (2007).
[63] See Richard Frase, 'State Sentencing Guidelines: Diversity, Consensus, and Unresolved Policy Issues' (2005) 105 *Columbia Law Review* 1190, 1196–7 (noting that 18 states plus the federal government have adopted sentencing guidelines that are relatively determinate but that a number of states have rejected the guidelines approach).
[64] 538 US 11 (2003). A three-strikes law imposes an enhanced penalty on an offender who has committed a third crime, usually a felony.
[65] Ibid 25.

DiFrancesco,[66] the offender argued that the prosecution should not be able to appeal a sentence imposed under a dangerous offender statute because, if it prevailed, his sentence would be enhanced beyond the term imposed by the sentencing court, an argument very similar to that made by M. However, consistent with the German Federal Constitutional Court's determination, the Supreme Court concluded that 'the argument that the defendant perceives the length of his sentence as finally determined when he begins to serve it, and that the trial judge should be prohibited from thereafter increasing the sentence, has no force where, as in the dangerous special offender statutes, Congress has specifically provided that the sentence is subject to appeal'.[67] *DiFrancesco* appears to stand for the proposition that, as long as the authorizing statute in existence at the time of sentencing permits changes in sentence, a lack-of-notice or rule of law claim against a sentence that is prolonged at some later point in time will not succeed.

These various holdings by the United States Supreme Court suggest the following answers to the two questions posed at the end of the last section (here answered in reverse order). If the legislature has authorized indeterminate, open-ended sentences the length of which depends solely upon back-end assessments of risk, the Constitution does not prohibit a criminal court from imposing such an indeterminate disposition. If instead, the government retains a determinate sentencing regime but authorizes post-sentence commitment, it may do so as long as the individual is shown to be dangerous beyond his control and the state makes some attempt to treat the individual.

It may be that, in practice, the same legal regime is permissible in Europe. That is, *M v Germany* may still permit post-sentence confinement of people with any broadly defined mental disorder, as well as preventive detention that occurs in connection with a sentence, so long as that sentence is imposed at the front-end.[68] However, the European Court's decision in *M* appears to be considerably more hostile toward post-conviction dispositions based solely on assessments of risk than *Hendricks* and its progeny, and a subsequent decision from that Court signaled that post-sentence preventive detention of offenders on mental disorder grounds must be restricted.[69] Furthermore, an expansive reading of *M*

---

[66] 449 US 117 (1980).
[67] Ibid 139.
[68] See above nn 25–30 (describing European Court's apparent endorsement of indeterminate sentencing).
[69] *Haidn v Germany* [2011] ECHR No 6587/04 (holding that where an offender is found to suffer from an 'organic personality disorder' (as distinguished, apparently, from a psychosis) and was housed in a prison rather than a psychiatric hospital, he does not have a 'true mental disorder' for purposes of Article 5, s 1(e) of the European Covenant). See also *Sullivan v. Government of the United States* [2012] EWHC (Admin) 1680, 103 (a decision by a UK appellate court refusing to extradite a fugitive to the US because he might be committed under a law that permits preventive detention even of those who "acted with full criminal responsibility")).

supports the argument that a sentence based on an assessment of risk must be time-limited in some way and must also be authorized by a court in a 'separate proceeding' focused specifically on the risk issue, as was the case with the ten-year enhancement in *M* itself.[70]

4.   THE *FARDON* CASE

Like *M* and *Hendricks*, *Fardon* involved a statute that permitted post-sentence commitment of offenders perceived to be dangerous.[71] The specific challenge to the statute was quite different, however, given the non-justiciability of human rights provisions in front of the Australian High Court and the absence in Australia of a constitutional provision akin to the due process clause found in the US Constitution. Australia does not have a Bill of Rights, so Fardon's advocates argued that the statute affronted the 'institutional integrity' of the judiciary because its requirement that courts be involved in making post-sentence commitment decisions was incompatible with the exercise of judicial power and instead constituted an executive or administrative decision.[72] Six of the seven justices on the Australian High Court rejected this argument, on the reasonable ground that Australian courts had long been involved in imposing preventive detention in various contexts, including sentencing.[73]

In the course of their opinions the six justices in the majority made points very similar to those found in *Hendricks*. For example, several of the justices stated, as one put it, that 'the Act is not designed to punish the prisoner'.[74] In contrast, the dissenting justice anticipated the conclusions subsequently reached in *M*, calling Fardon's post-sentence detention under the statute 'double punishment' both because the disposition took place in a prison and because treatment 'takes a distant second place (if any place at all) to the true purpose of the legislation, which is to provide for "the continued detention in custody . . . of a particular class of prisoner"'.[75] At the same time, even the dissenting justice reaffirmed the

---

[70]   See *M v Germany* [131] (stressing that the ten-year prevention-oriented addition to M's sentence was imposed after 'a separate procedure'). Cf *Specht v Patterson*, 386 U.S. 605 (1967) (holding that to the extent an indeterminate sentence imposed on a sex offender is based on dangerousness, it must be preceded by a formal hearing, with the right to counsel, cross-examine witnesses, etc.).

[71]   *Dangerous Prisoners (Sexual Offenders) Act 2003* (Qld) s 8 pt 2 div 3.

[72]   *Fardon v A-G (Qld)* (2004) 223 CLR 575 [1] (Gleeson CJ). The arguments of counsel for Fardon are set out in Patrick Keyzer, Cathy Pereira and Stephen Southwood, 'Pre-emptive Imprisonment for *Dangerousness in Queensland under the Dangerous Prisoners (Sexual Offenders) Act 2003*: The Constitutional Issues' (2004) 11 *Psychiatry, Psychology and Law* 244.

[73]   See eg, ibid [20] (Gleeson CJ).

[74]   Ibid [34] (McHugh J); see also [216] (Callinan J and Heydon J) ('Several features of the Act indicate that the detention in question is to protect the community and not to punish.').

[75]   Ibid [148], [156], [173] (Kirby J).

government's authority to detain preventively those with 'mental illness' and to impose sentences based on dangerousness.[76]

Fardon then petitioned the Human Rights Committee (HRC) established under article 28 of the International Covenant on Civil and Political Rights.[77] Compared to the European Court of Human Right's subsequent decision in *M*, the HRC's decision in *Fardon* was brief. Otherwise, however, it was remarkably similar to *M*, with the exception of the inevitable difference that it was decided under the International Covenant rather than the European Convention on Human Rights. The HRC concluded that Fardon's post-sentence confinement was 'penal in character' and thus, under Article 9, paragraph 1 of the Covenant, was 'not permissible in the absence of [another] conviction for which imprisonment is a sentence prescribed by law'.[78] Further, because the statute under which Fardon had been confined was enacted after his initial sentence, its application to his case was in essence an ex post facto law that violated Article 15 of the Covenant proscribing any penalty heavier than the one that existed at the time of sentence.[79] Finally, the HRC found that, given the difficulty of predicting risk, the State's failure to demonstrate that Fardon's 'rehabilitation could not have been achieved by means less intrusive than continued imprisonment or even detention' violated Article 20, paragraph 3 of the Covenant.[80] Two members of the Committee dissented, reasoning that because 'the Covenant does not limit the State party's capacity to authorize an indefinite sentence with a preventive component' Fardon's post-sentence confinement, based on the judicial finding that he represented a 'serious danger to the community,' was 'legitimate'.[81]

An HRC opinion is not binding on Australia, although the HRC can request that any party to the International Covenant provide a response as to how it plans to give effect to the Committee's view. To date, Queensland and the federal government of Australia have not seen fit to appreciably change the statute in question.[82] But regardless of the ultimate impact of the HRC's *Fardon* decision, it does not challenge the legitimacy of preventive sentencing. Furthermore, still unclear after the HRC opinion is whether post-sentence confinement is always

---

[76]   See ibid [154] (Kirby J).

[77]   *Fardon v Australia*, UN Doc CCPR/C/98/D1629/2007.

[78]   Ibid [7.4(1)].

[79]   Ibid [7.4(2)].

[80]   Ibid [7.4(4)]. The HRC also found that the process provided Fardon was inadequate [7.4(3)].

[81]   Appendix to *Fardon v Australia* [7.4] (Individual opinion of Committee members Mr Krister Thelin and Ms Zonke Zanele Majodina). Further analysis of *Fardon* is found in Patrick Keyzer, 'The United Nations Human Rights Committee's Views about the Legitimate Parameters of the Preventive Detention of Serious Sex Offenders' (2010) 34 *Criminal Law Journal* 283–291.

[82]   Bernadette McSherry, 'Post-Sentence Incapacitation of Sex-Offenders and the Ethics of Risk Assessment' in M Malsch and M Duker (eds), *Incapacitation: Trends and New Perspectives* (Ashgate, 2012) 77–96 (stating that the HRC opinion 'will have little impact'). See also the contribution of Gogarty, Bartl and Keyzer in this volume.

impermissible or whether, as recognized in *M* and its progeny, such confinement is authorized for people with mental disorder. In an effort to sort out where the law in Europe, the United States and Australia might go from here, the next section of this paper lays out a possible analytical framework.[83]

5. PRINCIPLES THAT MIGHT GOVERN THE STATE'S USE OF PREVENTIVE DETENTION

In other work,[84] I have developed seven principles, derived from both American and international law, that might govern the state's exercise of preventive intervention authority, whether exercised in the sentencing context or elsewhere:

(1) the principle of legality, which requires commission of a crime or imminently risky conduct before preventive detention takes place;

(2) the risk-proportionality principle, which requires that government prove a probability and magnitude of risk proportionate to the duration and nature of the contemplated intervention;

(3) the related least drastic means principle, which requires the government to adopt the least invasive means of accomplishing its preventive goals, and thus may well preclude confinement and at least requires treatment that reduces confinement;

(4) the principle of criminal justice primacy, which permits preventive detention in a separate system only when the criminal justice system does not have jurisdiction and even then only when limited to detention of those whose subsequent behavior is unlikely to be affected by a significant prospect of serious criminal punishment or serious harm;

(5) the evidentiary rule that, when government seeks preventive confinement, it may only prove its case using actuarial-based probability estimates or, in their absence, previous antisocial conduct;

---

[83]   Although not the focus of this paper, Canada is another country with relatively well-developed preventive detention law that, nonetheless, could use some rethinking. In *R v Lyons*, 2 SCR 309 (1987), the Canadian Supreme Court held that indeterminate sentences (based on dangerousness) in lieu of a normal sentence do not violate the Canadian charter provision prohibiting cruel and unusual punishment unless the sentence becomes 'grossly disproportionate'. In *R v LM*, 2 SCR 163 (2008), the Court sanctioned a ten-year term of community supervision appended to the end of a sentence under a 'long-term offender' statute, on the grounds that the supervision was not punishment. Neither case elaborated on the issues raised here.

[84]   A recent iteration of this work is found in Christopher Slobogin, 'Prevention as the Primary Goal of Sentencing: The Modern Case for Indeterminate Dispositions in Criminal Cases' (2011) 48 *San Diego Law Review* 1127. A similar treatment but integrating international law is Christopher Slobogin, 'Legal Limitations on the Scope of Preventive Detention' in B McSherry and P Keyzer (eds), *Dangerous People: Policy, Prediction, and Practice* (Federation Press, 2011) 37. The philosophical grounding for this work, not rehearsed here, is found in chapter 6 of Christopher Slobogin, *Minding Justice: Laws that Deprive People with Mental Illness of Life and Liberty* (Harvard University Press, 2006).

(6) the evidentiary rule that the subject of preventive detention may rebut the government's case concerning risk with clinical risk assessments, even if they are not as provably reliable as actuarial prediction;

(7) the procedural principle that a subject's risk and risk management plans must periodically be reviewed using procedures that assure voice for the subject and avoid executive branch domination of the decision making process.

5.1. PREVENTIVE DETENTION AS PART OF SENTENCING

Applied to sentences that are in whole or part focused on prevention, principles (1) through (3) and (5) through (7) play out along the following lines (principle (4) does not apply, because it deals with preventive detention outside the criminal process, about which more below). First, conviction for an offence satisfies principle one (the principle of legality). But there must be a conviction. An arrest, a suspicion, or the mere presence of a risk factor, no matter how predictive, is not enough. Otherwise, government would have too much power to intervene in the lives of people at will.[85]

Second, the nature and duration of any part of the sentence that is not based on retributive considerations would depend, under principles two and three, upon the probability and magnitude of the risk posed by the offender and the means available to diminish the risk. Relying on this risk-proportionality reasoning – alluded to and apparently endorsed in all of the German court decisions in *M v Germany*[86] – the initial confinement on preventive grounds might be limited to situations where the state can prove the offender poses a greater than 50% risk of committing a serious offence, and even then only if no less restrictive means (ankle monitors, intensive probation, registration requirements) can achieve the state's prevention aim.[87] A lower probability or lower magnitude risk would at most permit monitoring in the community. Furthermore, even if confinement is initially authorized, risk-proportionality reasoning would dictate that it could continue only if increasingly greater risk is demonstrated.

Regardless of the setting, principle three also requires that, for any portion of the sentence meant to accomplish preventive goals, the state provide treatment that can reduce risk of further offending and thus render less restrictive the

---

[85] For elucidation of this point, see Slobogin, *Minding Justice* above n 84, 115–22 and Slobogin, 'Prevention as the Primary Goal of Sentencing' above n 84, 1132–34.

[86] See German Criminal Code art 62 (requiring that all preventive measures be proportionate to the offender's dangerousness).

[87] The 50% figure comes from the American rule that arrest requires probable cause, which is often quantified around the 50% level. See Wayne R LaFave et al, *Criminal Procedure* (West, 5th ed, 2009) 167.

preventive intervention. The strong language of the European Court's decision in *M v Germany*, building on the briefer observations made by the Human Rights Committee in *Fardon*, best captures how this principle would operate. Specifically, trained personnel, individualized treatment plans, increasing opportunities for conditional release of confined individuals who adhere to these plans and continual updating of the rehabilitation regimen are essential aspects of such a regime.[88]

Principles five and six work in tandem in structuring how the government can meet the all-important proof requirements outlined above. Principle five states that the government's case-in-chief in cases seeking incarceration must rely on actuarial risk assessment instruments in proving the probability and magnitude of risk. While actuarial instruments have been much criticized, both conceptually and as a normative matter,[89] when validated on the relevant population they are superior to other means of proving risk, such as unstructured and structured clinical judgment. Compared to these latter types of risk assessment, actuarial assessments are more accurate, less likely to mislead the fact finder, and the best means of providing the factfinder with the concrete estimate of risk necessary to make the difficult normative judgment as to whether a person should be deprived of liberty. However, in recognition of the fact that actuarial instruments are based on group characteristics, principle six permits the offender to contest the actuarial probability estimate with an individualized clinical risk assessment, with the caveat that the government may respond in kind.[90]

Finally, principle seven requires that the proof process at sentencing be consistent with due process requirements, which at a minimum should probably include the rights to a neutral fact finder, counsel, and confrontation of the state's evidence,

---

[88] Another recent European Court decision that is highly relevant here is *Wells and Lee v U K*, Application Nos 25119/09, 57715/09 and 57877/09 (18 September 2012), which considered the validity of the United Kingdom's system of indeterminate sentences for the public protection ('IPP' sentences), meant to be imposed on certain classes of offenders who would then be subject to treatment programs and granted release when no longer considered a high risk. The Court held that the IPP sentences at issue in the case before it were invalid under Article 5 s 1 of the Convention. Noting that the government, by its own admission, had failed to fund the relevant treatment programs, the court stated that 'it would be irrational to have a policy of making release dependent on a prisoner undergoing a treatment course without making reasonable provision for such courses' [206].

[89] For a description of the conceptual debate, see Nicolas Scurich and Richard S John, 'A Bayesian Approach to the Group versus Individual Controversy in Actuarial Risk Assessment' (2011) 36(3) *Law and Human Behavior* 237. For a discussion of concerns about actuarial assessments from a normative perspective, see Christopher Slobogin, 'Risk Assessment' in Joan Petersilia and Kevin Reitz (eds), *The Oxford Handbook of Sentencing and Corrections* (Oxford University Press, 2012) 196.

[90] For more on risk assessment approaches, the rationale for the position taken in the text and the way principles five and six interact, see Christopher Slobogin, *Proving the Unprovable: The Role of Law, Science and Speculation in Adjudicating Culpability and Dangerousness* (Oxford University Press, 2007) 101–8, 115–29.

as well as an explanation of the ultimate decision and the right to appeal that decision, at least when there is no consensus during the initial review.[91] Principle seven further requires that a similar process take place at regular intervals to ensure adherence to the risk-proportionality and least drastic means principles. These periodic hearings presumably would often result in changes in the nature and duration of the intervention, including conditional and outright release.

5.2. PREVENTIVE DETENTION OUTSIDE OF THE CRIMINAL JUSTICE SYSTEM

The type of *post*-sentence commitment explicitly involved in *Hendricks* and *Fardon* and implicitly at issue in *M v Germany* would have to abide by all of these principles as well. Of particular interest for present purposes, however, is the additional stipulation, under principle four, that preventive detention outside the criminal justice system (including post-sentence commitment) is permissible only if (1) the criteria for criminal punishment do not apply and (2) the individual is unlikely to be affected by a significant prospect of serious criminal punishment or harm. This criminal justice primacy principle is meant to address those practices – ranging from civil commitment of people with mental disorder to quarantine and prisoner-of-war camps – that contemplate preventive detention in the absence of a criminal conviction or after a sentence has been served. It is submitted that the principle of criminal justice primacy does a better job of explaining and placing limitations on these practices than does either current law or current theory.

Consider first how extant law deals with preventive detention of people with mental disorder. Current doctrine – endorsed in Article 5, s 1(e) of the European Convention on Human Rights, *Hendricks* and the High Court's opinion in *Fardon* – holds that people 'of unsound mind' may be subject to preventive detention in a system separate from the criminal justice system. But the rationale for this doctrine is hard to discern from any of the relevant court rulings. In two cases, one decided one year after *M v Germany* and another decided in 2012, the European Court of Human Rights simply emphasized that the mental disorder referred to in s 1(e) must be a serious one, necessitating treatment in a psychiatric hospital.[92] *Hendricks* does not even require hospitalization, although it does require that confinement take place in a facility separate from prison and that the state provide

---

The relevant US Supreme Court decisions are *Gagnon v Scarpelli*, 411 US 778 (1973) and *Morrissey v Brewer*, 408 US 471 (1972), which set out due process rights in probation and parole revocation proceedings. Both cases emphasized that the complexity of the proceedings is a significant determinant of whether these rights should be extended to a particular proceeding. Risk assessments probably fall in the 'complex' category.

92   *Haidn v Germany* [2011] ECHR No 6587/04; *B v Germany* [2012] ECHR No 61261/09.

evidence of a 'mental abnormality' that renders the person 'dangerous beyond [his] control'.[93] *Fardon* does not require any type of mental disability for post-sentence detention, while also acknowledging the permissibility of preventive detention for those with mental disability.[94] None of these rulings attempt more than a shallow explanation for why people with mental disorder can be subjected to special preventive measures. Nor have these courts attempted to delineate the types of mental disorder or the specific functional impairments that will justify preventive detention.

Furthermore, none of these courts has adequately explained their apparent stance toward long-term preventive detention of dangerous people who do *not* have mental disorder. More specifically, they have not provided a way of reconciling those few situations in which such detention is accepted – ie, quarantine and wartime detention – with those situations in which it is not – ie, prisoners who are about to be released. Since people in all of these categories can be a significant threat to the public, why is preventive detention outside of criminal punishment permitted for the first two groups and not the third?

Scholars and a few lower courts have tried to provide the answers these high court decisions have yet to give, but have been unsuccessful at doing so. For instance, the usual justification advanced by scholars for preventive detention of people with mental disorder is that, while government should generally not be able to deprive people of liberty until they have acted on a rational choice, it may detain persons who are *incapable* of acting rationally; preventive detention does not de-value autonomy if the people so detained are not autonomous.[95] This lack-of-autonomy rationale clearly does justify detention of people with serious mental illness. But it does not provide a justification for other well-accepted forms of long-term preventive detention that involve *autonomous* actors, such as enemy combatants (detainable under international law)[96] and people with infectious diseases (a category of people detainable under Article 5, s 1(e) of the European Convention).[97]

---

93 *Hendricks*, 521 US 346, 358 (1997).
94 Even the dissent agreed with this position. See above n 76.
95 See, eg, Eric S Janus, 'Hendricks and the Moral Terrain of Police Power Civil Commitment' (1998) 4 *Psychology, Public Policy and Law* 297, 298 ('Properly understood, the *Hendricks* decision will limit civil commitment to those who are "too sick to deserve punishment"' (quoting *Millard v Harris*, 406 F 2d 964, 969 (DC Cir 1968))); Stephen J Morse, 'Uncontrollable Urges and Irrational People' (2002) 88 *Virginia Law Review* 1025, 1025–7, 1077 (arguing that sexual predator commitment should be limited to those who are 'nonresponsible').
96 See *Hamdi v Rumsfeld*, 542 US 507, 519–21 (2004): (The detention of enemy combatants to prevent their return to the battlefield is 'a fundamental incident of waging war' and consistent with 'longstanding law of war principles'.).
97 Cf *Jacobsen v Massachusetts*, 197 US 11 (1905): (permitting forcible vaccination).

A more expansive rationale that tries to encompass all three of these situations permits preventive detention when conviction of dangerous people is not possible.[98] On this view, because people with mental illness will be excused due to disability, people with contagious diseases are blameless for their condition, and wartime killing (outside of war crimes) is not subject to criminal punishment under the laws of war, preventive detention of the dangerous individuals within these groups can be considered justifiable. But if this 'unconvictability' rationale is taken seriously, then any dangerous person released from prison should be subject to preventive detention as well; after all, until that person commits another crime conviction is not possible.[99]

Alec Walen has tried to justify the unconvictability rationale on 'autonomy-respecting' grounds. But his efforts end up illustrating the uncabined nature of that approach. For instance, he states that people with contagious diseases have a duty to segregate themselves from the general population, and that detention simply enforces a duty they already have.[100] Apparently, this duty to accept quarantine exists because people with contagious diseases are dangerous. But then why wouldn't all persons who are prone to commit crime (eg. gang members) have a duty to detain themselves? Similarly, Professor Walen states that people who commit a 'very serious crime or a series of more or less serious crimes' may be preventively detained after serving their sentence because they have 'lost their status' as autonomous persons.[101] Even if limited to serious cases, this rationale has the potential to permit preventive detention of huge numbers of murderers and recidivists. Additionally, it does not explain why dangerous people who commit a moderately serious crime or a series of lesser crimes do not lose their autonomous status; presumably, what signals a willingness to exercise autonomy in the wrong direction and thus justifies ignoring the right to be treated as autonomous is the intentionality or number of one's crimes, not their seriousness.[102] Walen's scheme

---

[98] Cf Stephen J Schulhofer, 'Two Systems of Social Protection: Comments on the Civil-Criminal Distinction, with Particular Reference to Sexually Violent Predator Laws' (1996) 7 *Journal of Contemporary Legal Issues* 69: (preventive detention outside the criminal justice system is permissible 'when the state has a compelling interest that cannot be met through the criminal process'.); Alec Walen, 'A Unified Theory of Detention with Application to Detention for Suspected Terrorists' (2011) 70 *Maryland Law Review* 871, 880: (permitting preventive detention of suspected terrorists who are 'incapable of being adequately policed and held accountable for their choices', a situation that occurs when the alternative to preventive detention – deportation – results in the inadequate monitoring of the suspected terrorist).

[99] Note that detention of a person about to be released from prison does not violate the legality principle because of the crime that authorized the imprisonment. See *United States v DiFrancesco*, 449 US 117 (1980).

[100] Walen, above n 98, 921 ('One who has a dangerous, infectious disease, or even one who merely has reason to think there is a good chance he has such a disease, can ensure he does not harm others only by staying away from them. If this is true, then he has a duty to isolate himself from others.').

[101] Ibid 908.

[102] Ibid 911 (noting that lost status could attach to one-time thieves and robbers).

is not so much 'autonomy-respecting' as autonomy-ignoring. In effect, it states that autonomy is important, but only until the person presents a serious danger that cannot be punished by the criminal justice system, in which case it is not.[103]

The better rationale for these types of preventive detention (meant to be described by the principle of criminal justice primacy) is that the criminal justice system must be the response to antisocial behavior unless it *cannot work as a preventive mechanism.* This approach would not focus on autonomy or convictability but on deterrability, a state in which a person is either unable or unwilling to exercise autonomy in the right direction even if the consequences are grave and immediate. Consider the three categories of people just described. Individuals who are so mentally ill that they misperceive reality will not be concerned about criminal punishment (a point developed in more detail below). Similarly, assuming no reasonable medical alternative to confinement, people who suffer from highly contagious and deadly diseases cannot, no matter how hard they try, prevent infection as they go about their daily lives; thus, criminal punishment cannot do so either. Soldiers who are under orders to kill or be killed (or terrorists who have no compunction about dying in their efforts to assassinate others) are also unaffected by the prospect of criminal penalties; indeed, they are willing to risk death. In other words, the danger represented by these people is *undeterrable* through the criminal sanction; even if the proverbial cop were standing near their elbow, they would harm others (including, perhaps, the cop).[104] The undeterrability rationale also clarifies that the state's interest in protecting its citizens, while always significant, nonetheless only outweighs the un-convicted individual's liberty interest sufficiently to permit non-criminal confinement when the criminal justice system can have no impact. In short, the undeterrability rationale better explains why many nonautonomous actors may be subject to long-term prevention detention – their undeterrability, not their lack of autonomy or their unconvictability – and also explains why some autonomous actors may be so detained.[105]

---

[103] In the enemy combatant context, Professor Walen states in another work that '[a] precondition for someone having the right to be treated as autonomous is that the person be accountable for harmful acts that the state has a right to require them not to commit' and that enemy combatants do not meet that precondition. Alec Walen, 'Taking Autonomy Seriously (or Not): A Moral Mistake at the Core of Slobogin's Approach to Preventive Detention' in Michael Corrado (ed), *Preventing Danger: New Paradigms in Criminal Justice* (Carolina Press, 2013) 4–5. Although this reasoning makes sense, I would not call it "autonomy-respecting," but rather autonomy-ignoring. Professor Walen has offered a justification for preventive detention of enemy combatants despite their autonomy, again based on the perceived danger of waiting until the person has exercised their autonomy in the wrong direction.

[104] The 'policeman-at-the-elbow' test is one way in which the irresistible impulse prong of the insanity test has been operationalized in the United States. See Gary B Melton et al, *Psychological Evaluations for the Courts: A Handbook for Mental Health Professionals and Lawyers* (Guilford Press, 3rd ed, 2007) 216.

[105] Note that Article 14 of the Convention on the Rights of Persons with Disabilities provides in part that "States Parties shall ensure that . . . the existence of a disability shall in no case justify a

Applying this principle to a case of post-sentence commitment such as M's, the state would have to show that the individual is impervious to serious criminal sanction before preventive detention could take place. If the individual is suffering from psychosis, such a showing might easily be made. People with psychosis who commit crimes often do not know they are doing so or think they are acting in self-defense.[106] In these situations, fear of the criminal law can have no impact on their actions. On this view, a preventive detention system for psychotic individuals who have served their sentence or for people acquitted by reason of insanity is justifiable, as is involuntary civil hospitalization of people with psychosis (assuming the overt act requirement of principle one is met).

The absence of a psychotic disorder would not necessarily mean that post-sentence preventive detention is impermissible, however. Some offenders with severe impulse control problems, although not as compromised as people with psychosis, might also be said to be undeterrable at the time of their crime. However, the degree of undeterrability necessary to justify preventive intervention must be significant – akin, again, to the policeman at the elbow scenario. Otherwise, this reasoning could easily end up justifying preventive detention of ordinary recidivists as well – individuals whose actions *are* affected by the prospect of punishment. As the Minnesota Supreme Court held in a case involving preventive detention of a sex offender, such commitment requires proof not only of risk but also of 'an utter lack of power to control their sexual impulses'.[107] Other people who might fall into this category are those at the extreme end of the psychopathy spectrum – those who evidence complete disregard for the criminal law – and people with severe addictions who could be said to have disorders of desire.[108] Whether M or Fardon fits into this category is difficult to tell from the record in their cases. As noted

---

deprivation of liberty." Available at http://www.un.org/disabilities/convention/conventionfull.shtml. This language appears to prohibit preventive detention based on disability *per se*. See Office of the High Commissioner for Human Rights Thematic Study on Legal Measures for Ratification and Implementation of CRPD, A/HRC/10/48, paras. 48–49. If so, in defining who may be preventively detained signatory countries must rely on functional criteria rather than on diagnostic labels like "psychosis" or, to use the words of the European Convention, "unsound mind". The criminal justice primacy principle provides such a functional definition, one that rests not on a distinction between disability and non-disability but on undeterrability, applicable not only to those who are thought to be "disabled" but to other people as well.

[106] See Slobogin, *Minding Justice*, above n 84, 23–8.
[107] *In re Blodgett*, 510 NW 2d 910, 913 (Minn, 1994) (quoting *State ex rel Pearson v Probate Court*, 287 NW 297, 302 (1939) *affd* 309 US 270 (1940)) (internal quotation marks omitted); see also *Thomas v State*, 74 SW 3d 789, 791–2 (Mo, 2002): (holding that commitment requires proof of 'serious difficulty in controlling . . . behavior'); *In re Commitment of W Z*, 801 A 2d 205, 216–8 (NJ, 2002): (holding that commitment requires proof of an 'inability to control one's sexually violent behavior').
[108] Cf Stephen Morse, 'Preventive Detention of Psychopaths and Dangerous Offenders' (2011) 48 *San Diego Law Review* 1077, 1116: (arguing that psychopaths 'cannot grasp or be guided by the good reasons not to offend', an incapacity that could be expressed 'either as a cognitive or control defect' and also concluding that 'internal duress' or 'disorders of desire' might explain some crimes committed by addicts).

earlier, M was 51 by the time his case got to the European Court. While the rape for which Fardon was serving his sentence (of 14 years) occurred 20 days after his release from a 13-year prison sentence for a previous rape, no other information about his criminal history or psychological profile is provided in either the High Court's opinion or the HRC opinion.

However, Leroy Hendricks – who declared shortly before the end of his prison sentence (for his eighth and ninth acts of child molestation) that he could not 'control the urge' to molest children and that the only sure way he could keep from sexually abusing them was 'to die'[109] – probably did meet the undeterrability criterion. If so, the Supreme Court was right to permit his post-sentence commitment. Then there is the case of Garry David from Australia. David was sentenced to 14 years for shooting a woman and two police officers, conduct that occurred right after his release from a previous violent offence. While in prison he assaulted more than 15 inmates and guards. Noting that his diagnosis was antisocial personality disorder, a court found that, if released, David's underlying anger and resentment would be almost certain to rise to an explosive level as soon as he felt thwarted or subjected to stress.[110] David would also appear to have been eligible for post-sentence preventive detention.

6.   CONCLUSION

If preventive detention adheres to the foregoing principles it should be permitted, whether tacked on to the end of a sentence or designed as a substitute for it. Continued resistance to this authority in Europe might stem in part from the fact that Nazi Germany enthusiastically endorsed the idea of habitual offender laws, thus associating preventive detention with the worst sort of authoritarianism.[111] But the European Court of Human Rights rightly concluded in *M* that this fact did not undermine the conclusion that a post-sentence preventive disposition, properly limited, is not a penalty.[112]

This conclusion only stands, however, if all of the principles described above are followed. Detention for preventive purposes must be the least drastic means of achieving the government's public safety goals and may occur only if a significant probability of serious harm is proven through the best possible scientific evidence, and even then only if meaningful correctional efforts, along the lines suggested

---

[109]   *Hendricks*, 521 US 355.
[110]   For a description of this case, see C Robert Williams, 'Psychopathy, Mental Illness and Preventive Detention: Issues Arising from the David Case' (1990) 16 *Monash University Law Review* 161, 162, 170–78.
[111]   *M v Germany* [108].
[112]   Ibid [125].

by *M v Germany*, are made. Frequent periodic review is also essential. If these principles are followed, a system of liberty deprivation that permits preventive detention can be more humane than one that does not, not only because preventive measures will be strictly cabined and oriented toward treatment but also because governments will know that their most dangerous offenders will be sequestered and thus that the vast majority of offenders can be given short sentences.[113]

---

[113]   Cf ibid [116] (where the German government made a similar argument).

PREVENTIVE DETENTION IN ENGLAND AND WALES: A REVIEW UNDER THE HUMAN RIGHTS FRAMEWORK

Kris GLEDHILL

Various parts of this book feature preventive detention regimes put in place at the end of a punitive sentence, often modelled on the US laws governing sexually violent predators, that have been adopted in various parts of Australia and planned for New Zealand. England and Wales does not have such legislation, but part of this chapter will explain that an alternative legislative structure that achieves the same effect is in place in the form of the *Mental Health Act 1983*. This is supplemented by various orders designed to prevent future crime, together with a risk assessment framework. The chapter will also deal with the question of whether the arrangements in place are consistent with a human rights framework, the central elements of which are the state's duties to protect the victims of predictable crime, to avoid arbitrary detention or arbitrary interference with privacy autonomy rights and to ensure that due process is secured.

1. THE *MENTAL HEALTH ACT 1983*: PREVENTIVE DETENTION

1.1. DEFINITION OF MENTAL DISORDER

In the USA, the current wave of preventive detention laws[1] typically act as a supplement to the mental health provisions of the relevant state code. The original

---

[1]   These are reminiscent of the laws that became popular from the 1930s onwards, dealing with 'sexual psychopaths', broadly those with an unstable personality who were unable to comply with social norms and laws and had a compulsion to commit sexual offences. See John Kip Cornwell, 'Protection and Treatment: The Permissible Civil Detention of Sexual Predators' (1996) 53 *Washington and Lee Law Review* 1293; John M Fabian, 'Kansas v Hendricks, Crane and Beyond' (2003) 29(4) *William Mitchell Law Review* 1367.

model, enacted in 1990, is part of the mental illness section of the Washington Code[2] and targets the 'sexually violent predator':

> (16) 'Sexually violent predator' means any person who has been convicted of or charged with a crime of sexual violence and who suffers from a mental abnormality or personality disorder which makes the person likely to engage in predatory acts of sexual violence if not confined in a secure facility.[3]

In England and Wales, the definitions of mental disorder in its *Mental Health Act 1983* have always been wide enough to cover people who would meet this definition and have been widened by the *Mental Health Act 2007* in a way that puts this beyond doubt. So, the definition of mental disorder in section 1 of the 1983 Act is 'any disorder or disability of the mind'; prior to the 2007 Act, it was necessary for most purposes to find that the mental disorder amounted to mental illness, mental impairment, severe mental impairment or psychopathic disorder. The latter category is the most relevant for present purposes. There was one limitation, namely that the disorder had to be treatable in order to found longer-term detention.[4] However, this test was easy to meet because it required only that it be possible to stop a deterioration' and it was satisfied if the impact was only on the consequences of the disorder, even if the underlying condition was not affected.[5]

This categorization has been removed, leaving only the basic (and wide) definition of mental disorder. In addition, the 2007 Act removed a number of exclusions from the coverage of the statute. Originally, section 1(3) of the 1983 Act provided that mental disorder could not arise only from 'promiscuity or other immoral conduct, sexual deviancy or dependence on alcohol or drugs', but as amended by the 2007 Act, only dependence on alcohol or drugs is excluded. The aim of the government in removing the exclusion of sexual deviancy was expressly to ensure that disorders of sexual preference recognised clinically as mental disorders

---

[2]   *Mental Illness*, 71 Wash Rev Code ch 09 <http://apps.leg.wa.gov/RCW/>. The law is predicated on legislative findings that the existing mental health regime is inadequate to deal with the personality disorders that lead to repeat sex offending: *Mental Illness*, 71 Wash Rev Code ch 09 § 010.
[3]   Ibid ch 09 § 020. For another example (recently renamed from *Mental Health, Mental Retardation, and Substance Abuse Services*): *Behavioral Health and Development Services*, 37.2 Va Code Ann ch 9 <http://leg1.state.va.us/cgi-bin/legp504.exe?000+cod+TOC>.
[4]   *Mental Health Act 1983* (UK) ss 3, 20, 37 (as enacted).
[5]   See *Reid v Secretary of State for Scotland* [1999] 2 AC 512 at 531: Lord Hope commented that, when considered in the context of disorders to which the treatability test applied, medical treatment clearly covered treatment aimed to alleviate or to prevent a deterioration of the mental disorder, but extended to 'treatment which alleviates or prevents a deterioration of the symptoms of the mental disorder, not the disorder itself which gives rise to them'. See also Lord Hutton at 551.

are covered by the Act; 'paraphilias like fetishism or paedophilia' are given as examples in the Explanatory Notes to the *Mental Health Act 2007*.[6]

Moreover, the treatability requirement has been removed. What has been put in its place is a requirement that appropriate treatment be available, which is defined in section 3(4) of the 1983 Act[7] as 'medical treatment which is appropriate in his case, taking into account the nature and degree of the mental disorder and all other circumstances of his case'. What counts as medical treatment is also widely defined by section 145(1) of the 1983 Act; it 'includes nursing, psychological intervention and specialist mental health habilitation, rehabilitation and care'. By section 145(4), which was added by the 2007 Act,[8] it has to have as its purpose 'to alleviate, or prevent a worsening of, the disorder or one or more of its symptoms or manifestations'; it may meet this without any prospect of success.

1.2. DETENTION IN HOSPITAL BY ORDER OF THE CRIMINAL COURTS

The next point to note about the English regime is the ability of the criminal courts to impose a 'hospital order' to place a defendant in hospital at the end of a criminal process. Section 37 of the *Mental Health Act 1983* allows a hospital order to be made wherever the offence is one that carries imprisonment. In addition, it can be imposed if a defendant is found not guilty by reason of insanity but to have committed the conduct part of the offence charged or if the defendant is found not fit to stand trial but to have committed the act.[9] The criteria for an order are that there is mental disorder, that it is of a nature or degree making it appropriate for the defendant to be detained in hospital for medical treatment, that appropriate treatment is available and that it is the most suitable disposal in light of 'all the circumstances including the nature of the offence and the character and antecedents of the offender, and to the other available methods of dealing with him'. So there is a combination of clinical criteria and judicial discretion; in relation to the latter, the finding that hospital placement is the most suitable disposal, this may be made out even if there is no causal link between mental

---

[6]   *Explanatory Notes to the Mental Health Act 2007* (UK) [24].

[7]   Added by *Mental Health Act 2007* (UK), s 4(3).

[8]   Ibid s 7(2).

[9]   In the Crown Court, the jury trial court, these sentencing powers arise under a combination of the *Criminal Procedure (Insanity) Act 1964* and the *Criminal Procedure (Insanity and Unfitness to Plead) Act 1991*; for a more detailed account, see Gledhill, *Defending Mentally Disordered Persons* (Legal Action Group, 2012) ch 9, 12. In the summary court, the Magistrates Court, the main provision is section 37(3) of the *Mental Health Act 1983*, allowing the imposition of a hospital order without a conviction, which has been interpreted to allow processes similar to those followed under the specific statutes in the Crown Court; see Gledhill, *Defending Mentally Disordered Persons*, ch 10, 13.

disorder and the offending behaviour.[10] This permits a finding that a defendant who falls to be sentenced for an offence poses a risk of further offending by reason of a mental disorder, even if not implicated in the index offence, such that a hospital order disposal is proper.

A hospital order lasts for six months and can then be renewed under section 20(4)(c) of the Act, which applies also to civil patients, if the test for renewal is made out; these are the criteria for the imposition of the hospital order and a finding that 'it is necessary for the health or safety of the patient or for the protection of other persons that he should receive such treatment and it cannot be provided unless he is detained under this section'.[11] In short, once made, if the defendant has a mental disorder that poses an ongoing risk, detention can be indefinite. Of course, given that a civil order could be made in any event, the hospital order can be seen as just a way of securing the defendant's involvement in the hospital process by diverting him or her from the criminal justice system at the sentencing stage; an alternative view is that it is a method of securing preventive detention through the criminal justice system.

1.3. THE RESTRICTION ORDER REGIME

There is a second part of the hospital order regime to be noted, which is much more clearly a preventive detention regime, namely the restriction order under section 41 of the 1983 Act. This section provides that a hospital order can be combined with a restriction order where

> it appears to the court, having regard to the nature of the offence, the antecedents of the offender and the risk of his committing further offences if set at large, that it is necessary for the protection of the public from serious harm so to do …[12]

The effects of a restriction order are that: (i) the hospital order no longer lapses after six months (rather, it is in existence until it is discharged, which may be never); (ii) management decisions, such as the transfer of the patient or the granting of leave,

---

[10]   See, for example, *R v Paul Lee Smith* [2001] EWCA Crim 743, [2001] MHLR 46, where the sentencing judge's refusal to impose a hospital order because there was no connection between the offence (rape) and the defendant's mental disorder was overturned on the basis that the judge had placed undue weight on the lack of a causal link. However, this does not mean that a punitive sentence cannot be imposed on a defendant who has a mental disorder: see *R v Nafei* [2004] EWCA Crim 3238, [2006] MHLR 176, a drug importation case. For a fuller discussion, see Gledhill, above n 9, ch 18.

[11]   There is no necessity test at the time a section 37 order is made: if there were, it would exclude a defendant who was willing to be a voluntary patient in hospital.

[12]   This can only be made by the Crown Court, but magistrates have power to commit a defendant to the Crown Court for sentence if it is felt that a restriction order might be necessary: *Mental Health Act 1983* s 43.

require the consent of the Secretary of State for Justice; and (iii) release[13] may be made subject to conditions and the prospect of recall by the Secretary of State for Justice.[14] A restriction order lasts indefinitely, and so the defendant is subject to detention or recall for life; only if he or she is granted an absolute discharge by the Tribunal or Secretary of State will the effect of the restriction order come to an end. In short, this regime puts the patient under a dual administration, part of which is a therapeutic relationship with the treating clinician; but major decisions in this regime are subject to the secondary supervision of the executive, which has public safety as its governing feature.

In the central decision on when a restriction order is proper, *R v Birch*,[15] the Court of Appeal noted that, whilst a risk of anti-social recidivism could not lead to a restriction order, a relatively minor offence could lead to one:

> [T]here is nothing in the Act which requires a causal connection between the offender's mental state and what the professionals call the 'index offence'. It is sufficient for section 41 that the defendant is a convicted offender, and that the conditions of section 41 are satisfied … It would however be a mistake to equate the seriousness of the offence with the probability that a restriction order will be made. This is only one of the factors which section 41(1) requires to be taken into account. A minor offence by a man who proves to be mentally disordered and dangerous may properly leave him subject to a restriction.[16]

So, as examples, restriction orders have been upheld in relation to: an assault occasioning actual bodily harm from a punch when the medical evidence rather than prior conduct suggested that there might be an escalation (*R v Kamara*);[17] a burglary combined with medical evidence of command hallucinations and aggressive behaviour in hospital (*Jones v Isleworth Crown Court*);[18] a burglary by a man with drug abuse and mental health problems who was, as a result, inherently likely to commit further offences and so confront householders (*R v Golding*);[19] and several minor offences (theft of a pair of police gloves, shoplifting of food, possession of cannabis and breach of bail) by a man who had been involved in public disorder and had been aggressive in hospital in the context of a withdrawal from treatment but who had serious offending in the past and had spent time in

---

[13]   Which may be ordered by a judicial Tribunal or the Secretary of State for Justice.
[14]   It should be noted that civil patients may be released on a community treatment order and subject to recall, but this power is exercisable by a clinician who is in a therapeutic relationship with the patient not by a member of the executive whose function centres on public safety.
[15]   (1990) 90 Cr App R 78.
[16]   Ibid 88 (Mustill LJ).
[17]   [2000] MHLR 9.
[18]   [2005] EWHC 662 (Admin), [2005] MHLR 93.
[19]   [2006] EWCA Crim 1965, [2006] MHLR 272.

high secure hospital conditions on transfer from prison (*R v Steele*).[20] It is to be noted that a restriction order can be imposed even if the doctors do not support it; the assessment of risk is for the judge.

So, a judicial sentencing decision that a person poses a risk arising from mental disorder can lead to a life-long order involving preventive detention and, if the patient is released, control in the community with the prospect of recall to hospital.

1.4. TRANSFERS OF PRISONERS TO HOSPITAL

In addition to this, there are provisions that allow a serving prisoner to be transferred to hospital before the end of a custodial sentence and thereby be treated as if a hospital order had been made. This can cover patients whose mental disorder has become apparent during the sentence as well as those whose mental disorder could have led to a hospital order being made by the criminal court but who were sent to prison instead. Importantly, a prisoner transferred to hospital will not be released at the end of the sentence imposed. This regime arises under section 47 of the 1983 Act, which allows the Secretary of State for Justice to transfer a serving prisoner to hospital. The criteria are that medical evidence indicates the presence of mental disorder of nature or degree to make detention in hospital for medical treatment appropriate, the availability of appropriate medical treatment and that the Secretary of State deems transfer 'expedient'. This is a discretion, but one that has to take into account the interests of the detainee, who is entitled to the same level of mental health care as anyone else (since that is not a right lost by imprisonment).[21]

There have been examples of this expediency being based on concerns that the prisoner is too dangerous to be released at the end of a sentence in light of the risk of offending arising from mental disorder. In *SW London and St George's Mental Health NHS Trust v 'W'*,[22] the latter had been sent to prison on the basis that his personality disorder could not be treated, and so he did not meet the criteria then required for a hospital order (namely the treatability requirement which, as noted above, was removed by the *Mental Health Act 2007*). This opinion of non-treatability had been confirmed during his sentence, but immediately before he was due to be released from prison, W was transferred to hospital under section

---

[20]   [2010] EWCA Crim 605, [2010] MHLR 107.
[21]   Indeed, a failure to take reasonable steps to treat mental disorder could breach rights under the European Convention on Human Rights (see fn 52 infra), in particular Art 8 and also potentially Art 3 in an extreme case: see *R (D) v Home Secretary and National Assembly for Wales* [2004] EWHC 2857 (Admin), [2005] MHLR 17.
[22]   [2002] EWHC 1770 Admin, [2002] MHLR 392.

47. The basis for this was that he required a structured release plan to prevent him manifesting his disorder. Crane J held that this was all lawful; indeed, he recorded that there was no challenge to its use at the end of the sentence.[23] The factual context, it should be noted, was that W had been transferred to a secure hospital unit, and there was no immediate prospect of him being released.[24] In an earlier case, *R v Secretary of State for the Home Department ex p Gilkes*,[25] a challenge to the use of a transfer at the end of a sentence was dismissed as not unreasonable; Dyson J noted that late transfers were 'undesirable', but he specifically rejected an argument that such transfers could only be lawful in 'exceptional cases'.[26]

The use of the power at the end of the sentence has been upheld under the *Mental Health Act 1983* as amended in 2007 (as noted above, by removing the need for treatability of those with a psychopathic disorder but adding the requirement that appropriate treatment be available for all forms of disorder). In *R (SP) v Secretary of State for Justice*,[27] the Court of Appeal upheld the transfer to a high secure hospital of a prisoner who was a week away from release (from a sentence for serious driving and arson offences) and who was said to be suffering from a psychopathic disorder. He had not been offered any treatment in prison because the degree of his disorder excluded him from relevant programmes; the transfer was to ensure that he was able to access treatment in a setting where he would not be excluded. The point argued in the case was whether there was proper evidence that appropriate treatment was available, not the use of the power at the end of the sentence, even though an obvious question might be why he had not been transferred at the outset of his seven-year sentence.

As has been noted, the effect of a transfer at the end of a sentence of imprisonment is that the transferee remains detained; this is because section 47(3) provides that '[a] transfer direction with respect to any person shall have the same effect as a hospital order made in his case'. The patient's detention can then be renewed for so long as the criteria for detention remain.[28] In addition, the Secretary of State can add a restriction direction under section 49 of the Act, which means both that

---

[23]   Ibid [9].
[24]   There are other reported examples of transfers at the end of the sentence, including successful challenges on the basis that the treatability test was not met. See *R (F) v Secretary of State for Justice* [2008] EWCA Civ 1457, [2008] MHLR 370: transfer at end of sentence quashed because of failure of medical evidence to address issue of treatability. See also *R (DK) v Secretary of State* [2010] EWHC 82 (Admin), [2010] MHLR 64: transfer at the end of a sentence was quashed on the basis of inadequate reasons as to treatability.
[25]   [1999] MHLR 6.
[26]   Ibid [18]; he noted that it was a relevant factor in assessing expedience. In *R (F) v Secretary of State for Justice* [2008] EWCA Civ 1457, [2008] MHLR 370 [31], Waller LJ noted that transfers at the end of a sentence would 'hopefully ... only be in very exceptional cases', but the court did not have to consider the lawfulness of the practice.
[27]   [2010] EWCA Civ 1590, [2011] MHLR 65.
[28]   This is subject to review by a Tribunal.

the patient is treated as if a restriction order had been made and also that there can be a return to prison if the release date has not passed and the patient no longer needs to be in hospital.[29] Any such restriction direction ceases to have effect once the prison release date has passed, leaving just the equivalent of a section 37 order.

It should be noted that, whilst those who have a mental disorder and could have had a hospital order imposed might nevertheless be sentenced to imprisonment (on the basis that there was a need for punishment and a hospital disposal was not the most suitable), an addition to the range of options given to the courts has been to impose a prison sentence and secure the equivalent of a transfer under sections 47 and 49 (meaning that the defendant would move from hospital to prison if the need for hospitalisation ceased).

This hybrid order exists under section 45A of the 1983 Act, which was added by section 46 of the *Crime (Sentences) Act 1997*. Its purpose[30] was to deal with 'certain mentally disordered offenders for whom the present form of hospital order is unsatisfactory, particularly those who are considered to bear a significant degree of responsibility for their offences',[31] such that a fixed period in detention might be required 'because the offender is found to bear some significant responsibility for the offence notwithstanding his disorder, or because the link between the offending behaviour and the mental disorder is not clear at the time of sentencing'.[32] This would 'enable the courts to deal with some of the most difficult cases in a way which took proper account of the offender's need for treatment; the demands of justice; and the proper right of other people to be protected from harm'.[33] As enacted, it applied only to those with a psychopathic disorder; it was only extended to other forms of mental disorder when the *Mental Health Act 2007* removed the different categories and left only the general definition of mental disorder.

1.5. OTHER RISK BASED SENTENCING OPTIONS

This range of options available to the sentencing courts, combined with the administrative arrangement to transfer prisoners to hospital, means that there is a preventive detention regime and so no need for a separate sexually violent

---

[29] Being able to secure the objective of returning the patient to prison if he or she recovers means that there is no need for a level of risk such as would justify a restriction order under s 41, even though it has the same effect: see *R (T) v Home Secretary* [2003] EWHC 538, [2003] MHLR 239.
[30] *Protecting the Public: the Government's Strategy on Crime in England and Wales*, Cm 3190 (1996). The relevant discussion is in chapter 8, which for some reason dealt with sex offenders and mentally disordered offenders.
[31] Ibid [8.12].
[32] Ibid [8.13].
[33] Ibid [8.12].

predator law. To complete this picture, it should be noted that there are many other ways in which the English criminal justice system makes provision for preventive detention or otherwise takes preventive action.

So (i) for the most serious offences, namely those carrying life imprisonment, the accepted basis for the imposition of that life sentence is that the offender is dangerous and is so for an unpredictable period of time; (ii) there has been a significant experimentation with an expanded range of risk-based sentencing (involving both determinate and indeterminate terms); (iii) there has developed a significant range of preventive orders that are either ancillary to a sentence or can be made separately.

(i)   Life imprisonment

Expanding on these in turn, the sentence of discretionary life imprisonment[34] is proper if an offender commits a serious example of an offence carrying a maximum sentence of life, and the evidence was that he or she presented a risk of further serious offending over a time-scale that could not adequately be assessed by the court, such that a determinate sentence could not protect the public.[35] This could arise from mental disorder provided that the offence itself was serious enough;[36] so, in contrast to the restriction order assessment, it was not enough that there was evidence of an escalating pattern. (This provides a significant contrast between preventive detention in a hospital setting and that in a prison setting; the former has much lower criteria.)

(ii)   Imprisonment for Public Protection (IPP)

Second, there has been an experiment with an extended regime of preventive detention based on a finding of dangerousness. The experiment started with the legislature seeking to reduce the discretion of the judiciary not to impose a discretionary life sentence and then vastly increased the situations in which an indeterminate sentence was imposed. The legislature then had to roll back the regime because of serious concerns about it. The initial change was the automatic life sentence regime of section 2 of the *Crime (Sentences) Act 1997*, which required a life sentence for the second conviction for one of a list of several serious offences (all of which carried discretionary life imprisonment),[37] unless

---

[34]   There is a also a mandatory life sentence if the offence is murder: *Murder (Abolition of Death Penalty) Act 1965* (UK) s 1.

[35]   See *R v Chapman* [2000] 1 Cr App R 77. This built on *R v Hodgson* (1968) 52 Cr App R 113 and *AG's Ref No 32 of 1996 (Whittaker)* [1997] 1 Cr App R(S) 261.

[36]   See *R v Simmonds* [2001] EWCA Crim 167, [2001] MHLR 54.

[37]   The offences for England and Wales were set out in s 2(5) of the Act, and were: attempted murder, conspiracy to murder or incitement to murder, soliciting murder (s 4 of the *Offences Against the Person Act 1861* [UK]), manslaughter, wounding causing grievous bodily harm with

there were exceptional circumstances; in effect, the discretionary life sentence became a mandatory sentence unless these exceptional reasons could be found. This had to be imposed even if there was mental disorder justifying a hospital disposal (that not being exceptional),[38] though it could be a factor revealing that the defendant was not in fact dangerous (which would give a reason to find the case exceptional).[39]

When the extended dangerous offender regime was introduced by sections 224 and following of the *Criminal Justice Act 2003*,[40] the automatic life sentence was removed; but courts were now allowed to impose a hospital disposal instead of a dangerousness-based custodial disposal.[41] The new regime rested on a list of over 150 'specified offences' of a sexual or violent nature; if they carried ten years or more, they were 'serious offences'. On conviction for a specified offence, the court had to carry out an assessment of dangerousness. If that dangerousness was found to exist, an indeterminate sentence of imprisonment for public protection[42] was required if the offence was a serious specified offence; otherwise, it was necessary to impose an extended sentence of custody plus extended supervision in the community.[43] The key finding of dangerousness was made out by a significant risk to members of the public of serious harm occasioned by the commission of further specified offences. It is to be noted that these provisions were triggered by a single offence; if it was a second conviction for a specified offence, dangerousness was presumed unless that was an unreasonable view to take. As to the impact of mental disorder, in *R v Johnson*,[44] the Court of Appeal noted that, inter alia:

---

intent (s 18 of the *Offences Against the Person Act 1861*), rape or attempted rape, intercourse with a girl under 13 (s 5 of the *Sexual Offences Act 1956* [UK]), possessing a firearm with intent to injure, using a firearm to resist arrest, or carrying a firearm with criminal intent (ss 16, 17 and 18 of the *Firearms Act 1968* [UK]; and robbery using a firearm or imitation firearm within the meaning of that Act. Equivalent offences for Scotland and Northern Ireland were set out in ss 2(6) and (7).

[38] Section 37 of the *Mental Health Act 1983* was amended to make this point. In *R v Drew* [2003] UKHL 25, [2003] 1 WLR 1213, [2003] MHLR 282, it was found acceptable to sentence to prison a defendant who needed to be in hospital provided that there was an adequately quick section 47 transfer to hospital; otherwise there would be a breach of Article 3 of the ECHR. This was upheld by the European Court of Human Rights in *Drew v UK* appn 35679/03, [2006] MHLR 203. The Court did suggest that there were problems under Art 5, the right to liberty, from detention in a non-therapeutic setting (though this had not been argued in the domestic courts and so could not be a proper basis for challenge before it).

[39] For example, *R v Newnham* [2000] 2 Cr App R(S) 407: acute mental illness at time of incompetent armed robbery; illness then treated.

[40] Pt 12, c 5.

[41] Section 37 of the 1983 Act was amended to make it no longer subservient to the dangerous offender provisions.

[42] The discretionary life sentence remained available if the seriousness of the offence justified it.

[43] In relation to young offenders, an extended sentence was possible for a serious specified offence.

[44] [2006] EWCA Crim 2486, [2007] 1 WLR 585, [2006] 2 Prison LR 159.

inadequacy, suggestibility, or vulnerability ... may serve to mitigate the offender's culpability. In the final analysis however they may also serve to produce or reinforce the conclusion that the offender is dangerous. In one of the instant cases it was suggested that the sentence was wrong because an inadequate offender had suffered what was described as an 'aberrant moment'. But, as experience shows, aberrant moments may be productive of catastrophe. The sentencer is right to be alert to such risks of aberrant moments in the future, and their consequences.[45]

Unfortunately, the Court did not go on to note the possibility of a disposal by way of hospital order (though on the facts none of the defendants whose cases were being considered were suitable for a hospital order).

In practice, the dangerous offender sentencing provisions caused significant problems, in particular because large numbers of people were caught, even for relatively minor offending, such that a short minimum term was imposed as part of the indeterminate sentence to reflect the seriousness of the crime. Though their cases could be reviewed by the Parole Board once the minimum term had been served, they could not be released until their risk had been reduced. Such a finding depended on the completion of courses and interventions, but the resources for these were not forthcoming. In *R (Walker and James) v Secretary of State for Justice*,[46] it was held by the Court of Appeal that the failure to provide adequate resources meant that the bringing into force of the statutory regime was irrational and, so, illegal. This conclusion was not appealed when the case proceeded to the House of Lords (on a question relating to Article 5 of the ECHR [European Convention on Human Rights]).[47]

As a result, the regime was significantly rolled back. In sections 13 to 18 of the *Criminal Justice and Immigration Act 2008*: (i) the presumption as to the existence of dangerousness if a defendant was convicted of a second specified offence was removed; (ii) the duty to impose at least imprisonment for public protection for a serious specified offence by an adult on the finding of dangerousness became a matter of discretion and arose only if the offender had a previous conviction for one of 22 more serious specified offences or the tariff set to reflect the seriousness of the index offence and associated offending was at least two years; and (iii) the ambit of the extended sentence for adults was widened to make it an alternative.

---

[45]   Ibid [10](v) (Sir Igor Judge P).
[46]   [2008] EWCA Civ 30, [2008] 1 WLR 1977, [2008] Prison LR 63.
[47]   *R (James, Lee and Wells) v Secretary of State for Justice* [2009] UKHL 22, [2009] 2 WLR 1149, [2009] Prison LR 371. The House concluded that there was no breach of Art 5(1), but the European Court of Human Rights reached a contrary view, finding that detention based on dangerousness had to involve rehabilitation in order to be lawful: see *James, Wells and Lee v UK*, apps 25119/09 57715/09 57877/09, judgment of 18 September 2012.

The latest government has gone further: chapter 5 of part 3 of the *Legal Aid, Sentencing and Punishment of Offenders Act 2012* removes the indeterminate sentences for public protection (by section 123) and reworks the extended sentences. Section 122 of this Act adds a section 224A to the *Criminal Justice Act 2003* to require a life sentence for a second conviction for one of a list of offences that carry life imprisonment. However, this only occurs if the sentence for the previous offence was ten years or more or a life sentence with a minimum term of five years or more (which would be based on a ten-year determinate term, since early release is after a half of such a term) and the offence merits ten years or more. There is also an exception that it is not necessary to impose the life sentence if it would be unjust (which was similar to the exception to the automatic life sentence regime). This will presumably be interpreted as to allow a defendant to show that he or she is not dangerous despite the second conviction and so is outside the purpose of a life sentence.[48]

The reworked extended sentences remain based on a finding of a significant risk of the causing of serious harm from the commission of further specified offences. So there remains a commitment to risk assessment. This is interesting because the White Paper that led to the end of the sentence of IPP included amongst the reasons for changing the regime:

> The limitations in our ability to predict future serious offending also calls into question the whole basis on which many offenders are sentenced to IPPs and, among those who are already serving these sentences, which of them are suitable for release.[49]

(iii)   Ancillary orders

The final development in English sentencing has been the expansion of ancillary orders (and some free-standing ones not linked directly to a sentence) designed to prevent re-offending, combined with administrative arrangements for managing offenders thought to pose a risk. These also rest on abilities to predict future offending, which is accepted to be limited.

There are a significant number of these orders, and so this is merely a selected outline. Those convicted of sexual offences are required to register for monitoring purposes and can be subject to Sexual Offences Protection Orders, Foreign Travel Orders or Risk of Sexual Harm Orders under Part II of the *Sexual Offences Act*

---

[48]   As was the case in relation to the automatic life sentence: see *R v Offen and others* [2000] EWCA Crim 96, [2001] 1 WLR 253, [2001] Prison LR 283. This allowed the court to avoid imposing an arbitrary sentence that might otherwise breach Art 5 ECHR.

[49]   *Breaking the Cycle: Effective Punishment, Rehabilitation and Sentencing of Offenders*, Cm 7972 (2010) [186].

2003. These will also apply to a person who was unfit to stand trial or judged not guilty by reason of insanity but found to have committed the relevant act. These orders allow courts to provide restrictions on what people can do and are designed to meet risks they are said to pose, with breach being a criminal offence. Similar regimes are applicable to different sorts of behaviour, such as the Anti-Social Behaviour Order, which was introduced by the *Crime and Disorder Act 1998* and gradually extended since.[50] The regime allows magistrates to make orders prohibiting further anti-social conduct on an application by the police, a local authority or a social landlord, with a criminal penalty for breach; the central test on the merits is that making the order is necessary to prevent further anti-social conduct.

Drinking Banning Orders can be made to keep people away from places that sell alcohol (under part I of the *Violent Crime Reduction Act 2006*), Football Banning Orders can be made to keep hooligans away from soccer grounds (*Football Spectators Act 1989*), Travel Restriction Orders are available to prevent drug traffickers from travelling overseas (section 33 of the *Criminal Justice and Police Act 2001*), Financial Reporting Orders may be made in relation to those convicted of theft, fraud or money laundering (section 76 of the *Serious Organised Crime and Police Act 2005*), and Serious Crime Prevention Orders can be made to disrupt involvement in further crime (section 19 of the *Serious Crime Act 2007*) or by the High Court as a civil order without a conviction (section 1). Another civil order is the Violent Offender Order available from magistrates on the application of the police (Part 7 of the *Criminal Justice and Immigration Act 2008*).

In addition, there is a significant regime that does not turn on court orders but is administrative in nature: the Multi-Agency Public Protection Panel system established by section 67 of the *Criminal Justice and Court Services Act 2000*, which has established a system of risk assessment and management for sexual and violent offenders. In the most recent annual report from the Ministry of Justice,[51] it was noted that there are 55,000 offenders covered. This regime coordinates the administrative arrangements for various matters, including for the release from custody of those in hospital following such an offence (or to have committed the actus reus whilst insane, or having been found unfit to stand trial), and may control whether the relevant judicial body can release if a pre-requisite is that suitable accommodation is available.

---

[50] It may be replaced by a Criminal Behaviour Order, see *Putting Victims First: More Effective Responses to Anti-Social Behaviour*, Cm 8367 (2012).

[51] United Kingdom, Ministry of Justice, *Multi-Agency Public Protection Arrangements Annual Report* (25 October 2012) Ministry of Justice Website <http://www.justice.gov.uk/publications/statistics-and-data/prisons-and-probation/mappa.htm>.

2. THE HUMAN RIGHTS FRAMEWORK

Preventive detention regimes (supplemented by control in the community) have to be assessed against the human rights framework that is binding on most nations as a matter of international law and often incorporated into domestic law. There are three elements to this: first, there is the perspective of potential victims to be considered, in relation to whom there may be a duty to take preventive action; second, there are the rights of those against whom preventive action is taken, which will affect their rights to liberty and freedom of action; and finally, there is a need for due process to be followed before a decision is taken that might affect a fundamental right.

2.1. THE DUTY TO PROTECT

The United Kingdom is a party to the European Convention on Human Rights 1950[52] and the International Covenant on Civil and Political Rights 1966 (ICCPR),[53] both of which contain a duty to protect life and a prohibition on conduct that amounts to torture or inhuman or degrading treatment. From these elements, a duty to protect emerges, particularly from the case law of the European Court of Human Rights. The relevant texts are in the following terms:

> *ECHR Article 2 – Right to life:*
> 1. Everyone's right to life shall be protected by law. No one shall be deprived of his life intentionally save in the execution of a sentence of a court following his conviction of a crime for which this penalty is provided by law. ...[54]

> *ICCPR Article 6:*
> 1. Every human being has the inherent right to life. This right shall be protected by law. No one shall be arbitrarily deprived of his life.[55]

---

[52] *Convention for the Protection of Human Rights and Fundamental Freedoms*, opened for signature 4 November 1950, 213 UNTS 222 (entered into force 3 September 1953), as amended by Protocol No 11 to Convention for the Protection of Human Rights and Fundamental Freedoms, opened for signature 11 May 1994, ETS No 5 (entered into force 1 November 1998) ('ECHR') <http://conventions.coe.int/treaty/en/treaties/html/005.htm>.

[53] *International Covenant on Civil and Political Rights*, opened for signature 16 December 1966, 999 UNTS 171 (entered into force 23 March 1976) <http://treaties.un.org>.

[54] Article 2(2) provides for a limited set of circumstances in which, in addition to a judicial execution, there is no breach of Art 2, relating to self-defence, arrest, and quelling serious disorder but provided that the response involves using the least possible force.

[55] The equivalent of Article 2(2) ECHR is encompassed by the use of arbitrariness; sub-articles (2) and following of Article 6 regulate rights that must be secured around the use of the death penalty if not abolished.

ECHR Article 3 Prohibition of torture

No one shall be subjected to torture or to inhuman or degrading treatment or punishment.

ICCPR Article 7

No one shall be subjected to torture or to cruel, inhuman or degrading treatment or punishment. In particular, no one shall be subjected without his free consent to medical or scientific experimentation.

The important word that is part of the right to life is that it is a right that has to be *protected*: in short, there is not just an obligation on the state to secure the right by preventing deprivation of life outside a few limited circumstances when it is permitted, but there is also a positive duty on the state to protect life. And it has been made clear that this will include situations in which the danger is caused by the criminal actions of third parties, not just state agents. This is apt to cover preventive detention, but it is to be noted that the jurisprudence rests on the acceptance that it may be difficult to predict when there is a situation that demands such protective action.

The case law in which this duty to protect has been raised has been usefully summarised by the House of Lords in *R (Middleton) v West Somerset Coroner*:[56]

> 2. The European Court of Human Rights has repeatedly interpreted Art 2 of the European Convention as imposing on member states substantive obligations not to take life without justification and also to establish a framework of laws, precautions, procedures and means of enforcement which will, to the greatest extent reasonably practicable, protect life.[57]

The 'framework of laws' includes the criminalisation of homicide but extends further, for example, to laws relating to the possession of weapons. But that is not enough, since there must also be a 'framework of … precautions, procedures and means of enforcement' so as to protect life. This may extend to offering protection against individual assailants. This has been confirmed by the Grand Chamber of the European Court of Human Rights is *Mastromatteo v Italy*,[58] in which a member of the public was killed by prisoners who had absconded from prison leave, granted on the basis of a finding that they did not pose an undue risk. In

---

[56] [2004] UKHL 10, [2004] 2 AC 182, [2004] Inquest LR 17. The House also described, at [3], how there was a procedural obligation to investigate possible state fault, which was central to the case.

[57] The authorities cited are: *LCB v UK* (1998) 27 EHRR 212 [36]; *Osman v UK* (1998) 29 EHRR 245, [2000] Inquest LR 101; *Powell v UK* app no 45305/99, [2000] Inquest LR 19; *Keenan v UK* [2001] Inquest LR 8, [2001] Prison LR 180, (2001) 33 EHRR 913 [88]–[90]; *Edwards v UK* [2002] Inquest LR 27, [2002] Prison LR 161, (2002) 35 EHRR 487 [54]; *Calvelli and Ciglio v Italy* (app no 32967/96, 17 January 2002); *Öneryildiz v Turkey* app no 48939/99, 18 June 2002).

[58] [2002] Inquest LR 182, [2003] Prison LR 11, app no 37703/97.

considering whether this involved a breach of Article 2 of the ECHR, the Court set out the following principles:

> (i) the primary specific obligation arising under the duty to safeguard life was to put in place effective criminal-law provisions to deter offences against the person, backed up by law-enforcement machinery for the prevention, suppression and punishment of breaches of such provisions;
>
> (ii) there might also be a positive obligation on the authorities to take preventive operational measures to protect an individual whose life is at risk from the criminal acts of another individual;
>
> (iii) however, this obligation had not to be disproportionate in light of the difficulties involved in policing modern societies, the unpredictability of human conduct and the operational choices in relation to priorities and resources.

The Court summarised this operational obligation in the following terms:

> Accordingly, not every claimed risk to life can entail for the authorities a Convention requirement to take operational measures to prevent that risk from materialising. A positive obligation will arise, the court has held, where it has been established that the authorities knew or ought to have known at the time of the existence of a real and immediate risk to the life of an identified individual or individuals from the criminal acts of a third party and that they failed to take measures within the scope of their powers which, judged reasonably, might have been expected to avoid that risk.[59]

This was not breached on the facts: it was not shown that, in balancing the importance of reintegrating prisoners into the community and seeking rehabilitation,[60] the judicial system of determining release was inadequate from the point of view of the obligations under Article 2 or had been misapplied on the facts. The Court noted:

> 72. ... The court considers that this system in Italy provides sufficient protective measures for society. It is confirmed in this view by the statistics supplied by the respondent state, which show that the percentage of crimes committed by prisoners subject to a semi-custodial regime is very low, as is that of prisoners absconding while on prison leave.[61]

---

[59]   Ibid [68]; the authorities cited by the Court for the proposition are *Osman v UK* (1998) 29 EHRR 245, [2000] Inquest LR 101, s 116; *Edwards v UK* [2002] Inquest LR 27, [2002] Prison LR 161, (2002) 35 EHRR 487, s 55; and *Bromiley v UK*, app no 33747/96, 23 November 1999).

[60]   *Mastromatteo v Italy* [2002] Inquest LR 182, [2003] Prison LR 11, app no 37703/97 [72]: 'One of the essential functions of a prison sentence is to protect society, for example by preventing a criminal from re-offending and thus causing further harm.'

[61]   The figures that had been supplied by the government to the Court were set out at [49] of the judgment and showed that in the period 1991 to 2001 no more than 1.12% of prisoners on prison leave and no more than 2% of prisoners subject to the semi-custodial regime had

73. Accordingly, there is nothing to suggest that the system of reintegration measures applicable in Italy at the material time must be called into question under Article 2.[62]

Importantly, the Court was willing to look at statistical research to determine whether there was a systemic problem.

Two instances are worth noting, where a breach of the duty has been found. In *Paul and Audrey Edwards v UK*,[63] the deceased was a vulnerable man with mental health problems – the son of the applicants – who was remanded into custody charged with sexual harassment matters. He was placed in a cell with another remand prisoner with mental health issues and a past history of violence, who was facing assault charges and who killed Mr Edwards. The assailant, who was immediately transferred to a high secure psychiatric hospital, later admitted manslaughter on the grounds of diminished responsibility, on the basis that he was affected by mental illness at the time of the killing. However, this had not been picked up during assessments. There had been a series of errors, including a failure to transfer medical notes to the doctor who carried out the assessment of the assailant in the police station (which would have revealed that there was active consideration being given to placing him under the civil provisions of the *Mental Health Act 1983*), a failure to have him reassessed after bizarre and violent behaviour in the police station, a failure to give any information to the member of the prison health care service who screened new admissions to prison, and the emergency buzzer in the cell did not work. The European Court of Human Rights found a breach of the operational duty arising under Article 2: essentially, the death occurred following serious short-comings, which should have revealed a danger to the life of Mr Edwards from which he could have been protected.

More recently, the same principles have been applied in a situation involving a person who was released from custody and then killed. In *Tomašić and Others v Croatia*,[64] MM killed his former wife and their child. The circumstances were that he had been sentenced to five months' imprisonment for threatening to kill his family with a bomb but, in light of a psychiatric assessment that established MM had a profound personality disorder and was highly likely to repeat the

---

absconded; and in the years 1999, 2000 and 2001, the percentage of prisoners on the semi-custodial regime who had committed an offence whilst so subject was 0.26%, 0.71% and 0.12% respectively.

[62] At [76]–[78], it was noted that the information available did not suggest the prisoners involved would pose a real and immediate threat to life on release, nor could this be said to arise from the fact that one of the prisoners was released after a previous accomplice had absconded as there was no material suggesting that there was a conspiracy afoot. The failure of the police to arrest the abscondees was not shown to involve any negligence.

[63] [2002] Inquest LR 27, [2002] Prison LR 161, (2002) 35 EHRR 487.

[64] App no 4762/05, 15 January 2009, [2012] MHLR 167.

same or similar criminal offences, the sentencing court also ordered psychiatric treatment during imprisonment and afterward (but on appeal this was changed to treatment during sentence only). However, the only treatment received in prison was talking therapy; he was released without a risk assessment, and a few weeks later committed the killings by shooting before committing suicide. Despite the previous threats made, the police had not searched his car or house for a weapon. The combined features amounted to a breach of the operational obligation under Article 2: in short, it had not been enough to rely on the deterrent effect of the criminal law, and specific action should have been taken to prevent MM carrying out a threat that should have been known to be real and immediate. The reason for the latter finding was the assessment made at the sentencing stage; despite that, no reasonable steps were taken.[65]

Article 3 of the ECHR has also been determined to give rise to positive obligations to protect, including from the actions of others. For example, in *A v United Kingdom*,[66] there was a finding of a breach of Article 3 as a result of the failure of the UK to restrict the width of the defence of 'reasonable chastisement' and to criminalise punishment of a child by a parent – involving beating with a garden cane, producing actual bodily harm – that was inhuman and degrading. As another example, in *Z and Others v United Kingdom*,[67] the failure of social services to remove children from circumstances of neglect and abuse was held to breach Article 3.

Accordingly, there is a clear duty to protect arising from the duties to protect life and prevent treatment that is inhuman and degrading. Whilst the case law noted above has arisen under the ECHR, there is no reason to suggest that it would be different under the ICCPR. Indeed, the Human Rights Committee has expressly noted the importance of Article 7 ICCPR in relation to the prevention of corporal punishment and the need for protection from the actions of private persons.[68]

What is apparent from this is that the state has a duty to protect the victims of the criminal actions of others and has to do more than simply punishing after the event. It may be that, in many situations, the actions of the assailant will amount to an inchoate crime or will involve the commission of a separate offence, such as possession of an offensive weapon, which is criminal because of the risk of harm.

---

[65] For another example, see *Opuz v Turkey*, app no 33401/02, 27 BHRC 159, (2010) 50 EHRR 28, which involved a failure to protect a woman from domestic violence.
[66] (1999) 27 EHRR 611.
[67] (2002) 34 EHRR 97.
[68] See *Replaces General Comment 7 Concerning Prohibition of Torture and Cruel Treatment or Punishment (Art 7)* CCPR General Comment No 20 (10 March 1992) [2], [5] <http://www2.ohchr.org/english/bodies/hrc/comments.htm>; the Committee emphasised the need for a wide interpretation of the right to life and the need for positive measures: *The Right to Life (Art 6)* CCPR General Comment No 6 (30 April 1992).

But this will not cover all situations in which there is a duty to take preventive measures. Might it extend to preventive detention? *Tomašić* is clearly important in this context. The Court made no suggestion that the absence of a court order for detention of longer than five months or for ongoing treatment after release (that having been quashed by the appellate court) relieved the authorities of their obligations to protect. On the particular facts, there was a specific failing to find the weapon he used, possession of which might have been criminal; but the other failings identified, namely to treat adequately and to risk assess, suggest that ongoing intervention was necessary. Whether this required detention or some management in the community involves an assessment of the other rights that have to be balanced, namely those of the person identified as the potential assailant.

2.2.   AVOIDING ARBITRARY DETENTION OR INTERFERENCE WITH AUTONOMY

The intervention required under the duty to protect arises only in limited circumstances when particular threats have been identified. The absence of a duty to intervene will not, of course, be the end of the potential for intervention, since a state may exercise a power of intervention to protect potential victims even if there is no duty. Whether it can properly do so involves looking at the limitations on those interventions contained in the rights of the person affected under Articles 5 and 8 of the ECHR and Articles 9 and 17 of the ICCPR:

ECHR Article 5 Right to liberty and security
1. Everyone has the right to liberty and security of person. No one shall be deprived of his liberty save in the following cases and in accordance with a procedure prescribed by law:
   (e) the lawful detention of persons for the prevention of the spreading of infectious diseases, of persons of unsound mind, alcoholics or drug addicts or vagrants

ICCPR Article 9
1. Everyone has the right to liberty and security of person. No one shall be subjected to arbitrary arrest or detention. No one shall be deprived of his liberty except on such grounds and in accordance with such procedures as are established by law.[69]

ECHR Article 8 Right to respect for family and private life
1. Everyone has the right to respect for his private and family life, his home and his correspondence.

---

[69]   See also ECHR Art 5(4) and ICCPR Art 9(4), which require the provision of a court review of the lawfulness of ongoing detention.

2. There shall be no interference by a public authority with the exercise of this right except such as is in accordance with the law and is necessary in a democratic society in the interests of national security, public safety or the economic well-being of the country, for the prevention of disorder or crime, for the protection of health or morals, or for the protection of the rights and freedoms of others.

ICCPR Article 17
1. No one shall be subjected to arbitrary or unlawful interference with his privacy, family, home or correspondence, nor to unlawful attacks on his honour and reputation.
2. Everyone has the right to the protection of the law against such interference or attacks.

Again, the language of the ECHR and ICCPR is semantically different but substantively the same. In relation to liberty, the European text permits detention in certain circumstances only, whereas the UN Covenant allows any detention provided that is not arbitrary. However, the European Court of Human Rights has made clear that the purpose of the ECHR is to avoid detention that would be arbitrary. For example, in *Litwa v Poland*,[70] the Court summarised the point as follows:

72. The Court reiterates that under Art 5 of the Convention any deprivation of liberty must be 'lawful', which includes a requirement that it must be effected 'in accordance with a procedure prescribed by law'. On this point, the Convention essentially refers to national law and lays down an obligation to comply with its substantive and procedural provisions.

73. It also requires that any measure depriving the individual of his liberty must be compatible with the purpose of Art 5, namely to protect the individual from arbitrariness (see *K-F v Germany* 27 November 1997, § 63).[71]

What the Court also noted was that Article 5(1)(e), which was raised on the facts as Mr Litwa had been detained on account of intoxication, had a common theme that included public protection:

[A] predominant reason why the Convention allows the persons mentioned in paragraph 1(e) of Article 5 to be deprived of their liberty is not only that they are dangerous for public safety but also that their own interests may necessitate their detention.[72]

---

[70] [2000] MHLR 226, 33 EHRR 53.
[71] For another example, see *HL v UK*, 40 EHRR 761, [2004] MHLR 236.
[72] Also of potential relevance here is Art 5(1)(b), which allows detention to secure the fulfilment of any obligation prescribed by law: there is limited case law on this provision, and it may be that it requires a specific obligation rather than a more general obligation such as the need to

Again, this will be the same under the ICCPR, where the express test in Article 9(1) is arbitrariness; similarly, that is the test under Article 17 in relation to privacy and autonomy issues. The ECHR allows interventions, provided that they meet the proportionality test of Article 8(2), which is the obverse: a proportionate intervention is not arbitrary.[73]

From these human rights standards, it is suggested that there is a continuum: at one extreme is the duty to protect, which requires state intervention, and at the other end is the duty not to detain or interfere with autonomy rights when to do so is arbitrary. In the middle is a situation in which there is a power to intervene if the state has decided that it will do so.

2.3.   DUE PROCESS – FAIR TRIALS

The outline given above deals with what might be termed the merits of a decision as to whether or not to detain or take preventive management action in the community. The English statutory regime outlined above reflects a choice to set the balance in a way that reflects on the power of the state to offer protection in a way that seems to meet the controls of arbitrariness. So, it is difficult to suggest that the grounds for detention under the *Mental Health Act 1983* allow arbitrariness if properly applied; equally, the management techniques reflected in the various preventive orders that control what people can do in the community are designed to impose limitations to protect the rights of others. In any event, the UK has its *Human Rights Act 1998*, section 3, which requires that all statutory powers be construed in such a manner as to reflect the requirements of the ECHR, unless that simply is not possible in light of the statutory language.

However, there is a third element of the human rights framework, which is the need for fair trials before rights are determined: this is set out in ECHR Article 6 and ICCPR Article 14 and will include whether steps should be taken to interfere with fundamental rights discussed in the preceding section. This clearly links back to the operational aspect of the duty to protect; it is limited because of the unpredictability of human behaviour. Similarly, it has been made clear that questions of the lawfulness of detention on mental health grounds under Article 5(1)(e) of the ECHR involve adequate evidence. In *Winterwerp v Netherlands*,[74] whilst accepting that 'unsound mind' could not be given a definitive meaning,

---

obey the criminal law. In relation to the need for a restrictive interpretation, see *Engel v The Netherlands (No 1)*, 1 EHRR 647.

[73]   Freedom of movement rights can also be mentioned and will be of similar effect: see Article 12 of the ICCPR (which allows proportionate restrictions on this right) and Article 2 of Protocol No 4 to the ECHR (which has a similar test).

[74]   (1979) 2 EHRR 387.

the Court confirmed that it could not be made out 'simply because [the detainee's] views or behaviour deviate from the norms prevailing in a particular society'.[75] It added that the need for 'a true mental disorder' was something that had to be based on 'objective medical expertise' given to the body deciding on detention.[76] In other words, the substantive tests imply the need for due process, including adequate evidence, supplementing the express right to a fair trial.

This has been reflected in US jurisprudence relating to the sexually violent predator statutes. For example, in *Kansas v Hendricks*,[77] the Supreme Court found that the substantive test in the Kansas statute – a 'mental abnormality or personality disorder which makes the person likely to engage in the predatory acts of sexual violence'[78] – properly balanced the liberty rights of the defendant and the protection of the public. Thomas J noted that mental health detention was analogous and that

> [w]e have consistently upheld such involuntary commitment statutes *provided the confinement takes place pursuant to proper procedures and evidentiary standards.*[79] (Emphasis added.)

In another context, the Supreme Court has accepted that future criminality is difficult to predict. In *Jurek v Texas*,[80] it upheld the validity of a provision in Texas death penalty law to the effect that a finding that a defendant would pose a continuing threat to society from the probability of further criminal act could be made as an aggravating factor relevant to the imposition of the death penalty. It was noted, 'It is, of course, not easy to predict future behaviour. The fact that such a determination is difficult, however, does not mean that it cannot be made.'[81]

Slobogin and others[82] have commented that this authority suggests that any contention that the lack of predictive accuracy in the risk assessment tools means that detention is improper is likely to be rejected should the question reach the Supreme Court.

---

[75] Ibid [37].
[76] Ibid [39].
[77] (1996) 521 US 346.
[78] Ibid 352.
[79] Ibid 357.
[80] 428 US 262 (1976).
[81] Ibid 274–5. The court noted that the future has to be predicted all the time, for example in decisions as to bail.
[82] Christopher Slobogin, Arti Rai and Ralph Reisner, *Law and the Mental Health System* (Thompson West, 5th ed, 2009) 695.

(i)   The import of the difficulties of prediction

However, it is worth considering the difficulties of prediction of future criminality and the implications this has for the judicial function and the need for adequate certainty before orders are made that infringe fundamental rights. The Supreme Court's conclusion in *Jurek*, that it is difficult but may not be impossible, does not answer the many questions that arise. In short, the difficulty of prediction gives rise to questions of both substantive and procedural due process: how can the substantive test be met in light of difficulties of prediction? And how can a court fairly adjudicate on the substantive question?

As noted above, this difficulty of prediction is central to why the European Court of Human Rights has imposed only a very limited duty to protect; furthermore, it was a significant reason for the abandonment by the UK government of the IPP sentence, as described above. This has also been recognised by the Human Rights Committee of the United Nations and Kirby J of the High Court of Australia. The domestic case was *Fardon v Attorney-General*,[83] in which the Queensland provision for post-sentence detention – the *Dangerous Prisoners (Sexual Offenders) Act 2003*[84] – was challenged. The majority had no particular qualms about the use of detention based on predicted future crime. For example, Gleeson CJ accepted, 'No doubt, predictions of future danger may be unreliable, but … they may also be right.'[85] The alleged vagueness of the statutory test of an 'unacceptable risk' of further offending was in fact a reflection of a concept of there being a risk of a magnitude that justified an order, and it should not be given a greater degree of definition than it was capable of yielding.[86] The dissenting judgment of Kirby J, however, questioned the very basis of having a legal system make orders when the evidence presented to them was necessarily imprecise. He accepted that the statute was phrased in such a way as to strive for adequate certainty, but he concluded:

---

[83]   (2004) 223 CLR 575. The arguments advanced by Fardon are set out in Patrick Keyzer, Cathy Pereira and Stephen Southwood, 'Pre-emptive Imprisonment for Dangerousness in Queensland under the *Dangerous Prisoners (Sexual Offenders) Act 2003*: The Constitutional Issues' (2004) 11 *Psychiatry, Psychology and Law* 244.

[84]   Statutes are available at http://www.legislation.qld.gov.au/OQPChome.htm.

[85]   *Fardon v A-G (Qld)* (2004) 223 CLR 575 [12]. He relied on Veen v R (1979) 143 CLR 458, where a life sentence – which had been imposed on the basis of a finding of dangerousness following a conviction for a serious offence, namely manslaughter on the basis of diminished responsibility – was quashed on appeal by the High Court of Australia and replaced by a determinate term. The prisoner was duly released from that term and killed another person; this led to a further conviction for manslaughter on the basis of diminished responsibility (*Veen v R [No 2]* (1988) 164 CLR 465). The implication is that, as courts may get it wrong by not detaining people who turn out to be dangerous, they should err on the side of caution by detaining indeterminately.

[86]   *Fardon v A-G (Qld)* [2004] HCA 46 [22].

Even with the procedures and criteria adopted, the Act ultimately deprives people such as the appellant of personal liberty, a most fundamental human right, on a prediction of dangerousness, based largely on the opinions of psychiatrists which can only be, at best, an educated or informed 'guess'.[87]

This case proceeded to the Human Rights Committee as *Fardon v Australia*:[88] the Committee held that detention was arbitrary, and so in breach of Article 9 of the ICCPR, because Australia had not demonstrated why community supervision was inadequate.[89] Part of their reasoning is similar to that of Kirby J:

[P]redicted dangerousness to the community … is inherently problematic. It is essentially based on opinion as distinct from factual evidence, even if that evidence consists in the opinion of psychiatric experts. But psychiatry is not an exact science.

To avoid arbitrariness in detaining on the basis of future criminality, therefore, it was necessary to show why other action short of detention was inadequate.[90]

(ii)   Predicting future crime

It must, of course, be accepted that courts make many orders based on likelihoods as to future conduct: for example, decisions to remand a criminal defendant in custody on the basis of the risk of absconding or committing further offences. But this will involve a judicial skill-set of analysing a pattern of past behaviour (previous convictions), the seriousness of the current allegation and the strength of the evidence, and hence the likely penalty. That is not the same as the prediction of future criminality over a period of a number of years, and even if it is of the same nature as the bail decision, it is of such a very different degree as to be outside the judicial skill-set. Hence the involvement of expert evidence in relation to preventive detention: it is a key feature of the sexually violent predator laws in the USA and Australia and part of the mental health legislation that performs the same role in England and Wales.

---

87   Ibid [125].
88   CCPR/C/98/D/1629/2007; see also *Tillman v Australia* CCPR/C/98/D/1635/2007, which considered the equivalent legislation in New South Wales.
89   It also held that the action taken was a criminal penalty and had been imposed retrospectively, in breach of Art 15; and it had not been imposed in a manner consistent with a criminal process and, so, breached Art 14 as well. For further discussion and analysis see Patrick Keyzer, 'The United Nations Human Rights Committee's views about he legitimate parameters of the preventive detention of serious sex offenders' (2010) 34 *Criminal Law Journal* 283–291.
90   *Fardon v Australia* CCPR/C/98/D/1629/2007 [7.4(4)]. The test for breaches of autonomy rights is also one of arbitrariness: what is implicit in the conclusion of the Committee is that it may be easier to justify an intervention that is short of a loss of liberty.

However, the need for expert evidence beyond that of a probation officer was not required for IPP sentences in England and Wales, and the Court of Appeal had been reluctant to endorse cross-examination of that evidence, despite the existence of a criminal justice system based on adversarial cross-examination. In *R v Boswell*,[91] a challenge to a decision to impose IPP failed, one ground being that there had been an erroneous approach to risk assessment tools by the writer of a pre-sentence report (which suggested a significant risk of further offending). Dyson LJ set a singularly non-interventionist approach to the assessment of the reliability of these instruments, commenting at paragraph 12:

> Those tools are no doubt the product ... of a good deal of research and provide a satisfactory basis for reaching conclusions of the kind that were reached in this case.

In short, although the question was the propriety of indeterminate detention, there was almost an assumption as to the efficacy of the tools on which the evidence was based. It had already been established that there was no right to cross-examine the makers of the reports. In *R v S and Others*,[92] the Court of Appeal commented at paragraph 100 that, in relation to a challenge to an assessment of the seriousness of a risk of reoffending and causing harm in a pre-sentence report,

> It is only likely to be in very rare cases that it will be incumbent on a judge to permit the author of a pre-sentence report to be cross-examined in relation to assessment of seriousness. It is, of course, open to counsel to make submissions about the contents of a report in relation to a defendants' history of criminal offending and all other material matters.

This seems to understate the problem. The historical evidence is that judgment as to future violence is poorly correlated with actuality. This was demonstrated in the aftermath of a constitutional challenge that provided a chance for investigation. In *Baxstrom v Herold*,[93] detention in a prison hospital after the end of a sentence was found to be unconstitutional because the process followed (certification by a doctor) was not as stringent as that applicable to a person being detained from the community (jury trial); as such, there was differential treatment that breached the equal protection provisions of the Fourteenth Amendment to the United States Constitution.[94] As a result, many patients were transferred to civil

---

91 [2007] EWCA Crim 1587.
92 [2005] EWCA Crim 3616, [2006] 2 Prison LR 119.
93 (1966) 383 US 107.
94 § 1: 'No state shall ... deny to any persons within its jurisdiction the equal protection of the laws.'

mental hospitals and often then released;[95] this allowed research on whether the claims that they were dangerous were borne out. The recidivism rate for violent offending was found to be 11 per cent (though it is to be noted that about a third of the patients remained detained in civil hospitals).[96] This poor correlation between predictions of future crime and recidivism provides reasons for caution about the ability to predict the future and base action on such predictions.

(iii)   The new techniques of risk assessment

There was another response to the Baxstrom research, which was a decision to seek better risk assessment; the concentration has been on the development of actuarial models, which have long been accepted to be more reliable.[97] There are now many such tools:[98] the common theme is the collection of information about a large number of offenders and recidivism rates to give statements of probability of reoffending on the basis of an assessment of the presence or absence of certain factors.[99] Typically, the tools work by collating and scoring answers to a list of questions as to whether a given feature is definitely present, partially or probably present, or absent.[100] The overall score can then be compared against the scale developed in the research that gave rise to the tool, to provide a prediction of the risk of further offending.[101] In the UK, the probation service (and the prisons) have a standard tool, the Offender Assessment System (OASys).[102]

---

[95]   Tony Maden, *Treating Violence* (Oxford University Press, 2007) 28: 'New York State realized that 966 other detained patients in their hospitals for the criminally insane could petition … on the same grounds and could expect to win. They gave in gracefully and ordered that all 967 patients should be transferred to civil mental hospitals within the space of a few months.' There was another case, *Dixon v A-G (Pennsylvania)* (1971) 325 F Supp 966, which had a similar impact in that state.

[96]   See Thomas R Litwack et al, 'Violence Risk Assessment: Research, Legal and Clinical Considerations' in Irving Weiner and Allen Hess (eds), *The Handbook of Forensic Psychology* (Wiley and Sons, 3rd ed, 2006) 491: in relation to the *Baxstrom* and *Dixon* patients, 'Follow-up studies determined that only a small percentage had to be returned to secure facilities, and that only a small minority of patients ultimately released to the community were rearrested for violent offenses.' Therefore, 'determinations of dangerousness for the purpose of preventive detention warrant careful judicial scrutiny'.

[97]   Monahan et al, *Rethinking Risk Assessment (The Macarthur Study of Mental Disorder and Violence)* (Oxford University Press, 2001) 7, citing studies commencing in 1954.

[98]   A leading Australian text, Ian Freckelton and Hugh Selby, 'Prediction of Risk Evidence' in *Expert Evidence – Law, Practice, Procedure and Advocacy* (Lawbook, 4th ed, 2009) ch 39, lists 29 of them. Maden, above n 95, 92 speaks of a 'Risk Assessment Industry'.

[99]   Maden, above n 95, 79.

[100] Depending on the nature of the tool, it may involve reviewing files on the subject or assessing the subject at interview, or both.

[101] See, for example, Maden's description of two well-known instruments that use this scoring method, the PCL-R tool (the Hare Psychopathy Checklist, referred to above) that measures whether someone is a psychopath and the HCR-20 (Historical Clinical Risk-20) – above n 95, 88 and 105. Both involve 20 questions.

[102] For more information on this, see [4.90] and following of Creighton and Arnott, *Prisoners – Law and Practice* (LAG 2009); see also Prison Service Order 2205, Offender Assessment and Sentence Management <http://www.justice.gov.uk/offenders/psos>.

But the field is developing, as was recognised by Blaxell J of the Western Australia Supreme Court in *DPP (WA) v Moolarvie*:

> It is … clear from a number of published articles in reputable international journals … that these tools are at an early stage of development and involve an area of behavioural science which is the subject of some controversy.[103]

And there are disputes within the field as to whether tools based solely on static factors (ie ones that are fixed at the time of assessment – age, number of previous convictions, whether victims male or female etc) provide a superior outcome to those that incorporate dynamic factors (ie attitudes that might change over time, perhaps following intervention). Maden gives a hint of the dispute (and of his position):

> While enthusiasts argue that actuarial methods should supplant clinical estimation of risk, a more balanced review concludes that the proper place of such instruments is as an adjunct to good clinical practice.[104]

Several important things should be noted. First, the tool may produce risk ratings that are expressed as 'high', 'medium' or 'low'; but what that means must be assessed – for example, if a 'high' risk is 55%, that means there is a 45% chance of no reoffending. Secondly, the actuarial prediction is not an individual prediction: just as an actuary working in the life insurance industry cannot predict the death of an individual but is limited to saying what will happen on average to a group of people with the identified characteristics, so it is for violence risk assessments.[105] Accordingly, a conclusion that a defendant presents a 30% risk of committing a further offence within the next ten years means that 30% of people sharing the defendant's characteristics will commit a further offence if they act in the same way as the group on whom the study was based. The tool cannot say whether an individual will be one of the group who will or one of the group who will not.

---

[103] [2008] WASC 37 [41] <http://decisions.justice.wa.gov.au/supreme/supdcsn.nsf>.
[104] Maden, above n 95, 97. (The citations to the 'enthusiasts' and those who are 'more balanced' are omitted.) Still, both are better than those who merely rely on their professional judgment and provide 'unstructured clinical assessments', whom Maden describes as 'men in three-piece suits and half-moon glasses; unlikely gurus, perhaps, but they have the same reliance on charismatic authority. They are right because of who they are, and the classic response to challenge is: "And who are you?"'
[105] See Parry and Drogin, *Mental Disability, Law, Evidence and Testimony* (ABA, 2007) 276: 'actuarial predictions consider how people similar to the defendant have acted in the past in similar circumstances'.

Thirdly, there may be many questions that can be asked about the tool that has been used. For example,

(i) Given that the tool will be based on statistics obtained from studies of particular populations over a period of time (and perhaps even of secondary analyses of studies carried out for other purposes), there may be questions of whether there are alternative explanations for the figures so that apparent correlation is because of the existence of another feature that is causative?

(ii) What was the adverse outcome measured by the study: arrest, charge, or conviction? If the question for the court is the likelihood of further offending, a tool that is based on statistics of arrests or even charges is of questionable value.

(iii) Was the tool created on the basis of a specific population which has features that do not apply to the defendant (or the country where the tool is being applied) – eg different alcohol abuse patterns, different community support mechanisms.

(iv) Is the tool still valid in light of changes over time since it was created, including new policies and methods of managing offenders that were not present when the study was carried out?

(v) The training of the person using the instrument.

(vi) Any element of subjectivity in the scoring of the instrument.[106]

This makes it clear that the confidence of Dyson LJ in *Boswell*, noted above, that the risk assessment tools are 'the product ... of a good deal of research and provide a satisfactory basis for reaching conclusions of the kind that were reached in this case' is far from accurate. Rather, the tools are developing, are subject to continuing debate within the expert community, do not produce the individualised results that courts need, and produce results that have error rates.[107]

What should a court do in light of these features in seeking to do better than the English courts seem to have done in securing the right to a fair trial? Perhaps it should recognise the need for caution in admitting or attaching significant weight to such evidence. Certainly, it should accept that, as a guardian of substantive and procedural due process, it may not be possible to conclude that the relevant substantive test is met on the evidence available in light of the necessary qualifications as to that evidence.

---

[106] For an example, see *A-G (Qld) v McLean* [2006] QSC 37, where Dutney J was confronted with evidence from three experts who used the same tools and reached wildly different results. He was also confronted with tests developed for populations outside Australia and not validated for indigenous Australians, the group to which the defendant belonged.

[107] Indeed, in *Boswell*, there appears to have been an error. The report-writer is quoted at paragraph 6 of the judgment, 'Actuarial assessment tools used in the preparation of this report take into account Mr Boswell's extensive range of previous convictions and indicate that his likelihood of re-offending has been assessed to be of a high level'. This is the language of an individualised assessment, but this is not possible.

It is also important to ensure that expert witnesses who assist the courts carry out their tasks appropriately. In this regard, the High Court Rules in New Zealand[108] provide an example of good practice. Schedule 4 to the Rules, the Code of Conduct for Expert Witnesses, requires experts to include various matters in their evidence, including:

> 4. If an expert witness believes that his or her evidence or any part of it may be incomplete or inaccurate without some qualification, that qualification must be stated in his or her evidence.
>
> 5. If an expert witness believes that his or her opinion is not a concluded opinion because of insufficient research or data or for any other reason, this must be stated in his or her evidence.

This is clearly an appropriate and ethical approach, and it will help a court to answer the important question of whether the qualifications that must be made as to the assessment of the risk of future criminality are such that the order designed to meet that risk cannot properly be made without breaching the prohibition on arbitrary detention or arbitrary interference with autonomy rights. Procedural due process must not be forgotten when asking whether the seductive aim of protecting future victims of crime is attainable.

---

[108]   *Judicature Act 1908* (NZ) Schedule 2.

THE NEW FACE OF PREVENTIVE DETENTION IN NEW ZEALAND: PUBLIC PROTECTION ORDERS

Warren BROOKBANKS

1. INTRODUCTION

Preventive detention has been part of New Zealand's penal law for many years. As one of only two, truly indeterminate sentences available to the courts, preventive detention has been used sparingly, although its actual use has increased in recent years.[1] Although preventive detention is not a sentence of last resort,[2] sentencing courts have taken a cautious approach to the sentence, mindful of the reality that in many cases long, finite sentences may be expected to meet the public protection mandate underlying the sentence.[3] However, its utilization in relation to serious violent or sexual offences is generally associated with an offender history of violent or predatory sexual conduct so that its principal purpose is the incapacitation, rather than simply the punishment, of an offender.

While New Zealand can lay claim to a discrete sentence called preventive detention,[4] the generic expression 'preventive detention' also applies to other executive measures designed to ensure the indefinite detention of a person who is considered to present a significant risk of harm to the public or particular members of it. In particular, since 2004, New Zealand has had provision for 'extended supervision orders',[5] a form of executive control designed for pedophiles who, while having completed sentences of imprisonment, are considered to present a high risk of further sexual offending against juveniles. As this discussion will

---

[1]   The other sentence is life imprisonment. See *Sentencing Act 2002* (NZ) s 103. It is estimated that as at 30 June 2010 719 prisoners in New Zealand were serving indeterminate sentences. This compares with 54 in Victoria and 350 in Queensland at the same date. See Department of Corrections, 'Regulatory Impact Statement' (Wellington, 20 March 2012) [34] n 4.

[2]   See *R v Rameka* [1997] NZCA 178 (18 June 1997). '[T]he statutory test is not to be burdened by the notion that preventive detention is a sentence of last resort.'

[3]   *R v Leitch* [1998] 1 NZLR 420, 428 (Richardson J).

[4]   See *Sentencing Act 2002* (NZ) s 87.

[5]   *Parole Act 2002* (NZ) pt 1A.

show, the relationship between extended supervision and preventive detention is complex and has been the subject of judicial consideration.

More recently, however, the New Zealand Government has signaled its intention to enact legislation to provide for yet another form of preventive detention, namely, a 'public protection order'. The legislation[6] was introduced to Parliament on 18 September 2012 and at the time of writing had not been subjected to select committee scrutiny. However, its passage through the legislative process seems likely, given current populist sentiment favouring indeterminate sentencing for sexual offenders. The Bill would establish a new regime of civil detention allowing courts to impose a Public Protection Order with secure residences situated within prison precincts. It is anticipated that such orders would be used in between five and 12 cases over a ten-year period, including some people currently subject to the most intensive form of extended supervision.[7] The scope, structure and rationale for Public Protection Orders will be the principal focus of this chapter.

It should also be noted, however, that preventive detention is also the basis of therapeutic orders that may be made under criminal justice and mental health legislation. Under current New Zealand law, an offender acquitted on account of insanity may be made subject to an order for detention as either a 'special patient' or as a 'special care recipient', depending on whether the offender was mentally impaired or intellectually disabled at the time of the offending and whether such an order was 'necessary' in the interests of the public, any person or class of persons who may be affected by the court's decision.[8] In the case of a special patient, such detention is indefinite and may endure as long as the Minister of Health considers the defendant's continued detention is necessary to safeguard the defendant's own interest, those of the public or the safety of a person or class of persons.[9] Special care recipients are managed under a separate statutory protocol of 'compulsory care' and may be detained in a secure facility for a period of three years, renewable upon application to the family court.[10]

Finally, pursuant to mental health legislation a civilly committed psychiatric patient may be made subject to a 'restricted patient' order, where the patient presents special difficulties because of the danger he or she poses to others.[11] Such orders are rare in New Zealand and, like special patient orders made under the *Criminal Procedure (Mentally Impaired Persons) Act (CP (MIP) Act)*, are subject to the non-clinical decision-making of senior politicians in relation to applications

---

[6] *Public Safety (Public Protection Orders) Bill* (NZ).
[7] Department of Corrections, above n 1, cl 27.
[8] *Criminal Procedure (Mentally Impaired Persons) Act 2003* (NZ) s 24(1)(c).
[9] Ibid s 33(4).
[10] See *Intellectual Disability (Compulsory Care and Rehabilitation) Act 2003* (NZ) ss 46(2) and 85.
[11] *Mental Health (Compulsory Assessment and Treatment) Act 1992* (NZ), s 54(1).

for change of status or leave.[12] Preventive detention operating within mental health settings might properly be characterized as 'anticipatory containment', since its purpose is not to punitively detain but rather to provide secure care for those whose mental impairment is considered to present a high risk of future assaultive and other dangerous behaviour.

In this chapter, however, because of their potentially broad scope, I will not be examining further issues around mental health detention. Rather, the discussion will be principally focussed on the different manifestations of preventive detention, but in particular, the proposed public protection order regime.

The chapter will commence with an account of the operation of and policy behind the sentence of preventive detention in s 87 of the *Sentencing Act 2002*. It will then consider extended supervision orders and their role in preventive crime control. The next, and most substantial, section will consider the Public Safety (Public Protection Orders) Bill, examining its principal elements and the policy behind the Bill. The chapter will conclude with a discussion of the human rights implications of New Zealand's preventive detention regime and its consistency or otherwise with international norms.

2. PREVENTIVE DETENTION

Preventive detention has a long history in New Zealand criminal justice. It has existed, in one form or another, for over 100 years, having first been enacted as legislation targeting 'Habitual criminals and Offenders'.[13] A judge could declare a person to be a 'habitual offender' where a person had been convicted of a nominated class of offence, namely Class 1 offences (generally serious sexual offences) or Class 2 offences (offences of violence and other serious crimes, including robbery, burglary, theft and extortion).[14] Declaration of habitual criminal status in respect of a Class 1 offence was triggered where the offender had at least two previous convictions for a Class 1 offence. In respect of Class 2 offences, the declaration could only be made where the offender had at least four previous convictions for either Class 1 or Class 2 offences. Declaration as an habitual offender gave the court the discretionary power to direct that on the expiry of their sentence the person be detained in a 'reformatory prison' under the *Crimes Act 1908*.[15]

Specific provision for preventive detention was first made in sections 24–26 of the *Criminal Justice Act 1954*. Eligibility for the sentence of preventive detention

---

[12]   Ibid s 81.
[13]   See *Crimes Act 1908* (NZ), s 29.
[14]   Ibid s 29(3).
[15]   Ibid s 30(3). The provision re-enacted s 4 of the *Habitual Criminals and Offenders Act 1906*.

was tied to three categories of offending, in descending order of seriousness. In the first instance, provided a person was not less than 25 years of age, had at least one previous conviction for a sexual offence against a child since the age of 17, and had been convicted again of a sexual offence against a child, a Supreme Court judge (now the High Court) could order his or her detention subject to a sentence of preventive detention. The court had to be satisfied that the person should be detained in custody 'for a substantial period'.[16] The habitual offender character of the sentence was reflected in that a person could also be made subject to preventive detention of more than three years imprisonment for a new offence where he or she had at least three previous convictions since age 17 for offences punishable by imprisonment for three years or more and had been sentenced to imprisonment at least twice or sent to reformative training, 'borstal' or corrective training. Sexual offending was not a necessary component of the preventive detention sentence imposed.

Under this model, a person sentenced to preventive detention was detained in a prison until released on the recommendation of the Parole Board after having served at least three years. Generally, detention was for a maximum of 14 years, unless the offender had received preventive detention for a sexual offence against a child, in which case detention was indeterminate.[17]

The legislation governing preventive detention was amended in 1967. Under the 1954 Act, the sentence had not been used extensively and by the mid-1960s had all but disappeared.[18] During the period 1965–1966, only five people had received the three-to-14-year sentence, which had been shown to have an unsettling effect on inmates. The sentence was often excessive in relation to the offences to which it applied.[19] It was also recognized that it was difficult to judge the unlikelihood of an offender continuing to offend, the release criterion, in a custodial setting.[20] Law change was, therefore, considered necessary.

The *Criminal Justice Amendment Act 1967* removed preventive detention from all offences except sexual offences. Its role became purely custodial. The maximum period of 14 years (which, in any event, only applied to non-sexual offending) was abolished, and the minimum period of detention increased from three to seven years. During the period 1968–1978, very few people were sentenced to preventive detention. The few that were served an average of thirteen years in custody,[21] thus

---

[16] *Criminal Justice Act 1954* (NZ), s 24(2).
[17] Ibid s 26.
[18] G Newbold, *Punishment and Politics: The Maximum Security Prison in New Zealand* (Oxford University Press, 1989) 125.
[19] Ibid.
[20] Ibid.
[21] Ibid.

vindicating the legislation's goal of achieving custody 'for a substantial period'. The sentence was thus primarily incapacitative, and little or no thought was given to its rehabilitative potential.

In 1985, a new *Criminal Justice Act* was enacted. The sentence of preventive detention was carried over from the 1954 Act but with significant amendment. In particular, it applied only to offenders not less than 25 years of age who were convicted of another sexual offence since attaining the age of 17. The limitation to sexual offences 'against a child' was removed, but the qualification that the sentence be expedient 'for the protection of the public' and warranting detention in custody 'for a substantial period' was retained.[22] However, the section was soon to be amended again in the elusive pursuit of a formula allowing detention of offenders at an appropriate age, nominating appropriate qualifying offences and nominating an appropriate offence history. As has been observed, 'The repeal and substitution of s 75 by the *Criminal Justice Amendment Act (No 2) 1987* and its amendment by the *Criminal Justice Amendment Act 1993* are further episodes in a saga which commenced early this century and which has seen successive widening and narrowing of the range of offenders to whom the sentence of preventive detention is applicable.'[23]

Amendments in 1987 and 1993 effected significant changes to the provision by expanding the provision's scope to include nominated sexual and violent offences[24] and to require that the sentencing judge be satisfied on the basis of psychiatric evidence that there is a 'substantial risk' that the offender would commit a specified offence upon release. The use of the expression 'specified offence' was new to the Act as amended in 1987 and indicated the extended range of qualifying offences.[25] The purpose of the new provision was one of crime prevention by placing incorrigible violent or dangerous and incorrigible sexual offenders 'out of circulation'.[26] There was no longer, however, any requirement that such offenders be 'habitual'. Concern for the prolixity of an offender's offending history was replaced by official concern for its gravity and risk of repetition.

Since its inception, preventive detention has been sparingly used, although there is evidence of an increased use of the sentence in recent years. As at 6 August 1993, 51 detainees were serving preventive detention sentences. However, its use since then has fluctuated. From 1997 to 2002, the number of sentences of preventive detention was, on average, about 12 per year. However, in the year

---

22 *Criminal Justice Act 1985* (NZ), s 75(2).
23 G Hall, *Sentencing Guide* (Butterworths, 1994) D/792.
24 These were described as 'specified offence[s]' and included serious sexual offences against children and a range of other serious violent offences in the *Crimes Act 1961* (NZ).
25 G Hall, above n 23 p D/793.
26 Ibid.

2004 it jumped to 33 and in 2008 to 24. This variation in its use is not easily explained. It is possible that its increased use may be due to the reduction in the minimum term or other changes in the eligibility criteria introduced by the *Sentencing Act 2002*. As at 31 March 2011, 11% of the sentenced population were subject to indeterminate sentences.[27] These include both preventive detention and life sentences that have no end date. Of these, the vast majority (74.2%) are on minimum, low or low-medium security. Twenty-two point eight percent (22.8%) are on maximum or high security.

2.1. CHANGES ARISING FROM THE *SENTENCING ACT 2002*

The *Sentencing Act* has expanded the range of offenders who may be eligible for preventive detention. Three principal changes are noted. First, the age of eligibility is lowered from 21 years to 18 years and over at the time the offence was committed. Second, the range of qualifying offences has been increased. Third, there is no longer a requirement that violent or sexual offenders have had any previous convictions.[28] The section makes clear that the primary purpose of the sentence is public protection rather than punishment. It can only be imposed in order to protect the community from further offending.[29] The sentence can only be imposed by the High Court,[30] although if a District Court considers such a sentence is warranted it may decline jurisdiction and commit the person to the High Court for sentence.[31]

There are three pre-conditions for the imposition of preventive detention. The offender must:

- have committed a qualifying offence;
- [be] aged 18 or older;
- and be likely to commit another qualifying offence on release.[32]

---

[27] See *Prison Facts and Statistics* – March 2011 (Department of Corrections, Wellington, 2011) <http://corrections.govt.nz/about-us/facts_and_statistics.html >.
[28] See *Sentencing Act 2002* (NZ), s 87(2).
[29] *R v Johnson* [2004] 3 NZLR 29 (2003) 21 CRNZ 196 (CA).
[30] *Sentencing Act 2002* (NZ), s 87(3).
[31] Ibid s 90.
[32] Ibid s 87(2).

The list of relevant 'qualifying offences' has been expanded from earlier iterations of the preventive sentence provisions to include all major sexual offences (including compelling an indecent act with an animal and bestiality) and to include a broad range of violent offences. These range from manslaughter to assault with intent to rob and include acid throwing, abduction and kidnapping.[33]

While the minimum age of eligibility has been lowered from 21 to 18, courts have been reluctant to impose the sentence on offenders just over the age threshold.[34] In *R v Kale* the Court of Appeal accepted the appropriateness of the sentencing Judge's decision to impose preventive detention because 'no other course was open to him', despite the Court's concern about the offender's young age at the time of sentence.[35]

2.2. PUNISHMENT VERSUS PROTECTION

The stated purpose of preventive detention in New Zealand is 'to protect the community from those who pose a significant and ongoing risk to the safety of its members'.[36] Reflecting on this legislative purpose in *R v Johnson*,[37] the New Zealand Court of Appeal held that preventive detention is a sentence with a 'specifically protective' purpose and may only be invoked for protective reasons. Furthermore, the New Zealand statute requires the Court to be satisfied, before imposing such a sentence, that the person is 'likely to commit another qualifying sexual or violent offence' on release from a finite sentence.[38] In *Johnson*, the Court of Appeal held that, because preventive detention is protective not punitive in intent, the statutory requirement that the minimum period of imprisonment imposed under the section must be the longer of the minimum period of imprisonment required to reflect the *gravity* of the offence. It was necessary to provide *punishment* for an offence where the period required for that purpose is longer than the minimum five years provided for in s 89(1) of the *Sentencing Act 2002*.

---

33   See ibid s 87(5).
34   See eg *R v Kale* (1993) 9 CRNZ 575 (CA); *R v Puaga* (1993) 9 CRNZ 685 (CA).
35   The offender had recently turned 21, when the age threshold for eligibility then prevailing was 21.
36   *Sentencing Act 2002* (NZ), s 87(1).
37   [2004] 3 NZLR 29, [22].
38   *Sentencing Act 2002* (NZ), s 87((2)(c).

The Court noted that the absence of an upper limit for a minimum term imposed in relation to indefinite sentences was a matter of deliberate legislative intent. The Court said:

> The legislature clearly envisaged that some offences which warrant a sentence of preventive detention might be so grave as to take them outside the ten year cap which applies in respect of minimum terms imposed in relation to finite sentences.[39]

In considering how gravity is to be assessed for the purposes of the minimum term (in the context of a sentencing regime that fixes a lower limit of five years but, jurisdictionally, permits a minimum term exceeding any human lifespan), the Court cautioned that, in the absence of a 'principled evaluation of gravity', there was a risk of the law being applied 'arbitrarily'.[40]

It should be said that while the stated purpose of preventive detention may be protective and not punitive, punishment is surely a matter of perception and experience, and it will be of no consolation to offenders sentenced to preventive detention that we are not punishing them but protecting the public from them. Inevitably, offenders facing significant loss of liberty on account of criminal conviction and sentencing would prefer the certainty of a finite sentence and a clearly defined, minimum non-parole period than the inherent uncertainties associated with the indeterminacy of preventive detention. However, because preventive detention *is* indeterminate and its duration unknown in advance, it is important that the parameters for its imposition are clarified to the greatest degree possible in the interests of fair process and fairness generally. An area of significant concern in this regard is the question of how risk is assessed in determining whether an offender is a proper candidate for the sentence. This will be considered in more detail in relation to the Public Safety (Public Protection Orders) Bill.

3.   EXTENDED SUPERVISION

In 2004, New Zealand introduced legislation to manage the long terms risks posed by child sex offenders living in the community. The *Parole (Extended Supervision) Amendment Act 2004* amended the *Parole Act 2002* to allow the post-sentence supervision of high-risk child sex offenders under a regime of 'extended supervision orders' (ESOs). The expressed purpose of the legislation was 'to protect members of the community from those who, following receipt of a

---

[39]   *R v Johnson* [2004] 3 NZLR 29, at [27].
[40]   Ibid [28].

determinate sentence, pose a real and ongoing risk of committing sexual offences against children or young persons'.[41] The ESO process was triggered when the Chief Executive of the Department of Corrections applied to the sentencing court (either the District Court or High Court) for an extended supervision order in respect of an 'eligible offender'. Such orders may last for up to 10 years subject to standard conditions and special conditions imposed by the Parole Board.[42] New Zealand courts have accepted that the availability of an extended supervision order should be taken into account in determining whether a finite sentence would suffice for the purposes of public protection and have held that, if a determinate sentence combined with an ESO would adequately protect the public, it is to be preferred to preventive detention.[43]

Extended supervision allows correctional authorities to detain an inmate in home-detention-like conditions for the first 12 months of the order, so that the offender may not leave their approved address without the permission of a probation officer. There may be restrictions on movement and restrictions on association, in particular of juveniles under the age of 16. Recent amendments to the ESO legislation mean that part-time residential restrictions (electronically monitored curfew) can be imposed beyond the first 12 months of an ESO, and the Parole Board may impose residential restrictions beyond the first 12 months of an ESO.[44]

3.1. EXTENDED SUPERVISION AND THE *BILL OF RIGHTS*

Since the enactment of Part 1A of the *Parole Act 2002*,[45] there has been a significant amount of litigation challenging such matters as the scope of the legislation,[46] the contents of mandated health assessors' reports,[47] risk assessment methodology[48] and the nature of rights engaged by the ESO application. The latter has become

---

[41]   *Parole Act 2002* (NZ), s 107 I (1).
[42]   Ibid s 107A.
[43]   See *R v Mist* [2005] 2 NZLR 791; (2005) 21 CRNZ 490 (CA). See also *R v Parahi* [2005] 23 NZLR 356; (2005) 21 CRNZ 754 (CA).
[44]   See Parole Act 2002, s 107K as amended by s 4 of the Parole (Extended Supervision Orders) Amendment Act 2009.
[45]   Part 1A was inserted by s 11 *Parole (Extended Supervision) Amendment Act 2004*.
[46]   See eg *Chief Executive of the Department of Corrections v J* HC Wellington CRI-2009-485-100, 9 November 2009 concerning whether the legislation was principally concerned with recidivist offending.
[47]   See *Grieve v Chief Executive of the Dept of Corrections* (2005) 22 CRNZ 20 (CA) and see *Chief Executive of the Dept of Corrections v McDonnell* HC Auckland CRI-2005-404-239, 19 May 2008.
[48]   *R v Peta* [2007] 2 NZLR 627; (2007) 22 CRNZ 925 (CA) where the new Zealand Court of Appeal reviewed risk assessment methodology and best practice with the aim of providing guidance for health assessors and judges.

a matter of some controversy, given the fact that the legislation is expressly retrospective[49] and gives rise to significant human rights concerns. These were highlighted in *Belcher v Chief Executive of the Department of Corrections*,[50] an appeal against the making of an ESO based on both evidentiary and human rights grounds. In dealing with the appellant's argument that the provisions in the *Parole Act 2002* relating to ESOs were unjustifiably inconsistent with the *New Zealand Bill of Rights Act 1990* (the *NZBORA*), the Court acknowledged that the imposition through the criminal justice system of significant restrictions (including detention) on offenders, in response to criminal behaviour, amounted to punishment. Consequently, ss 25 and 26 of the *NZBORA* were engaged. Section 25 prescribes minimum standards of criminal procedure, including the right, if convicted of an offence where the penalty has been varied between the commission of the offence and sentencing, to the benefit of the lesser penalty. Section 26 proscribes retrospective penalties and double jeopardy. The Court held that, while the retrospective nature of the ESO scheme is not justified as a 'reasonable limit' on the rights contained in ss 25 and 26, in terms of s 5 of the *NZBORA*, it was nonetheless clear that the Legislature intended the ESO legislation to have retrospective effect. Nevertheless, the Court refrained from making a declaration of inconsistency, an issue it reserved for future consideration.[51] The Court, however, in considering the question of whether a ten-year ESO was justified in the circumstances, reaffirmed the approach that the focus of the legislation is protective. This has been held to mean that ESOs are not to be made for the minimum period required to facilitate *treatment* but for the minimum period required to achieve *active protection* of vulnerable community members.[52]

It is now clear that the making of an ESO, despite its highly restrictive character, does not engage the full panoply of procedural rights and protections that might typically be associated with criminal justice proceedings. In *McDonnell v Chief Executive of the Department of Corrections*,[53] the Court of Appeal dealt with a number of challenges to the lawfulness of the ESO procedure and considered the rights applicable to offenders considered eligible for placement under the regime. The Court observed that it was not appropriate to treat an ESO application as analogous to bringing a fresh charge against the offender. For example, the right to be presumed innocent of the offence for which the offender was made subject to an ESO made no sense since the offender had already been through the trial

---

[49] See *Parole Act 2002* (NZ), s 107C(2): 'To avoid doubt, and to confirm the retrospective application of this provision, despite any enactment or rule of law'.

[50] [2007] 1 NZLR 507.

[51] The matter was subsequently considered by the New Zealand Supreme Court, which essentially confirmed the Court of Appeal's approach of describing the inconsistency but making no declaration. See *Belcher v Chief Executive of the Department of Corrections* [2007] NZSC 54.

[52] See *Chief Executive of the Department of Corrections v McIntosh* HC Christchurch CRI 2004-409-162, 8 December 2004, [27].

[53] [2009] NZCA 352 (2009) 8 HRNZ 770.

and found guilty. Similarly, the right to jury trial was inapplicable. Nevertheless, because the ESO process was analogous with the sentencing process, other rights applicable to sentencing, guaranteed by s 24 of the *NZBORA*, were equally applicable to the ESO process. This was held to include the same right to legal representation that a prisoner facing sentence enjoyed but not the right to legal representation at the interview with a health assessor, since the latter was not the equivalent of a police interview.[54] But the Court agreed that a Court tasked with determining whether or not to make an ESO must comply with s 27(1) of the *NZBORA* – the right to observance of the principles of natural justice 'by any tribunal or other public authority which has the power to make a determination in respect of [a] person's rights, obligations or interest protected or recognized by law'. In *McDonnell*, although the Court of Appeal agreed that the appellant had not been given a fair opportunity to participate in the health assessor's interview for the purposes of a health assessor report mandated by the Act, the failure to involve the Applicant in the preparation of the report did not render the report invalid or remove the Court's jurisdiction to make an ESO.[55] The assessment was conducted in his absence and without his consent. However, the Court held that any procedural failures in that regard did not invalidate the report, even though they might affect the weight to be given to the report.[56]

While the jurisprudence around extended supervision orders continues to develop in New Zealand, the particular legislative context has proven to be a difficult and complex environment in which to develop an affirmative rights discourse. In a sense, like the ESO orders themselves, the legislative context is neither fish nor fowl. While it is not wholly averse to the articulation and application of rights, nor is it wholly sympathetic to rights claims and, as the discussion on non-retrospectivity has shown, is positively dismissive of some fundamental rights. We will consider this problem further as we move now to examine the most recent manifestation of preventive detention in New Zealand, namely, the proposed public protection order regime.

4.   *THE PUBLIC SAFETY (PUBLIC PROTECTION ORDERS) BILL*

The Public Safety (Public Protection Orders) Bill was introduced by the Minister of Justice, the Hon Judith Collins on 18 September 2012. The Bill establishes a new regime of civil detention through the use of a Public Protection Order. This allows for offenders with a high risk of serious sexual or violent offending and who have

---

54   Ibid [40].
55   *McDonnell v Chief Executive of the Department of Corrections* [2009] NZCA 352 at [53]. See *Parole Act 2002* (NZ), s 107F(2).
56   *Adams on Criminal Law – Sentencing* (Thomson/Brookers, 2007) PA107F 10.

completed a prison sentence to be detained within a secure residence located in the precincts of a prison. The legislation is the outcome of an investigation by the Department of Corrections of the most appropriate means of managing offenders 'who, at the end of their sentence, or while on the most intensive form of extended supervision order, still present a very high risk of imminent and serious sexual or violent re-offending'.[57] Five options were identified. They included:

- A strengthened extended supervision order permitting offenders to be closely managed in the community until their risk is reduced.
- Expansion of the scope of the Intellectual Disability (Compulsory Care and Rehabilitation) [IDCCR] Act 2003 to enable offenders with borderline intellectual disability to be managed in a secure facility until their risk is reduced.
- A new civil detention order under which people (including offenders) would be detained in a secure facility in the community until their risk was reduced.
- A continuing detention order under which offenders would be detained in prison until their risk is reduced.
- A new form of civil detention using public protection orders.

The strengthened extended supervision order and *IDCCR Act* options were rejected because neither would cover the whole target group. In the case of the *IDCCR Act* option, because the definition of intellectual disability would need to be amended, this would create an inconsistency with the internationally accepted clinical definition of intellectual disability. For this reason, the *IDCCR Act* option was rejected.

The drafters of the 'Regulatory Impact Statement' rightly noted that, while a civil detention order could have been structured to meet international obligations and the *New Zealand Bill of Rights Act 1990*, drafting legislation that did not reference previous offending and detain a larger group than the target group 'would be difficult'.[58] New Zealand's rejection of the ill-fated Mental Health (Compulsory Assessment and Treatment) Amendment Bill in the early 1990s (which attempted to provide a regime of anticipatory containment for high-risk persons with intellectual disability and psychopaths) is eloquent testimony to the unacceptability of that model of containment.

The continuing detention model was rejected because of its likely conflict with the *NZBORA* and other international obligations but was favoured by the Department of Corrections because it would provide 'the best means of improving public safety'.[59]

---

[57] Department of Corrections, above n 1, [5].
[58] Ibid [7].
[59] Ibid [8].

4.1.   RATIONALE FOR PUBLIC PROTECTION ORDERS

The principal rationale for the Public Protection Order model is the concern that, under current New Zealand legislation, there are no means of responding officially to offenders who present a very high risk of imminent and serious sexual or violent offending who are released from prison on the expiry of their finite sentence. Such offenders, albeit small in number, are considered to present a risk to public safety sufficiently serious to warrant a new approach to their management. While the new orders were 'expected' to apply to between five and 12 offenders over a ten-year period, actual anticipated numbers are notoriously non-specific. Nor is there any clear basis upon which the numbers are calculated. We are simply told that the Department expects that the numbers of offenders who, as they near the end of their sentence, present a very high risk of imminent and serious sexual or violent re-offending 'is likely to be very low'.[60] However, granted that according to the Department's own figures New Zealand has significantly more prisoners serving indeterminate sentences than the states of Victoria and Queensland put together, it could be argued that the projected five to 12 over ten years may be a serious underestimate. Unexpectedly high numbers of inmates receiving public protection orders could have serious a impact on both the cost of administering the new regime and the quality of rehabilitation services available for such persons, further entrenching the proposed regime's incompatibility with international human rights norms.

The reason why the public protection order is now favoured is that it offers the prospect of maintaining high-risk offenders on a short leash post release. A perceived problem with existing regimes of offender management lies in the fact that offenders serving finite jail terms may be released on parole after having served either a third of their sentence or the non-parole period, whichever is the longer.[61] While the Parole Board may only release a person on parole if satisfied that the offender does not present an undue risk to public safety, once an offender has reached his or her sentence expiry date they must be released, regardless of their risk profile.[62] The concern is that if the risk level of a prisoner due for release on their sentence expiry date has not reduced, there is a risk that a small number of such offenders may be released while the risk of serious offending remains very high. It is argued that less restrictive, existing forms of supervision are inadequate for preventing almost certain, further offending by this cohort. In particular, while extended supervision may effectively manage child sex offenders at high risk of re-offending, it has no application to high-risk offenders whose offending is not against children or juveniles. Similarly, supervision subject to the most intensive

---

[60]   Ibid [27].
[61]   See *Parole Act 2002* (NZ), s 84(1), (2).
[62]   Ibid s 86(2).

form of an extended supervision order[63] applies only to child sex offenders, and while its highly restrictive monitoring is undoubtedly instrumental in reducing the risk of re-offending, it has not prevented further offending. Nor does it have any application beyond this cohort.

For these reasons, the public protection order model is favoured by government above other available options. It is said to meet the needs of public safety and, it is claimed, would present virtually no risk to public safety. Furthermore, the cost of detention is estimated to be relatively low although likely to be higher than detention in prison because of the lack of scale. Because detention would be located in prison precincts and would have access to prison resources, the average costs are estimated to be lower that those associated with a civil detention order, requiring the construction of new detention facilities in the community. However, it is acknowledged that, because public protection orders are indeterminate and apply to people already convicted of and punished for a crime, significant human rights issues arise. These will be considered in more detail in the final section of the chapter.

4.2. THE STRUCTURE AND SCOPE OF PUBLIC PROTECTION ORDERS

To be eligible for the imposition of a public protection order for indefinite detention, an offender must have committed a serious sexual or violent offence (that is to say, an offence for which the person would be eligible for preventive detention).[64] The person must aged 18 years or older, be detained in prison for a serious sexual or violent offence and must be released from detention not later than six months after the date on which the chief executive of Corrections applies for a public protection order against the person.[65] Alternatively, the person may already be subject to an extended supervision order with a condition of full-time accompaniment and monitoring imposed under the *Parole Act 2002*, ss 33(2)(c) and 107K(2).

---

[63]   The most intensive form of an extended supervision order includes a special condition imposed by the Parole Board requiring the offender to be at a specified residence at all times and to be accompanied and monitored 24 hours a day by an authorized person. See 'Regulatory Impact Statement', above n 1.

[64]   The definition of 'serious sexual or violent offence' in the bill nominates sexual offences under Part 7 of the *Crimes Act 1961*, including having sexual contact with or organizing 'sex tours' in respect of children and young people outside of New Zealand (see ss 144A and 144C), punishable by seven or more years of imprisonment. It also includes manslaughter, attempted murder and a raft of other serious violent offences.

[65]   See Public Safety (Public Protection Orders) Bill cl 7.

Other bases upon which the threshold for imposition of a public protection order may be triggered are where:

- the person is subject to a condition of long-term full-time placement in the care of an appropriate agency for the purposes of a programme under the Parole Act 2002, ss 15 (3)(b) or 16(c); or
- the person is subject to a protective supervision order; or
- the person has arrived in New Zealand within 6 months of ceasing to be subject to a sentence or order imposed for serious sexual or violent offending by an overseas court, has been in new Zealand for less than 6 months, and intends to reside in New Zealand.[66]

In each case, it is only the chief executive of the Department of Corrections who may apply for a public protection order where a person meets the threshold of a 'very high risk of imminent serious sexual or violent offending by the person'.[67] The application must be supported by at least two health assessor reports, including at least one by a registered psychologist, addressing the nature and seriousness of the risk.

The Court may also call for an independent health assessor assessment of the prisoner, who may also request an assessment by an independent health assessor. In either case, the report must address the question of whether the prisoner presents a very high risk of imminent serious sexual or violent offending.[68] The Judge or a High Court Registrar is empowered to issue a summons for the respondent prisoner to attend at a specified date and time for the hearing of the public protection order application. While the respondent is entitled to apply for legal aid for the purposes of defending the PPO application,[69] the cost of any independent health assessor report requested by the respondent under cl 10(2) must be met out of the legal aid grant. Given the current crisis in legal aid funding for criminal law work in New Zealand, this proposal does not fit well and will inevitably put further pressure on criminal defence lawyers who struggle to make ends meet with the current legal aid fee structure. Nevertheless, granted the highly restrictive and indeterminate nature of PPOs, it will clearly be essential that respondents are adequately represented in order, where appropriate, to challenge the making of an order. This right may well be compromised if a grant of legal aid is further eroded by having to meet the costs of independent health assessor reports.

---

66   See ibid cl 7(b)(ii), (c),(d).
67   Ibid cl 8.
68   Ibid cl 10.
69   See ibid cl 10(5).

4.3.   REVIEW

The legislation provides for review both by a review panel and by the High Court. The review panel, consisting of two health assessors and four people with experience in the operation of the Parole Board, must review the continuing justification of the order within one year of the making of the order and within every succeeding year after the most recent previous review. Where the review panel considers the relevant risk no longer exists, it may direct the chief executive to apply to the High Court for a further review of the order. Such a review must take place within five years after the order is made and, subsequently, within five years after the order is made and at intervals of not more than five years. The Court may direct that the chief executive apply for any subsequent reviews at intervals of not more than ten years.[70] The person subject to a PPO may also, with leave of the court, apply to the court for a review of the order. No time frame is specified as to when such an application may be made.

The court review of a public protection order would appear to be a Judge-led inquiry, where the Court may consider a range of documentation and reports from nominated personnel. These include:

- the chief executive;
- the manager of the residence that the person is required to stay in;
- the manager of the prison, if the person is detained in a prison;
- any health assessor.[71]

After considering all available reports, the Court is required to consider whether the subject person is eligible for release. Eligibility for release is governed by clause 80 of the bill. If the person is successful in persuading the court that there is no longer a very high risk of imminent serious sexual or violent offending, the court must cancel the PPO and impose a 'protective supervision order' on the person. Although it is not stated in the bill, it is assumed that the protective supervision order (PSO) operates upon the person's release into the community. In making such an order, the court may 'load' it with 'any requirements it considers necessary' to reduce the risk of reoffending by the person, to facilitate and promote rehabilitation and reintegration into the community, and to provide for the reasonable concerns of victims.[72]

Notice of any such requirements must be provided in writing to the person under a PSO, the chief executive and the police but may be varied, or the order discharged,

---

[70]   Ibid cl 15(2).
[71]   Public Safety (Public Protection Orders) Bill 2012, cl 17(1).
[72]   Ibid cl 81.

at any time on application to the court. The Review panel, on application by the person or the chief executive, may also modify the requirements if satisfied the modification will render the requirement less restrictive.

4.4. LEGAL REPRESENTATION

Although the bill says nothing about legal representation at a PPO review hearing under clause 17, the rules of natural justice would seem to demand it, especially given the weighty liberty interests that are at stake in the making or downgrading of such an order. Since legal aid is clearly available for defending an application for a PPO,[73] it would seem to follow that it should also be available to defend a review application and to make submissions in respect of the making of a less restrictive protective supervision order. For this purpose, counsel would have an important role in challenging the basis of any report that may be relied upon by the court and in cross-examining expert health assessors in respect of quantification and level of risk alleged to constitute the continuing justification for a PPO or why a PSO may be considered not to be appropriate. While the procedure for making a PPO and reviewing the same seems to imply an inquisitorial model of investigation, there may be powerful reasons why zealous advocacy, including vigorous cross-examination, will from time to time be a necessary feature of such inquiries.

Furthermore, recent case law developments in England should put on notice public officials and those administering the new legislation that failure to provide adequate rehabilitation for offenders under PPOs and PSOs may render the government liable to the accusation that such continuing detention is arbitrary, unlawful and in breach of both the New Zealand Bill of Rights and obligations at international law.[74] In particular, it may be argued that any failure by the state to provide appropriate resources so that prisoners have real opportunity to participate in rehabilitative courses enabling them to progress through the prison system and show that they are no longer dangerous would at least be in breach of their right not to be arbitrarily detained and other rights at international law. These will be considered in more detail later in the chapter.

4.5. ASSESSING FUTURE RISK

As with the sentence of preventive detention and extended supervision orders, risk assessment will be a critical component of the public protection order regime

---

[73] See ibid cl 10–(5).
[74] See *James, Well and Lee v United Kingdom* ECHR, applications 25119/09, 57715/09, 57877/09; *Johnson v SSHD* [2007] EWHC Civ 427; *Walker v SSHD* [2007] EWHC 1835 Admin. See also D Rhodes, 'Governments Ignored IPP Warnings' (2012) 156(36) *Solicitors Journal* 13.

in the event that the legislation is enacted. Much has been said and written on this topic. My purpose here is simply to highlight current areas of concern in order to achieve greater transparency in decision-making around preventive detention and to reduce the risk of arbitrariness in the use of the sentence.

Earlier iterations of the preventive detention provisions in New Zealand required that the court be satisfied the offender presented a 'substantial risk' of committing a specified offence on release.[75] Risk was assessed on the basis of expert reports, which addressed, among other things, the person's predisposition towards particular types of behaviour, likely amenability to formal treatment interventions, degree of risk of reoffending and general future prognosis. Such evaluations depended greatly on clinical experience and intuition and, in the early period, were not referenced to actuarial risk assessment tools.

However, the situation has now changed and, in relation to both preventive detention and extended supervision, risk assessment is increasingly reliant on the use of actuarial instruments by expert health assessors. With regard to preventive detention, the threshold for the third jurisdictional prerequisite for the imposition of the sentence is the Court being satisfied that the offender was 'likely' to commit another qualifying or violent offence if released on parole after a finite term of imprisonment.[76] This requires an assessment of 'the likelihood, type and seriousness of the offending, at an appreciably remote future time'.[77] While health assessors regularly employ actuarial risk assessment tools in assessing relevant risk for the purposes of preventive detention, it is also true that in this domain health professionals are reluctant to offer predictions of future offending:

> [A]ssessment of risk behaviour is inaccurate and inexact and the prediction of behaviour in the future is far more uncertain than prediction of behaviour in the short term.[78]

These limitations are well known to sentencing judges and appellate courts and, for this reason, while health assessor reports must address their statutory purpose, the final assessment of the likelihood of the offender committing a further sexual or violent offence is a judicial one.[79] This suggests that, in respect to preventive detention, judges have a much more 'hands on' role in the assessment of risk than in other contexts where a judicial determination of risk is required.

---

[75]   See eg *Criminal Justice Act 1985*, s 75(2) and *R v Leitch* [1998] 1 NZLR 420, 429.
[76]   *Sentencing Act 2002* (NZ), s (2)(c).
[77]   *R v Pairama* CA216/97, 8 September 1997, 4.
[78]   *R v Exley* CA279/06 [2007] NZCA 393 [32].
[79]   *Adams on Criminal Law*, above n 56, SA87.10. See also *R v Exley* CA279/06 [2007] NZCA 393, [32]; *R v Peta* [2007] 2 NZLR 627 at [50]–[51] (CA).

4.6. RISK ASSESSMENT AND PUBLIC PROTECTION ORDERS

As noted above the imposition of a public protection order depends on proof of a risk of the highest order of magnitude, namely 'a very high risk of imminent serious sexual and violent offending by the person'.[80] The risk must be assessed by at least two health assessor reports, of whom at least one is a registered psychologist, and must address two questions:

(1) whether the respondent exhibits 'to a high level' the following characteristics:
   (a) an intense drive or urge to commit a particular form of offending;
   (b) limited self-regulatory capacity, evidenced by general impulsiveness, high emotional reactivity, and inability to cope with, or manage, stress and difficulties;
   (c) absence of understanding or concern for the impact of offending on actual or potential victims;
   (d) poor interpersonal relationships or social isolation or both; and
(2) A very high risk of imminent serious sexual or violent offending by the respondent.

The characteristics in (1) above must be evidence of a 'severe disturbance in behavioural functioning' so that mere evidence that the respondent has intense drives, limited self-regulatory skills, or a lack of empathy for victims etc will not, of themselves, reach the level of risk required under the legislation. They must be established in the context of what amounts to profound behavioural abnormality.

However, unlike the assessment of risk for the purposes of preventive detention, and to a lesser extent, extended supervision, risk assessment for the purposes of public protection orders is concerned with the likelihood of dangerous behaviour occurring within the immediate short term following the completion of a finite sentence. Because assessment of short-term risk is a matter around which clinicians may express a greater degree of confidence, it seems likely that actuarial assessments will be more determinative of risk than is the case with preventive detention. However, as Andrew Geddis astutely observes,[81] the methods of making determinations as to who really is a 'dangerous' prisoner who will reoffend in a violent or sexual manner upon release are not infallible. He offers the following cautionary quote on the dangers of reliance on actuarial tools to assess risk for serious violent and sexual offences:

---

[80] Public Safety (Public Protection Orders) Bill 2012, cl 8.
[81] A Geddis, 'No Doubt the Precogs Have Already Seen This' *Pundit* (8 November 2011) <http://www.pundit.co.nz/print/2145>.

In terms of risk assessment, it has been established that actuarial tools drawn from the statistical analysis of data on offenders, are generally more reliable than the clinical judgments of professionals alone, but even then, while the accuracy of actuarial tools will be high for frequent minor offences, for serious sexual and violent offences their accuracy is not high and there are significant numbers of false positive. As a result, the ability of actuarial risk assessment tools to accurately predict risk in terms of dangerousness is less powerful than is commonly assumed.[82]

Such assessment tools work by collating and scoring answers to set questions as to whether a given risk feature is definitely present, probably present or absent.[83] An overall score is then compared against the scale developed in research giving rise to the tool and may be used to predict the risk of further offending. However, the assessment of risk based on a cohort that shares relevant characteristics of the defendant cannot predict whether the individual will be one of the group who will commit further offences or not. Kris Gledhill has observed:

> It should be readily apparent that the use of these risk assessment tools raises issues for the prediction of dangerousness in relation to an individual: the tools are developing, are subject to continuing debate within the expert community, do not produce the individualized results that courts need , and produce results that have error rates; but their development is predicated on the frailties of professional judgment in predicting the future behaviour of individuals. What the courts should do in the light of these features should be a subject for debate.[84]

While I agree entirely with this assessment, it is regrettable that such a debate is unlikely to occur before the current proposals for public protection orders are decided upon. This is because the appetite for predictive certainty is not strong as compared to the desirability of having empirical tools that have the appearance of scientific validity and offer some promise of predictive capture.

5.   HUMAN RIGHTS ISSUES

In addressing human rights concerns, it has been acknowledged that the introduction of the continuing detention order model in New Zealand is 'likely to be controversial both in New Zealand and internationally, and is likely to be found to be inconsistent with the [*New Zealand Bill of Rights Act*] and New Zealand's

---

[82]   Ibid.

[83]   K Gledhill, 'Preventive Sentences and Orders: The Challenge of Due Process' [2011] *Journal of Commonwealth Criminal Law* 78, 86.

[84]   Ibid 87.

international obligations'.[85] Furthermore, the Regulatory Impact Statement noted that if continuing detention is introduced in New Zealand it is likely that some person who is made subject to such an order could bring a complaint before the UN Human Rights Committee. While a complaint before the Human Rights Committee could find a breach by New Zealand of its international commitments, the Statement notes that such criticism or complaint 'would have no binding effect, but would have implications for New Zealand's international reputation'.[86]

On this basis, it seems clear enough that the proposed Public Protection Order regime is destined to experience a rocky road through the legislative process and, if ultimately enacted, in its eventual implementation. The problems are potentially far-reaching. It is now clear enough that the proposal will be in breach of the *New Zealand Bill of Rights Act 1990*. In particular, the retrospective character of the legislation appears to breach s 26 of the *NZBORA*, which endorses the right to be free from retroactive penalties and double jeopardy. It is suggested that the way this will operate will be to apply current criteria for preventive detention to prisoners sentenced for offending that occurred when preventive detention was not possible for them. So, where the Parole Board believes a prisoner currently serving a finite sentence for serious sexual or violent offending poses a significant risk of committing further such crimes on release, the Crown would be empowered to apply to the High Court to effectively suggest that the prisoner's sentence ought to be changed to one of preventive detention using contemporary tests.[87]

Geddis also suggests that the proposal is also 'almost certainly' a breach of the rule of law because it potentially subjects someone to a legal rule that is different from that which applied when he or she committed the act governed by that rule. It has been observed that the prohibition of retroactivity gives expression to the 'essential temporal condition of the principal of legality: the required criminal law must have existed when the conduct in issue occurred'.[88] The importance of this principle led Hall to make the further observation that 'there has probably been no more widely held value-judgment in the entire history of human thought than the condemnation of retroactive penal law'.[89]

Such an approach to prevention of crime is a far cry from what different international human rights bodies have held to be acceptable by way of national legislation. In recent jurisprudence arising from the European Court of Human Rights, the Court has held that a prisoner's preventive detention ordered by a

---

85   Department of Corrections, above n 1, [75].
86   Ibid.
87   A Geddis, above n 80.
88   J Hall, *General Principles of Criminal Law* (Bobbs-Merrill, 2nd ed, 1960) 58–59.
89   Ibid 59.

sentencing court did not violate the European Convention of Human Rights.[90] This was because preventive detention as ordered by the sentencing court was warranted under the Convention as detention 'after conviction'. As such, it did not breach Article 5 of the Convention (right to liberty and security). However, for the purposes of the present discussion, it is of interest that, at the same time as these cases were heard, the European Court welcomed a recent leading judgment of the German Federal Constitutional Court declaring all provisions on the retrospective extension of preventive detention and on the retrospective order of such detention incompatible with the German Basic Law. The incompatibility lay in the fact that the law failed to comply with the constitutional protection of legitimate expectations guaranteed in a State governed by the rule of law, read in conjunction with a constitutional right to liberty. It hardly needs be stated that such retrospective extension is precisely what is proposed in the New Zealand model.

As Andrew Geddis notes, both the European Court of Human Rights and the United Nations Human Rights Committee have said it is 'OK' for a country to sentence someone to an indefinite period of detention for something they have done (together with a justified fear of what this indicates they may do upon release). But, as he further notes, altering a person's prison sentence once it has been imposed purely because of fears the person may do "a bad thing in the future" is a no-no from a human rights perspective.[91]

The UN Human Rights Committee has given careful consideration to the international law implications of legislation similar to that currently proposed for New Zealand.[92] In *Tillman v Australia*,[93] the Committee considered the applicant's claim that his detention pursuant to a continuing detention order made under the *Crimes (Serious Sex Offenders) Act 2006 (NSW)* (CSSOA) section 17(1b) constituted arbitrary detention under article 9, paragraph 1 of the International Covenant on Civil and Political Rights and violated the prohibition against double punishment (article 14, paragraph 7). The Committee upheld the author's communication and declared that the State party had violated article 9 paragraph 1 of the Covenant. Accordingly, it was under an obligation to provide the author with an effective remedy, including the termination of his detention under CSSOA. The Committee made some important observations about the legalities of the impugned detention. These have a direct bearing on the Public

---

[90]　See *Schmitz v Germany* (application no 30493/04; *Mork v Germany* (application nos 31047/04 and 43386/08).

[91]　A Geddis, 'No Doubt the Precogs Have Already Seen This (Redux)' *Pundit* (11 April 2012).

[92]　For a summary of the decisions prepared by counsel, see Patrick Keyzer, 'The United Nations Human Rights Committee's views about the legitimate parameters of the preventive detention of serious sex offenders' (2010) 34 *Criminal Law Journal* 283–291.

[93]　CCPR/C/98/D/1635/2007.

Protection Order model proposed for New Zealand. Because of their significance, I will cite the most important of the Committee's reasons *in extensu*:

> 7.4...(1) The author had already served his 10-year term of imprisonment and yet continued, in actual fact, to be subjected to imprisonment in pursuance of a law which characterizes his continued incarceration under the same prison regime as detention. This purported detention amounted, in substance, to a fresh term of imprisonment which, unlike detention proper, is not permissible in the absence of a conviction for which imprisonment is a sentence prescribed by law.

> (2) Imprisonment is penal in character. It can only be imposed on conviction for an offence in the same proceedings in which the offence is tried. The author's further term of imprisonment was the result of Court orders made, some ten years after his conviction and sentence, in respect of predicted future criminal conduct which had its basis in the very offence for which he had already served his sentence. This new sentence was the result of fresh proceedings, though nominally characterized as 'civil proceedings', and fall within the prohibition of Article 15, paragraph 1, of the Covenant. In this regard the Committee further observes that, since the CSSOA was enacted in 2006 shortly before the expiry of the author's sentence for an offence for which he had been convicted in 1998 and which became an essential element in the Court orders for his continued incarceration, the CSSOA was being retroactively applied to the author. This also falls within the prohibition of article 15, paragraph 1, of the Covenant, in that he has been subjected to a heavier penalty 'than was applicable at the time when the criminal offence was committed.' The Committee therefore considers that detention pursuant to proceedings incompatible with article 15 is necessarily arbitrary within the meaning of article 9, paragraph I, of the covenant.

> ...

> (4) The 'detention' of the author as a 'prisoner' under the CSSOA was ordered because it was feared that he might be a danger to the community in the future and for purposes of his rehabilitation. The concept of feared or predicted dangerousness to the community applicable in the case of past offenders in inherently problematic. It is essentially based on opinion as distinct from factual evidence, even if that evidence consists of the opinion of psychiatric experts. But psychiatry is not an exact science. The CSSOA, on the one hand, requires the Court to have regard to the opinion of psychiatric experts on future dangerousness but, on the other hand, requires the Court to make a finding of fact of dangerousness. While Courts are free to accept or reject expert opinion and are required to consider all other available relevant evidence, the reality is that the Courts must make a finding of fact on the suspected future behaviour of a past offender which may or may not materialize. To avoid arbitrariness, in these circumstances, the State party should have demonstrated that the author's rehabilitation could not have been achieved by means less intrusive that continued imprisonment or even detention, particularly as the State party had a continuing obligation under article 10, para-

graph 3, of the Covenant to adopt meaningful measures for the reformation, if indeed it was needed, of the author throughout the 10 years during which he was in prison.[94]

This ruling highlights what is both material and problematic with the proposed public protection order regime. Quite apart from the danger of over-predicting risk that may never materialize, such actuarially-based models risk serious conflict with established human rights principles. This problem has recently been highlighted in the UK in relation to sentences of indeterminate imprisonment for public protection (IPP), first introduced in 2005.[95] Under this legislation, sentences are imposed upon offenders deemed 'dangerous' according to statutory criteria. A tariff sentence is set by the sentencing judge, after the expiry of which the offender is eligible for release. However, that will only occur once the Parole Board is satisfied he or she no longer poses a danger to the public.[96] The problem that has emerged is that with large numbers of prisoners being placed by the courts under IPP orders, courses and training required by the Parole Board to satisfy the mandate for rehabilitation are simply not available for many prisoners or are simply inadequate. This has resulted in large numbers of prisoners languishing in prison well beyond their tariff date but without any means of demonstrating they meet release criteria.[97]

This has led to litigation before the European Court of Human Rights where the applicants have argued that their right to liberty and security under article 5(1) of the European Convention on Human Rights has been breached.[98] Although the court failed to find IPPs unlawful per se, the state's failure to provide sufficient rehabilitative courses produced what amounted to arbitrary detention once the minimum tariff had been served.[99]

What is of interest, from the perspective of the New Zealand's proposal, is that IPPs are already on the way out.[100] The IPP has been abolished by the *Legal Aid, Sentencing and Punishment of Offenders Act 2012*,[101] in favour of a new model of extended sentence. The extended sentences are non-custodial and involve releasing an offender on licence for a period of up to eight years.

The legal challenge to the IPP regime has placed the UK Government under considerable pressure to ensure that the detention of IPP inmates complies

---

[94] Ibid.
[95] See *Criminal Justice Act 2005* (UK) s 225.
[96] See J Lorimer, 'Picking up the IPP Pieces' (2012) 156(37) *Solicitors Journal* 9.
[97] Ibid.
[98] See *James, Well and Lee v United Kingdom* ECHR, applications 25119/09, 57715/09, 57877/09.
[99] Lorimer, above n 92.
[100] Ibid.
[101] See *Legal Aid, Sentencing and Punishment of Offenders Act 2012* (UK) s 123.

with article 5(1) of the ECHR, which will mean committing sufficient (and considerable) funds into the prison system to provide suitable and adequate courses and assessment processes for offenders serving IPPs. The decision of the UK Government to now abolish IPPs should give pause to the New Zealand Government as it now embarks on a plan to introduce an analogous type of order. One may hope that wisdom will prevail and that it will be seen that the cost of the introduction, both in terms of human rights values and fiscal realities, is simply too high. Other alternatives need to be explored.

6. CONCLUSION

Preventive detention, in all its forms, represents a significant intrusion upon the fundamental rights and freedoms of individuals deemed sufficiently dangerous to justify indeterminate detention. Yet as this discussion has shown, detention for preventive purposes is often associated with over-prediction of risk, with the result that significant numbers of those so detained may never actualize the risk for which the detention is warranted.

There is also the risk that legislation made hastily and in reaction to perceived public dangers may prove to be seriously non-compliant with international human rights norms and may generate social problems at least as far-reaching as the mischief they were designed to remedy.

In New Zealand, state officials have been quick to respond to the opportunities presented for sentencing and disposition involving the use of preventive sentencing tools, including preventive detention and extended supervision. In each case, their parameters are sufficiently broad to capture the worst offending by criminals whose behaviour meets the relevant eligibility criteria. There is no evidence that these methodologies have been either over- or under-inclusive in targeting the particular cohorts addressed in the legislation, although there is some evidence of an increased use of preventive detention in recent years. It is not suggested, however, that this has been excessive. The addition, as from June 2010, of a 'Three Strikes' sentencing regime in New Zealand,[102] has added an additional means of preventively detaining serious sexual and violent offenders, especially where on a third 'strike' the offender serves the statutory maximum sentence without parole eligibility. However, because of its primarily punitive focus, this regime has not been discussed in this chapter. It is adequately described elsewhere.[103]

---

[102] See ss 86A–86I, *Sentencing Act 2002* (NZ), as inserted from 1 June 2010 by s 6 *Sentencing and Parole Reform Act 2010*.
[103] See W J Brookbanks and R Ekins, 'The Case Against the "Three Strikes" Sentencing Regime' [2010] *New Zealand Law Review* 689.

Granted the availability and operational effectiveness of existing preventive detention regimes in New Zealand, it must be seriously doubted whether a further incapacitatory model is warranted at this time. The proposal to introduce public protection orders permitting the indefinite detention of offenders released at the end of a finite prison sentence (but who have committed no further offences warranting punishment) goes significantly further in impugning fundamental rights and freedoms than any measure previously contemplated by a New Zealand government. It is highly doubtful that the case for doing so has been conclusively established.

THE REHABILITATION OF PREVENTIVE DETENTION

Brendan GOGARTY, Benedict BARTL and Patrick KEYZER

1.   INTRODUCTION

The right to liberty is a fundamental human right,[1] entrenched as a customary right and enshrined in numerous international human rights covenants through the protection of the individual against arbitrary interference by the State.[2] The right to liberty can be traced through the common law back to the Magna Carta of 1215.[3] Nevertheless, the right to personal liberty is not absolute, with the state also having a legitimate right to ensure public safety.[4] The inherent tension between these competing rights has generally been reconciled through an acceptance that the state can detain people for appropriate reasons where the detention has been established in law and so long as the reasons for the detention and/or the practice of the detention is not arbitrary. In some cases, preventive detention is ordered as part of a criminal sentence. This variety of preventive detention gives rise to no human rights issues, per se. However, in some circumstances, individuals have been subject to preventive detention based not on offences they have committed but, rather, with respect to offences they *might* commit in the future.

Over the last few decades, however, legislatures around the world have increasingly implemented preventive detention regimes, and in a wider and wider variety of circumstances. Andrew Ashworth has identified three themes of criminology that help explain the political shift toward preventive detention:[5] the growth

---

[1]   *Kurt v Turkey* (European Court of Human Rights, Application No 15/1997/799/1002, 25 May 1998) [122]–[123]; *A v Secretary of State for the Home Department* [2004] UKHL 56 [36].

[2]   Article 3 of the *Universal Declaration of Human Rights*; article 9(1) of the *International Covenant on Civil and Political Rights*; article 6 of the *African Charter on Human and Peoples' Rights*; article 7(1) of the *American Convention on Human Rights*; article 5(1) of the *European Convention for the Protection of Human Rights and Fundamental Freedoms*.

[3]   D Clark, 'The Icon of Liberty: The Status and Role of Magna Carta in Australian and New Zealand Law' (2000) 24(3) *Melbourne University Law Review* 866–92.

[4]   See eg, Article 9(1) of the *International Covenant on Civil and Political Rights*.

[5]   A Ashworth, 'Criminal Law, Human Rights and Preventative Justice' in B McSherry, A Norrie and S Bronitt (eds), *Regulating Deviance: The Redirection of Criminalisation and the Futures of Criminal Law* (Hart Publishing, 2009) 87–108. This material was summarised by Bernadette

of 'actuarial justice' whereby governments encourage 'techniques to identify, classify, and manage groupings sorted by dangerousness';[6] the rise of the 'risk society' whereby governments focus on the risks presented by certain individuals or circumstances and act to minimise them;[7] and 'the shift from managing risk towards the necessity to take protective action when the precise nature and scope of potential threats are unknown'.[8]

In the political context of policy-making, Lucia Zedner has observed that criminal justice policy has shifted from a post-crime focus to a pre-crime focus.[9] Exclusionary strategies are developed based on the 'precautionary principle'.[10] This then 'ousts evidence-based approaches to public policy'.[11] Richard Ericson has argued that the 'criminalization of uncertainty' is preferred today because of our 'limited knowledge about threats'.[12]

The shift to the pre-crime society has resulted in the diminution of ancient and fundamental protections of both liberty and due process. This has not gone unnoticed. A range of commentators and critics have argued that preventive detention provisions may be in breach of international human rights provisions. This criticism has recently been given voice within the European Court of Human Rights (ECHR) and the United Nations Human Rights Committee (UNHRC) in respect of post-sentence preventive detention in Germany and Australia, respectively. Those tribunals both found that, where there has been no fresh criminal trial, such detention is incompatible with the right to liberty and other human rights. This chapter considers the decisions of both human rights decision-making bodies to focus on the rehabilitation of the offender and argues that the findings also have implications for other countries with preventive detention measures.

McSherry in Bernadette McSherry and Patrick Keyzer, *Sex Offenders and Preventive Detention* (Federation Press, 2009) ch 2.

[6] M Feeley and J Simon, 'The New Penology: Notes on the Emerging Strategy of Corrections and its Implications' (1992) 30(4) *Criminology* 449–74; M Feeley and J Simon, 'Actuarial Justice: The Emerging New Criminal Law' in D Nelken (ed), *The Futures of Criminology* (Sage, 1994) 173–201.

[7] R Ericson and K Haggerty, *Policing the Risk Society* (Oxford University Press, 1997); B Hudson, *Justice in the Risk Society* (Sage, 2003).

[8] P O'Malley, 'Globalizing Risk? Distinguishing Styles of 'Neo-liberal' Criminal Justice in Australia and the USA' (2002) 2(2) *Criminal Justice* 205–22; R Ericson, *Crime in an Insecure World* (Polity Press, 2007).

[9] L Zedner, 'Pre-crime and Post-criminology?' (2007) 11(2) *Theoretical Criminology* 261–81, 262.

[10] S M Gardiner, 'A Core Precautionary Principle' (2006) 14(1) *The Journal of Political Philosophy* 33–60; C R Sunstein, *Laws of Fear: Beyond the Precautionary Principle* (Cambridge University Press, 2005).

[11] Bernadette McSherry and Patrick Keyzer, *Sex Offenders and Preventive Detention* (Federation Press, 2009) ch 2.

[12] R Ericson, 'Governing through Risk and Uncertainty' (2005) 34(4) *Economy and Society* 659–72, 669.

This chapter begins with an overview of the right of liberty and its particular application to indefinite and preventive detention measures. It provides short histories of the indefinite and preventive detention regimes in Germany and Australia and the recent findings of both the ECHR and the UNHRC that the use of preventive detention in both countries was incompatible with human right covenants. It concludes with an outline of how indefinite and preventive detention measures can continue to be implemented in a manner that is also compatible with human rights.

2.   DETENTION AND THE RIGHT TO LIBERTY

In his 1869 treatise 'On Liberty', John Stuart Mill wrote that '[o]ver himself, over his own body and mind, the individual is sovereign',[13] arguing that the basis of tyranny – be it of the ruler or of the majority – was the deprivation of individual liberty. In a civilised society the only basis for the interference of individual or collective liberty, Mill argued, 'is to prevent harm to others'.[14] Indeed, over the next century Mill's thesis would be born out in a succession of tyrannical regimes who utilised the court system to silence opponents and dissidents under the guise of the administration of justice. As Lord Scott has noted, the arbitrary and secretive deprivation of liberty by the state has long been the 'stuff of nightmares', associated with the most oppressive and despotic regimes throughout history, but particularly in the 20th Century.[15]

Nevertheless, there can be legitimate and compelling grounds for the state to remove individual liberty, and even Mill accepted that in certain circumstances the public interest might permit state detention, at least to the extent that it would achieve the protection of 'society or its members from injury and molestation'.[16] Indeed, even the most liberal and democratic states regularly incarcerate individuals who are considered a risk to the safety of others and, to a lesser extent, to themselves. The question, of course, is the inherent tension between the state's obligation to refrain from interfering with the liberty of individuals and its concurrent obligation to protect public safety and order.

The *Universal Declaration of Human Rights* (*UDHR*) was declared in response to the human rights abuses and atrocities perpetrated during the Second World War, at a time when the nations of the world were particularly cognisant of how unjustifiable deprivations of liberty might be employed by despotic regimes to gain and consolidate power. Article 3 subsequently declares that amongst the

---

[13]   J S Mill, *On Liberty* (Walter Scott, 1989) 18.
[14]   Ibid.
[15]   *A v Secretary of State for the Home Department* [2005] 2 AC 68, 148–9.
[16]   Mill, above n 13, 141.

inherent and inalienable rights which all human beings share is the 'right to liberty and security of the person'.[17] Whilst this is a particularly emphatic declaration of the individual right to liberty of the person, it does, of course, evidence the inherent tension between the obligation of the state with respect to that right and concurrent obligation of the state to protect the security of persons from harm, including harm from others in society. Article 9, therefore, qualifies these rights by implying the state does have the right to deprive individuals of their liberty so long as the process to which they are subjected is not 'arbitrary'.[18] The human rights covenants that followed the *UDHR* contained similar balancing principles. Article 9(1) of the *International Covenant on Civil and Political Rights (ICCPR)* provides:[19]

> Article 9
>
> (1) Everyone has the right to liberty and security of person. No one shall be subjected to arbitrary arrest or detention. No one shall be deprived of his liberty except on such grounds and in accordance with such procedure as are established by law.

The legitimate deprivation of liberty through detention, therefore, requires that it be established in law,[20] and in circumstances that do not amount to arbitrary detention.[21] Although on occasion there will be overlap between lawfulness and arbitrariness, both elements must be independently established. For example, whilst detention that is illegal domestically may well also be arbitrary, it is possible for detention to be lawful domestically but still arbitrary under international

---

[17]   Adopted and proclaimed by General Assembly Resolution 217A (III) of 10 December 1948, preamble, article 3. Although not a legally binding instrument, the *UDHR* is generally recognised as 'the basic catalogue of fundamental human rights which should be respected by all states': Helena Cook, 'Preventive Detention – International Standards and the Protection of the Individual' in Stanislaw Frankowski and Dinah Shelton (eds), *Preventive Detention – A Comparative and International Law Perspective* (Martin Nijhoff, 1992) 2.

[18]   Article 9 of the *Universal Declaration of Human Rights* noting that '[n]o one shall be subjected to arbitrary arrest, detention or exile'.

[19]   See also article 6 of the *African Charter on Human and Peoples' Rights*; article 7(2) of the *American Convention on Human Rights* and article 5(1) of the *European Convention for the Protection of Human Rights and Fundamental Freedoms*. For the purposes of this chapter, the 'human rights covenants' are those international instruments noted above and the *International Covenant on Civil and Political Rights*.

[20]   See, for example, Human Rights Committee, *Views: Communication No 702/1996*, UN Doc GAOR/ A/52/40 (18 July 1997) 230–1 [5.5] ('*C McLawrence v Jamaica*'). See also *I-A Court HR, Gangaram Panday Case v Suriname, judgment of January 21, 1994*, in OAS doc. OAS/Ser.L/V/ III.31, doc. 9, Annual Report of the Inter-American Court of Human Rights 1994, p. 32, para 47.

[21]   Human Rights Committee, *General Comment No 8: Right to Liberty and Security of Persons*, 16th sess, CCPR (30 June 1982). Whilst article 5 of the European Convention does not expressly prohibit 'arbitrary' detention, the ECHR has noted in case law that 'in a democratic society subscribing to the rule of law, no detention that is arbitrary can ever be regarded as 'lawful'': *Winterwerp v The Netherlands* (1979) Eur Court HR (ser A) para 39.

---

law.[22] In practice, this has meant that human rights decision-making bodies will look to the 'quality of the law' to ensure that the detention 'is sufficiently accessible, precise and foreseeable in its application, in order to avoid all risk of arbitrariness'.[23] Whilst the meaning of 'arbitrary' is not defined in any of the international covenants, the United Nations Human Rights Commission made clear in the leading case of *Van Alphen v The Netherlands* that the term is to be defined broadly:[24]

> 'arbitrariness' is not to be equated with 'against the law', but must be interpreted more broadly to include elements of inappropriateness, injustice and lack of predictability. This means that remand in custody... must be necessary in all the circumstances, for example to prevent flight, interference with evidence or the recurrence of crime.

Whether the deprivation of liberty amounts to arbitrary detention in law is determined in light of a variety of factors, including 'the type, duration, effects and manner of implementation'.[25] This goes beyond simply considering whether a person is imprisoned or restrained in the traditional sense. For example, in *Guzzardi v Italy* a requirement to live on part of an island amounted to a loss of liberty.[26] Additionally, the United Nations has made clear that in circumstances in which human rights are restricted, such as the deprivation of liberty, the principles of proportionality and parsimony must be met, such that 'the least intrusive intervention amongst those which might achieve the desired result' must be adopted.[27]

---

[22] Cook, above n 17, 8. See also *Steel and Others v the United Kingdom*, (European Court of Human Rights, Application No 67/1997/851/1058, 23 September 1998), 2735 [54] and the references collected in Patrick Keyzer, 'The "Preventive Detention" of Serious Sex Offenders: Further Consideration of the International Human Rights Dimensions' (2009) 16 *Psychology, Psychiatry and Law* 262–70.

[23] *Nasrulloyev v Russia*, (European Court of Human Rights, Application No 656/06, 11 October 2007) para 71; *AS v Poland* (European Court of Human Rights, Application No 39510/98, 20 June 2006) para 73; *Amuur v France*, (European Court of Human Rights, Application No 17/1995/523/609, 25 June 1996) para 50.

[24] Human Rights Committee, *Communication No 305/88*, UN Doc CCPR/C/39/D/305/1988 (23 July 1990) para 5.8 ('*Van Alphen v The Netherlands*'). See also Human Rights Committee, *Communication No 560/1993*, UN Doc CCPR/C/59/D/560/1993 (30 April 1997) para 9.2 ('*A v Australia*'); Human Rights Committee, *Communication No 1128/2002*, UN Doc CCPR/C/83/D/1128 (18 April 2005) para 6.1 ('*Rafael Marques de Morais v Angola*'). With regard to the American Convention on Human Rights, see Velasquez Rodriguez Case, Judgment of the Inter-American Court of Human Rights 29 July, 1988. See also Claire Macken, 'Preventive Detention and the Right of Personal Liberty and Security under the International Covenant on Civil and Political Rights 1966' (2005) 26 *Adelaide Law Review* 1.

[25] *Guzzardi v Italy* (1980) Eur Court HR (ser A) para 92. See also *Engel and Others v the Netherlands* (1976) Eur Court HR (ser A) 24 [58]–[59].

[26] *Guzzardi v Italy* (1980) Eur Court HR (ser A) para 96.

[27] Human Rights Committee, *Communication No 488/1992*, UN Doc CCPR/C/50/D/488/1992 (25 December 1991) para 8.3 ('*Nicholas Toonen v Australia*'); Human Rights Committee, *Communication No 900/1999*, UN Doc CCPR/C/76/D/ 900/1999 (25 December 1991) para

Whilst exceptions to the deprivation of liberty have long been recognised in case law, only the *European Convention for the Protection of Human Rights and Fundamental Freedoms* expressly lists these exceptions:

> 5. Right to liberty and security
>
> (1) Everyone has the right to liberty and security of person. No one shall be deprived of his liberty save in the following cases and in accordance with a procedure prescribed by law:
>
> (a) the lawful detention of a person after conviction by a competent court;
>
> (b) the lawful arrest or detention of a person for non-compliance with the lawful order of a court or in order to secure the fulfillment of any obligation prescribed by law;
>
> (c) the lawful arrest or detention of a person effected for the purpose of bringing him before the competent legal authority on reasonable suspicion of having committed an offence or when it is reasonably considered necessary to prevent his committing an offence or fleeing after having done so;
>
> (d) the detention of a minor by lawful order for the purpose of educational supervision or his lawful detention for the purpose of bringing him before the competent legal authority;
>
> (e) the lawful detention of persons for the prevention of the spreading of infectious diseases, of persons of un-sound mind, alcoholics or drug addicts or vagrants;
>
> (f) the lawful arrest or detention of a person to prevent his effecting an unauthorized entry into the country or of a person against whom action is being taken with a view to deportation or extradition.

The European Court of Human Rights (ECHR) has consistently refused to expand the scope of article 5(1), concluding that this section sets out an exhaustive list of exceptions and 'must be interpreted strictly'.[28] Importantly, article 5(1)(c) of the ECHR expressly provides that detention may be lawful 'when it is reasonably considered necessary to prevent his committing an offence'.[29] In practice, this has

---

8.2 ('*C v Australia*'). See also UN Commission on Human Rights, *The Siracusa Principles on the Limitation and Derogation Provisions in the International Covenant on Civil and Political Rights*, 41st sess, UN Doc E/CN4/1985/4 (28 September 1984).

[28] *Bouamar v Belgium* (1988) Eur Court HR (ser A) 19 [43]. See also *Winterwerp v The Netherlands* (1979) Eur Court HR (ser A) para 37; *Ireland v the United Kingdom* (1978) Eur Court HR (ser A) 74 [194]; *Engel and Others v the Netherlands* (1976) Eur Court HR (ser A) 24 [57].

[29] Similar measures have been upheld in the commentary arising from other human rights covenants. For example, United Nations Special Rapporteur on Prevention of Discrimination and Protection of Minorities Mr Louis Joinet has previously noted, '... contrary to what one might suppose, administrative detention is not banned on principle under international rules': United Nations Economic and Social Council, Commission on Human Rights, Sub-Commission on Prevention of Discrimination and Protection of Minorities, 'Revised Report on the Practice of Administrative Detention, submitted by Mr Louis Joinet', E/CN4/Sub 2/1990/29. See also Human Rights Committee, *General Comment No 8: Right to Liberty and Security of Persons*, 16th sess, CCPR (30 June 1982) which provides that where 'so-called

meant that detention may be imposed for an indefinite period but only by a court and only when the matter is *sub judice*, that is, during the sentencing process.[30] Further, where liberty is to be deprived for preventive purposes, the court has interpreted the section narrowly and in a manner which limits the capacity of states to establish a general policy of preventive detention against either an individual or group on the basis of a propensity to commit offences. Rather, the court must be satisfied that the State has adopted the measure in order to prevent a 'concrete and specific offence'.[31] Additionally, all the major human rights decision-making bodies have insisted that procedural guarantees be afforded before detention based on preventive grounds can be sanctioned.[32]

In summary, international human rights covenants expressly guarantee the right to liberty from unlawful or arbitrary detention. Further, human rights decision-making bodies have placed strict limits on what might be considered lawful detention where liberty is deprived for ostensibly preventive purposes, requiring that such detention only be used as a last resort and subject to periodic court reviews to confirm the continued necessity of the detention.

Having set out the principles established in international human rights law, the chapter now turns to an analysis of the indefinite and preventive detention measures in Germany and Australia and their review by the ECHR and the UNHRC.

3. A SHORT HISTORY OF THE INDEFINITE AND PREVENTIVE DETENTION SYSTEM IN GERMANY

Following the lead set by many European countries,[33] Germany introduced indefinite detention provisions in 1933, with an estimated 16,000 offenders

---

preventive detention is used … it must not be arbitrary, and must be based on grounds and procedures established by law'. As found in Cook, above n 17, 11.

[30] Human Rights Committee, *Communication No 1090/2002*, UN Doc CCPR/C/79/D/1090/2002 (6 November 2003) para 7.3 ('*Rameka v New Zealand*').

[31] *Guzzardi v Italy* (1980) Eur Court HR (ser A) para 102.

[32] *Ciulla v Italy* (1989) Eur Court HR (ser A) 16 [38]. See also Human Rights Committee, *Communication No 66/1980*, UN Doc CCPR/C/OP/2 (15 March 1980) para 18.1 ('*David Alberto Campora Schweizer v Uruguay*'). See also article 9(2)–(5) of the *International Covenant on Civil and Political Rights*; Human Rights Committee, *General Comment No 8: Right to Liberty and Security of Persons*, 16th sess, CCPR (30 June 1982) which provides that 'if, in addition, criminal charges are brought in such cases, the full protection of articles 9(2) and (3), as well as article 14, must be granted'.

[33] Sweden was the first European country to introduce preventive detention provisions in 1927, followed by the Netherlands, Norway and the former Yugoslavia in 1929, Italy, Denmark and Belgium in 1930 and Poland and Finland in 1932.

sentenced to indefinite detention between 1934 and 1945.[34] Surprisingly, this large number did not include political opponents or other dissidents of the regime; around 85 per cent of those sentenced to indefinite detention were sentenced for repeated petty crime, most often property crime.[35] Following World War II, the indefinite detention provisions remained relatively unchanged in the Federal Republic of Germany[36] but were rarely used,[37] with the relatively small numbers continuing to be repeat petty criminals[38] who were required to serve an additional indefinite detention of three to four years following their term of imprisonment.[39]

During the 1960s, a major review of the *Criminal Code* led to indefinite detention provisions being limited to people who had committed serious offences and not simply petty criminals.[40] The reforms introduced included a higher threshold being set before offenders could be sentenced to preventive detention as well as a maximum sentence of ten-years preventive detention.[41] There was a significant reduction in the number of offenders sentenced to indefinite detention in the ensuing decades: 718 people were indefinitely detained in 1970, dropping to 208 in 1980 and 182 in 1990, following which an average of 30 to 40 offenders were sentenced to indefinite detention.[42] The narrowing of the offence range to

---

[34]   This enormous number can be contrasted with the estimated 800–1000 offenders to whom commentators believed the provisions would apply: J Hellmer, 'Hangtäterschaft und Berufsverbrechertum', (1961) 73(3) *Zeitschrift für die gesamte Strafrechtswissenschaft* 441–62, 442.

[35]   T Weichert, 'Sicherungsverwahrung – verfassungsgemäß' (1989) 6 *Strafverteidiger* 265–74, 267. See commentators noting that the provision was probably not applied to dissidents because they were summarily sent to concentration camps with no opportunity for a court process: Jan-David Jansing, *Nachträgliche Sicherungsverwahrung* (Lit Verlag, 2004) 29–30.

[36]   The death penalty, which had been available as a sentencing option for preventive detention was abolished: T Weichert, above n 35. In East Germany, the provisions were held to be 'invalid' by the highest court in the German Democratic Republic and were repealed: Heinrich Laufhütte, Ruth Rissing-van Saan and Klaus Tiedemann (eds), *Strafgesetzbuch: Leipziger Kommentar* (De Gruyter, 12th ed, 2006) vol 3, 413.

[37]   For example, there were 673 preventive detention detainees in 1961, 899 in 1966 and 718 in 1970. As found in Laufhütte, Rissing-van Saan and Tiedemann, ibid.

[38]   For example, according to one report, 49.1 per cent of those sentenced to preventive detention in 1956 had been sentenced to repeated theft; 20.1 per cent to receiving stolen goods and fraud and 23.1 per cent for indecency offences: Werner Geisler, Die *Sicherungsverwahrung im englischen und deutschen Strafrecht* (Duncker and Humblot, 1967) 209. Another study found that between 1958 and 1961 55 per cent of those sentenced to preventive detention had been convicted of theft and 20 per cent to fraud: G Grünwald, 'Sicherungsverwahrung, Arbeitshaus, vorbeugende Verwahrung und Sicherungsaufsicht im Entwurf 1962' (1964) 76(4) *Zeitschrift für die gesamte Strafrechtswissenschaft* 633–68, 643. See also Jansing, above n 35, 59.

[39]   Grünwald, ibid 641.

[40]   Laufhütte, Rissing-van Saan and Tiedemann, above n 36, 414. The reformed section 66(1) relevantly provided that preventive detention could be imposed in circumstances where an offender had a tendency to commit serious offences that would severely damage the victim psychologically or physically or which, because of serious economic loss, were dangerous to the general public.

[41]   The threshold requirement for preventive detention was that offenders were found guilty of at least two offences with a minimum custodial sentence of at least one year imposed.

[42]   Statistisches Bundesamt, Fachserie 10 Reihe 4.1, 2010. See also Jansing, above n 35, 63.

which preventive/indefinite sentencing provisions applied also saw significant changes in the types of offenders incarcerated. A study published in 1997 found that 78 per cent of those sentenced to indefinite detention had been convicted of serious offences – which include homicide or sexual offence or robbery – and only 14.4 per cent had committed either burglary or fraud.[43]

The trend towards the diminution in the use and scope of indefinite detention in Germany began to reverse in the mid-to-late 1990s as the result of a number of high–profile sexual assault cases there and in neighbouring countries.[44] Those cases provoked community outrage and sensationalist media attention, making indefinite detention a central and highly politicised issue in the lead up to the September 1998 elections. The Government sought to seize the initiative by pushing through amendments which broadened the scope of indefinite detention as well as making the sentences more severe. The amendments included the ten-year maximum indefinite detention sentence becoming both indeterminate and retrospective and the prerequisites for the imposition of indefinite detention being relaxed.[45] Further amendments, introduced in 2002 and 2004, reduced the age that someone could be indefinitely and preventively detained from 21 to 18 years old.[46]

---

[43]   J Kern, 'Aktuelle Befunde zur Sicherungsverwahrung – Ein Betrag zur Problematik des § 66 StGB' (1997) 47 *Zeitschrift für Strafvollzug und Straffälligenhilfe* 19–25, 19. Similar figures are also available for 2010 with the German Bureau of Statistics noting that, of the 536 persons currently serving preventive detention orders, 86.9 per cent had been convicted of serious offences: Statistisches Bundesamt, Strafvollzug – demographische und kriminologische Merkmale der Strafgefangenen 2010, Reihe 4.1 at 23.

[44]   These cases included an 18-year-old woman called Stephanie Karl who was kidnapped, sexually abused and murdered in 1995 by a 35-year-old man with a history of sexual offending as well as the 1996 case of a 7-year-old girl called Natalie Astner who was raped and murdered in a small Bavarian village by an offender who had been paroled only months prior to the killing for earlier sexual assault convictions. Both of these cases were preceded by the Dutroux case in neighbouring Belgium in 1995 in which the offender abducted, sexually abused and killed at least four children. See, for example, Michael Petrunik and Linda Deutschmann, 'The Exclusion-Inclusion Spectrum in State and Community Response to Sex Offenders in Anglo-American and European Jurisdictions' (2008) 52(5) *International Journal of Offender Therapy and Comparative Criminology* 499, 507. See also J Kinzig, 'An den Grenzen des Strafrechts – Die Sicherungsverwahrung nach den Urteilen des BverG' (2004) 57 *Neue Juristische Wochenschrift* 911–14, 912.

[45]   The amendment to Section 66a Criminal Code ('vorbehaltene Sicherungsverwahrung') meant that preventive detention detainees who had already served two-thirds of their detention terms could be ordered to reappear before the courts, where a decision could be made about the detainees further detention. The amendment was defended on the grounds that, in the period between the detainees being sentenced to detention and the subsequent court hearing, important evidence either in support of the further preventive detention or the release of the detainee could be collected. Number of prior offences relaxed from the previous requirement of two separate prior convictions to only one being required to trigger an indefinite detention.

[46]   The amendment to Section 66b Criminal Code ('nachträgliche Sicherungsverwahrung') could be relied upon when during the custodial sentence it became apparent that the offender was likely, upon their release, to commit offences that could harm.

Harsher indefinite detention and the introduction of preventive detention measures saw the number of detainees climb dramatically, from 176 indefinite detention detainees in 1998 to 536 indefinite and preventive detention detainees in 2010.[47] In just over a decade, the number of offenders sentenced to indefinite and preventive detention in Germany had more than tripled.

Criticism of the reforms followed, particularly the perception that the reforms were more focused on appeasing the public than the rehabilitation of the detainees.[48] The European Committee for the Prevention of Torture and Inhuman or Degrading Treatment or Punishment, for example, argued in 2005:[49]

> Due to the potentially indefinite stay for the small (but growing) number of inmates held under *Sicherungsverwahrung*, there needs to be a particularly clear vision of the objectives in this unit and of how those objectives can be realistically achieved. The approach requires a high level of care involving a team of multi-disciplinary staff, intensive work with inmates on an individual basis (via promptly-prepared individualised plans), within a coherent framework for progression towards release, which should be a real option. The system should also allow for the maintenance of family contacts, when appropriate.

Despite similar recommendations being repeated a year later by the European Commissioner for Human Rights,[50] the indefinite and preventive detention provisions were not amended. Consequently, and amidst growing frustration about the conditions in which they were being held, a number of indefinitely and preventively detained people filed cases with the courts.

---

[47] Statistisches Bundesamt, Strafvollzug – demographische und kriminologische Merkmale der Strafgefangenen 2010, Reihe 4.1 at 23; Laufhütte, Rissing-van Saan and Tiedemann, above n 36, 415.

[48] For example, an author noted that the sexually motivated murders of children have 'not increased but remained rare with absolute figures oscillating between 1 and 7 cases per year'. This led to the authors' conclusion that the amendments were 'driven by public and media demands...': H-J Albrecht, 'Dangerous Criminal Offenders in the German Criminal Justice System' (1997) 10(2) *Federal Sentencing Reporter* 69–73, 73.

[49] European Committee for the Prevention of Torture and Inhuman or Degrading Treatment or Punishment (CPT), *Report to the German Government on the visit to Germany by the European Committee for the Prevention of Torture and Inhuman or Degrading Treatment or Punishment (CPT) from 20 November to 2 December 2005* (Strasbourg, 18 July 2007) para 100 <http://www.cpt.coe.int/documents/deu/2007-18-inf-eng.pdf >.

[50] Thomas Hammarberg, *Report by the Commissioner for Human Rights Mr Thomas Hammarberg on His Visit to Germany 9–11 and 15–20 October 2006* (Strasbourg, 11 July 2007) para 8.2 <https://wcd.coe.int/wcd/ViewDoc.jsp?id=1162763>.

4. PREVENTIVE DETENTION IN GERMANY AND THE EUROPEAN COURT OF HUMAN RIGHTS

The case of *M v Germany*[51] concerned a psychologically impaired offender with a long history of criminal conduct who in 1986 was sentenced to five years imprisonment and ten years indefinite detention for robbery and attempted murder. Whilst the detainee was serving his indefinite detention order, preventive detention amendments were introduced ensuring that M remained in detention upon completion of his 15-year, original sentence. Following failed hearings before Germany's appellate courts, including the Constitutional Court,[52] M filed a complaint with the European Court of Human Rights. There he argued that his continued detention breached both his right to liberty and the prohibition against a retrospectively harsher sentence under articles 5(1)(a) and 7(1) of the *European Convention for the Protection of Human Rights and Fundamental Freedoms*, respectively.

In December 2009, the ECHR upheld M's complaint, rejecting Germany's argument that M's continued detention was valid because it took place after his original conviction. The Court held that there was 'not a sufficient causal connection' between the imposition of the original sentence and the ongoing detention.[53] Had there been no amendment to the *Criminal Code* in 1998, in which the maximum term of ten-years indefinite detention was abolished, M would have been released following his 15-year sentence. Hence, his continued detention was a consequence of legislative amendments only, and not a proof of guilt or ongoing risk to the community. The ECHR found this breached both M's right to liberty and article 7(1) of the Convention, namely the prohibition against retrospective sentences:

---

[51]   (European Court of Human Rights, Application No 19359/04, 17 December 2009) <http://www.hrr-strafrecht.de/hrr/egmr/04/19359-04.php?referer=db>. For a more detailed outline of M's case, see the contribution of Christopher Slobogin in this volume.

[52]   Bundesverfassungsgericht [German Constitutional Court], 2 BvR 2029/01, 5 February 2004. See, in particular, paragraph 145 of the judgment in which the court found that a custodial sentence and a preventive detention order pursue different aims. Consequently, the court concluded that preventive detention is not a punishment. The judgment was criticised by some commentators including J Kinzig, 'An den Grenzen des Strafrechts – Die Sicherungsverwahrung nach den Urteilen des BverG' (2004) 57 *Neue Juristische Wochenschrift* 911–14, 913; D Best, 'Das Rückwirkungsverbot nach Art. 103 Abs. 2 GG und die Maßregeln der Besserung und Sicherung' (2002) 114(1) *Zeitschrift für die gesamte Strafrechtswissenschaft* 88–129, 107.

[53]   *M v Germany* (European Court of Human Rights, Application No 19359/04, 17 December 2009) [100]. See also *Van Droogenbroeck v Belgium* (1982) 4 EHRR 443 where the court adopted the 'sufficient connection' test.

7. No punishment without law

(1) No one shall be held guilty of any criminal offence on account of any act or omission which did not constitute a criminal offence under national or international law at the time when it was committed. Nor shall a heavier penalty be imposed than the one that was applicable at the time the criminal offence was committed.

In its earlier decision, the German Constitutional Court had held that the preventive detention provisions did not amount to a 'penalty' but rather were measures necessary for the rehabilitation of the offender and the protection of the public.[54] In support of its finding, the Court noted that section 67e of the *Criminal Code* allowed the court to review an offender's preventive detention order 'at any time'. On this basis, the Court distinguished the measure from an ordinary criminal sanction.

The ECHR disagreed, finding that: [55]

> ... there is no substantial difference between the execution of a prison sentence and that of a preventive detention order... in particular ... there appear to be no special measures, instruments or institutions in place, other than those available to ordinary long-term prisoners, directed at persons subject to preventive detention and aimed at reducing the danger they present and thus at limiting the duration of their detention to what is strictly necessary in order to prevent them from committing further offences.

In the view of the Court, a lack of concrete measures capable of leading to the offender's rehabilitation meant that preventive detention was a punitive measure, a penalty and therefore a breach of Article 7(1) of the Convention. Or, in the words of one commentator, 'the Court confirmed the suspicion of 'false labeling' that had been leveled against preventive detention since the 1920s'.[56]

---

[54] Bundesverfassungsgericht [German Constitutional Court], 2 BvR 2029/01, 5 February 2004.
[55] *M v Germany* (European Court of Human Rights, Application No 19359/04, 17 December 2009) [127].
[56] J Kinzig, 'Das Recht der Sicherungsverwahrung nach dem Urteil des EGMR in Sachen M. gegen Deutschland' (2010) 30 *Neue Zeitschrift für Strafrecht* 233–9, 237.

5.   PREVENTIVE DETENTION AND GERMANY'S CONSTITUTIONAL COURT

On 4 May 2011, the German Constitutional Court having considered the decision of the ECHR, held the preventive detention provisions in the German Criminal Code to be unconstitutional.[57] The Court determined that, in light of the ECHR decision, it was clear that the legitimacy and future viability of Germany's preventive detention system required an *Abstandsgebot*: that is, a clear separation between those prisoners sentenced to custodial sentences and persons ordered to undertake preventive detention. Physical separation and the establishment of differentiated work and recreational activities would go some way towards establishing the necessary barriers between those sentenced to custodial sentences and those subject to preventive detention.[58] Further, the Court recommended the implementation of 'a freedom-orientated and therapy-focused master plan',[59] the focus of which would be the coordination of individualised programs that provided detainees in preventive detention with 'a realistic prospect of release'.[60] According to the Court, this goal would be made possible when:[61]

–   the lives of preventive detention detainees were tailored as far as possible to 'general living conditions'; and
–   professionally trained personnel were made available; and
–   family and social contact was maintained through regular visits.

The constitutional decision marks a relatively large departure from pre-existing German jurisprudence, which had consistently held an opposing view to that ultimately determined by the ECHR. It is also noteworthy that, rather than attempting to justify its previously contradictory position to the ECHR, the German Constitutional Court embraced it and called for greater 'judicial dialogue' on questions of human rights:[62]

> The openness of the [German] Constitution to public international law is… an expression of sovereignty, integrated in inter- and supranational contexts and whose evolution is not precluded but rather assumed and expected. Against this background it is clear that the 'last word' of the German Constitution is not in conflict with the judicial dialogue of international and European courts but rather sees the decisions of such bodies as its normative basis.

---

[57]   Bundesverfassungsgericht [German Constitutional Court], 2 BvR 2365/09, 4 May 2011 <http://www.bundesverfassungsgericht.de/entscheidungen/rs20110504_2bvr236509.html>.
[58]   Ibid [115].
[59]   Ibid [130].
[60]   Ibid [109].
[61]   Ibid [115].
[62]   Ibid [89].

The decision was lauded by the European Court of Human Rights, which in two recently published decisions welcomed:[63]

> the Federal Constitutional Court's approach for interpreting the provisions of the Constitution also in the light of the Convention and this Court's case-law, which demonstrates that court's continuing commitment to the protection of fundamental rights not only on a national, but also on European level.

Notably, these German developments echoed decisions relating to Australian preventive detention regimes that had been challenged in the United Nations Human Rights Committee.

6. INDEFINITE AND PREVENTIVE DETENTION IN AUSTRALIA

In Australia, whilst indefinite detention provisions have been a longstanding feature of the criminal justice system in most States and Territories,[64] such provisions have, until recently, been limited in scope and application and generally 'the power to impose an indefinite sentence [in Australia] is one "to be sparingly exercised, and then only in clear cases"'.[65] Whilst exceptions to this rule exist,[66] in general, preventive detention was not legislatively proscribed until Victoria and New South Wales introduced legislative instruments in the early 1990s in an attempt to keep particular individuals in preventive detention.[67] The Victorian legislation was aimed at Garry David, and he died in custody before the Act could

---

[63]   *Schmitz v Deutschland* (European Court of Human Rights, Application No 30493/04, 9 June 2011) [41]; *Mork v Deutschland* (European Court of Human Rights, Application Nos 31047/04, 43386/08, 9 June 2011) [54].

[64]   See section 18A of the *Sentencing Act 1991* (Vic); section 163 of the *Penalties and Sentences Act 1992* (Qld); section 98 of the *Sentencing Act 1995* (WA); sections 22 and 23 of the *Criminal Law (Sentencing) Act 1988* (SA); section 19 of the *Sentencing Act 1997* (Tas) and; section 65 of the *Sentencing Act 1995* (NT): all allow for an order for indefinite detention to be passed at the time of sentence. See also Bernadette McSherry, Patrick Keyzer and Arie Frieberg, *Preventive Detention for 'Dangerous' Offenders in Australia: A Critical Analysis and Proposals for Policy Development* (Criminology Research Council, 2006) 10; Eileen Baldry et al, 'Imprisoning Rationalities' (2011) 44(1) *Australian and New Zealand Journal of Criminology* 24–40.

[65]   *Buckley v R* (2006) 224 ALR 416 per Gleeson CJ, Gummow, Kirby, Heydon & Crennan JJ.

[66]   These exceptions include detention in remand pending trial, detention in cases of mental illness or infectious disease, and detention of non-citizens while migration claims are assessed or pending deportation: *Lim v Minister for Immigration* (1992) 176 CLR 1, 23 per Brennan, Deane & Dawson JJ.

[67]   *Community Protection Act 1990* (Vic); *Community Protection Act 1994* (NSW). The Acts authorised the respective Supreme Courts to order the continued detention of Garry David (Victoria) and Gregory Wayne Kable (NSW) if their respective Supreme Courts were satisfied that the person posed a continued danger to the public.

be applied.[68] The High Court ruled that the New South Wales legislation, which singled out an offender named Gregory Wayne Kable, was unconstitutional because it required the Supreme Court of New South Wales, a court capable of exercising federal jurisdiction in a national constitutional characterised by the separation of judicial power, to exercise a power that impermissibly interfered with the independence of that court.[69] Justice Gaudron, one of the four majority judges, described 'indefinite detention, based on an opinion that a person is more likely than not to commit a serious act of violence in the future, as "the antithesis of the judicial process"'.[70]

Although a number of attempts were made to challenge legislation on the basis of what came to be known as the *Kable* principle,[71] it was not until 2004 that a preventive detention regime would once again come before the High Court. The Queensland *Dangerous Prisoners (Sexual Offenders) Act* 2003 did not single out any particular prisoner, but instead applied to offenders serving a period of imprisonment for a serious sexual offence.[72] Section 8 of the Act authorises the Supreme Court of Queensland to make 'an order that the prisoner undergo examinations by 2 psychiatrists named by the court who are to prepare independent reports'. Pursuant to s 11, the two psychiatrists make an assessment of the level of risk that a prisoner will commit another serious sexual offence if they are released, or released under supervision. The Attorney can then make an application under s 13 of the Act for a 'continuing detention order' (referred to as a 'Division 3 order'):

> 13 Division 3 orders
> (1) This section applies if, on the hearing of an application for a division 3 order, the court is satisfied the prisoner is a serious danger to the community in the absence of a division 3 order (a serious danger to the community).
>
> (2) A prisoner is a serious danger to the community as mentioned in subsection (1) if there is an unacceptable risk that the prisoner will commit a serious sexual offence –
> (a) if the prisoner is released from custody; or

---

[68] B McSherry, 'Sex, Drugs and "Evil" Souls: The Growing Reliance on Preventive Detention Regimes' (2006) 32(2) *Monash University Law Review* 237–74, 240.

[69] *Kable v DPP (NSW)* (1996) 189 CLR 51. The Victorian legislation was never challenged as it was directed at a particular offender who later committed suicide.

[70] Cited by Crennan J in *Gypsy Jokers Motorcycle Club Inc v Commissioner of Police*, (2008) 234 CLR 532, 594.

[71] See Patrick Keyzer, *Principles of Australian Constitutional Law* (LexisNexis, 3rd ed, 2010) ch 19.

[72] For the purposes of the Act, it was irrelevant whether or not the person was sentenced to imprisonment before or after the commencement of the Act. The Schedule to the *Dangerous Prisoners (Sexual Offenders) Act 2003* (Qld) defines a serious sexual offence as an offence of a sexual nature involving violence or against children.

(b) if the prisoner is released from custody without a supervision order being made.

(3) On hearing the application, the court may decide that it is satisfied as required under subsection (1) only if it is satisfied –
(a) by acceptable, cogent evidence; and
(b) to a high degree of probability; that the evidence is of sufficient weight to justify the decision.

(4) In deciding whether a prisoner is a serious danger to the community as mentioned in subsection (1), the court must have regard to the following –
(aa) any report produced under section 8A; [73]
(a) the reports prepared by the psychiatrists under section 11 and the extent to which the prisoner cooperated in the examinations by the psychiatrists;
(b) any other medical, psychiatric, psychological or other assessment relating to the prisoner;
(c) information indicating whether or not there is a propensity on the part of the prisoner to commit serious sexual offences in the future;
(d) whether or not there is any pattern of offending behaviour on the part of the prisoner;
(e) efforts by the prisoner to address the cause or causes of the prisoner's offending behaviour, including whether the prisoner participated in rehabilitation programs;
(f) whether or not the prisoner's participation in rehabilitation programs has had a positive effect on the prisoner;
(g) the prisoner's antecedents and criminal history;
(h) the risk that the prisoner will commit another serious sexual offence if released into the community;
(i) the need to protect members of the community from that risk;
(j) any other relevant matter.

(5) If the court is satisfied as required under subsection (1), the court may order –
(a) that the prisoner be detained in custody for an indefinite term for control, care or treatment (continuing detention order); or
(b) that the prisoner be released from custody subject to the requirements it considers appropriate that are stated in the order (supervision order).

(6) In deciding whether to make an order under subsection (5)(a) or (b) –
(a) the paramount consideration is to be the need to ensure adequate protection of the community; and
(b) the court must consider whether –
    (i) adequate protection of the community can be reasonably and practicably managed by a supervision order; and

---

[73] Section 8A authorises the 'chief executive of the Attorney-General' to prepare a report indicating whether supervision of an offender in the community is reasonably practicable.

    (ii) requirements under section 16 can be reasonably and practicably managed by corrective services officers.

(7) The Attorney-General has the onus of proving that a prisoner is a serious danger to the community as mentioned in subsection (1).

Having regard to the matters raised in s 13(4), the Supreme Court of Queensland must decide whether it is 'satisfied' that 'the prisoner is a serious danger to the community'. When the court decides that it is satisfied that the prisoner is a serious danger to the community, it must be persuaded 'by acceptable, cogent evidence' and 'to a high degree of probability' that 'the evidence is of sufficient weight to justify the decision'. The judicial inquiry must focus on the risk of re-offending and make a prediction about future conduct based upon matters that largely deal with propensity, which would not ordinarily be admissible in a trial where the person was liable to be imprisoned. [74]

The Explanatory Memorandum to the legislation contemplated that the Attorney General might, in the final six months of an offender's custodial sentence, apply to the court for a risk assessment in order 'to ensure that the prisoner is able to take full advantage of any opportunities for rehabilitation offered during the term of imprisonment'.[75]

Robert Fardon was the first person dealt with under the Act. In 1967, Fardon was convicted of one count of attempted carnal knowledge of a girl under the age of ten. He was sentenced to a good behaviour bond operational for three years. [76] During the following decade, Fardon was convicted of ten counts of stealing and one count of vagrancy (1968), driving under the influence of alcohol or a drug (1974), break, enter and steal (1974), stealing (1975), assault occasioning actual bodily harm (1977), driving under the influence of alcohol or a drug and driving disqualified (1975) and unlawful use of a motor vehicle. [77]

In October 1980, Fardon was convicted on own plea of guilty of one count of unlawful and indecent dealing with a girl under the age of 14 years, one count of rape and one count of unlawfully wounding the girl's sister; he was sentenced to 12 months imprisonment on the first count, 13 years imprisonment on the second and six months imprisonment on the third, all to be served concurrently. These offences were committed on 18 December 1978. The rape, in particular, was

---

[74] See ss 13(4) and (6). The reference to 'detention in custody' is under s 50 of the Act, 'taken to be a warrant committing the prisoner into custody for the Corrective Services Act 2006', that is, a continuing detention order is served in prison.
[75] Explanatory Memorandum, *Dangerous Prisoners (Sexual Offenders) Bill 2003* (Qld), 5.
[76] *A-G (Qld) v Fardon* [2003] QSC 331.
[77] Ibid.

described by the sentencing judge as 'brutal' and the circumstances of the rape as 'horrific'. [78]

Fardon was released on parole after serving eight years. Within three weeks he had committed another serious sexual offence. Fardon pleaded guilty to the offences of sodomy and unlawful assault of a woman he had met in a bar. He pleaded not guilty to a charge of rape of the same woman on the ground of consent. On 27 June 1989, Fardon was convicted of all three charges and sentenced to 14 years for rape, 14 years for sodomy and three years for unlawful assault, all to be served concurrently. The sentences of imprisonment for these offences expired on 27 June 2003.

On 6th June 2003, three weeks before Fardon's release for the 1989 convictions, the *Dangerous Prisoners (Sexual Offenders) Act* (Qld) came into force. The legislation was enacted without dissent (and only one abstention) by the (unicameral) Queensland Parliament after being introduced on the 3rd of June.

The *Dangerous Prisoners (Sexual Offenders) Act* was the subject of a constitutional challenge.[79] Australia does not have a constitutional bill of rights, but its constitutional court, the High Court of Australia, had held that it is implicit that the separation of judicial power effected by the Australian Constitution prohibits any parliament in Australia from enacting legislation that would be repugnant to the autonomy and integrity of a court. Members of the Court had previously held that the involuntary detention of a person in prison is penal or punitive in character and exists only as an incident of the exclusively judicial function of adjudging and punishing criminal guilt.[80] Members of the High Court had also held that it is an elementary principle of the rule of law in Australia that a person may only be punished for a breach of the law, but can be punished for nothing else.[81]

Relying on these statements of principle, it was argued that an order of imprisonment could only be made by a court,[82] following the commission of a

---

[78] Ibid.
[79] The case is *Fardon v A-G (Qld)* (2004) 223 CLR 575. The arguments advanced on behalf of Mr Fardon are set out by his counsel in P Keyzer, C Pereira and S Southwood, 'Pre-emptive Imprisonment for Dangerousness in Queensland under the *Dangerous Prisoners (Sexual Offenders) Act 2003*: The Constitutional Issues' (2004) 11(2) *Psychiatry, Psychology and Law* 244–53 and were reflected, in an elaborated form, in the dissenting judgment of Kirby J in *Fardon v A-G (Qld)* (2004) 223 CLR 575, 631–2.
[80] *Chu Kheng Lim v Minister for Immigration* (1992) 176 CLR 1, 26–29; *Kable v DPP (NSW)* (1996) 189 CLR 51, 97, 131.
[81] *Chu Kheng Lim v Minister for Immigration* (1992) 176 CLR 1, 27–28.
[82] Ibid 26–28.

criminal offence, a charge being proven beyond reasonable doubt[83] following a fair trial[84] (a plea of guilty aside), and the person being found guilty of the offence with which he or she was charged.[85] The presumption of innocence must apply.[86] The reason why these powers were exclusive to courts, and could not be excluded from courts, was to maintain the rule of law and preserve liberty.[87]

Taking these principles into account, it was argued that there could be no order of imprisonment on the basis of a prediction of risk that a person would commit a crime. There needs to be a crime first. Fardon had served his sentence for his crimes and was, therefore, entitled to release. It was also argued that it would be inconsistent with the separation of judicial power and the integrity of a court to authorise them to punish a person twice for the same crime and that this legislation achieved that unconstitutional objective.[88]

The High Court upheld the law. Unlike the *Kable* decision, the legislature in *Fardon* had not specifically addressed the legislation to the indefinite detention of an individual but rather a class of individuals, and a majority of the High Court concluded that the Queensland Parliament had provided a set of evaluative criteria against which the court could exercise its discretion to determine whether the relevant prisoner presented an ongoing threat to public safety. This ensured that the integrity of the decision-making court was not preserved, so the law was upheld.[89]

The majority dedicated little attention to the impact of a continuing detention order on the rights of the individual subject to such an order. Indeed it avoided the question of whether retrospective or double punishment might be constitutionally prohibited by framing preventive detention as 'protective of the community' rather than aimed at punishing the offender *per se*.[90]

---

[83] *Azzopardi v The Queen* (2001) 205 CLR 50, 64–65; *RPS v The Queen* (2000) 199 CLR 620, 630, 634.

[84] *Dietrich v The Queen* (1992) 177 CLR 292.

[85] *Azzopardi v The Queen* (2001) 205 CLR 50, 64–65.

[86] See, for example, *State v Coetzee* [1997] 2 LRC 593, 677–8 [220], cited in *R v Lambert* [2001] 3 WLR 206, 218–9; *The People v O'Callaghan* [1966] IR 501, 508, 516 (cited with approval in *Ryan v DPP* [1989] IR 399, 404–5).

[87] *Wilson v Minister for Aboriginal Affairs* (1996) 189 CLR 1, 11 per Brennan CJ, Dawson, Toohey, McHugh and Gummow JJ.

[88] This argument was based on observations made by a majority of the High Court in *Kable v DPP (NSW)* (1996) 189 CLR 51, 96–7, 106, 120, 132. It is set out in detail in Keyzer, Pereira and Southwood, above n 79.

[89] *Fardon v A-G (Qld)* (2004) 223 CLR 575. The majority comprised Gleeson CJ, McHugh, Gummow, Hayne, Callinan und Heydon JJ with Kirby J the sole dissenter.

[90] Ibid 592, 597, 610, 647, 654. For analysis of the High Court's decision, see Patrick Keyzer, 'Preserving Due Process or Warehousing the Undesirables: To What End the Separation of Judicial Power of the Commonwealth?' (2008) 30 *Sydney Law Review* 101, 104–5; Kate Warner, 'Sentencing Review 2002–2003' (2003) *Criminal Law Journal* 325.

In a scathing judgment the sole dissenter Justice Kirby noted:[91]

> Simply calling the imprisonment by a different name (detention) does not alter its
> true character or punitive effect… If the real objective of the Act were to facilitate
> rehabilitation of certain prisoners… significant, genuine and detailed provisions
> would have appeared in the Act for care, treatment and rehabilitation. There are
> none. Instead, the detainee remains effectively a prisoner. He or she is retained in
> a penal custodial institution, even as here the very prison in which the sentences of
> judicial punishment have been served. After the judicial sentence has concluded,
> the normal incidents of punishment continue. They are precisely the same.

Following the High Court's decision and, consequently, the exhaustion of all
domestic remedies, communications were lodged with the United Nations
Human Rights Committee (UNHRC).[92] There it was argued that the complainant
was subject to prohibitions of the *International Covenant* on *Civil and Political
Rights*, including arbitrary detention and double punishment because he had
been convicted twice for the same offence. Based on the earlier case law of human
rights decision-making bodies, the complainant argued that the use of a prison for
offenders sentenced to preventive detention was neither suitable nor proportionate
for rehabilitative purposes, proposing that special treatment facilities should be
made available for persons subject to preventive detention.[93] Unsurprisingly, the
Australian Government rejected the complainant's assertions, submitting that
'the complainant has access to the best available rehabilitative resources and
facilities within the prison system'.[94]

In March 2010, the UNHRC having reviewed the complaints, held in two 11–2
judgments that the complainants' preventive detention was incompatible with
the prohibition against arbitrary detention under Article 9(1) of the *ICCPR*.[95]
The UNHRC pointed to four significant factors leading to their conclusion that
the detention was arbitrary. These factors included that there was nothing to

---

[91]   *Fardon v A-G (Qld)* (2004) 223 CLR 636, 643–4.
[92]   Kenneth Tillman, who was subject to a preventive detention order in New South Wales,
       also filed a communication with the United Nations Human Rights Committee. New South
       Wales and Western Australia had introduced preventive detention measures following the
       High Court's upholding of the Queensland laws. Both the Tillman and Fardon decisions
       were handed down by the United Nations Human Rights Commission on the same day with
       substantially similar findings: Human Rights Committee, *Communication No 1629/2007*,
       UN Doc 1629/2007 (10 May 2010) ('*Fardon v Australia*') <http://www.unhcr.org/refworld/
       docid/4c19e97b2.html>; Human Rights Committee, *Communication No 1635/2007*, UN Doc
       1635/2007 (10 May 2010) ('*Tillman v Australia*').
[93]   *Fardon v Australia* [3.3].
[94]   Patrick Keyzer, '*Attorney-General (Qld) v Lawrence [2008] QSC 230 – The Dangerous Prisoners
       (Sexual Offenders) Act* – Are "the Best Available Rehabilitative Resources" Available?' (2009)
       33 *Criminal Law Journal* 175–83, 175.
[95]   *Fardon v Australia*.

distinguish the complainant's preventive detention from a custodial sentence, thereby ensuring that the 'detention amounted, in substance, to a fresh term of imprisonment'.[96] Other factors included the imposition of retrospectively harsher punishment (contrary to Art 15) and the removal of due process guarantees (contrary to Art 14); in particular, a person subjected to criminal punishment must have a criminal trial. In other words, the complainant had been sentenced twice for the same offence in circumstances in which procedural guarantees were lacking and was subject to a retrospectively harsher custodial sentence. Finally, the UNHRC addressed the 'inherently problematic' concept of future dangerousness holding that the State had failed to establish that rehabilitation could not have been achieved by 'means less intrusive than continued imprisonment or even detention'.[97] According to the UNHRC, this finding was reinforced in the acknowledgement that the 'penitentiary system shall comprise treatment of prisoners the essential aim of which shall be their reformation and social rehabilitation'.[98]

Having found that article 9(1) of the *ICCPR* had been breached, the UNHRC did not go on to determine other breaches. Nevertheless, they opined, without deciding the matter, that the punitive nature of the post-sentence detention of the complainant may also contravene the prohibition against double punishment[99] and retrospective punishment.[100]

7.   HUMAN RIGHTS BODIES AND THE TREND TOWARDS REHABILITATION

The judgments of both the ECHR and the UNHRC have reaffirmed the importance of the rights of the individual and in the process provided a framework for detention regimes around the world that is compatible with human rights. Most significantly, both the ECHR and the UNHRC have demanded a clear separation between offenders sentenced to a custodial sentence and persons detained on a preventive detention order. The reasoning of both decision-making bodies is based on the distinction that must be adopted between a custodial sentence and a preventive detention order. That is, whereas the aim of a custodial sentence is punishment achieved through a loss of liberty, the aim of a preventive detention order must be the detainee's further rehabilitation and subsequent reintegration into the community achieved through provision of an individually tailored rehabilitative program.

---

[96]   Ibid [7.4]; *Tillman v Australia* [7.4].
[97]   Ibid.
[98]   Article 10(3) of the *International Covenant on Civil and Political Rights*.
[99]   Article 14(7).
[100]   Article 15(1).

Dealing with serious offenders is, unquestionably, a highly fraught and challenging responsibility for governments. The crimes, as the account of Mr Fardon's criminal history above demonstrates, can be exceptionally serious and abhorrent. But the decisions of the ECHR and the UNHRC are to be welcomed, not least because of the potential for contemporary state practice to blur the line between community protection and criminal punishment. That is not least because of the great amount of public pressure that can be brought to bear on those governments to keep high profile, notorious or infamous offenders permanently out of society. The tendency of governments to yield to that pressure is understandable, yet it must be guarded against. Criminal sanctions must be publicised, prospective and proportional; their breach must be determined by a fair, independent and impartial court or tribunal, subject to procedural and evidential protections.[101] Such rules are fundamental; indeed, in 1830 Blackstone wrote that the 'confinement of the person, in any wise, is an imprisonment ... To make imprisonment lawful, it must ...be by process from the courts of judicature'.[102] The removal or diminution of these safeguards threatens the institutional integrity of the legal system, and, arguably, public trust in its administration and willingness to submit to its authority.

In Kirby J's dissent in *Fardon* he noted the common law tradition that:[103]

> [t]he categories of exception to deprivations of liberty treated as non-punitive may not be closed; but they remain exceptions. They are, and should continue to be, few, fully justifiable for reasons of history or reasons of principle developed by analogy with the historical derogations from the norm. Deprivation of liberty should continue to be seen for what it is. For the person so deprived, it will usually be the worst punishment ... reserved to the judiciary in a case following an established breach of the law.

People must be 'ruled by the law, and by the law alone' and may be 'punished for a breach of law, but he can be punished for nothing else'.[104] The *Fardon* and *Tillman* communications draw a sharp distinction between imprisonment and post-sentence preventive detention, which now must take place in a non-punitive environment.

---

101 Article 14 of the *International Covenant on Civil and Political Rights*.
102 William Blackstone, *Commentaries on the Laws of England (1765–1769)* (Clarendon, 17th ed, 1830) book 1, paras 136–7, relying on the authority of Sir Edward Coke, *Institutes of the Laws of England* (Clarke and Sons, 1809) pt 2, 589.
103 *Fardon v A-G (Qld)* (2004) 223 CLR 575 [175].
104 Albert Venn Dicey, *Introduction to the Study of the Law of the Constitution* (Macmillan, 10th ed, 1959) 202.

The blurring between punitive and protective detention is plain from the objects clauses of the Australian legislation, which provide that the objectives of preventive detention orders are 'to provide continuing control, care or treatment of a particular class of prisoner to facilitate their rehabilitation'.[105] The difficulty with this terminology is that it provides the legislature with an opportunity to 'control' persons through detention[106] but to argue that it is actually for their care or treatment. [107] In future, it ought not to be sufficient for state parties to simply point to legislative reassurances as demonstrative that rehabilitation of persons on preventive detention orders within the prison is taking place. Both human rights bodies have made very clear that the aims and objectives of the two systems must be clearly separated. State parties run the risk that, if they are unable to clearly show that required rehabilitation services are being offered, their reassurances could be seen as lip-service, giving rise to a finding that the detention is in actual fact a punishment and, consequently, a breach of human rights covenants.

Whilst the German authorities have acted quickly, making public a draft of the new preventive detention system in September 2011, the reaction of the Australian Government to the decision of the UNHRC has been less encouraging. Australia has rejected the finding of the Committee, consistently stating that the continued detention of sexual offenders past their custodial sentence is reasonable and necessary and that no less restrictive means are available to it to protect the community.[108] Given that the same legislative regime makes provision for supervision orders, the position of the Australian government is questionable.[109] Moreover, the practice, resources and funding dedicated to actual rehabilitation and treatment in such schemes seems to undermine the Government's claim that the scheme is not punitive in nature. In Queensland, there are presently a limited number of places for the treatment of sexual offenders, a limited number of prisons in which treatment of sexual offenders can take place and a waiting list of offenders wanting treatment.[110] In addition, post-prison transition and

---

[105]   See the Long Title of the *Dangerous Prisoners (Sexual Offenders) Act 2003*.

[106]   This conclusion is confirmed in a reading of the legislative purposes. The *Dangerous Prisoners (Sexual Offenders) Act 2003* has the protection of the community in the foreground: *A-G (Qld) v Downs* [2005] QSC 16. See also *A-G (Qld) v Lawrence* [2008] QSC 230; *A-G (Qld) v Hynds* [2009] QSC 355.

[107]   Keyzer, above n 94.

[108]   Australian Government Attorney-General's Department, *Response of the Australian Government to the Views of the Committee in Communication No. 1635/2007 Tillman v Australia And Communication No. 1629/2007 Fardon v Australia*.

[109]   *Dangerous Prisoners (Sexual Offenders Act) 2003*, sections 13, 13A, 15 and 16A-16D.

[110]   Patrick Keyzer, 'The United Nation Human Rights Committee's Views about the Legitimate Parameters of the Preventive Detention of Serious Sex Offenders' (2010) 34(5) *Criminal Law Journal* 283–91, 289–90.

reintegration planning is characterised by inappropriate accommodation solutions, inadequate services and a lack of funding.[111]

In these circumstances there seems to be little in evidence of intent by the state to treat offenders and reduce the alleged risk upon which their ostensibly protective detention has been justified.[112] At best, there is lacklustre political, financial and institutional support for treatment regimes aimed at reducing the risk that individuals pose to the community and eventually returning their liberty to them. In such circumstances, it appears that such offenders continue to be detained past the term of their sentence simply because of what they have done, rather than what they pose a risk of doing. Given the decisions of both the ECHR and the UNHRC, that is clearly contrary to international law.

Australia, like Germany, has weathered the global financial crisis relatively well, so its apparent recalcitrance in responding to determinations that it is in breach of its international obligations cannot be attributed to financial difficulties. Hence, its response – or indeed lack thereof – must be seen as largely political. Neither case is adequate justification for breach of international obligations in any case. Germany's response must be the preferred one. Whether other countries, parties to the same human rights conventions, follow Germany's example and clearly delineate between protective and punitive detention of sexual offenders is yet to be seen. However, as we have sought to argue, this important distinction should not be narrowly construed as applicable only to those countries with preventive detention systems but rather is also likely to have a significant bearing on all countries in which indefinite detention systems are in place. It is difficult to imagine a more serious public policy challenge than this; it should be addressed conscientiously and with human rights principles squarely applied.[113]

8.   CONCLUSION

The decisions of the European Court of Human Rights and the United Nations Human Rights Committee have provided a foundation for the return of prisoner rights. Sex offences are abhorrent and there is no question that offenders should be punished, and severely, for such offences. It is understandable that governments would respond in a punitive fashion in the circumstances. However liberty is sacrosanct. It is important to remember that the offenders imprisoned under the German and Australian regimes discussed in this chapter had already been

---

[111]   Patrick Keyzer and I Coyle, 'Realising the Legitimate Objective of Reintegration: A Critical Analysis of Queensland's New "Public Protection Model" for Serious Sexual Offenders' (2009) 34(1) *Alternative Law Journal* 27–31.

[112]   Keyzer, n 94, 177-8.

[113]   See also the contribution of Astrid Birgden in this volume.

subject to the judicial and correctional systems, and had been punished with long prison sentences. Even if we might think these sentences were inadequate, the retrospective infliction of further punishment infringes international human rights principles. To continue to punish such offenders after the service of their custodial sentence undermines the very purpose of the criminal justice system, the authority of the court or tribunal that determined the sentence, and indeed the rule of law. So much is clear from international human rights conventions and the determinations of the international tribunals considered in this chapter.

ANTI-TERROR PREVENTIVE DETENTION AND THE INDEPENDENT JUDICIARY

Rebecca WELSH

Australia's approach to terrorism has developed rapidly and has been characterised by a dual focus on prevention and prosecution. The federal government responded to the international terrorist attacks of the first few years of the 21st century with an approach Professor Kent Roach labels 'hyper-legislation'.[1] In ten years, Australia transitioned from having no national anti-terror laws to boasting more anti-terror Acts than any other Western democracy.[2] Terrorism was identified as an imminent threat requiring urgent, broad-spectrum legislation aimed at prevention as much as prosecution. As then Attorney-General Philip Ruddock observed: 'The law should operate as both a sword and a shield – the means by which offenders are punished but also the mechanism by which crime is prevented.'[3] A key challenge for governments in Australia and elsewhere has been the implementation of effective anti-terror laws without compromising fundamental rights. This chapter considers Australia's anti-terror preventive detention schemes and considers whether the primary constitutional means by which these schemes may be challenged, the separation of judicial power, presents an effective tool for protecting the basic rights and liberties of citizens.

1. AUSTRALIAN ANTI-TERROR PREVENTIVE DETENTION

There are four kinds of preventive orders within Australia's vast anti-terror law framework that may be classified as preventive detention. The first two fall within the Australian Security Intelligence Organisation's ('ASIO's') 'special powers' relating to terrorism offences in Part 3 Division 3 of the *Australian Security Intelligence Organisation Act* 1979 (Cth) ('ASIO Act'). These provisions empower

---

[1]   K Roach, *The 9/11 Effect* (Cambridge, 2011) 309.
[2]   G Williams, 'A Decade of Australian Anti-Terror Laws' (2011) 35 *Melbourne University Law Review* 1136.
[3]   P Ruddock, 'Legal Framework and Assistance to Regions' (Regional Ministerial Counter-Terrorism Conference, Bali, February 2004) [49].

ASIO to seek two kinds of anti-terror warrants. The first is a 'questioning warrant', enabling ASIO to question adult non-suspects for up to a total of 24 hours (over the course of up to 28 days)[4] and requiring the production of records or other things.[5] Children aged 16 or 17 may also be subject to a questioning warrant if they are suspected of involvement in a terrorism offence.[6] The second is a 'questioning and detention warrant'. This warrant is identical to a questioning warrant, with the additional allowance that the person may be detained virtually incommunicado by ASIO for up to seven days. A person being questioned and/or detained under one of these warrants has no right to silence, no privilege against self-incrimination and may be subjected to body and strip searches.[7] The person's rights to contact third parties, including legal representatives, are severely circumscribed.[8] A number of disclosure and non-compliance offences punishable by imprisonment of up to five years attach to the provisions.[9] To date, 16 questioning warrants and no questioning and detention warrants have been issued.

The further two kinds of anti-terror order that may be described as preventive detention are preventive detention orders (PDOs) and control orders, introduced into Divisions 105 and 104, respectively, of the *Criminal Code Act* 1995 (Cth) in 2005. A PDO allows for the incarceration of an individual for up to 48 hours for the purpose of preventing an imminent terrorist act (that is, one expected to occur within 14 days) or to protect evidence of a recent terrorist act (one occurring within the last 28 days). Significant restrictions on contact apply to a detainee under a PDO, though unlike persons subject to an ASIO warrant the detainee may not be interrogated. Control orders allow for an extensive array of restrictions and obligations to be imposed on an individual, falling short of imprisonment, for up to 12 months.[10] Control orders are issued on the basis that the order would substantially assist in preventing a terrorist act or that the person has been involved in training with a terrorist organisation.[11] Each term of a control order must be 'reasonably necessary and reasonably appropriate and adapted' for

---

4   *Australian Security Intelligence Organisation Act* 1979 (Cth) s 34E(5)(b) ('ASIO Act').
5   Ibid ss 34D, 34E.
6   Ibid s 34ZE.
7   J McCulloch and JC Tham 'Secret State, Transparent Subject: The Australian Security Intelligence Organisation in the Age of Terror' (2005) 38 *The Australian and New Zealand Journal of Criminology* 400, 402.
8   *ASIO Act* ss 34J(1)(e), 34K(1), (9)–(11), 34G(5)–(6), 34E(3), 34ZO, 34C(3B), 34D(4A), 34TA, 34U, 34CU. See also, McCulloch and Tham, ibid; A Palmer, 'Investigating and Prosecuting Terrorism: The Counter-Terrorism Legislation and the Law of Evidence' (2004) 27 *University of New South Wales Law Review* 373 at 381.
9   Ibid ss 34L, 34ZS. For further discussion on the non-disclosure aspects of the provisions, see JC Tham, 'Critique and Comment Casualties of the Domestic "War on Terror": A Review of Recent Counter-Terrorism Laws' (2004) 28 *Melbourne University Law Review* 512; McCulloch and Tham, ibid.
10   Ibid ss 104.5(f), 104.16(d).
11   Ibid s 104.4(1)(b)-(c).

the purpose of protecting the public from a terrorist act.[12] Two control orders have been issued, one against Jack Thomas and the second against David Hicks on his release from prison following his detention by US forces at Guantanamo Bay.

Clearly, ASIO anti-terror warrants, PDOs and control orders challenge not only the rights and liberties of citizens but also broader notions of due process and punishment. In Australia, there are few legal mechanisms by which Parliaments' powers to enact legislation may be challenged. An avenue of challenge that is of key importance in the preventive detention context is the separation of judicial power derived from Chapter III of the Constitution. Beyond protections that may be drawn from Chapter III, governments' powers to preventively detain are largely unconstrained. It may seem odd that a fairly technical set of constitutional principles focussing solely on judicial power and independence provides the basis for determining the nature and limits of preventive detention. However, in the absence of a national Bill or Charter of rights, the separation of judicial power has been increasingly appreciated as a fertile source of rights protection, including some rights to due process.

Each of Australia's anti-terror detention schemes involves serving judges in important ways and thus invokes constitutional protections with respect to the independence and integrity of those judges. In the next section, I introduce the separation of judicial power and describe some of the ways in which it has been interpreted to protect rights and liberties. The remainder of the chapter canvasses how separation of judicial power principles may provide an avenue to challenge the four anti-terror preventive detention schemes described and queries the effectiveness of this means of restraining parliament's power to preventively detain.

2.   THE SEPARATION OF JUDICIAL POWER

Since 1901, Australia has developed a particularly strict separation of judicial power in order to preserve the independence and impartiality of federal courts. This separation is based on the premise that judicial and non-judicial powers ought not be vested in the same body, except where a non-judicial function is incidental or ancillary to a judicial one. The separation of functions is governed by two 'separation rules'. The first separation rule is that 'judicial power' may only be vested in courts. The second, more controversial[13] and ultimately more flexible, separation rule restricts federal courts to the exercise of judicial power

---

[12]   Ibid s 104.4(1)(d).
[13]   See, *R v Joske; ex parte Australian Building Construction Employees and Builders Labourers Federation* (1974) 130 CLR 87, 90 (Barwick CJ); J Stellios, 'Reconceiving the Separation of Judicial Power' (2011) 22 *Public Law Review* 113.

and ancillary non-judicial functions.[14] Thus, the constitutional allocation of functions depends almost entirely upon their definition as judicial or otherwise.

At first blush, the separation rules produce an extreme result.[15] The nebulous nature and considerable breadth afforded to the concept of judicial power has, however, lent the rules significant practical flexibility. Indeed, it is accepted that the concept of judicial power defies, or 'transcends', abstract conceptual analysis[16] and that exclusive, exhaustive definition of even the core of judicial power is neither possible nor desirable.[17] The classic starting point in defining judicial power is Griffith CJ's 1908 definition:[18]

> [Judicial power is] the power which every sovereign must of necessity have to decide controversies between its subjects, or between itself and its subjects, whether the rights relate to life, liberty or property. The exercise of this power does not begin until some tribunal which has power to give a binding and authoritative decision (whether subject to appeal or not) is called upon to take action.

This definition identifies a number of characteristics subsequently harnessed by the High Court to distinguish judicial from non-judicial powers, namely: a binding decision, resolving a controversy, about existing rights. It is accepted that none of the indicia are generally determinative and that, in order to define a power, the decision-maker will weigh present indicia against absent and contrary indicia in an often unpredictable balancing exercise.[19] The key or 'core' characteristic of judicial power is the resolution of a controversy about *existing rights or duties*, although even this characteristic may be ignored when the function is of a kind traditionally exercised by courts.[20]

---

[14] *R v Kirby; Ex parte Boilermakers' Society of Australia* (1956) 94 CLR 254, 296 (Dixon CJ, McTiernan, Fullagar, Kitto JJ). Affirmed on appeal: *Attorney-General (Cth) v The Queen* (1957) 95 CLR 529, 540–1.

[15] Arguably, a situation of extreme formalism: P Gerangelos, *The Separation of Powers and Legislative Interference in Judicial Process* (Hart Publishing, 2009) 22.

[16] *R v Trade Practices Tribunal; Ex parte Tasmanian Breweries Pty Ltd* (1970) 123 CLR 361 at 394 (Windeyer J). See also, Gerangelos, ibid.

[17] *Nicholas v The Queen* (1998) 193 CLR 173, 219 (McHugh J), 207 (Gaudron J); *Precision Data Holdings Ltd v Willis* (1991) 173 CLR 167, 188 (Mason CJ, Brennan, Deane, Dawson, Toohey, Gaudron and McHugh JJ).

[18] *Huddart, Parker & Co Pty Ltd v Moorehead* (1909) 8 CLR 330, 357 ('*Huddart Parker*').

[19] D Dalla-Pozza and G Williams, 'The Constitutional Validity of Declarations of Incompatibility in Australian Charters of Rights' (2007) 12 *Deakin Law Review* 1, 10–11.

[20] On the importance of this 'core' factor, see: *Ha v New South Wales* (1997) 189 CLR 465, 504 (Brennan CJ, McHugh, Gummow and Kirby JJ); *Huddart, Parker* (1909) 8 CLR 330, 357; L Zines, *The High Court and the Constitution* (4th ed, Federation Press, 1997) 171; J Stellios, *The Federal Judicature: Chapter III of the Constitution – Commentary and Cases* (LexisNexis, 2010) 108–111. Cf, *Thomas v Mowbray* (2007) 233 CLR 307, 328–9 (Gleeson CJ) ('*Thomas*').

An important and long-standing exception to the second separation rule restricting judges to judicial tasks is the 'persona designata' exception. This exception builds upon the assertion that the separation of powers does not bind federal judges in their personal capacity (as designated persons or 'personae designatae') and so enables non-judicial functions and titles to be conferred on judges individually. By the 1980s, the exception was supported by extensive practice which, sometimes controversially, had seen serving judges appointed to administrative positions such as Ambassador and Royal Commissioner.[21]

In the 1995 case of *Grollo v Palmer*[22] – an unsuccessful challenge to provisions enabling telecommunication interception warrants to be issued by judges personally – the High Court established a limit on the persona designata exception, namely: 'no function can be conferred that is *incompatible* either with the judge's performance of his or her judicial functions or with the proper discharge by the judiciary of its responsibilities as an institution exercising judicial power'.[23] As this statement suggests, incompatibility may be established by an actual conflict between the function in question and the judge's personal integrity or practical capabilities. Incompatibility may also be established if the conferral of the function on a serving judge would injure the actual or perceived independence or integrity of the judicial institution as a whole. In *Wilson v Minister for Aboriginal and Torres Strait Islander Affairs*,[24] the appointment of Justice Jane Mathews as 'reporter' to the Minister (regarding whether certain areas should be classified as Aboriginal heritage sites) was found to be incompatible on this final basis, as the High Court found the role of reporter was so entwined with the executive as to diminish public confidence in the judiciary as a whole. In reaching this determination, a majority of the Court elaborated on this kind of incompatibility, saying it could be indicated by: the function being 'an integral part of, or closely connected with, the functions of the legislative or executive government'[25] and either reliance upon non-judicial instruction, advice or wish, or the exercise of discretion on political grounds (that is, on grounds not expressly or impliedly confined by law).[26]

A second relevant limitation on the separation rules is that they apply only to federal courts. Thus, there is no direct constitutional restriction on Parliaments' abilities to confer functions on State courts or judges.[27] However, in the 1990s the High Court developed an important limitation in this respect based on the

---

21   For a history of this practice and its controversy, see AJ Brown, 'The Wig or the Sword? Separation of Powers and the Plight of the Australian Judge' (1992) 21 *Federal Law Review* 48.
22   (1995) 184 CLR 348 ('*Grollo*').
23   Ibid 365 (Brennan CJ, Deane, Dawson and Toohey JJ) (emphasis added).
24   (1996) 189 CLR 1 ('*Wilson*').
25   Ibid 17 (Brennan CJ, Dawson, Toohey, McHugh and Gummow JJ).
26   Ibid 17 (Brennan CJ, Dawson, Toohey, McHugh and Gummow JJ).
27   Throughout this paper, 'State' should be taken refer to both States and Territories.

acknowledgment that State courts are vested with limited federal jurisdiction and, to that extent, their independence and integrity is entitled to constitutional protection.[28] Similarly, State courts form part of an integrated national court system, which further entitles them to a degree of constitutional protection.[29] Like the limit on the permissible functions of judges persona designata, State courts may only be vested with powers that are not incompatible with their institutional independence and integrity. Gleeson CJ summarised the principle as follows:[30]

> [S]ince the Constitution established an integrated Australian court system, and contemplates the exercise of federal jurisdiction by State Supreme Courts, State legislation which purports to confer upon such a court a function which substantially impairs its institutional integrity, and which is therefore incompatible with its role as a repository of federal jurisdiction, is invalid.

Determining incompatibility at the State level is an 'evaluative process'[31] ultimately considering whether the function is seriously repugnant to the institutional independence and integrity of the court[32] and, thus, infringes the 'minimum requirement' that a State court be independent and impartial.[33] Recent High Court incompatibility cases have turned on whether the challenged provisions enabled the executive to dictate or compel an essential attribute of the court's function,[34] or compromised an essential feature of the court's independent processes.[35] The abovementioned tests from *Grollo* and *Wilson* have also been applied to determine incompatibility in the State courts context.[36] In 2011, the High Court confirmed that when a non-judicial function is conferred on a State judge persona designata, this will merely form a factor to weigh into the overall process of determining incompatibility; it will not avoid potential incompatibility or even present a weighty factor in the ultimate determination.[37]

---

[28]   *Kable v Director of Public Prosecutions (NSW)* (1996) 189 CLR 51, 103 (Toohey J), 82 (Dawson J) ('Kable').

[29]   *Kirk v Industrial Relations Commission (NSW)* (2010) 239 CLR 531, [95]–[100] (French CJ, Gummow, Hayne, Heydon, Crennan, Kiefel and Bell JJ).

[30]   *Fardon v Attorney-General (Qld)* (2004) 223 CLR 575, [15] ('Fardon').

[31]   *K-Generation Pty Ltd v Liquor Licensing Court* (2009) 237 CLR 501, [88] (French CJ).

[32]   Ibid [256] (Kirby J).

[33]   *North Australian Aboriginal Legal Aid Service Inc v Bradley* (2004) 218 CLR 146, [29]–[30] (McHugh, Gummow, Kirby, Hayne, Callinan and Heydon JJ); *Forge v Australian Securities and Investments Commission* (2006) 228 CLR 45, [41] (Gleeson CJ).

[34]   *International Finance Trust Co Ltd v New South Wales Crime Commission* (2009) 240 CLR 319, [4] (French CJ), [152], [155], [160] (Heydon J), [96]–[98] (Gummow and Bell JJ); *Gypsy Jokers Motorcycle Club Inc v Commissioner of Police* (2008) 234 CLR 532, [7] (Gleeson CJ); *South Australia v Totani* (2010) 242 CLR 1, [100], [142] (Gummow J) ('Totani').

[35]   *Wainohu v New South Wales* (2011) 243 CLR 181, [7] (French CJ and Kiefel J), [109] (Gummow, Hayne, Crennan and Bell JJ) ('Wainohu').

[36]   See, eg, ibid [94] (Gummow, Hayne, Crennan and Bell JJ), [21]–[43] (French CJ and Kiefel J).

[37]   R Welsh, '"Incompatibility" Rising? Some Potential Consequences of *Wainohu v New South Wales*' (2011) 22 *Public Law Review* 259; Ibid [36], [49] (French CJ and Kiefel J), [105]–[107] (Gummow, Hayne, Crennan and Bell JJ).

In summary, a legislative provision will be unconstitutional if it:

– confers judicial power on a body other than a court;
– confers non-judicial power (that is not incidental or ancillary to a judicial function) on a federal court;
_ confers non-judicial power on a judge persona designata or on a State court that is incompatible with the institutional independence or integrity of the judiciary.

Australia's anti-terror preventive detention schemes variously invoke each of these bases of challenge. Ordering preventive detention has been held to be capable of either judicial or non-judicial order. The High Court has indicated that only punitive detention necessarily requires judicial determination of criminal guilt and therefore must be ordered by a court as such.[38] The Court has adopted a starkly deferential position to determining whether detention is punitive or preventive, looking first and foremost to the annunciated purpose in the relevant Act. As anti-terror preventive detention orders have a clearly preventive, not punitive purpose, it is highly unlikely that a court would find them to require judicial process.

PDOs and ASIO warrants are issued by judges in their personal capacity, posing the question of whether this role is 'incompatible' with judicial independence. Judges appointed persona designata also oversee exercises of power under the two ASIO warrants, posing the same questions of potential incompatibility. Control orders, on the other hand, are issued by federal courts and, thus, will be valid only if the function is judicial in nature. These constitutional questions are dealt with in turn below.

3.   PREVENTIVE DETENTION ORDERS

The *Criminal Code* creates two kinds of PDOs. The first, an initial PDO, may authorise detention of up to 24 hours and is initiated and administered entirely within the ranks of the Australian Federal Police ('AFP'). The second kind of order is a continued PDO. Continued PDOs are issued on application by the AFP to an 'issuing authority' and may extend detention to up to 48 hours from the point the detainee was first taken into custody.

In the case of continued PDOs the issuing authority is a consenting qualified person appointed to the position by the Attorney-General.[39] The Attorney-

---

[38]   *Fardon* (2004) 223 CLR 575.
[39]   *Criminal Code Act* 1995 (Cth) s 105.2(1) ('*Criminal Code*').

General may appoint: a practicing or retired judge of a Federal, Family, or State or Territory Supreme Court; a Federal Magistrate; or a President or Deputy President of the Administrative Appeals Tribunal.[40] When issuing a continued PDO, the issuing authority is acting in his or her personal capacity.

There are two possible grounds upon which a PDO may be issued. The first ground focuses on the prevention of an imminent act of terrorism.[41] This ground provides that: making the order would substantially assist in preventing an imminent terrorist act; detaining the person for the requested period is reasonably necessary to prevent that terrorist act; and there are reasonable grounds to suspect the person will either engage in a terrorist act, possesses a thing that is connected with the preparation for, or engagement in, a terrorist act, or has done an act in preparation for, or planning, a terrorist act.[42] The second ground on which a PDO may be issued is that it is reasonably necessary to detain the person in order to preserve evidence of, or relating to, a terrorist act that has occurred in the previous 28 days.[43]

The application for a PDO includes a summary of the grounds on which the applying officer considers the order should be made, as well as the outcomes of any previous orders (such as control orders) sought against the detainee.[44] The summary provided in the AFP's application will not contain any information the disclosure of which is likely to prejudice national security, within the meaning of the *National Security Information (Criminal and Civil Proceedings) Act 2004* (Cth) ('NSIA').[45] Applications for continued PDOs will also include any information given to the officer by the detainee.[46] This is the only opportunity that the detainee has to inform the issuing authority, and the detainee must be informed of their right to provide information to the issuing authority in this way.[47]

A detainee under a PDO is subject to significant restrictions on their contact with third parties, including legal representatives, and may be subject to a prohibited contact order, which can restrict their contact more broadly.[48] Officers are not

---

[40]   Ibid ss 105.2(1), 100.1(1). The President of the AAT will necessarily also be a Judge of a federal court: *Administrative Appeals Tribunal Act 1975* (Cth) s 7(1).
[41]   Ibid s 105.4(5).
[42]   Ibid s 105.4(4).
[43]   Ibid s 104.4(6).
[44]   Ibid ss 105.7(2), 105.11(2).
[45]   Ibid s 105.11(3A). 'Likely to prejudice national security' is defined as 'a real, and not merely a remote, possibility that the disclosure will prejudice national security', and 'security' is broadly defined as Australia's defence, security, international relations or law enforcement interests: *National Security Information (Criminal and Civil Proceedings) Act 2004* (Cth) ss 8, 17 ('NSIA').
[46]   Ibid s 105.11(5).
[47]   Ibid s 105.10A(b).
[48]   Ibid s 105.14A.

permitted to question a detainee under a PDO except to confirm the detainee's identity, ensure his or her wellbeing or to enable the fulfilment of the terms of the PDO.[49] Conversely, a person charged with a terrorism offence or held under an ASIO warrant may be interrogated.

Against this backdrop, it can be seen that PDOs fill a very slight gap in the anti-terror legislative arsenal. Their role appears to be to allow for urgent detention in the absence of sufficient evidence to support an arrest and when questioning would not substantially assist a terrorism investigation (thus allowing them to be interrogated under an ASIO warrant). It is perhaps no wonder then that after seven years, and despite urgent enactment, the PDO provisions have never been used. PDOs, however, remain a key aspect of Australia's anti-terror legislation. Their close relationship, but distinct differences, to ASIO warrants discussed below and to terrorism offences more broadly highlights that PDOs are designed to enable the detention of individuals outside the usual criminal, or even intelligence gathering, processes and paradigms.

The involvement of serving judges as issuing authorities for continued PDOs begs the constitutional question: is the issuing of PDOs by judges persona designata compatible with the maintenance of judicial independence and integrity? There are strong indications that the power to issue a continued PDO would be considered compatible with judicial independence and integrity. The power to issue a PDO bears similarities to other powers upheld by the High Court as compatible with judicial power, in particular the issuing of telecommunications intercept warrants in *Grollo*. Like the power upheld in *Grollo*, the issuing of PDOs requires the assessment of an application made by the AFP in closed proceedings. Moreover, the power requires assessment of a similar set of criteria to that determined to be 'judicial' in *Thomas v Mowbray* in respect of control orders, discussed below.[50] The task of issuing a PDO is exercised independently, at arms-length from the AFP officers seeking the order, and does not incorporate the judge into the executive branch of government. Moreover, the power to issue a PDO based solely on predicted risk rather than past the wrongdoing of the detainee is not necessarily incompatible with judicial independence. Such powers were upheld in *Fardon v Attorney-General (Qld)*[51] and *Baker v The Queen*.[52]

Notwithstanding the overall similarities between the power to issue PDOs and the similar powers to issue intercept warrants and order the continued detention of serious offenders (each upheld by the High Court as constitutional),[53] there

---

49   Ibid s 105.42.
50   *Thomas* (2007) 233 CLR 307.
51   (2004) 223 CLR 575.
52   (2004) 223 CLR 513.
53   *Grollo* (1995) 184 CLR 348; *Fardon* (2004) 223 CLR 575.

are some indications that the power to issue PDOs could be incompatible with judicial independence and integrity. The Court has traditionally considered imprisonment to be particularly deserving of a fair and proper process, as the involvement of judges in ordering imprisonment outside the criminal trial process poses a unique risk to the maintenance of courts' independence and integrity.[54] In this context, the extent to which a power complies with the hallmarks of due process is pivotal to determining compatibility; this was a basis on which the post-sentence preventive detention scheme in *Kable v Director of Public Prosecutions (NSW)* was invalidated and the similar scheme in *Fardon* upheld.[55] The High Court has repeatedly acknowledged that a power which can be exercised in a manner contrary to the core elements of procedural fairness may be incompatible with judicial power.[56]

The process by which a PDO is made lacks the hallmarks of procedural fairness. Orders are made in a closed proceeding to which the rules of evidence do not apply. The issuing authority is not able to hear directly from the detainee. The decision to make a PDO may be based on secret evidence, never disclosed to the detainee. The issuing authority need only provide a summary of the grounds on which the order was made, not a detailed set of reasons. Once again, information the disclosure of which might prejudice national security need not be included in this summary, meaning the detainee could never know the reason why they were detained.

This is an even greater departure from ordinary judicial standards than the powers to order preventive detention of potentially dangerous prisoners upon their release from prison considered in *Fardon*, and even in *Kable*. Those Acts compromised fair process in a number of important respects, but nonetheless permitted the detainee to contest their detention in an open hearing, with full legal representation and a more substantial notice period and information to enable him or her to build and put a case.[57] A PDO also has more severe consequences for individual liberty than other non-judicial functions which have previously been

---

[54]   See, eg, *Chu Kheng Lim v Minister for Immigration* (1992) 176 CLR 1, 23 (Brennan CJ, Deane and Dawson JJ), [128] (Gummow J); *Kable*, 106–107 (Gaudron J); *Fardon* (2004) 223 CLR 575, 612 [79] (Gummow J).

[55]   *Fardon* (2004) 223 CLR 575, 655 (Callinan and Heydon JJ). For consideration of the constitutional arguments advanced in *Fardon* and a critique of the compliance of the DPSOA regime with the separation of judicial power, see: Patrick Keyzer, 'Preserving Due Process or Warehousing the Undesirables: To What End the Separation of the Judicial Power of the Commonwealth?' (2008) 30 *Sydney Law Review* 101.

[56]   *Wainohu* (2011) 243 CLR 181, [99], [103].

[57]   For further discussion and critique of the access to justice dimensions of the dangerous prisoners regime see: Patrick Keyzer and Suzanne O'Toole 'Time, Delay and Nonfeasance: *The Dangerous Prisoners (Sexual Offenders) Act 2003* (Queensland)' (2006) 31 *Alternative Law Journal* 198; Patrick Keyzer and Bernadette McSherry, *Sex Offenders and Preventive Detention: Politics, Policy and Practice* (The Federation Press, 2009) 78–79.

upheld by the Court as compatible, such as the issue of intercept warrants which itself imposes significantly on the privacy and property rights of the individual.[58] These distinctions could support a finding that PDOs go too far; by appointing serving judges to order imprisonment in proceedings lacking fairness, openness and equality of arms the provisions infringe the independence and integrity of the judicature. Therefore, there is some doubt as to whether the involvement of judges in the PDO regime is constitutionally valid.

If the function can be shown to be incompatible, the conferral of the role on serving judges will be unconstitutional. The ultimate outcome of constitutional invalidity in this respect is merely that the function could be conferred on certain practitioners and retired judges – the provisions themselves would remain largely intact. The authoritative acknowledgment that the function in incongruous with core constitutional principles may potentially achieve broader aims of delegitimizing PDOs. However, the fact remains that even if the main constitutional limit on governments' powers to preventively detain was invoked and was successful, it would only serve to alter *who* was issuing the orders, not actually affect the nature of the orders or enhance the rights of detainees under the orders. This primary avenue for constitutional challenge to uphold citizens' rights to due process ultimately provides for less than satisfactory protection.

4. AUSTRALIAN SECURITY INTELLIGENCE ORGANISATION WARRANTS

Serving members of the State and federal judiciaries play a significant role in both questioning and questioning and detention warrants under the ASIO Act. Each kind of warrant is issued by a federal judge persona designata.[59] As with PDOs, this involvement of serving judges prompts the constitutional question of whether issuing an ASIO warrant is compatible with judicial independence and integrity.

Both questioning and questioning and detention warrants are issued on the basis that the issuing authority is satisfied, first, that there are reasonable grounds to believe the questioning will 'substantially assist the collection of intelligence that is important in relation to a terrorism offence'[60] (the 'Questioning Threshold') and, second, that the Attorney-General has consented to the request.[61] As with the issuing of PDOs, the process of issue presents a substantial departure from due process, in that the decision to issue a warrant is made in secret, on the basis of information provided solely by the applicant and not open to challenge, and

---

[58]   *Grollo* (1995) 184 CLR 348, [26] (McHugh J).
[59]   *ASIO Act* s 34AB.
[60]   Ibid s 34ZE.
[61]   Ibid ss 34E(1), 34G(1).

substantial reasons are not given for the decision. Where the issuing authority's decision results in a questioning warrant (that does not allow for incarceration), it is unlikely that incompatibility could be established. The same arguments as to the compatibility of issuing PDOs would apply, without the heightened due process requirements invoked where the order results in incarceration. In short, the cases of *Grollo* (upholding persona designata issuance of intercept warrants) and *Thomas* (upholding the issuance of control orders as 'judicial') would weigh heavily in favour of the validity of persona designata issuance of ASIO questioning warrants.

Where the issuing authority's decision, however, results in the detention of the individual, the departures from procedural fairness may be argued to cause substantial detriment to the independence and integrity of the issuing judge. This argument would be along the same lines as that developed above in respect of PDOs but would be strengthened by: the longer period of detention available under an ASIO questioning and detention warrant (7 days rather than 48 hours); the fact that the issuing authority is not required to turn his or her mind to the appropriateness or necessity of the detention; and the additional allowance for intensive interrogation under an ASIO warrant. The outcome of a challenge would depend upon how much weight the court saw fit to place on the arms-length distance between the judge and the applicant and the links between due process and judicial integrity. As with PDOs, if it could be established that issuing an ASIO warrant was incompatible with a serving judge's independence and integrity, the result would merely be that the list of potential appointees as issuing authority would be shortened. The provisions would otherwise remain intact.

Serving judges are involved in ASIO anti-terror warrants in another, more unique, way. Once the warrant has been issued, the detainee is immediately brought before a 'prescribed authority' who has broad powers to oversee and supervise all exercises of power under the warrant[62] and who may be a serving State judge.[63] A primary feature of the prescribed authority's role is the making of 'directions'. The prescribed authority may make directions within the scope of the warrant relating to: any arrangements for the person's detention including commencement, continuation and release; breaks in questioning; continuation of questioning; contact with third parties including family members, legal representation and interpreters; and disclosure of information to third parties.[64] The prescribed authority may also make directions outside the scope of the warrant with the Attorney-General's consent or if the direction is for the purpose of addressing a concern of the Inspector General of Intelligence and Security

[62] Ibid ss 34H, 34J(3).
[63] Ibid s 34B.
[64] Ibid s 34K(1).

('IGIS').[65] The prescribed authority may even direct that the person be detained, or further detained, if satisfied that if they are not immediately detained the person may alert someone involved in a terrorism offence that the offence is being investigated, may not appear for questioning, or may destroy or damage evidence.[66] The ASIO Act provides that such a direction is not necessarily at odds with the terms of a questioning warrant.[67]

It is interesting to note that, despite the provisions being federal in nature, the role of prescribed authority is conferred on State judges personae designata. This may reflect the greater risk such a role presents to judicial independence and integrity. Until 2011, it was unresolved whether any constitutional restrictions existed on the kinds of functions that could be conferred on State judges personae designata. In fact, there were some indications that Parliaments' powers with respect to State judges were virtually unlimited.[68] In 2011, however, the High Court found that the same incompatibility limit applied regardless of whether a power was conferred on a State court or judge. The fact the judge is appointed personally merely forms a factor to weigh into the overall process of determining incompatibility.[69]

The role of prescribed authority is truly unique within Australia, and no similar role has been subject to constitutional challenge. Thus, any consideration of whether the appointment of serving judges as prescribed authorities would be incompatible with their independence or integrity remains, to some extent, conjecture. On one hand, the prescribed authority retains considerable independence in the fulfilment of his or her role. The appointee's discretions are broad; the judge retains general control over the entire process. This general position of independence may be sufficient to maintain compatibility. However, there are many features of the role of prescribed authority that indicate a strong basis for a challenge on incompatibility grounds. The prescribed authority may not interrogate or detain the person held under the warrant, but he or she does play a key role in administering, guiding and controlling the interrogation and detention. At the prescribed authority's discretion, legal representatives and third parties become involved, questioning and detention commences, is deferred and ceases, and any other arrangements for the person's detention may be altered. Unlike judicial or even Tribunal proceedings, the exercises of powers under an ASIO warrant is not governed by rules or legal principles, nor does it aim to fairly voice and balance the interests involved to reach a determination. ASIO

---

[65]   Ibid s 34Q(1)–(3).
[66]   Ibid s 34K.
[67]   Ibid s 34K(3).
[68]   *Kable* (1996) 189 CLR 51, 118 (McHugh J); Fardon (2004) 223 CLR 575, [15] (Gleeson CJ), [32] (McHugh J); *Forge v Australian Securities Investments Commission* (2006) 228 CLR 45, [61]–[66] (Gummow, Hayne and Crennan JJ).
[69]   *Wainohu* (2011) 243 C.L.R. 181, [50] (French CJ and Kiefel J), [105] (Gummow, Hayne, Crennan and Bell JJ).

warrants are conducted to facilitate an intelligence gathering exercise. The prescribed authority plays an authoritative role throughout the interrogation,[70] unlike the role of issuing authority for intercept or other warrants. The prescribed authority is ultimately fulfilling an executive role, the conduct of which is at times dependent upon the consent of the Attorney-General, the concerns of the IGIS and submissions made by ASIO. The appointee thus occupies a position both authoritative over and submissive to the executive officers involved, both supervisory and responsive.

Moreover, the presence and involvement of a judge as the 'master of ceremonies' within the interrogation room conveys that all three arms of government are simultaneously authorising the course of interrogation and detention under the warrant. The integrated involvement of the prescribed authority in the scheme arguably submerges the judge in the investigation process. Consistent involvement of executive officers in the exercise of the prescribed authority's functions could be argued to metaphorically dress the persona designata in the uniform of the intelligence services and borrow the judge's reputation for objectivity to condone and authorise executive will throughout the process. Thus, despite formal independence, the prescribed authority is integrated into every facet of the intelligence gathering process from the initial exercise of powers under the warrant until the warrant's completion. The closest relevant analogue may then be the appointment of Justice Mathews as 'reporter' to the Minister, an independent but ultimately integrated role and consequently found to be incompatible with the independence and integrity of the judicature.[71] Unlike the reporter, the prescribed authority does not maintain his or her position at the whim of the executive, but ASIO warrants' uniquely invasive, secretive and severe incursions on the rights of persons not necessarily suspected of any wrongdoing present additional factors challenging the independence and integrity of the appointee. All in all, reasonable arguments could be mounted to indicate constitutional invalidity of the appointment of serving judges to this role.

The ASIO Act provides that the prescribed authority is usually a retired judge. The appointment of a retired judge to the position of prescribed authority would be, generally, uncontroversial and is certainly the preferable option. Only if the Attorney-General forms the view there are an insufficient number of consenting retired judges available for appointment may a consenting serving judge of a State Supreme or District Court be appointed.[72] If the appointment of serving judges to the position of prescribed authority was found to be incompatible, and thus unconstitutional, the ASIO anti-terror warrant schemes would thus

---

[70]   *ASIO Act* s 34K(6).
[71]   *Wilson* (1996) 189 CLR 1.
[72]   *ASIO Act* s 34B.

remain otherwise intact; the inclusion of serving judges in the list of potential appointees could be excised from the remainder of the Act. Thus, despite the potential for a reasonably strong challenge to such a key feature of the ASIO warrant scheme, such a challenge would not address the most troubling features of the warrants. The scheme would remain, as former High Court Chief Justice Sir Gerard Brennan described it, as providing for a person to be 'detained in custody, virtually incommunicado without even being accused of involvement in terrorist activity, on grounds which are kept secret and without effective opportunity to challenge the basis of his or her detention'.[73]

5. CONTROL ORDERS

In contrast to PDOs and ASIO anti-terror warrants, control orders are judicial orders ordered by federal courts. Also unlike the orders considered above, control orders have been subject to constitutional challenge in which they were upheld as in keeping with the separation of judicial power.

Control orders in the *Criminal Code* are modelled on the United Kingdom's anti-terror control order provisions,[74] though they contain key differences such as the absence of a special advocates scheme. They also lack some of the broader supporting mechanisms such as the United Kingdom and European human rights frameworks.[75] Under a control order, adult non-suspects or children aged 16 or 17 may be subject to restrictions or obligations for up to 12 months[76] regarding: their presence at certain places; contact with certain people; use of telecommunication devices or technology; possession of things or substances; activities; wearing a tracking device; reporting to certain people at particular times and places; fingerprinting and photographing for the purpose of ensuring compliance with the order; and participation in consensual counselling or education.[77]

The Australian control order regime provides senior members of the AFP with a three-stage process to obtain a final 'confirmed' control order against an individual. First, the AFP must obtain the consent of the Attorney-General, then commence an ex parte application for an interim control order from an issuing court and, finally, engage in proceedings to confirm the control order.[78] The

---

[73] G Brennan, 'The Law and Justice Address' (Speech delivered at the Justice Awards, Parliament House, Sydney, 31 October 2007).
[74] *Prevention of Terrorism Act 2005* (UK).
[75] For comparative analysis, see A Lynch, 'Control Orders in Australia: A Further Case Study in the Migration of British Counter-Terrorism Law' (2008) 8 *Oxford University Commonwealth Law Journal* 159.
[76] Ibid ss 104.5(f), 104.16(d).
[77] *Criminal Code* s 104.5(3).
[78] Where an urgent control order is sought, the first two steps are reversed: Ibid s 104.10.

provisions appoint federal courts as 'issuing courts', responsible for determining both interim and confirmation proceedings.[79] Though the procedural contexts differ, the role of the issuing court is almost identical in interim and confirmation proceedings. The issuing court considers the same criteria in determining whether to issue an interim or confirmed order and in determining applications to revoke, renew or vary the terms of the order.[80] In each instance, the issuing court determines whether, on the balance of probabilities, it is satisfied that making the order would substantially assist in preventing a terrorist act *or* the controlee has been involved in training with a terrorist organisation.[81] Once satisfied on one or both of these grounds, the issuing court determines whether each term of the requested order is reasonably necessary and reasonably appropriate and adapted for the purpose of protecting the public from a terrorist act.[82] In reaching its determination, the Court must take into account the impact of the obligations, prohibitions and restrictions on the controlee's circumstances, including financial and personal.[83] It is not necessary that the controlee be suspected of, or charged with, any wrongdoing.

In accordance with the Constitution's strict separation of judicial power, federal courts may only exercise judicial power. Accordingly, if the task of issuing interim or confirmed control orders is not judicial, the appointment of federal courts as issuing courts is unconstitutional. As outlined above, judicial power is characterised by the binding determination of a controversy regarding existing rights under law. In control order proceedings the issuing court does not consider whether laws have been breached or engaged thus enlivening a judicial resolution or remedy. Rather, the role of the issuing court is to consider whether the circumstances of the application justify the creation of new rights and obligations between the controlee and the state. In this way, the power conferred on the issuing court lacks the key characteristics of judicial power; it does not resolve a controversy about existing rights and duties.

In *Thomas*, a majority of the High Court (Kirby and Hayne JJ dissenting) concluded that the power to make an interim control order was judicial and did not require the court to exercise its powers in a manner at odds with its fundamental independence.[84] The Court found that, although the function of issuing control orders lacked the key characteristics of judicial power, it was

---

[79]   Issuing Courts are the Federal Court of Australia, the Family Court of Australia or the Federal Magistrates Court of Australia: Ibid s 100.1.
[80]   Ibid ss 104.4(1), 104.16(1)(a).
[81]   Ibid s 104.4(1)(b)–(c).
[82]   Ibid s 104.4(1)(d).
[83]   Ibid s 104.4(2).
[84]   This finding has been analysed, and criticised, at length elsewhere. See for example A Lynch, 'Thomas v Mowbray: Australia's "War on Terror" Reaches the High Court' (2008) 32 *Melbourne University Law Review* 1183.

sufficiently analogous to accepted judicial tasks and constrained by familiar legal standards to be included within the ambit of 'judicial power'. The Court stressed the similarities between the task of issuing control orders and the issuance of peace bonds, denials of bail, apprehended violence orders and preventive post-sentence detention, all of which create rights and obligations rather than determine existing legal rights in dispute. These analogies were systematically rejected by the dissenting justices, particularly by Kirby J,[85] and attracted pointed criticism in subsequent commentary.[86] These critiques distinguished the majority's analogues on the bases that they were not federal powers or were in fact incidental to core judicial roles (such as the conduct of a criminal trial). Gleeson CJ acknowledged the analogies his Honour relied upon were 'not exact' but relied on them nonetheless to establish that the power to issue control orders was not 'antithetical to the judicial function'.[87]

Having found that the imposition of restrictions absent a legal controversy regarding existing rights was an acceptable form of judicial power, the majority justices drew upon these same analogies to show that predictive reasoning was a familiar aspect of judicial power. Hayne and Kirby JJ in dissent placed considerable weight on the fact that the issuing court's role was entirely predictive;[88] however, the majority found predictive reasoning in itself to be congruent with judicial power, provided that prediction was constrained by legal standards.[89] The majority emphasised that control orders were issued according to 'the balance of probabilities', 'reasonable necessity' and proportionality, each a legal criterion.[90] For Hayne and Kirby JJ these 'opaque' legal criteria were simply insufficient to render the power of the issuing court 'judicial'.[91] As Hayne J summarised, courts rely on evidence to assist their predictions and, in the control order context, that evidence would likely be in the form of intelligence. His Honour continued:[92]

> Rarely, if ever, would [intelligence information] be information about which expert evidence, independent of the relevant government agency, could be adduced. In cases where it could not be tested in that way (and such cases would be the norm rather than the exception) the court, and any party against whose interests the information was to be provided, would be left with little practical choice except to act upon the view that was proffered by the relevant agency. ... [T]o the extent that federal courts are left with no practical choice except to act upon a view

---

85   *Thomas* (2007) 233 CLR 307, 422–425 (Kirby J).
86   See Lynch, above n 83, 1202–1203; D Meyerson, 'Using Judges to Manage Risk: The Case of *Thomas v Mowbray* (2008) 36 *Federal Law Review* 209.
87   *Thomas* (2007) 233 CLR 307, 329 (Gleeson CJ).
88   Ibid 468–469 (Hayne J), 432 (Kirby J).
89   Ibid 328 (Gleeson CJ), 345–6 (Gummow and Crennan JJ).
90   Ibid 331–333 (Gleeson CJ), 346–8 (Gummow and Crennan JJ).
91   Ibid 417 (Kirby J).
92   Ibid 477–478 (Hayne J).

proffered by the Executive, the appearance of institutional impartiality and the maintenance of public confidence in the courts are both damaged.

Hayne J's observations go to the heart of one of the key challenges preventive detention schemes pose to judicial independence. Ultimately, however, this view was not shared by the majority of the Court.

In essence, the decision of the High Court upholding the issuance of control orders as judicial confirms that the imposition of severe restrictions on liberty on the basis of predicted risk is in keeping with constitutional protections, provided the power involves the application of familiar legal standards. This decision arguably expands notions of judicial power considerably beyond the characteristics identified in Griffith CJ's classic definition quoted earlier. Gleeson CJ suggested this outcome may present an advancement in rights protection[93] as, 'the evident purpose of conferring this function on a court if to submit control orders to the judicial process, with its essential commitment to impartiality and its focus on the justice of the individual case'.[94] This view has some appeal, particularly having considered the PDO and ASIO schemes that provide for detention in circumstances entirely outside the judicial process. Indeed, the involvement of courts in ordering restraints on liberty is preferable to an entirely internal police process, for example. However, this must be viewed in light of the substantial compromises to due process the High Court in *Thomas* was willing to permit. For the dissenting justices, court issuance of control orders may have been preferable to an executive process, but not at the expense of what these justices perceived as essential features of due process.

Interim control orders are issued ex parte, on the basis of information provided by the AFP (including the Attorney-General's consent to the order) and without notice to the affected person. Urgent interim control orders may be issued in response to an application by phone, fax or email.[95] Once the Court has issued the order, it will be in force from the time it is personally served on the person subject to the order (the 'controlee').[96] This must be done as soon as practicable and not less than 48 hours before the time of the confirmation hearing.[97] This provision suggests the interim order is not intended to endure for very long, implicitly counter-balancing the inherent unfairness of the ex parte interim proceedings. However, a direct effect of the provision is to guarantee the controlee only 48 hours notice of the confirmation hearing. Along with the order, the controlee

---

[93] Ibid 329 (Gleeson CJ).
[94] Ibid 335 (Gleeson CJ).
[95] *Criminal Code* s 104.6.
[96] Ibid s 104.5(1)(d).
[97] Ibid ss 104.12(a), 104.5(1A).

receives a summary of the grounds on which the order was issued.[98] If the AFP elects to confirm the interim order, an officer must serve the order personally on the controlee as well as information enabling the controlee to understand and respond to the substance of the facts, matters and circumstances on which the confirmation application will be based.[99] Documents may be excluded from service if their disclosure would be likely to: prejudice national security (within the meaning of the the the NSIA);[100] be protected by public interest immunity; put at risk ongoing operations by law enforcement agencies or intelligence agencies; and/ or put at risk the safety of the community, law enforcement officers or intelligence officers.[101] Confirmation proceedings take place in open court, allowing the controlee to contest the confirmation of the interim order by cross-examination, evidence and submissions.[102] The AFP or the controlee may apply to an issuing court at any time seeking revocation or variation of the order.[103] There are no limits on seeking consecutive control orders over an individual.

The ex parte, without notice nature of the interim proceedings and the limited time and information available to the controlee upon which to build a case for the confirmation hearing demonstrated, for Kirby J, that the power to issue control orders was exercised in a manner at odds with judicial independence.[104] On the other hand, a majority of the High Court was satisfied that the 'interlocutory' nature of the interim proceedings and the open and fair nature of the subsequent confirmation hearing overcame any potential invalidity arising from the inherent unfairness of the interim proceedings.[105] Thus, it appears that the Constitution will tolerate substantial compromises to the usual processes of courts, provided a full open hearing is held at some stage of the proceedings.

Following *Thomas*, a number of Australian States created new control order schemes, extending the reach of the preventive paradigm into the traditional ambit of the criminal law, namely, serious organised crime and gangs.[106] Two successful constitutional challenges to the control order schemes of the Australian States focussed squarely on the executive's novel attempts to usurp key aspects of the

---

[98] Ibid s 104.5(1).
[99] Ibid s 104.12A(2).
[100] *NSIA* ss 8, 17.
[101] *Criminal Code* s 104.12A(3).
[102] Ibid s 104.14.
[103] Ibid ss 104.18–104.26.
[104] *Thomas* (2007) 233 CLR 307, 433–6 (Kirby J).
[105] Ibid 335 (Gleeson CJ), 340 (Gummow and Crennan JJ).
[106] See, eg, *Serious and Organised Crime (Control) Act 2008* (SA) (invalidated in part in *Totani* (2010) 242 CLR 1); *Crimes (Criminal Organisations Control) Act 2009* (NSW) (invalidated in *Wainohu* (2011) 243 CLR 181; *Criminal Organisation Act 2009* (Qld); *Serious Crime Control Act 2009* (NT).

court's functions.[107] Importantly, in the course of its reasons in these cases, the High Court applied and reinforced the decision in *Thomas* upholding the issuance of control orders as generally in keeping with accepted notions of judicial power and independence.

Throughout the High Court's decisions on control orders, the orders have been carefully distinguished from 'detention' orders providing for incarceration in a state facility. Therefore, the now well-established validity of control orders, even when issued following a process with a non-judicial flavour, may not impact directly on the validity of orders resulting in imprisonment. Notwithstanding this distinction, *Thomas* indicates that preventive restraints on liberty according to predictive reasoning and in circumstances falling short of providing full fairness and equality are in keeping with the constitutional separation of judicial power.

6. CONCLUSIONS

The preventive detention paradigm is expanding. It was harnessed quickly and enthusiastically by the federal government in response to the threat of terrorism. Now, it is spreading throughout Australia in the broader criminal justice and serious crime spheres. There is little to demonstrate that the preventive detention schemes considered have proved necessary or effective, particularly in the case of PDOs and ASIO questioning and detention warrants, which have never been used.

As preventive detention schemes become an entrenched feature of Australia's legal landscape, the question of how to protect citizens from arbitrary or unjust detention becomes increasingly pertinent. The strict separation of federal judicial power is frequently cited as an effective source of rights protection in arguments against the introduction of a national Bill or Charter of rights. It is far from clear whether such a Bill or Charter could effectively protect rights and freedoms, but it is certainly clear that the separation of judicial power is a woefully inadequate and, at best, tangential and awkward tool in achieving this aim. The complexity of the issues involved in mounting a separation of powers challenge, and the fact that these challenges merely address *whom* is ordering the detention rather than the broader issues posed by the detention scheme itself, suggest that the separation

---

[107] *Totani* (2010) 242 CLR 1 in which invalidity was limited to the provision rendering the issuing of a control order by the Supreme Court mandatory upon the Court finding an individual was a 'member' of a 'declared organisation' deemed by the Attorney-General to be such; *Wainohu* (2011) 243 CLR 181 in which the Act's invalidity rested on the removal of the obligation to give reasons for a judge's decision (exercised in a personal capacity but with the appearance of court proceedings) to 'declare' an organisation, prior to the Supreme Court control order proceedings.

of judicial power cannot be considered a particularly effective means of ensuring citizens' basic rights are protected from legislative encroachment. What is more, as Fergal Davis argues,[108] judicial review may ultimately legitimise and thus facilitate the expansion of a challenged scheme, certainly if the court upholds the provisions (as in *Thomas*), but also if invalidity is based on a discreet aspect of the provisions, as is almost always the case in Chapter III matters.

As mentioned at the outset of this chapter, beyond protections that may be drawn from Chapter III, the government's power to preventively detain is largely unconstrained. This brief consideration of Australia's anti-terror detention schemes indicates that, absent substantial developments in constitutional jurisprudence, the Constitution offers meagre protections, barely capable of protecting the fundamental rights of citizens against governments' capacities to preventively detain. It appears then that if there is an effective mechanism by which Australians' rights may be upheld in the face of preventive detention laws, it may not arise from the Constitution.

---

[108] F de Londres and F Davis, 'Controlling the Executive in Times of Terrorism: Competing Perspectives on Effective Oversight Mechanisms' (2010) 30 *Oxford Journal of Legal Studies* 19.

REDRESS FOR UNLAWFUL IMPRISONMENT

Ian FRECKELTON

1.   INTRODUCTION

When preventive or other detention by custodial authorities is unlawful, those who are the victims of such detention are profoundly disempowered. Given that the circumstances of such illegal deprivation of liberty frequently involve persons with a mental illness, an intellectual disability, a brain injury or persons who have been imprisoned for a criminal offence, the law has been required to explore creative options to devise remedies to facilitate detainees' capacity to assert their rights and properly mount a case that their detention should be brought to an end. Much has depended on the initiative and industry of legal representatives. The means of redress for persons whose liberty rights have been infringed have traditionally centred upon the writ of habeas corpus but in some jurisdictions now include other forms of remedy, including financial.

This chapter reviews a range of scenarios in which persons who have been unlawfully detained have asserted rights to secure their freedom, to secure more humane conditions of incarceration, and in some instances to receive compensation.

2.   HABEAS CORPUS

The common law knew seven writs known as habeas corpus.[1] The most famous and the one that has survived into the modern era is the last, habeas corpus *ad subjiciendum*, sometimes known as habeas corpus *ad subjiciendum et recipiendum*. The prerogative writ of habeas corpus is a writ with an ancient lineage[2] – even

---

[1]   'Habeas corpus *ad deliberandum et recipiendum*, habeas corpus *ad respondendum*, habeas corpus *ad satisfaciendum*, habeas corpus *ad testificandum*, habeas corpus *ad faciendum et recipiendum*, habeas corpus *ad prosequendum* and habeas corpus *ad subjiciendum*': see *J by his litigation guardian Vardanega v Australian Capital Territory* [2009] ACTSC 170 [29].
[2]   See PD Halliday, *Habeas Corpus* (Harvard University Press, 2010).

having origins that preceded the Magna Carta.[3] William Howe[4] in his *Studies in the Civil Law and Its Relations to the Law of England & America* traced its use back to the Pandects of Justinian I.

It was formalised by the Magna Carta 1297 (Imp), Clause 39 of which provided that:

> No freeman shall be taken or imprisoned, or be disseised of his freehold, or liberties or free customs, or be outlawed or exiled, or any other wise destroyed; nor will we pass upon him, or condemn him, but by lawful judgment of his peers, or by law of the land. We will sell to no man, we will not deny or defer to any man either justice or right.[5]

The writ received legislative reinforcement by the *Habeas Corpus Act 1679* (Imp)[6] and the *Habeas Corpus Act 1816* (Imp). It began as a means of bringing a person to court, but the habeas corpus *ad subjiciendum* evolved into a mechanism for protecting citizens against the unlawful restraint of liberty, generally by an organ of the state. Blackstone[7] described it as 'the great and efficacious writ in all manner of illegal confinements':

> directed to the person detaining another, and commanding him to produce the body of the prisoner with the day and cause of his capture and detention ... to do, to subject to, and receive whatever the judge or court authorised to do by some rule of common law or statute.

He described it as 'that great bulwark of our constitution'.[8] Gradually a number of forms of the habeas corpus writs fell into disuse.

In 1890 Lord Halsbury, though, captured the modern approach to the remedy, pronouncing in *Cox* v *Hakes*, 'For a period extending as far back as our legal history the writ of *habeas corpus* has been regarded as one of the most important safeguards of the liberty of the subject.'[9]

---

[3] See eg J Farbey et al, *The Law of Habeas Corpus* (Oxford University Press, 3rd ed, 2008).
[4] William Howe, *Studies in the Civil Law and Its Relations to the Law of England & America* (Little Brown, 1896) 54.
[5] Clauses 39 and 40 of the Magna Carta 1215 (Imp) provided that: '39. No freeman shall be taken, or imprisoned, or disseized, or outlawed, or exiled, or in any way harmed – nor will we go upon or send upon him – save by the lawful judgment of his peers or by the law of the land. 40. To none will we sell, to none deny or delay, right or justice.'
[6] *Habeas Corpus Act 1679* (Imp) <http://www.constitution.org/eng/habcorpa.htm>.
[7] William Blackstone, *Commentaries on the Laws of England* (Clarendon, 1765) vol 1, 120.
[8] Ibid vol 4, 431.
[9] (1890) 15 App Cas 506, 514. Similarly, in *Secretary of State* v *O'Brien* [1923] AC 603, 609 Lord Birkenhead said:

The writ of habeas corpus came to Australia with English settlement,[10] and Australian Supreme Courts have issued it on many occasions, including in diverse factual scenarios.

An early Australian example of the invocation of the writ occurred in the decision of Forbes CJ of the New South Wales Supreme Court in 1831 in *In re Canney*.[11] An application for habeas corpus was directed to the keeper of the Sydney gaol to 'bring up' the body of a female named Catherine Canney, a prisoner in his custody. The application and supporting affidavits stated that that the applicant was a native of the Colony and married to Mrs Canney. Owing to a family dispute, Mrs Canney left her husband and hired herself to the owners of the *Lord Liverpool* cutter, a regular trader between Sydney and Newcastle, in whose service she remained, employed as a female steward mending and washing the cabin furniture, until the cutter was partially wrecked. After a time she was brought before Dr Brooks, a Newcastle magistrate, charged by her husband with cohabiting as a prostitute with the steward of the *Lord Liverpool* and sentenced for three months to the female factory at Parramatta to work in a house-of-correction.

It was contended in the Supreme Court that the warrant did not set out an offence that could justify Mrs Canney's detention and that the magistrate could not legally sentence Canney, a free woman, to be confined in the factory as that was a place exclusively for female prisoners under sentence of transportation. The Chief Justice granted the writ.

Shortly afterwards (in 1832), Forbes CJ and Dowling J heard another application for habeas corpus[12] by the father of a girl of about nine whose mother he had married (after the birth of their daughter) in Van Diemen's Land. However, after they cohabited for a short time 'she eloped from him' and disappeared for about four years. He discovered she had 'conducted herself in a disreputable manner', amongst other things becoming the mother of another child. As she had no means of maintaining the child she had had with him, he applied for a writ of habeas corpus so that his daughter could be restored to him. The Court concluded

---

We are dealing with a writ antecedent to statute, and throwing its roots deep into the genius of our common law. It is perhaps the most important writ known to the constitutional law of England, affording as it does a swift and imperative remedy in all cases of illegal restraint or confinement. It is of immemorial antiquity, an instance of its use occurring in the thirty-third year of Edward 1. It has through the ages been jealously maintained by courts of law as a check upon the illegal usurpation of power by the Executive at the cost of the liege.
See also *In Re Storgoff*, 1945 CanLII 17 (SCC), [1945] SCR 526, 546; *May v Ferndale Institution*, 2005 SCC 82, [2005] 3 SCR 809 [19]–[21].

[10]   See eg *Ex parte Nichols* [1839] SCC 123, 128; *Ex parte Lo Pak* (1888) 9 NSWR 221 at 227, 234 and247; *Zwillinger v Schulof* [1963] VR 407; *PR v Department of Human Services* [2007] VSC 338 [8]; *Re Bolton; Ex parte Beane* [1987] HCA 12; (1987) 162 CLR 514.

[11]   [1831] NSWSupC 22.

[12]   *Storey v Storey* [1832] NSWSupC 62.

that the writ did not lie; the father had no right to have the child delivered up to him – he had 'no more than the natural right to maintain it'.

Discussing clause 39 of the Magna Carta and comparable provisions, Isaacs J of the Australian High Court in 1925[13] stated that the writ recognised three basic principles:

(1) primarily every free man has an inherent individual right to his life, liberty, property and citizenship;
(2) his individual rights must always yield to the necessities of the general welfare at the will of the State;
(3) the law of the land is the only mode by which the State can so declare its will.

More recently, in *Chu Kheng Lim v Minister for Immigration, Local Government and Ethnic Affairs*,[14] Brennan, Deane and Dawson JJ emphasised the protection that it affords against oppressive conduct by the state:

> Under the common law of Australia and subject to qualification in the case of an enemy alien in time of war, an alien who is within this country, whether lawfully or unlawfully, is not an outlaw. Neither public official nor private person can lawfully detain him or her or deal with his or her property except under and in accordance with some positive authority conferred by the law. Since the common law knows neither lettre de cachet[15] nor other executive warrant authorizing arbitrary arrest or detention, any officer of the Commonwealth Executive who purports to authorize or enforce the detention in custody of such an alien without judicial mandate will be acting lawfully only to the extent that his or her conduct is justified by valid statutory provision. [citations omitted]

They made reference to a passage in the important judgment of Deane J in *Re Bolton; Ex parte Beane*[16] where he said:

> [I]t is the plain duty of any such officer to satisfy himself that he is acting with the authority of the law in any case where, in the name of the Commonwealth, he directs that a person be taken and held in custody. The lawfulness of any such administrative direction, or of actions taken pursuant to it, may be challenged in the courts by the person affected: by application for a writ of habeas corpus where it is available or by reliance upon the constitutionally entrenched right to seek in

---

13   *Ex parte Walsh and Johnson; In re Yates* [1925] HCA 53; (1925) 37 CLR 36, 79.
14   [1992] HCA 64; (1992) 176 CLR 1[19].
15   The 'lettre de cachet' was a letter signed by the king and countersigned by a secretary of state, used primarily to authorise someone's imprisonment. It was a controversial instrument of administration under the ancien régime in France. Lettres de cachet were greatly abused during the 17th and 18th centuries. See F M Fling, 'Mirabeau: A Victim of the Lettres de Cachet' (1897) 3(1) *The American Historical Review* 19.
16   [1987] HCA 12; (1987) 162 CLR 514, 528–9.

this Court an injunction against an officer of the Commonwealth. It cannot be too strongly stressed that these basic matters are not the stuff of empty rhetoric. They are the very fabric of the freedom under the law which is the prima facie right of every citizen and alien in this land. They represent a bulwark against tyranny.

The writ does not issue as of right. Typically, application is made by summons or notice of motion ex parte for the writ, supported by affidavit. This is similar to the pre-1780 procedure. If the judge hearing the matter is satisfied that there is an arguable case for the writ, the case is adjourned so that proper notice can be given to the respondent and any relevant parties. It is possible for the court to issue the writ on this ex parte application but this is not normally done, mostly for want of evidence and procedural fairness.[17] Thus the application consists of two steps: the making of an order nisi for the issue of a writ of habeas corpus, which requires the person holding the detainee to bring the detainee to the court and show cause why the detention is lawful.[18] If, on the hearing, the detention cannot be justified, the order nisi is made absolute, and the court orders that the detainee be released.[19] Chief Justice Miles of the ACT Supreme Court[20] observed:

> A writ is not an order of a court. A writ is a command made by the Sovereign as part of the prerogative power requiring the person to whom it is directed to act according to its terms. Some writs, including a writ of habeas corpus, issue through the medium of a superior court and are regarded as part of its process. A writ of habeas corpus (or, more precisely, a writ of habeas corpus ad subjiciendum, one of the five varieties of a writ of habeas corpus) requires the person to whom it is directed to produce to the court the body of another whom he has in custody so that a decision may be made according to law relating to the liberty of the person in custody. As a matter of procedure, a writ of habeas corpus does not issue as

---

[17] J by his litigation guardian Vardanega v Australian Capital Territory [2009] ACTSC 170 [36].

[18] The starting point is important. As Tamberlin J in Hicks v Ruddock [2007] FCA 299 [54]–[55] observed:
Authorities support the proposition that in habeas corpus applications, the detaining party bears the onus of showing the lawfulness of that detention: Abbasi v Secretary of State [2002] EWCA Civ. 1598 at [66] (and cases cited therein); The King v Carter; Ex parte Kisch [1934] HCA 50; (1934) 52 CLR 221 at 227 per Evatt J; Regina v Governor of Brixton Prison; Ex parte Ashan (1969) 2 QB 222 at 233, 237, and 248; R v Governor of Metropolitan Gaol; Ex parte Di Nardo [1963] VR 61 at 62; and, regarding the need for evidence, Greene v Home Secretary [1942] AC 824. See also Aronson, Dyer and Groves, Judicial Review of Administrative Action (3rd ed., 2004) at 777–779. Cases which impose the general onus upon a respondent as to the legality of detention include: The King v Carter; Ex parte Kisch [1934] HCA 50; (1934) 52 CLR 221 at 227, where Evatt J said that the duty of the Court was to see if any legal ground is made out to justify detention; Naumovska v Minister for Immigration and Ethnic Affairs (1982) 60 FLR 267 at 278, where Sheppard J left the question open; R v Governor of Metropolitan Gaol; Ex parte Di Nardo [1963] VR 61 at 62; and Regina v Governor of Brixton Prison; Ex parte Ashan (1969) 2 QB 222 at 233, 237.

[19] Victorian Council for Civil Liberties Incorporated v Minister for Immigration & Multicultural Affairs [2001] FCA 1297 [54] (North J).

[20] R v the Superintendent of the Belconnen Remand Centre; Ex Parte Jack Victor Diamond Also Known As Victor Grzeszkiewicz [1986] ACTSC 76.

of course, unlike a writ of summons and the now abolished writs of subpoena. Long ago in New South Wales it was held that where the respondent takes part in proceedings leading to the granting of a rule authorising the issue of a writ of habeas corpus, all matters may be dealt with upon the return of the rule nisi which could be dealt with upon the return of the writ itself: *Ex parte Lo Pak* (1888) 9 NSWR 221.

Nonetheless, the writ has been held to be 'a basic protection of liberty, and its scope is broad and flexible'.[21] It has been called in aid, for instance, in cases where a marriage under duress has been suspected, in order to ascertain the true wishes of the proposed 'bride'.[22]

However, a writ of habeas corpus does not lie where the applicant is in custody pursuant to a judgment in due course of law, which has not been shown to be unlawful.[23] Nor is it available as a means of collaterally impeaching the correctness of a judgment or order made by a court of competent jurisdiction, which is not shown to be a nullity.[24]

The writ of habeas corpus can be issued in broad circumstances in the interests of justice. Lord Justice Atkin[25] observed in 1923 that:

> Actual physical custody is obviously not essential. 'Custody' or 'control' are the phrases used passim in the opinions of the Lords in *Barnardo v Ford* [1892] AC 326, and in my opinion are a correct measure of liability to the writ ... In testing

---

[21] *Al-Kateb v Godwin* [2004] HCA 37; (2004) 219 CLR 562 [25] (Gleeson CJ). In *Hicks v Ruddock* [2007] FCA 299 [35] Tamberlin J observed that:
A fundamental principle of English law is that no member of the executive can interfere with the liberty of a British subject, except on the condition that the legality of the interference is established as lawful before a court of justice: *R v Home Secretary, Ex parte Khawaja* [1984] 1 AC 74 at 110 per Lord Scarman. This principle is deeply embedded in the common law. It applies in war as in peace: see *Liversidge v Anderson [1941] UKHL 1;* [1942] AC 206 at 244. The writ of habeas corpus was described by Supreme Court Justice Brennan in *Fay v Moia* (1963) 372 US 391 at 400, quoting Lord Birkenhead in *Secretary of State for Home Affairs v O'Brien* [1923] AC 603 at 609, in these terms: 'It is a writ antecedent to statutes, and throwing its roots deep into the genius of our common law... It is perhaps the most important writ known to the constitutional law of England, affording as it does a swift remedy in all cases of illegal restraint or confinement.'
[22] *Re SK (Proposed Plaintiff) (An Adult by way of her Litigation Friend)* [2004] EWHC 3202 (Fam), [2005] 2 FLR 230.
[23] See eg *Williams, In re* [1934] HCA 48; (1934) 51 CLR 545, 548 (Starke J); *Re Writ of Habeas Corpus Ad Subjiciendum; Ex Parte Hooker* [2005] WASC 29 [19] (Le Miere J).
[24] *Officer in Charge of Cells, ACT Supreme Court, Re; Ex parte Eastman* [1994] HCA 36; (1994) 123 ALR 478 [6] (Deane J); *Rich v The Secretary to the Department of Justice* [2011] VSC 413 [13]–[14] (Buchanan JA); *Re Writ of Habeas Corpus Ad Subjiciendum; Ex Parte Hooker* [2005] WASC 292. See also *R v Sarson* 135 DLR (4th) 402;107 CCC (3d) 21.
[25] *R v Secretary of State for Home Affairs ex p O'Brien* [1923] 2 KB 361, 398.

the validity of the order the question is as to the legal right to control; in testing the liability of the respondent to the writ the question is as to de facto control.

A similarly broad approach was followed by the United States Supreme Court in *Jones v Cunningham*,[26] a prisoner's rights decision, where the Court observed that:

> the King's Bench, as early as 1722, held that habeas corpus was appropriate to question whether a woman alleged to be the applicant's wife was being constrained by her guardians to stay away from her husband against her will (*R v Clarkson* (1722) 1 Str 444, 93 ER 625). The test used was simply whether she was 'at her liberty to go where she please[d].' (Str at 445; ER at 445, 93 ER at 625). So also, habeas corpus was used in 1763 to require the production in court of an indentured 18-year-old girl who had been assigned by her master to another man 'for bad purposes.' (*R v Delaval* (1763) 3 Burr 1434, 97 ER 913. Although the report indicates no restraint on the girl other than the covenants of the indenture, the King's Bench ordered that she 'be discharged from all restraint, and be at liberty to go where she will.'(Burr at 1437; ER at 914) And more than a century ago, an English court permitted a parent to use habeas corpus to obtain his children from the other parent, even though the children were 'not under imprisonment, restraint, or duress of any kind.' (*Earl of Westmeath v. Countess of Westmeath*, as set out in a reporter's footnote in *Lyons v. Blenkin* (1821) 1 Jac 245 at 264, 37 ER 842 at 848; *accord, Ex parte M'Clellan* (1831) 1 Dowl 81). These examples show clearly that English courts have not treated the *Habeas Corpus Act* of 1679, 31 Car. II, c. 2 – the forerunner of all habeas corpus acts – as permitting relief only to those in jail or like physical confinement.

It held that 'the use of habeas corpus has not been restricted to situations in which the applicant is in actual physical custody'[27] and emphasised that the scope of the writ should reflect its fundamental purpose:

> History, usage and precedent can leave no doubt that, besides physical imprisonment, there are other restraints on a man's liberty, restraints not shared by the public generally, which have been thought sufficient in the English-speaking world to support the issuance of habeas corpus. ... Of course, that writ always could and still can reach behind prison walls and iron bars. But it can do more. It is not now and never has been a static, narrow, formalistic remedy; its scope has grown to achieve its grand purpose – the protection of individuals against erosion of their right to be free from wrongful restraints upon their liberty.[28]

---

[26] 371 US 236 (1963), interpreting US Const Art I, § 9: 'The Privilege of the Writ of Habeas Corpus shall not be suspended, unless when in Cases of Rebellion or Invasion the public Safety may require it.' See further A Gertmenian 'Criminal Procedure: The Custody Requirement for Habeas Corpus Relief in the Federal Courts' (1963) 51(1) *California Law Review* 228.

[27] *Jones v Cunningham* 371 US 236 (1963), 239.

[28] Ibid 240, 243.

This decision was followed in Australia by North J in litigation involving asylum seekers on board the Tampa.[29]

A significant decision that illustrates the limitations of the writ was the Tasmanian Supreme Court decision of *Re T*,[30] in which the Governor and the Director of Corrective Services were called upon to show cause why they should not produce to the court a man found not guilty by reason of insanity of murder and detained at a Security Hospital. At the request of the detainee, the Attorney-General referred his case to the Mental Health Review Tribunal, which recommended that he no longer be subject to restriction. However, its advice was not acted upon. It was submitted on behalf of the man that the Governor ought to have been satisfied that the restriction order deemed to have been made in respect of the man was no longer required for the protection of the public and that, therefore, he ought to have directed that it cease to have effect.

However, Zeeman J found that, in order for the applicant to be successful, it was necessary for him to show that some illegality attached to his continued detention and that he had been unable to demonstrate this. Applying Canadian authority,[31] he accepted that the detention decision of the Executive needed to be reached in accordance with procedural fairness but found that, in the absence of evidence, the Governor's discretion was improperly exercised – the writ did not lie.

3. HABEAS CORPUS AS A PROTECTION FOR PERSONS WITH MENTAL ILLNESSES

Many decisions by superior courts have dealt with applications for habeas corpus in respect of persons with mental illness whose liberty was denied to them or where their freedom of movement was circumscribed. Those with a mental illness can only be detained in hospital for treatment as permitted by statute and 'liberty may be violated only to the extent permitted by law and not otherwise'.[32] Good intentions to safeguard vulnerable persons have been held not to constitute a legitimate reason to curtail freedom of movement,[33] although courts on occasion

---

[29] *Victorian Council for Civil Liberties Inc v Minister for Immigration and Multicultural Affairs* (2001) 110 FCR 452 [83].

[30] [1993] TASSC 17.

[31] *Re McCann* (1982) 67 CCC (2d) 180, 187–8; see also *Re Brooks' Detention* (1962) 38 WWR 51, 53 suggesting that if the writ were exercised arbitrarily and without proper evidence, the writ may also lie.

[32] *Re S-C (Mental Patient: Habeas Corpus)* [1996] QB 599, 603; see also *R v East London and the City Mental Health NHS Trust* [2003] UKHL 58; [2004] 2 AC 280 [6].

[33] See *R v Board of Control; Ex parte Rutty* [1956] 2 QB 109. In *HL v The United Kingdom* [2004] ECHR 720, a case in which habeas corpus was sought in relation to the informal detention of a person with autism, the European Court of Human Rights held that 'an individual cannot be deprived of his liberty on the basis of unsoundness of mind unless three minimum conditions

have permitted continuing detention for a time, such as where it was suspected that otherwise the detainee 'may do a very harmful act to someone'.[34]

An important decision on the subject is that of Eastman J in *Re C (Mental Patient: Contact)*[35] where there was a dispute between parents as to their adult daughter's living arrangements. The parents had separated and their daughter remained in her father's care. The mother complained that the father had prevented her from seeing her daughter. The mother applied to stay contact with her and for an order that the mother could lawfully enter the father's home to take her daughter for contact. She also sought a declaration that the father could not lawfully obstruct or prevent contact. The preliminary question of whether there was jurisdiction to grant such relief came before Eastham J. He agreed that the court did have jurisdiction and observed:[36]

> It is submitted … that interference by a custodial parent with the other parent's access to a child is capable of being remedied by habeas corpus. That is a view with which I agree, and … if this is a case in which either contrary to the will of C if she is able to express her will, or, if contrary to her best interests as found by the court she is not being allowed to see her mother and not being allowed to have access and is otherwise being restrained, then habeas corpus would definitely be available.

He added:[37]

> I have come to the conclusion that if the plaintiff had wished there was material, if her contentions are right, to found an application for habeas corpus, and I am inclined to agree with the submission that if the grounds apply for relief in that drastic form it does support very much the contention that there should be relief available by way of the lesser declaration.

In *A Local Authority v MA*,[38] a case involving evaluation of the capacity of a deaf and dumb 18-year-old female to consent to marriage, Mumby J observed that the writ

> is a means not merely of testing the legal right to detain or control; inasmuch as it requires the 'gaoler' to bring the 'body' before the court, it is also a means

---

    are satisfied: he must reliably be shown to be of unsound mind; the mental disorder must be of a kind or degree warranting compulsory confinement; and the validity of continued confinement depends upon the persistence of such a disorder'.

[34]   *In re Gregory* (1899) 25 VLR 539.
[35]   [1993] 1 FLR 940.
[36]   Ibid 944.
[37]   Ibid 945.
[38]   *A Local Authority v MA* [2005] EWHC 2942 (Fam) [75]–[79].

of ascertaining whether someone is in fact being kept confined, controlled, coerced or under restraint. And if, by means of a habeas corpus, the court can, as Singer J put it, secure the attendance of a young adult at court, so that the judge may ascertain her true wishes and, if coercion is established, ensure her release, then, for the reasons given by Eastham J in *Re C (Mental Patient: Contact)* [1993] 1 FLR 940, the same result can equally be achieved by recourse to the inherent jurisdiction.

This leaves the onus upon a person who is encroaching upon the liberty of another with the onus of justifying its lawfulness.[39] The writ issues as of right upon cause being shown.[40] Justice Eames in *Murray v Director-General, Health and Community Services and Superintendent, Larundel Psychiatric Hospital*[41] affirmed this proposition, determining that 'if the detention is unlawful then there is no discretion and the writ must issue'.

4.   *ANTUNOVIC V DAWSON*

Zeljka Antunovic, a woman of 33, was made an involuntary patient in purported compliance with the criteria in Victoria's *Mental Health Act 1986* ('the Act') in 2008.[42] She was placed on a community treatment order ('the order') in the same year by Dr Louise Dawson, an authorised psychiatrist. The order was extended in 2009 and then again in 2010. The 2010 version of the order was scheduled to expire on 2 May 2011.

Under s 14(3)(b) of Victoria's mental health legislation a community treatment order issued by an authorised psychiatrist (or an order under s 36(4) by the Mental Health Review Board) may specify where a person must live, 'if this is necessary for the treatment of the person's mental illness'. This is generally known as a 'residence condition'. However, no such condition was placed on the order relating to Ms Antunovic, and the orders applying to her were never varied to include such a condition. A treatment plan[43] had been prepared in relation to Ms Antunovic. However, for no apparent reason other than its inadequacy, the plan also made no mention of her wish to cease living at her residence or of her earnest and oft-repeated desire to go home to live with her mother.

Victoria's Mental Health Review Board reviewed the community treatment order applying to Ms Antunovic on 18 June 2010. It received oral evidence from her and

---

[39]   See eg *R v Davey; Ex parte Freer* (1936) 56 CLR 381, 385.
[40]   See eg *Ruddock v Vadarlis* (2001) 110 FCR 491 [91].
[41]   Unreported, Supreme Court of Victoria, 23 June 1995 [27].
[42]   [2010] VSC 377.
[43]   Under s 19A of the *Mental Health Act 1986* (Vic).

medical evidence from a medical practitioner, Dr Dawson, who did not appear before the Board. It decided to continue the community treatment order and to review it again six weeks later, stating that it was not satisfied the treatment plan made for Ms Antunovic complied with the requirements stipulated under the Act. It specifically referred to the absence of any reference to Ms Antunovic's wish to cease residing at the community care unit where she was living and to go home to live with her mother. The Board did not impose any residential condition on Ms Antunovic's community treatment order.

Ms Antunovic took action before Bell J in Victoria's Supreme Court in relation to an obligation imposed upon her but not specified in her order or treatment plan that she reside in a community care unit ('CCU'), although she wished to live in her mother's house. Under Order 57.03 of Victoria's *Supreme Court (General Civil Procedure) Rules 2005*, the Court was empowered to issue a writ of habeas corpus *ad subjiciendum* or an order that Ms Antunovic, as a person restrained, be released.

Before Bell J it was agreed that Ms Antunovic had been instructed by Dr Dawson to live at the Norfolk Community Care Unit ('the CCU'). Such units were created in 1989 in Victoria 'for clients who have a severe or longer term mental illness, or who need a period of residential monitoring while their treatment is adjusted'.[44]

Ms Antunovic had a measure of freedom, which meant that her confinement was not absolute – she was allowed to go out during the day but was obliged to return at night. The key issue was that she was not allowed to live at her mother's house, although she had asked on numerous occasions to be allowed to do so. This position on the part of Dr Dawson persisted even after the concerns expressed by the Board. The Mental Health Legal Service, on Ms Antunovic's behalf, repeatedly also asked Dr Dawson and the CCU to allow Ms Antunovic to be allowed to live at home but was refused. Justice Bell inferred that Ms Antunovic felt unable to go home without the permission of Dr Dawson by reason of the power and control exercised over her by Dr Dawson and the CCU.[45]

It was submitted on behalf of Ms Antunovic that it was all the more important for the common law habeas corpus jurisdiction to be exercised because that would be consistent with protecting her human rights under Victoria's Charter of Human Rights and Responsibilities. Justice Bell accepted the submission and found that Antunovic's involuntary status engaged her human rights to freedom

---

[44]   L Neville MP, 'Community Care Units Expanded for Melbourne's East' (Media Release, 19 March 2008) <http://archive.premier.vic.gov.au/newsroom/2021.html>.
[45]   *Antunovic v Dawson* [2010] VSC 377 [174].

of movement under s 12 of the Charter and to liberty and security of the person under s 21.

Under s 12 of the Charter, every person 'has the right to move freely within Victoria and to enter and leave it and has the freedom to choose where to live'. Under s 21 every person has 'the right to liberty and security'. It prevents 'arbitrary arrest or detention'. Section 21(3) provides that no one can be deprived of their liberty 'except on grounds, and in accordance with procedures, established by law'. Justice Bell observed that these rights are recognised in a variety of international human rights instruments, including Articles 9 and 12(1) of the International Covenant on Civil and Political Rights, to which Australia is a signatory.

He held that the obligation to act compatibly with human rights depends in the first instance on whether a right is engaged. This occurs when a public authority makes a decision affecting, or acts toward, a person in a way that apparently limits their human rights. Then the question becomes whether the decision or conduct is compatible with human rights, this depending on whether any limitation is demonstrably justified according to the general limitations provision of s 7(2) of the Charter.

Justice Bell analysed the bases under Victoria's mental health legislation for the imposition of community treatment orders and, in particular, residential conditions attached to such orders. He observed that the powers 'to place people on such orders plainly interfere with their human rights and fundamental rights and freedoms in substantial ways. Therefore, this is only authorised in certain circumstances where it is necessary in the person's medical interest.'[46] He emphasised that a treatment plan 'is not a vehicle for imposing residence requirements on a person' and noted that the plan in question did not incorporate such a condition for Ms Antunovic. However, nor did it specify Ms Antunovic's wish to stop living at the unit and to return home to live with her mother. He observed that a policy of Victoria's mental health legislation (as a result of going some distance toward meeting the 1991 United Nations Principles for the Protection of Persons with Mental Illness and the Improvement of Mental Health Care) was to provide the least restrictive and intrusive treatment possible and that that incorporated provision of such treatment, where possible.[47]

Justice Bell accepted that Ms Antunovic was not

> in close-custody in the sense of being under arrest, imprisoned or detained. She
> has considerable freedom of movement during the day, but her freedom in that

---

[46]   [2011] VSC 377 [155].
[47]   *Mental Health Act 1986* (Vic), s 4(2), s 6A(b).

respect is limited by the requirement that she must live at the unit and be there at night. At night, her freedom of movement is limited by that requirement.[48]

Although he found this not to constitute 'a total restraint', he classified it as 'substantial'.[49] He inferred that she felt unable to go home without permission of Dr Dawson because of the authority Dr Dawson held over her as an authorized psychiatrist and because the unit was where she was being treated for her mental illness:

> Because of the power which the doctor and the unit have over her, Ms Antunovic feels unable simply to leave the unit and go home. I think she is being subjected to 'power' and 'control' within the applicable legal test of restraint.[50]

Justice Bell found that this restraint of Ms Antunovic's movement engaged the human right to freedom of movement under s 12 of the Charter and was unlawful. He concluded that the restraint, albeit partial, was

> amenable to habeas corpus because [it is] not shared by the general public who, under the common law, can generally choose where to live, and go to and from their home, at will. Being able to do so is an important aspect of the private and social life and the development of the individual, including that which occurs within their own family.[51]

He concluded that because of the breadth and flexibility of the writ of habeas corpus and its underlying function to protect personal liberty, it was available and constituted the most efficacious remedy for Ms Antunovic. He made orders for the release of Ms Antunovic by Dr Dawson and the Unit.

Justice Bell made such orders, having satisfied himself that:

> Were Ms Antunovic to go home to live with her mother, she would have access to and take her medication. I was satisfied that she could obtain her medication from a point close to her mother's inner-Melbourne home. There was no dispute that she would take it. She has been doing so voluntarily for some years. Nor was this a case in which there was a risk of Ms Antunovic harming herself or other people.[52]

---

48   *Antunovic v Dawson* [2010] VSC 377 [173].
49   Ibid.
50   Ibid [174].
51   Ibid [176].
52   Ibid [188]. See I Freckelton, 'Habeas Corpus and Involuntary Detention of Patients with Psychiatric Disorders' (2011) 18(4) *Psychiatry, Psychology and Law* 473.

5. REPERCUSSIONS OF THE *ANTUNOVIC* DECISION

The decision of Bell J contains an extensive scholarly analysis of the law of habeas corpus, particularly the law relating to the writ's application to persons detained involuntarily, either within hospitals or in the community, by reason of mental illness. For this reason alone, it is a significant decision to which recourse is likely to be made for many years.

The outcome of the case was not surprising. There was no warrant for the encroachment on Ms Antunovic's liberty that was imposed by Dr Dawson and the Unit. It had no basis in a residential condition in the community treatment order issued in relation to her. Nor did it appear in her treatment plan. Moreover, the requirement for her to live at the community care unit was contrary to her oft-stated wishes, which ought to have been represented in her treatment plan.

An important aspect of the decision is that the habeas corpus application was permitted although Ms Antunovic had significant freedom of movement – she was not wholly confined within the unit.[53] However, this aspect of the decision, too, was grounded in sound precedent with United States and United Kingdom authority supporting a broad reading of the preconditions for habeas corpus to include situations where a person's freedom is controlled or reduced by another without lawful justification. The decision signals that the writ, which Bell J described as having the purpose of protecting the bedrock value of personal liberty,[54] as well as orders for release from unlawful restraint, have the potential to play an important continuing role in regulating community treatment of persons with mental illness and associated encroachments upon their liberties.

Justice Bell's decision is significant in its emphatic acknowledgment of the significance of freedom of movement and decision-making for persons with psychiatric disorders. It builds upon his 2009 analysis in *Kracke v Mental Health Review Board*[55] and is a powerful endorsement of 'the personal liberty which mentally ill people have to choose where to go and live in the community'.[56] The words employed in the judgment at times constitute something akin to a call to arms to protect the rights of those members of the community who have disabilities:

---

[53]   Compare the facts in *HM v Switzerland* no 39187/98, s 48, ECHR 2002-II.
[54]   *Antunovic v Dawson* [2010] VSC 377 [195].
[55]   [2009] VCAT 646; I Freckelton and S McGregor, 'Human Rights and the Review of Persons with Mental Illnesses' (2010) 17(2) *Psychiatry, Psychology and Law* 173; S Tully, 'Kracke v Mental Health Review Board [2009] VCAT 646' (2009) 16 *Australian International Law Journal* 289.
[56]   *Antunovic v Dawson* [2010] VSC 377 [188].

When a court determines a habeas corpus … application, both the body of the person and the body of the law are at stake, for nothing tears to shreds more completely the whole idea of the rule of law than unlawfully restraining the personal liberty of the individual.[57]

6. THE *HL* DECISION

There is a problematic tradition in the provision of care and treatment to persons with disabilities that decision-making has been paternalistic and variously justified by convenience, necessity and what have been asserted to be the best interests of the person concerned.

Repudiation of these rationalisations found their high point in the decision of the European Court of Human Rights in *HL v The United Kingdom*.[58] HL had been admitted for treatment. He had autism from birth and was self-harming and at times violent towards others. He was unable to speak and had very limited understanding of his circumstances. The practice in the United Kingdom was to categorise persons in HL's situation, namely unable to consent to treatment but not explicitly objecting to it, as 'informal patients' who could be detained within psychiatric institutions. The European Court overturned United Kingdom decisions[59] in relation to HL and found that this method of detaining patients breached Article 5(1) of the European Convention for the Protection of Human Rights and Fundamental Freedoms. The Convention had been incorporated into United Kingdom law by the *Human Rights Act 1998* (UK), which provides that '[e]veryone has the right to liberty and security of person. No one shall be deprived of his liberty save in the following cases and in accordance with a procedure prescribed by law: (e) the lawful detention … of persons of unsound mind…' The Court observed:

[A]s a result of the lack of procedural regulation and limits, the hospital's health care professionals assumed full control of the liberty and treatment of a vulnerable incapacitated individual solely on the basis of their own clinical assessments completed as and when they considered fit: as Lord Steyn remarked, this left 'effective and unqualified control' in their hands. While the Court does

---

[57]   Ibid [192].
[58]   [2004] ECHR 720. See K Diesfeld, 'Criteria for Discharge of Persons with Learning Disabilities: A Comparative Analysis' in K Diesfeld and I Freckelton (eds), *Involuntary Detention and Therapeutic Jurisprudence* (Ashgate, 2003).
[59]   *R v Bournewood Community and Mental Health NHS Trust, ex parte L* [1998] 2 WLR 764 (CA); *R v Bournewood Community and Mental Health NHS Trust, ex parte L* [1999] AC 458 (HL). See K Gledhill, 'The Filling of the "Bournewood Gap"' and I Freckelton, 'Brain Injuries and Coercive Care' in B McSherry and I Freckelton (eds), *Coercive Care: Law and Policy* (Routledge, 2013).

not question the good faith of those professionals or that they acted in what they considered to be the applicant's best interests, the very purpose of procedural safeguards is to protect individuals against any 'misjudgments and professional lapses'.[60]

Similar issues arise with respect to many persons with congenital disabilities, brain injuries and dementias, who are routinely de facto detained as involuntary inpatients across a wide range of institutions.

The decisions of the European Court and of Bell J in *Antunovic v Dawson* raise the potential for habeas corpus action to be taken in respect of the encroachments on liberty generated by such practices.

7. REMEDIES FOR OPPRESSIVE CUSTODIAL CONDITIONS

Attempts have been made on a number of occasions to invoke the writ of habeas corpus where it has not been detention itself but prisoners' conditions of incarceration that have been challenged as unfair, unreasonable or oppressive. In the important Canadian Supreme Court decision of *R v Miller*,[61] le Dain J (for the Court) held:

> The general importance of this remedy as the traditional means of challenging deprivations of liberty is such that its proper development and adaptation to the modern realities of confinement in a prison setting should not be compromised by concerns about conflicting jurisdiction. ... There cannot be one definition of the reach of *habeas corpus* in relation to federal authorities and a different one for other authorities. Confinement in a special handling unit, or in administrative segregation ..., is a form of detention that is distinct and separate from that imposed on the general inmate population. It involves a significant reduction in the residual liberty of the inmate. It is in fact a new detention of the inmate, purporting to rest on its own foundation of legal authority. It is that particular form of detention or deprivation of liberty which is the object of the challenge by *habeas corpus*. It is release from that form of detention that is sought. ... I can see no sound reason in principle, having to do with the nature and role of *habeas corpus*, why *habeas corpus* should not be available for that purpose. I do not say that *habeas corpus* should lie to challenge any and all conditions of confinement in a penitentiary or prison, including the loss of any privilege enjoyed by the general inmate population. But it should lie in my opinion to challenge the validity of a distinct form of confinement or detention in which the actual physical constraint

---

[60]   *HL v The United Kingdom* [2004] ECHR 720 [121].
[61]   (1985) 24 DLR (4th) 9 [35].

or deprivation of liberty, as distinct from the mere loss of certain privileges, is more restrictive or severe than the normal one in an institution[62].

The *Miller* decision was relied upon by the applicants in *Prisoners A to XX Inclusive v New South Wales*[63] where it was alleged on behalf of 50 prisoners that the Department of Corrections' failure to supply them with condoms constituted a breach of its duty of care to them. They sought a declaration that the non-supply policy was unreasonable. They also sought a writ of habeas corpus. At first instance, Dunford J declined the writ and held that the writ of habeas corpus does not extend beyond the lawfulness of detention to the conditions of confinement. The prisoners appealed against this decision to the New South Wales Court of Appeal, maintaining that their confinement was made unlawful by the unreasonableness of the conditions of their imprisonment, including the risk of their being infected with HIV and hepatitis.

Ultimately, the Court of Appeal refused leave to amend the pleading to incorporate the writ of habeas corpus, observing that the provisions of the Magna Carta did not avail the prisoners:

> [W]hatever may have been intended by the drafter of the Magna Carta in 1212 or on the occasions when it was subsequently confirmed, it has influenced the development of current common law. It does not however, in my opinion, provide a statutory basis for saying that the denial by prison authorities of access by prisoners to condoms is unlawful.[64]

The decision, however, remains an important authority on the role of habeas corpus as a potential safety net for the conditions of prisoners.[65] It also highlights the limitations of both the writ of habeas corpus and of other remedies to protect the rights of sentenced prisoners in Australia.

– *Plata v Brown*

Another form of redress was sought in the United States in *Brown v Plata*,[66] a landmark ruling of the United States Supreme Court concerning the health of those detained in Californian prisons. In a 5:4 decision the Court declared that if a prison deprives prisoners of adequate medical care, it violates the obligation to refrain from cruel and unusual punishment (the Eighth Amendment to the

---

62 Compare *R v Deputy Governor of Parkhurst Prison; Ex parte Hague* [1992] 1 AC 58, 165–6; *Presider v Rodriguez*, 411 US 475 (1973).
63 (1994) 75 A Crim R 205 (Dunford J); (1995) 38 NSWLR 622.
64 Ibid 634–5.
65 See Matthew Groves, 'The Use of Habeas Corpus to Challenge Prison Conditions' (1996) 19(2) *University of New South Wales Law Journal* 281.
66 <Http://www.supremecourt.gov/opinions/10pdf/09-1233.pdf>.

United States Constitution)[67] and that the courts have a responsibility to remedy such a violation. It did so by affirming the unusual order of an inferior court that California reduce its prison population to 137.5% of design capacity within two years.

For instance, the United Kingdom for some time has identified the human rights dimensions of any form of detention of persons with mental illnesses.[68] The *Plata v Brown* decision emanates from a jurisdiction with a recent history of extraordinary levels of incarceration that inevitably have impacted upon the living conditions of prisoners in an egregious way – the United States has 25% of the world's prisoners, although it only represents 5% of the global population, and the numbers of those incarcerated (currently in the order of 2.4 million people) have increased six-fold since the 1970s.[69] The exploding prisoner population has brought with it a dramatic increase in the incarceration of persons with mental illnesses, intellectual disabilities and substance dependencies and, in spite of the burgeoning prison-building industry, inevitably a troubling incidence of prison conditions that are inhumane and grossly substandard.[70] This has a range of human rights ramifications.

There is ample reason to fear that the outcome of *Brown v Plata* will be no more than a modest reduction in numbers of the Californian prison population and, instead, a dispersal of prisoners to out-of-state penal facilities and county jails (as well as a further fillip to prison construction). However, the decision is extremely important symbolically and from a jurisprudential point of view. It shines a bright and embarrassing light (including annexing photographs) upon a hidden aspect of society that does not readily engage community sympathy and which, historically and too often still, is characterised by inhumanity justified by the notion that prisoners are an inferior form of citizen. The decision fundamentally divided the United States Supreme Court on ideological grounds. It raises internationally the issue of the extent to which the right to be free from 'cruel and unusual

---

[67] 'Excessive bail shall not be required, nor excessive fines imposed, nor cruel and unusual punishments inflicted.'

[68] See eg K Akuffo, 'The Involuntary Detention of Persons with Mental Disorder in England and Wales – A Human Rights Critique' (2004) 27 *International Journal of Law and Psychiatry* 109.

[69] See generally M Schlanger, '*Plata v Brown* and Realignment: Jails, Prisons, Courts, and Politics' (2013) 48(1) *Harvard Civil Rights – Civil Liberties Law Review*; J Lobel, 'Cruel and Unusual Punishment: Litigating under the Eighth Amendment: Prolonged Solitary Confinement and the Constitution' (2008) 11 *University of Pennsylvania Journal of Constitutional Law* 115; M A Geer, 'Human Rights and Wrongs in Our Own Backyard: Incorporating International Human Rights Protections under Domestic Civil Rights Law – A Case Study of Women in United States Prisons' (2000) *Harvard Human Rights Journal* 72; M C Friedman, 'Cruel and Unusual Punishment in the Provision of Prison Medical Care: Challenging the Deliberate Indifference Standard' (1992) 45 *Vanderbilt Law Review* 921.

[70] See eg J Bonta and P Gendreau, 'Reexamining the Cruel and Unusual Punishment of Prison Life' (1990) 14(4) *Law and Human Behavior* 347.

punishments' will henceforth operate as a protection for disadvantaged sectors of the community, such as those with mental illnesses both inside prisons and in other contexts, particularly when those affected have serious disabilities likely to be adversely affected by confinement. It also raises the potential for countries such as Australia to utilise the writ of habeas corpus to achieve a comparable outcome.

8. THE HISTORY OF THE *PLATA V BROWN* LITIGATION

In *Coleman v Brown*,[71] filed in 1990, a District Court of California found, after a 39-day trial, that prisoners with serious mental illness were not receiving minimal, adequate care. It concluded that California prisons had failed to implement necessary suicide prevention procedures,[72] with mentally ill inmates languishing 'for months, or even years, without access to necessary care. ... They suffer from severe hallucinations [and] they decompensate into catatonic states.'[73] A Special Master appointed to oversee remedial efforts reported 12 years later that the state of mental health care in California's prisons was deteriorating due to escalating rates of overcrowding.

In *Plata v Schwarzenegger*,[74] filed in 2001, a District Court of California, upon concessions from the State of California, concluded that deficiencies in prison medical care violated prisoners' rights to be free from cruel and unusual punishment under the United States Eighth Amendment to the Constitution. It stipulated a remedial injunction.

By 2005, the State of California had not complied with the injunction. This led the District Court to appoint a Receiver to oversee remedial efforts. The Court made the damning and dramatic finding, apparently frustrated at the State's lack of responsiveness, that 'it is an uncontested fact that, on average, an inmate in one of California's prisons needlessly dies every six to seven days due to constitutional deficiencies in the medical delivery system'. It concluded that prisons were unable to retain sufficient numbers of medical staff, that medical facilities lacked necessary equipment and did not meet basic sanitation standards, and that there was a dangerous incidence of doctors even failing to disinfect examination tables where prisoners with communicable diseases were treated. However, little progress continued to be made in prison conditions, and in 2008, the Receiver described continuing deficiencies:

---

[71]   912 F Supp 1282 (ED Cal).
[72]   Ibid 1315.
[73]   Ibid 1316.
[74]   USDC ND, Cal No C01-1351 THE.

> Timely access [to health care] is not assured. The number of medical personnel has been inadequate, and competence has not been assured. … Adequate housing for the disabled and aged does not exist. The medical facilities when they exist at all, are in an abysmal state of disrepair. Basic medical equipment is often not available or used. Medications and other treatment options are too often not available when needed. … Indeed, it is a misnomer to call the existing chaos a 'medical delivery system' – it is more an act of desperation than a system.

This led the *Coleman* and *Plata* plaintiffs to apply to their District Courts to convene a three-judge court under the *Prison Litigation Reform Act 1995* (US) ('the *PLRA*') to seek an order for reduction of the Californian prison population. The *PLRA* allowed for such an order but provided:

> Prospective relief in any civil action with respect to prison conditions shall extend no further than necessary to correct the violation of the Federal right of a particular plaintiff or plaintiffs. The court shall not grant or approve any prospective relief unless the court finds that such relief is narrowly drawn, extends no further than necessary to correct the violation of the Federal right, and is the least intrusive means necessary to correct the violation of the Federal right. The court shall give substantial weight to any adverse impact on public safety or the operation of a criminal justice system caused by the relief (18 USC 3626 (1)(A)).

The judges in both actions granted the request, and the cases were consolidated before a single three-judge court, which undertook a 14-day hearing and made extensive findings of fact about the state of the Californian penal system. It acceded to the applications by the *Coleman* and *Plata* plaintiffs and ordered California to reduce its prison population to 137.5% of design capacity within two years. It also ordered California to formulate a compliance plan and submit it for court approval. The order left the choice of means to reduce overcrowding to state officials. The State of California appealed the decision to the Supreme Court.

At the time of the hearing by the United States Supreme Court, California's correctional facilities held some 156,000 inmates, nearly double the number they were designed to hold. The 137.5% reduction required 46,000 persons to be reduced. California had succeeded in lessening the numbers by 9,000.

9.   THE HUMAN RIGHTS ISSUES IN *PLATA V BROWN*[75]

Justice Kennedy gave the court's decision for the majority which also consisted of Justices Ginsburg, Breyer, Sotomayor and Kagan. The majority accepted that, because of their conduct, prisoners can be deprived of the rights that others in the community have. However, they emphasised that the law and the United States Constitution 'demand recognition of certain other rights. Prisoners retain the essence of human dignity inherent in all persons. Respect for that dignity animates the Eighth Amendment prohibition against cruel and unusual punishment.'[76] They noted that the act of incarceration renders prisoners dependent on the State for food, clothing and necessary medical care, applying previous Supreme Court authority[77] that failure to provide such sustenance may produce 'torture or a lingering death'.[78] They emphatically held: 'A prison that deprives prisoners of basic sustenance, including adequate medical care, is incompatible with the concept of human dignity and has no place in civilized society.'[79]

The majority observed: 'Overcrowding has overtaken the limited resources of prison staff, imposed demands well beyond the capacity of medical and mental health facilities; and created unsanitary and unsafe conditions that make progress in the provision of care difficult or impossible to achieve.'[80] They commented: 'Prisoners are crammed into spaces neither designed nor intended to house inmates. As many as 200 prisoners may live in a gymnasium, monitored by as few as two or three correctional officers',[81] conditions so unsatisfactory as to lead the then-Governor Schwarzenegger to declare a state of emergency in the prisons in 2006.

The majority found that:[82]

> Prisoners in California with serious mental illness do not receive minimal, adequate care. Because of a shortage of treatment beds, suicidal inmates may be held for prolonged periods in telephone-booth sized cages without toilets ... A psychiatric expert reported observing an inmate who had been held in such a cage for nearly 24 hours, standing in a pool of his own urine, unresponsive and nearly catatonic. Prison officials explained they had 'no place to put him'. ... Other inmates awaiting care may be held for months in administrative segregation,

---

75   131 S Ct 1910 (2011).
76   Ibid 1928.
77   *Estelle v Gamble*, 429 US 97, 103 (1976), quoting *In re Kemmler*, 136 US 436, 447 (1890).
78   131 S Ct 1910, 1928 (2011).
79   Ibid 1928.
80   Ibid 1923.
81   Ibid 1924.
82   Ibid 1924–5.

where they endure harsh and isolated conditions and receive only limited mental health services. Wait times for mental health care range as high as 12 months. ... In 2006, the suicide rate in California's prisons was nearly 80% higher than the national average for prison populations; and a court-ordered Special Master found that 72.1% of suicides involved 'some measure of inadequate assessment, treatment, or intervention, and were therefore most probably foreseeable and/or preventable.'

They noted that living in crowded, unsafe and unsanitary conditions has the potential to cause prisoners with latent mental illnesses to worsen and to develop overt symptoms.

They found that, similarly, prisoners with physical illnesses in California received comparably deficient care, causing multiple deaths from delay in provision of medical care. In addition, overcrowding requires excessive reliance on lockdowns to keep order, in turn impeding effective delivery of care. An associated issue that they identified was that during lockdowns staff had either to escort prisoners to medical facilities or bring medical staff to prisoners: 'Either procedure puts additional strain on already overburdened medical and custodial staff. Some programming for the mentally ill even may be canceled altogether during lockdowns and staff may be unable to supervise the delivery of psychotropic medication.'[83] They found that such problems have the potential to be particularly acute in reception centres that process new and returning prisoners.

The majority rejected the argument by the State of California that the evidence presented at trial and before the three-judge court was unfair in that the State had not had a proper opportunity to adduce its own evidence. They held too that the three-judge court had found that reduction in overcrowding would not wholly cure the violations of the Eighth Amendment but concluded that this did not detract from the proposition that overcrowding was the principal cause. They accepted that the failure of California's prisons to provide adequate medical and mental health care could be ascribed to a number of factors other than overcrowding, including 'chronic and worsening budget shortfalls, a lack of political will in favor of reform, inadequate facilities, and systemic administrative failures'.[84]

The majority accepted that before the three-judge court could order a reduction in prisoner numbers, it was obliged by the enabling statute to determine that 'no other relief will remedy the violation of the Federal right':[85] no prospective relief can be issued with respect to prison conditions unless it is narrowly drawn,

---

[83] Ibid 1934.
[84] Ibid 1936.
[85] Ibid 1937.

extends no further than necessary to correct the violation of a federal right, and is the least intrusive means necessary to correct the violation.[86]

However, they found that the evidence adduced supported their conclusion that an order limited to other remedies would not provide adequate relief to the constitutional rights breach. They expressed doubts about whether out-of-state transfers qualified as a population limit for the purposes of the legislation but noted that, in any case, California had made 'no effort to show that it has the resources and the capacity to transfer significantly larger numbers of prisoners'[87] on the basis that receiving prisons would be in compliance with Eighth Amendment conditions. They found that further building of sufficient facilities was not financially viable given California's fiscal crisis: 'The Court cannot ignore the political and fiscal reality behind this case. California's Legislature has not been willing or able to allocate the resources necessary to meet this crisis absent a reduction in overcrowding. There is no reason to believe it will begin to do so now'.[88] That led them to conclude that without the proposed reduction in the level of overcrowding 'there will be no efficacious remedy for the unconstitutional care of the sick and mentally ill in California's prisons'.[89]

The majority determined that the population limit was not illegitimate by reason of failure to comply with the 'narrow tailoring test', a test under the *PLRA* that requires a court to adopt a remedy that is 'narrowly tailored' to the constitutional violation and that gives 'substantial weight' to public safety.[90] They accepted that reducing overcrowding would have a variety of beneficial consequences for prisoners, other than facilitating timely and adequate access to medical care, including reducing the incidence of prison violence and ameliorating unsafe living conditions.[91] However, they found that this did not detract from the order of the three-judge court. They concluded that the order was neither overbroad nor inflexible as it left it to the State of California to accommodate differences between institutions. The majority observed that the State had not proposed any 'realistic alternative' to the order and held:[92]

---

[86]   18 USC 3626(a).
[87]   Ibid 1938. Compare the initiative by the Supreme Court of India in *Vishaka v State of Rajasthan* (1997) 6 SCC 241, after the rape of a social worker, to direct that nominated guidelines and norms be strictly observed in all work places for the preservation and enforcement of the right to gender equality of the working women with the force of law 'until suitable legislation is enacted to occupy the field'.
[88]   Ibid 1939.
[89]   Ibid 1939.
[90]   18 USC 3626(a). 131 S Ct 1910, 1939 (2011).
[91]   Ibid 1940.
[92]   Ibid 1941.

The State's desire to avoid a population limit, justified as according respect to state authority, creates a certain and unacceptable risk of continuing violations of the rights of sick and mentally ill prisoners, with the result that many more will die or needlessly suffer. The Constitution does not permit this wrong.

The majority found that ample expert evidence supported the three-judge court's order and that its weighing of evidence was not clearly erroneous. Thus, the two-year timeframe issued by the court (which did not take effect until the decision of the Supreme Court) was reasonable.[93] It noted that it was open to the State of California to move for modification of the timeframe or to amend its order on the basis of suitable expert evidence. It concluded that as the State of California 'makes further progress [toward reduction of its prison population], the three-judge court should evaluate whether its order remains appropriate'.[94]

Four of the Supreme Court's judges, including the Chief Justice, recorded emphatic dissents. Justices Scalia and Thomas, for instance, denounced the majority's position as the affirmation by the Court of 'perhaps the most radical injunction issued by a court in our Nation's history'.[95] They classified the proceedings that led to the decision of the three-judge court as a 'judicial travesty' and maintained that the decision of the majority of the Supreme Court took 'federal courts wildly beyond their institutional capacity'.[96]

Justices Scalia and Thomas held that it was insufficient for the plaintiffs to assert either that they were part of a medical system so defective that some of the plaintiffs inevitably would be injured by incompetent medical care, or that they had each suffered an Eighth Amendment violation merely by being a patient in a poorly run prison system. They argued that most of the plaintiffs 'will not be prisoners with medical conditions or severe mental illness; and many will undoubtedly be fine physical specimens who have developed intimidating muscles pumping iron in the prison gym'.[97] They recorded their dissent from the issuing of 'structural injunctions', which they denounced as 'turning judges into long-term administrators of complex social institutions' and as playing a role 'essentially indistinguishable from the role ordinarily played by executive officials'.[98]

Justices Scalia and Thomas accepted that the findings by the three-judge court had been open to it on the facts but maintained that the judges:[99]

---

93   Ibid 1943.
94   Ibid 1944.
95   Ibid 1950.
96   Ibid 1951.
97   Ibid 1953.
98   Ibid 1953.
99   Ibid 1954.

Of course were relying largely on their own beliefs about penology and recidivism. … What occurred here is no more judicial factfinding in the ordinary sense than would be the factual factfinding that deficit spending will not lower the unemployment or that the continued occupation of Iraq will decrease the risk of terrorism (emphasis in original).

They expressed the view that structural injunctions do not simply invite judges to indulge policy preferences but to indulge incompetent preferences. They denounced the prospect of judges running social institutions, especially prisons, and even more so when they make decisions to release convicted criminals. They also contended that the majority had grasped authority that appellate courts should not have in raising the option for the State of California to return to the three-judge court to seek modification of its order.

Justice Alito, supported by Chief Justice Roberts, also dissented, holding that the Constitution does not give federal judges the authority to run a penal system and that the Eighth Amendment imposes only a limited restraint on state authority. They found that the three-judge court exceeded its authority under the Constitution and the *PLRA*, the order for release of 46,000 prisoners being premature and unnecessary. They found the evidence relied upon by the three-judge court to be outdated and inappropriate by reason of their failing to permit the State of California to adduce fresh evidence. They accepted that general overcrowding contributed to many of the problems within the Californian penal healthcare system but found that 'it by no means follows that reducing overcrowding is the only or best or even a particularly good way to alleviate those problems'.[100] They noted that the Special Master had stated that even releasing 100,000 inmates (two thirds of the California system's entire inmate population) would leave the problem of providing mental health treatment 'largely unmitigated'.[101] They found that the three-judge court:[102]

– did not properly assess the alternative remedies proposed by the State;
– failed to distinguish between conditions desirable as a matter of public policy and conditions not meeting the minimum level mandated by the Constitution; and
– wrongly rejected remedies that would have taken a more extended period of time than prompt discharge of prisoners.

Justice Alito and Chief Justice Roberts noted that this was not the first occasion on which courts had ordered a release of prisoners. During the early 1990s,

---

[100]   Ibid 1963.
[101]   Ibid 1963.
[102]   Ibid 1963–4.

federal courts enforced a cap on the number of inmates in the Philadelphia penal system and thousands of inmates were set free: 'Although efforts were made to release only those prisoners who were least likely to commit violent crimes, that attempt was spectacularly unsuccessful. During an 18-month period, the Philadelphia police rearrested thousands of these prisoners for committing 9,732 new crimes.'[103] In dissent, they held that the three-judge court's reliance on expert testimony that the release in California would not produce a similarly dangerous experience was 'a fundamental and dangerous error' appropriate for correction, as the degree of deference applicable generally on appeal did not apply to such questions. They concluded:[104]

> The prisoner release ordered in this case is unprecedented, improvident, and contrary to the PLRA. In largely sustaining the decision below, the majority is gambling with the safety of the people of California. Before putting public safety at risk, every reasonable precaution should be taken. The decision below should be reversed, and the case should be remanded for this to be done.

10. CRUEL AND UNUSUAL PUNISHMENT

The Eighth Amendment to the United States Constitution and similar provisions in other jurisdictions and under international law trace their language and their spirit to the *Bill of Rights* of 1689, in which the English Parliament declared that 'excessive bail ought not to be required, nor excessive fines imposed, nor *cruel and unusual punishments inflicted*'[105] (emphasis added). The provision was largely inspired by the draconian punishments inflicted on Titus Oates,[106] an English perjurer who fabricated the 'Popish Plot', an alleged Catholic conspiracy to kill King Charles II, and who had made a variety of extraordinary and devastating accusations.[107] The punishments visited upon him by the High Court were as follows:

---

[103] Ibid 1966.
[104] Ibid 1967–8.
[105] (UK) 1 Wm & M sess 2, c 2 <http://australianpolitics.com/democracy-and-politics/bill-of-rights-1689>. See A F Granucci, '"Nor Cruel and Unusual Punishments Inflicted": The Original Meaning' (1969) 57(4) *California Law Review* 839.
[106] See J Lane, *Titus Oates* (A Dakers, 1949); J Pollock, *The Popish Plot* (Cambridge University Press, 2010).
[107] Amongst other things, Oates made 43 allegations against various members of Catholic religious orders, including over 500 Jesuits, accused the Queen's physician and the secretary to the Duchess of York of planning to assassinate the King, as well as accusing multiple members of the nobility and even the Queen of plotting to poison the King, Many of his allegations were directed toward what he alleged were the machinations of the Jesuits.

Ian Freckelton

First, The Court does order for a fine, that you pay 1000 marks upon each Indictment.

Secondly, That you be stript of all your Canonical Habits.

Thirdly, the Court does award, That you do stand upon the Pillory, and in the Pillory, here before Westminster-hall gate, upon Monday next, for an hour's time, between the hours of 10 and 12; with a paper over your head (which you must first walk with round about to all the Courts in Westminister-hall) declaring your crime. And that is upon the first Indictment.

Fourthly, (on the Second Indictment), upon Tuesday, you shall stand upon, and in the Pillory, at the Royal Exchange in London, for the space of an hour, between the hours of twelve and two; with the same inscription.

You shall upon the next Wednesday be whipped from Aldgate to Newgate.

Upon Friday, you shall be whipped from Newgate to Tyburn, by the hands of the common hangman.

But, Mr. Oates, we cannot but remember, there were several particular times you swore false about; and therefore, as annual commemorations, that it may be known to all people as long as you live, we have taken special care of you for an annual punishment.

Upon the 24th of April every year, as long as you live, you are to stand upon the Pillory and in the Pillory, at Tyburn, just opposite to the gallows, for the space of an hour, between the hours of ten and twelve.

You are to stand upon, and in the Pillory, here at Westminster-hall gate, every 9th of August, in every year, so long as you live. And that it may be known what we mean by it, 'tis to remember, what he swore about Mr. Ireland's being in town between the 8th and 12th of August.

You are to stand upon, and in the Pillory, at Charing-cross, on the 10th of August, every year, during your life, for an hour, between ten and twelve.

The like over-against the Temple gate, upon the 11th.

And upon the 2d of September, (which is another notorious time, which you cannot but be remember'd of) you are to stand upon, and in the Pillory, for the space of one hour, between twelve and two, at the Royal Exchange; and all this you are to do every year, during your life; and to be committed close prisoner, as long as you live.[108]

Oates' appeal to the House of Lords failed, but shortly afterwards the House of Commons resolved that 'the prosecution of Titus Oates, upon two counts of perjury by the court of King's-bench, was a design to stifle the Popish plot,

---

[108]   (1685) 10 St Tr 1227, 1316–7; [1685] KB 1316: <http://books.google.com.au/books?id=px2KCNCWwsIC&pg=PT629&dq=titus+oates&hl=en&ei=XvP5TYyvGo_wvwPWg_WVAw&sa=X&oi=book_result&ct=result&resnum=4&ved=0CDsQ6AEwAw#v=onepage&q=titus%20oates&f=false>. See also <http://press-pubs.uchicago.edu/founders/documents/amendVIIIs1.html>. In addition, the provision needs to be seen in the context of the 'Bloody Assizes': see J Tutchin, J Bent and J Dunton, *The Bloody Assizes* (J W Hodge, 1929).

and that the verdicts given thereupon were corrupt, and the judgments given thereupon were cruel and corrupt'.[109]

The Eighth Amendment, which was enacted in almost identical terms to the English Bill of Rights, was adopted as part of the United States Bill of Rights just under a century later in 1791. Article 5 of the United Nations Declaration of Human Rights in 1948 in due course was formulated to state, 'No one shall be subjected to torture or to cruel, inhuman or degrading treatment or punishment.' Article 7 of the International Covenant on Civil and Political Rights (ICCPR), adopted by the United Nations General Assembly on 16 December 1966 and in force from 23 March 1976, similarly was drafted to provide that: 'No one shall be subjected to torture or to cruel, inhuman or degrading treatment or punishment. In particular, no one shall be subjected without his free consent to medical or scientific experimentation.'[110] In 1984, the United Nations adopted the Convention against Torture and other Cruel, Inhuman or Degrading Treatment or Punishment.[111] Similarly, there are the 1987 European Convention for the Prevention of Torture and Inhuman or Degrading Treatment or Punishment (as amended by the 1993 Protocols) and the 1985 Inter-American Convention to Prevent and Punish Torture.[112]

The United Nations Human Rights Committee has stated that the purpose of Article 7 of the ICCPR is 'to protect both the dignity and the physical and mental integrity of the individual' and that its prohibition relates to acts that cause either physical pain or mental suffering to a victim, extending therefore to corporal punishment, potentially to prolonged solitary confinement of a detained or imprisoned person, and intended to protect, children, pupils and patients in a variety of institutions.[113]

In Victoria and the Australian Capital Territory, Australia, this has translated to s 12 of the *Charter of Human Rights and Responsibilities Act 2006* (Vic) (the

---

[109]   (1685) 10 St Tr 1227 at 1329.

[110]   See S Joseph, J Schultz and M Castan, *The International Covenant on Civil and Political Rights* (Oxford University Press, 2nd ed, 2004) ch 9. See also Article 3 of the European Convention on Human Rights (ECHR); M Amos, *Human Rights Law* (Hart Publishing, 2006) 205ff. See also *R (on the application of Munjaz) v Mersey Care NHS Trust* [2003] EWCA Civ 1036, [2004] QB 395, in relation to supervised confinement of patients for the protection of others from significant harm.

[111]   *Convention against Torture and other Cruel, Inhuman or Degrading Treatment or Punishment*, <http://www2.ohchr.org/english/law/cat.htm>.

[112]   See generally R K M Smith, *International Human Rights* (Oxford University Press, 2nd ed, 2005) ch 14.

[113]   Human Rights Committee, General Comment, Art 7 (47th session, 1992), Compilation of General Comments and General Recommendations Adopted by Human Rights Treaty Bodies, UN Doc HRI\GE1\Rev 1 an 30 (1994): <http://www1.umn.edu/humanrts/gencomm/hrcom20.htm>.

Charter) and s 10 of the *Human Rights Act 2008* (ACT), which are framed in substantively the same terms. Section 12 of the Charter provides that:

> A person must not be-
> (a) subjected to torture; or
> (b) treated or punished in a cruel, inhuman or degrading way; or
> (c) subjected to medical or scientific experimentation or treatment without his or her full, free and informed consent.[114]

Relevant too is s 22(1) of the Charter, which prescribes that those deprived of liberty have the right to be 'treated with humanity and with respect for the inherent dignity of the human person'.[115] However, even in Victoria (and the Australian Capital Territory), which has a level of human rights protection accorded by legislation, enforcement of such rights is highly problematic. The principal mechanism for protection against abuses of the kind described in *Plata v Brown* would probably be via an injunction against a continuing commission of negligence, if a personal injuries action had already been filed in court.

In the United States, the Eighth Amendment has more teeth in certain circumstances, such as those facilitated by the *Prison Litigation Reform Act 1995* (US). The Eighth Amendment, which has been held to apply to the States,[116] has been the subject of extensive and controversial jurisprudence, much of it concerning the imposition of the death penalty. In *Furman v Georgia*,[117] Justice Brennan held that there are four principles by which a particular punishment may be evaluated to determine whether it is 'cruel and unusual':

–   The primary principle, the 'essential predicate', is that a punishment must not be so severe as to be degrading to the dignity of human beings.
–   The State must not arbitrarily inflict a severe punishment.
–   A severe punishment must not be unacceptable to contemporary society.
–   A severe punishment must not be excessive in the sense of being unnecessary.[118]

---

[114]   This is identical to 12(1)(e) of the *Constitution of the Republic of South Africa 1996*. Section 10 of the *Human Rights Act 2004* (ACT) is in almost identical terms.

[115]   See too *Human Rights Act 2004* (ACT), s 19(1); Article 10(1) of the ICCPR. See generally C Evans and S Evans, *Australian Bills of Rights* (Lexis Nexis, 2008) 1.107ff; N O'Neill, S Rice and R Douglas, *Retreat from Injustice: Human Rights Law in Australia* (Federation Press, 2004) ch 10.

[116]   *Robinson v California*, 370 US 660 (1962). See generally O'Neill, Rice and Douglas, ibid.

[117]   408 US 238, 271–82 (1972).

[118]   For a useful early analysis of such matters, see M J Radin, 'The Jurisprudence of Death: Evolving Standards for the Cruel and Unusual Punishments Clause' (1978) 126 *University of Pennsylvania Law Review* 990.

In *Trop v Dulles*,[119] Chief Justice Earl Warren highlighted the plasticity of its application: 'The [Eighth] Amendment must draw its meaning from the evolving standards of decency that mark the progress of a maturing society.' Thus, by contrast with execution by firing squad, drawing and quartering, public dissecting, burning alive, and disembowelling would all constitute breaches of the Eighth Amendment.[120] The death penalty has been held to be constitutional[121] (with two justices dissenting) but not for rape,[122] even child rape.[123] Prison officials have been held to violate the Eighth Amendment if they have acted with 'deliberate indifference' to inmate safety or health but only when aware that a consequence of their conduct is likely to be a substantial risk of serious harm and they disregard the risk by failing to take reasonable measures to abate it.[124]

Along similar lines, in *Tyrer v United Kingdom*,[125] the European Court of Human Rights held the birching of a 15-year-old boy was degrading punishment inconsistent with Article 3 of the ECHR and contrary to 'present-day conditions' and the development of 'commonly accepted standards'. However, in *Soering v United Kingdom*[126] it held that developments in penal and social policy had not reached a point that warranted the interpretation of Article 3 as inconsistent with the death penalty, although it did determine that it was a violation to extradite a person with a mental illness to the United States to face a charge of murder for which he could be convicted and sentenced to death.

Justice Ackermann in the South African case of *Dodo v The State*[127] has held that 'the impairment of human dignity, in some form and to some degree, must be involved' in a breach of the South African preclusion on cruel and inhuman treatment.

In *Kracke v Mental Health Review Board*,[128] Bell J held that the purpose of the Victorian right to freedom from cruel, inhuman or degrading treatment or punishment is:

> to protect people from various forms of ill-treatment which, although not torture, still attain a minimum level of severity and intensity in the suffering inflicted. The right expresses the fundamental values of the personal dignity and integrity of the

---

119 356 US 86, 101 (1958).
120 *Wilkerson v Utah*, 99 US 130 (1878).
121 *Furman v Georgia*, 408 US 238 (1972); see too *Gregg v Georgia*, 428 US 153 (1976).
122 *Coker v Georgia*, 433 US 584 (1977).
123 *Kennedy v Louisiana*, 554 US 407 (2008).
124 See *Wilson v Seiter*, 501 US 294 (1991); *Farmer v Brennan*, 511 US 825 (1994).
125 [1978] ECHR 2; (1979) 2 EHRR 1.
126 [1989] ECHR 14; (1989) 11 EHRR 439.
127 2001 (3) SA 382 [35].
128 [2009] VCAT 646 [574]–[575].

individual and the physical and psychological inviolability of their person, but on a broader plane than the right to freedom from torture.

11. THE REPERCUSSIONS OF *BROWN V PLATA*

As Terry Carney[129] has observed: 'Mental health law concerns "citizenship" in its wider sense – of respect for civil rights and social participation.' The contested majority decision of the United States Supreme Court in *Brown v Plata* will have more symbolic value than actual effect upon the component of the custodial population of California that has or potentially has a mental illness. The decision written by Justice Kennedy is a landmark activation of the preclusion on cruel and unusual punishment and an assertive response of the highest court in the United States to a violation of the right to be free from punishment of the kind against which the English Parliament took a stand in the aftermath of the sentencing of Titus Oates 1685. Arguably, it is the most significant flowering of a right which dates back to the English Bill of Rights.

For persons who are incarcerated, the *Brown v Plata* decision is a powerful statement that sentenced prisoners are not a second-class component of the community without entitlements to dignity and care.[130] Perhaps most importantly, and controversially, the decision constitutes a robust assertion that it is the business of the courts to do that which is necessary to protect such rights, even to the extent that such enforcement involves fundamental and radical structural injunctions to change the functioning of the custodial system.

For those committed to humane penal reform, the decision will provide an important fillip as the majority's denunciation of the dreadful conditions of overcrowding in California prisons graphically reveals the consequences of excessively congregate living – inevitable barbarity of confinement and unacceptable risks to the health of those compelled not just to live away from the remainder of the community but in oppressive conditions. The majority asserted the right of prisoners to be treated with dignity and denounced their brutal treatment. It is to be hoped that the decision will encourage rethinking of excessive resort to imprisonment in an era that has been strongly attracted to simplistic 'law and order politics' and to punishment and community protection as the principal purposes of sentencing. The *Brown v Plata* decision should

---

[129] T Carney, 'Mental Health Law in Postmodern Society: Time for New Paradigms?' (2003) 10(1) *Psychiatry, Psychology and Law* 12.

[130] See also the protection, albeit somewhat limited, extended in the decision of *Kudla v Poland, 2000.* ECtHR Application no 30210/96. Judgment 20 October 2000. See also P M Prior, 'Mentally Disordered Offenders and the European Court of Human Rights' (2007) 30 *International Journal of Law and Psychiatry* 546.

sensitise those working in the correctional environment and lawyers who purport to act in defence of human rights; the 'cruel and unusual punishment' preclusion existing in legislation in a number of jurisdictions and in many international human rights instruments has the potential to provide real and meaningful protection to vulnerable persons behind bars who rely upon the State for their dignity and wellbeing.

12. VINDICATORY DAMAGES

There are occasions when deprivations of liberty take place in a way that breaches fundamental rights and freedoms. In certain Commonwealth countries, there has been a dalliance in such cases with the potential for 'vindicatory damages' to be awarded to the victim. In *Attorney General of Trinidad and Tobago v Ramanoop (Trinidad and Tobago)*,[131] for instance, the Privy Council accepted that, when exercising its constitutional jurisdiction, a court:

> is concerned to uphold, or vindicate, the constitutional right which has been contravened. A declaration by the court will articulate the fact of the violation, but in most cases more will be required than words. If the person wronged has suffered damage, the court may award him compensation. ... An award of compensation will go some distance towards vindicating the infringed constitutional right. But how far it goes will depend on the circumstances, but in principle it may well not suffice. The fact that the right violated was a constitutional right adds an extra dimension to the wrong. An additional award, not necessarily of substantial size, may be needed to reflect the sense of public outrage, emphasise the importance of the constitutional right and the gravity of the breach, and deter further breaches. ... Although such an award, where called for, is likely in most cases to cover much the same ground in financial terms as would an award by way of punishment in the strict sense of retribution, punishment in the latter sense is not its object. Accordingly, the expressions 'punitive damages' or 'exemplary damages' are better avoided as descriptions of this type of additional award.

In *Ashley v Chief Constable of Sussex*,[132] Lord Ashley held in obiter that vindicatory damages could be awarded for the tort of battery or trespass when conduct of the police had caused the death of the victim. However, the Supreme Court in *Lumba (WL) v Secretary of State for the Home Department*[133] doubted the availability of such damages more generally. It did so in the context of applications for compensation for the detention of persons pending deportation technically being

---

[131]   [2005] UKPC 15. See also *Merson v Cartwright and Attorney General* [2005] UKPC 38; *Fraser v Judicial and Legal Services Commission* [2008] UKPC 25; *Inniss v Attorney General* [2008] UKPC 42; see also *Taunoa v Attorney-General* [2008] 1 NZLR 429.

[132]   [2008] UKHL 25; [2008] 1 AC 962 [22].

[133]   [2011] UKSC 12.

determined to constitute false imprisonment. Lord Dyson (with whose judgment Lords Hope, Walker, Collins and Kerry and Lady Hale agreed) emphasized, 'Exemplary damages apart, the purposes of damages is to compensate the victims of civil wrongs for the loss and damage that the wrongs have been caused.'[134] He commented:

> [T]he implications of awarding vindicatory damages in the present case would be far-reaching. Undesirable uncertainty would result. If they were awarded here, then they could in principle be awarded in any case involving a battery of false imprisonment by an arm of the state. I see no justification for letting such an unruly horse loose on our law.[135]

Lord Collins, to similar effect, held that

> [t]o make a separate award for vindicatory damages is to confuse the purpose of damages awards with the nature of the award. A declaration, or an award of nominal damages, may itself have a vindicatory purpose and effect. So too a conventional award of damages may serve a vindicatory purpose.[136]

The majority awarded only nominal damages. A consequence of the decision is that vindicatory damages in false imprisonment cases will generally not be available, and only orthodox compensatory damages will be awarded by courts.

13. CONCLUSIONS

It is cold comfort to detainees whose human rights are infringed to achieve notional acknowledgment of such infringement without meaningful redress being accorded to them. The Supreme Court of the United Kingdom decision in *Lumba* highlights the limitations of pecuniary awards for breaches of rights for persons who are in lawful detention.

However, there can be no doubt that habeas corpus actions remain the most effective form of assertion of rights in the form of securing release from unlawful detention when persons are detained in any form of custody that is contrary to law. In Australia, the *Antunovic v Dawson* decision has been a useful reminder of this.

---

134   Ibid [95].
135   Ibid [101]
136   Ibid [236].

While Canadian and some United States jurisprudence have contemplated the potential for the writ to be used where conditions within such custody are unlawful or oppressive, there is no clear authority to such effect in Australia or the United Kingdom. Thus decisions, such as that of *Plata v Brown* by the United States Supreme Court, are significant as they create the potential for such custody to be determined to be a breach of the right to be free of cruel, inhuman or degrading punishment and thereby to be unlawful. It is to be hoped that such jurisprudence will continue to evolve internationally, spurred on by the robust and humane statements of principle from the majority in *Brown v Plata*.

HUMPTY DUMPTY AND RISK ASSESSMENT: A REPLY TO SLOBOGIN

Ian Coyle and Robert Halon

When is preventive detention[1] justified on the basis that an individual convicted of a serious sexual or violent offence is considered likely to commit other offences in the future? This issue, at the most basic level, involves the interaction of the law with psychology. Although psychology and the law are uneasy bedfellows, the need for constant dialogue between the two disciplines is obvious. Nowhere is this dialogue more important than when dealing with preventive detention, since legal decisions in this domain are incontrovertibly founded on psychological assessment and statistical evidence as to the likelihood of recidivism of those whom the state seeks to detain at the expiration of their sentence or otherwise sanction with preventive detention.

Simplistically, psychological assessment and the application of the law in this domain revolve around the concept of an unacceptable risk to the community should sexual and violent offenders be released to or allowed to remain in the community by virtue of their likelihood of committing further serious offences. From the early 1990s, the legal response to dealing with the risk of recidivism posed by sexual and violent offenders has been codified under sexually violent predator (SVP) legislation in the USA. The various states in the Commonwealth of Australia enacted substantially similar legislation in the first decade of the new millennium.[2]

---

[1] In the USA, this is referred to as civil commitment: the effect is the same for those who are incarcerated or have their liberty otherwise curtailed irrespective of the legal terminology applied to these strictures. Throughout this article, the term 'preventive detention' is used for economy of language where appropriate.

[2] The *Dangerous Prisoners Sexual Offenders Act* 2003 (Qld); *Dangerous Sexual Offenders Act* 2006 (WA); *Crimes (Serious Sex Offenders) Act* 2006 (NSW); *Serious Sex Offenders (Detention and Supervision) Act* 2009 (VIC). For analysis, see the contribution of Gogarty, Bartl and Keyzer in this volume.

Since legal standards of proof and evidence[3] inform the bases upon which psychological assessments of such offenders are to be made, it is apposite to deal with these issues first.[4] A convenient place to start with this is the argument advanced by Slobogin[5] in this book, wherein he advances seven grounds, the conjoint operation of which would warrant preventive detention. Two of them are the focus of this chapter:

> (5) The evidentiary rule that, when government seeks preventive confinement, it may only prove its case using actuarial-based probability estimates or, in their absence, previous antisocial conduct; (6) the evidentiary rule that the subject of preventive detention may rebut the government's case concerning risk with clinical risk assessments, even if they are not as provably reliable as actuarial prediction...

In evaluating these propositions, it is necessary to consider the legal and statistical bases of proof. These bases of proof are quite different and, in fact, may never be reconciled since the law is verbally based and not amenable to categorical reduction, whereas the scientific standard of proof is mathematically based. Nonetheless, in the domain of SVP risk assessment they are inextricably interwoven. Reconciliation, at least of sorts, between these bases of proof is then fundamental to the integrity of the evidentiary rules posited by Slobogin, iterated above.

In what follows, this reconciliation is attempted without recourse to mathematical theorems wherever possible precisely because the law is verbally based. Experts in SVP cases are required to be able to explain statistical and epistemological concepts so that the triers of fact can understand the concepts involved without recourse to statistical formulae which most venire jurors–and judges for that matter–cannot be expected to understand. Judicial education can only go so far when complex statistical concepts are involved and empirical evidence vis-à-vis assessment of dangerousness is rapidly evolving.

To further compound the difficulty in explaining statistical and epistemological concepts to the triers of fact, there is evidence that the way in which statistical information from actuarial instruments is presented affects the likelihood that

---

[3]   For a more thorough exposition of the legal concepts involved see, generally: C Slobogin, *Proving the Unprovable – The Role of Law, Science and Speculation – Adjudicating Culpability and Dangerousness* (Oxford University Press, 2007); B McSherry and P Keyzer, *Sex Offenders and Preventive Detention – Politics, Policy and Practice* (Federation Press, 2009).

[4]   Codes of Ethics adopted by Psychological Societies are also germane here, but they are subordinate to the law and, where relevant, legally adopted Codes of Conduct. It is beyond the scope of this chapter to deal with these issues.

[5]   See Christopher Slobogin's contribution to this volume.

venire jurors will use an actuarial risk estimate in their decision to civilly commit a particular respondent.[6]

This point has loomed large in a number of seminal English and Welsh cases where the England and Wales Court of Criminal Appeal has robustly rejected the application of Bayesian analysis[7] to non-DNA cases (*R v Denis Adams* [1996] 2 Cr App R 467; *R v Adams* (No 2) [1998] 1 Cr App R 377; *R v Doney* [1997] 1 Cr App R 369).

There are two underlying themes evident in the judgments on which this rejection is founded. First, the statistical basis for calculating Bayes Theorem in many non-DNA cases involving pattern recognition is startlingly weak or non-existent. This decision is hard to disagree with.[8] Second, as Rose LJ noted in *Adams*:

> Quite apart from these general objections, as the present case graphically demonstrates, to introduce Bayes Theorem, *or any similar method* (emphasis added), into a criminal trial plunges the jury into inappropriate and unnecessary realms of theory and complexity deflecting them from their proper task.[9]

This begs the question: what is the proper task of the jury? Rose LJ asserted in *Adams* that it is to 'assess the evidence by common sense and their knowledge of the world and not by reference to a formula'.[10]

The thrust of these decisions has been recently affirmed in a heavily redacted, recent judgment of the England and Wales Court of Appeal (*R v T* EWCA Crim 2439 (2010)) involving a forensic scientist giving evidence as to the comparison between types of footwear where it was determined that:

> [i]n the light of the strong criticism of this court in the 1990s of using Bayes theorem (sic) before the jury in cases where there was no reliable statistical evidence, the practice of using a Bayesian approach and likelihood ratios to formulate opinions

---

[6] J Monahan, N Scurich and R S John, 'Innumeracy and Unpacking: Bridging the Nomothetic/Idiographic Divide in Violence Risk Assessment' (University of Virginia School of Law Public Law and Legal Theory Working Paper Series 2012–04, in press *Law and Human Behavior*) <http://ssrn.com/abstract=1993261>.

[7] It is, perhaps, necessary to point out that Bayes' Theorem has stood the test of mathematical time since it was posthumously presented to the Royal Society in 1763.

[8] See generally: W C Thompson and S A Cole, 'Psychological Aspects of Forensic Identification Evidence' in M Costanzo, D Krauss and K Pezdek (eds), *Expert Psychological Testimony for the Courts* (Routledge, 2006) 31–68; D M Risinger et al, 'The Daubert/Kumho Implications of Observer Effects in Forensic Science: Hidden Problems of Expectation and Suggestion' (2002) 90 *California Law Review* 1–56.

[9] *R v Denis Adams* [1996] 2 Cr App R 467; *R v Adams* (No 2) [1998] 1 Cr App R 377 [481].

[10] Ibid.

placed before a jury without that process being disclosed and debated in open court is contrary to principles of open justice.[11]

Considerable comment has been made on the problems of relying on common sense, ill defined as it is generally and in criminal trials specifically, when the application of life experiences and common sense can lead the triers of fact into unavoidable error.[12] Yet nowhere are the well-known problems with the triers of fact relying on their general knowledge of the world and common sense more likely to lead to error than in the contentious area of risk assessment of dangerousness. This requires a deep understanding of complex epistemological and statistical concepts such that matters involving preventive detention must proceed on the bases of expert evidence if miscarriages of justice are to be avoided.[13]

Despite the perorations of the England and Wales Court of Criminal Appeal, Bayes' Theorem is incontrovertibly correct, albeit that the results from its application are counterintuitive and defy common sense. It is also incontrovertibly apposite to apply in SVP cases, *provided that the statistical bases on which it rests in any particular case are explicated in evidence.*[14] Indeed, the application of Bayes' Theorem to actuarial approaches to risk assessment in SVP cases has been argued for most recently.[15] This aside, whichever way one looks at *R v T* and those precedents upon which it is founded, it demonstrates the import of attempting to reconcile the legal and scientific bases of proof in SVP cases. This follows.

---

[11]   *R v T EWCA* Crim 2439 (2010) [108 iii].

[12]   See, generally: A Tversky and D Khaneman, 'Judgment under Uncertainty: Heuristics and Biases' (1974) 185 *Science* 4157, 1124–31; I R Coyle, D Field and G Miller, 'The Blindness of the Eye-Witness' (2008) 82 *The Australian Law Journal* 471–98. I R Coyle, 'The Cogency of Risk Assessments' (2011) 18(2) *Psychiatry, Psychology and Law* 270–96; I R Coyle and D Field, 'Psychology from the Bench' (2011) *Psychiatry, Psychology and Law*, iFirst publication: <http://dx.doi.org/10.1080/13218719.2011.622430>.

[13]   Coyle, above n 12.

[14]   Parenthetically, it might be noted that the expert involved in *R v T* gave different definitions of likelihood ratios. These definitions were conflated with probabilities and, with a stunningly egregious example of muddle-headed thinking, verbal descriptors for the proposition that latent and exemplar specimens matched were equated with a 'Value of likelihood ratio'. For example, 'Moderate Support' was equated to a 'Value of likelihood ratio' of 10–100. There is no scientific basis for applying this verbal descriptor to such a ratio, assuming that it means anything in the first instance: none whatsoever. In short, from a scientific viewpoint the judgment is sound, although the implications of it, by extension, to the putative admissibility of a significant branch of statistics are troubling, if not clearly in error.

[15]   N Scurich and R S John, 'A Bayesian Approach to the Group versus Individual Prediction Controversy in Actuarial Risk Assessment' (2012) 36(3) *Law and Human Behavior* 237–46.

1. SCIENTIFIC AND LEGAL STANDARDS OF PROOF

The default position in science is unambiguous: for a proposition to be proven it has to be proven to at least 95% accuracy (p=0.95).[16] Recently, in recognition of the problems posed in SVP assessment, statistical standards to lower degrees of certainty have been incorporated in various references where actuarial instruments are considered.[17]

From a legal perspective, determining whether an individual poses an unacceptable level of risk is by no means clear-cut. Resolution of the apparently straightforward proposition that an individual must exhibit a certain amount of dangerousness to warrant preventive detention hinges upon the legal concept of *degrees of certainty*. What, it might be asked, is a reasonable degree of certainty from a legal perspective and how can this be established? Guidance on these points provided by the superior courts in jurisdictions that have embraced the common law is anything but clear.

The 'balance of probabilities' or 'the preponderance of the evidence' is the minimum standard of proof required in most civil matters. This may, for the purpose of this article, be considered as equating to a probability of above chance to the slightest degree: that is above 50%.[18] In criminal matters, the standard of proof is 'beyond a reasonable doubt'. This is not easily equated to a statistical probability, and it is not defined in any authoritative judgments of the superior courts in Common Law jurisdictions in terms of statistical probability.[19] However, studies on jurors in the USA indicate that this is equated with a probability of

---

[16]   This is not entirely correct. In science, the null hypothesis is disproved, to a defined standard of certainty, which enables the obverse hypothesis to be accepted. The null hypothesis is a hypothesis of no difference; it is formulated for the express purpose of being capable of rejection. If is rejected the alternative hypothesis may be accepted. Suppose, for example, that one wished to test the hypothesis that all humans born with hands had five fingers. The only way this could be completely proven would be to observe every human on the planet. However, one could disprove the opposite or null hypothesis, to a specific degree of certainty or probability, by observing a sufficiently large sample of humans, which would then imply that the original hypothesis was correct. The degree of certainty in such a process is never absolute; it may approach a probability of 1.0 (ie 100%) but it can never obtain this level of certainty unless all members of a class (in these case humans) are observed. This example is not far-fetched or fanciful since polydactyly (having more that five digits on either hand or foot) clearly exists, albeit that it is rare.

[17]   See, for example: T S Donaldson, B R Abbott and C Michie, 'Problems with the Static-99R Prediction Estimates and Confidence Intervals' (2012) 4 *Open Access Journal of Forensic Psychology* 1–23.

[18]   In statistical terms, probability (p) ranges from p=0 to p=1.0: these probabilities are equivalent to 0% and 100%. By convention, an event which has, even by the most minute amount, a greater than 50% probability of occurring may be expressed as p > 0.5.

[19]   Indeed, it is tantamount to legal heresy in Australia to try and equate standards of proof such as 'beyond reasonable doubt' with percentages or probabilities: see, generally: *Green v The*

---

approximately 90% (p = 0.90). Professor Slobogin[20] also cites this figure with approbation.

In cases involving preventive SVP detention, referred to with an act of legal legerdemain as 'civil' commitment in the USA, a 'middle ground' standard of proof is adopted; 'clear and convincing' proof is adopted (*Addington v Texas* 441 U.S. 418 (1979)) in many states. In *Addington*, the appellant was described, according to expert psychiatric testimony, as suffering from 'psychotic schizophrenia and had paranoid tendencies'.[21] He had also caused substantial property damage both at his own apartment and at his parents' home, refused to attend outpatient treatment programs and had escaped several times from mental hospitals. The US Supreme Court has not ruled that the 'clear and convincing' standard of proof applies to sexual and violent (SVP) offenders who do not require commitment to a hospital or equivalent institution, but it is likely that the same minimum standard would be held to apply. In part, this is because the US Supreme Court has also ruled that one of the conditions for such civil commitment is the existence of a mental abnormality that affects volitional control (*Kansas v Hendricks* 521 US 346 (1997)). Mental abnormality does not necessarily equate to the psychotic state of the appellant in *Addington* but might be founded upon what simply may be personality disorders included in nosologies of mental disorders such as the Diagnostic and Statistical Manual of Mental Disorder (DSM-IV-TR being the current version).[22] In 2002, the US Supreme court circumscribed the application of the *Kansas* law to those having 'serious difficulty in controlling behavior'.[23] However, some states have chosen to require the 'beyond a reasonable doubt' standard for SVP commitment.

It is even more problematic to try to assign a probability to the 'clear and convincing' standard of proof, but studies on jurors indicate that this is perceived to be somewhere around 70% (p > 0.70). Professor Slobogin[24] also cites this figure with approbation. A similar 'middle ground' standard of proof exists in Australia

---

    Queen (1971) 126 CLR 28 [at 31–33]; *R v Cavkic, Ahtanasi & Clarke* [2005] VSCA 182 (2 August 2005).

20   Slobogin, above n 3, 119.
21   *Addington v Texas* 441 US 418, 441 (1979).
22   There is debate about whether personality disorders are mental disorders within the ambit of SVP legislation in the USA. There is also the issue that there is no evidence that having a personality disorder affects volitional control *per se*. These issues, although doubtless important, are beyond the scope of this chapter.
23   *Kansas v Crane* 534 US 407 (2002).
24   Slobogin, above n 3, 119.

in civil[25] matters: the *Briginshaw* standard.[26] However, whether this applies to preventive detention in Australia is impossible to tell from consideration of the legislation.

In Australia, the standard of proof required before an individual can be preventively detained is opaque. Legislation that is more or less parallel with that adopted by the 20 US states having provisions for civil commitment has been adopted in the various states of the Commonwealth of Australia. However, no two jurisdictions define the requisite standard of proof in the same way, albeit that the standards of proof in Western Australia and Queensland are substantially similar.[27] Thus, the Western Australian Legislation indicates that the court has to be satisfied per s 7(2)(a) 'by acceptable and cogent evidence' and per s 7(2)(b) 'to a high degree of probability' that the offender poses 'a serious danger to the community' and 'that there is an unacceptable risk that, if the person were not subject to a continuing detention order or a supervision order, the person would commit a serious sexual offence'. In other states in Australia, the position is very different.

For example, the *Crimes (Serious Sex Offenders) Act* 2006 (NSW) provides, per s 2, that:

> [a]n extended supervision order may be made if and only if the Supreme Court is satisfied to a high degree of probability that the offender poses an unacceptable risk of committing a serious sex offence if he or she is not kept under supervision. And, in s 2(A): The Supreme Court is not required to determine that the risk of a person committing a serious sex offence is more likely than not in order to determine that the person poses an unacceptable risk of committing a serious sex offence.

In New South Wales, then, an unacceptable risk does not equate to a probability of more than 50% (p > 0.5) for the purpose of this legislation. This of course raises the question: what does 'unacceptable risk' equate to in percentage/probability terms? It also raises the prospect that the gravity of harm that an offender, if released into the community, may commit is conflated with the risk of recidivism.

---

[25] Adopting the same legal ledgermain as has been employed in the USA, some preventive detention legislation regimes enacted in the various states, such as Victoria, operate under a quasi-civil basis.
[26] *Briginshaw v Briginshaw* (1938) HCA 60 CLR 336; as a matter of law it is not entirely correct to state that the *Briginshaw* test changes the level of certainty required. It actually deals with the weight of the evidence adduced in civil matters such that the persuasiveness of one's case may have to increase in proportion the seriousness of the allegations – but in practical terms the result is the same.
[27] See n 2.

The Victorian *Sex Offenders (Detention and Supervision) Act 2009* is a standout in terms of obfuscation. Coyle[28] provides a detailed consideration of this egregious legislation, the thrust of which follows:

> In considering whether an offender 'poses an unacceptable risk of committing a relevant offence if a supervision order is not made' in accordance with the provisions of s 9(1) the conjoint operation of ss 9(2)-9(6) need to be considered. Promisingly, s 9(2) states:
> 'On hearing the application the court may decide that it is satisfied as required by subsection (1) only if it is satisfied (a) by acceptable, *cogent* evidence; and (b) to a high degree of probability that the evidence is of sufficient weight to justify the decision (emphasis added).'

> The promise held out by this section is negated by s 9(5), which states:
> 'For avoidance of doubt the court may determine under subsection (1) that an offender poses an unacceptable risk of committing a relevant offence even if the likelihood than the offender will commit a relevant offence is less than a likelihood of more likely than not.'

> The *reductio ad absurdum* arrived at by considering the conjoint operation of these sections is readily apparent. In Victoria, at least in the law courts where this act is applied, 'a high degree of probability' does not mean 'likely', 'likely' does not mean more probable than not and 'sufficient weight' becomes a meaningless legal abstraction.

One can only imagine how jurors would interpret this legislation and the difficulties a judge would have in trying to give them directions on this point.[29] However, unlike in the USA,[30] a judge sitting alone always makes decisions on preventive detention in Australia.

The legal tests then for 'dangerousness' and 'unacceptable risk' are anything but clear. Navigation through the legal maze erected by various legislations makes it clear that the standards of proof can range, in statistical terms, from significantly below 50% ($p < 0.5$) to above 90% ($p > 0.9$). To state the blindingly obvious, this is an extraordinary range of legal standards of proof for what may be exactly the same ostensible offences and risks. But this is not the end of the matter as far as proof is concerned. To reiterate, in the USA determination of a mental abnormality, even if such abnormality is relatively minor, is a prerequisite to preventive detention, but this is not the case in Australia. This difference might not be of import in all

---

[28]   Coyle, above n 12, 278–9.
[29]   For more detailed comment on these problems, see Coyle, above n 12, 279–80.
[30]   In the USA, either the defence or prosecution can request trial by jury in SVP civil commitment matters.

cases, but it surely is in some. For example, if an offender is considered to have Paraphilia Not Otherwise Specified (PNOS) in accordance with DSM-IV-TR, this would satisfy the grounds of mental abnormality and, thus, the issue of risk of recidivism could then be considered. In Australia no such diagnosis is necessary before considering the issue of risk, a point that is considered later.

2.   RELEVANCE, ADMISSIBILITY AND SUFFICIENCY OF EXPERT EVIDENCE

It is trite to state that evidence must be relevant to the issue at hand before it can be admitted; so much is axiomatic at law. It must also satisfy other tests of admissibility.[31] There are numerous legal tests that can apply in any particular matter, but in the context of this chapter it is meaningful to focus on a few that are pertinent to SVP cases. For a start, the probative value of any evidence that the defence or prosecution seek to be adduced must exceed its prejudicial value. In addition it must satisfy what may be termed the sufficiency test.[32]

Slobogin cites a well-known treatise on the law of evidence[33] in the USA on this point:

> Whether the entire body of one party's evidence is sufficient to go to the jury is one question. Whether a particular item of evidence is relevant to the case is quite another ... Thus, the common objection that the inference for which the fact is offered 'does not necessarily follow' is untenable. It poses a standard of conclusiveness that very few single items of circumstantial evidence ever could meet. A brick is not a wall.

Commenting on this, Slobogin observes:

> One might note, however, that in a substantial majority of sentencing and commitment cases the expert prediction testimony is the entire body of evidence. In such cases, the testimony is both the brick and the wall. Then shouldn't the sufficiency and admissibility enquires be merged? ... If so, two other responses, one empirical and one legal, are possible.

---

[31]   The difference between the two has not been appreciated by some authors writing from a psychological/statistical perspective, as is discussed later in this chapter.

[32]   The situation that obtains, for the purposes of this chapter, is identical in the USA and Australia vis-à-vis relevance, admissibility and sufficiency, or sufficient weight (often abbreviated to weight) as it is commonly referred to in Australia. See, generally: D Field, *Queensland Evidence Law* (LexisNexis Butterworths, 2nd ed, 2011) 3–15.

[33]   *McCormick on Evidence*, 1999 [at 640–641] cited in Slobogin, above n 3, 119.

It is hard to disagree with the initial proposition iterated: in SVP cases expert prediction testimony is paramount. Leaving this to one side for the moment, Slobogin[34] then proceeds to argue, considering the clear and convincing evidence standard, that 'expert prediction testimony might be considered clear and convincing proof any time the AUC value for the methodology in question is .75 or higher' for the empirical test. The legal test is, so he avers, dealt with by defining 'dangerousness' 'in such a way that error rates are minimized'. As an example, he posits that:

> [i]f the word 'likely' is equated with a 51% probability, then proving beyond a reasonable doubt that a person is dangerous under this definition would only require a 46 percent likelihood (0.9x.51) that this person would harm another.

Both of these arguments are specious, as is discussed in what follows.

3. THE COGENCY OF RISK ASSESSMENTS

At the risk of simplification, the legal tests of relevance, admissibility and sufficiency may be subsumed under the *en globo* heading of cogency: that which is capable of proving. The courts must decide, in each and every case involving preventive detention, whether *that particular individual* poses a risk of dangerousness. From a scientific perspective, the issue is to provide the triers of fact with cogent information to assist them in their deliberations. Since examination of the tests that Slobogin[35] proposes needs to be conducted in this light, it is apposite to deal first with the empirical tests he proposes against which the cogency of actuarial instruments may be judged.

The proposition that the product of the probabilities adopted for 'beyond reasonable doubt' (0.9) and 'likely' (0.51) is sufficient to prove beyond a reasonable doubt that a person is dangerous and would harm another is a complete travesty of mathematics and logic. The act of multiplication does not change the multiplier and the multiplicand since this would render basic arithmetic meaningless; 'beyond reasonable doubt' remains just that, as does 'likely'. Otherwise, language takes on an 'Alice through the Looking Glass' quality wherein Humpty Dumpty says: 'When I use a word... it means what I want it to mean – neither more nor less.'[36]

[34] Slobogin, above n 3, 119.
[35] Slobogin, above n 7.
[36] Lewis Carroll, *Through the Looking Glass and What Alice Found There* (Macmillan, 1872) 44 <www.alice-in-wonderland.net>.

The statistical parameter Area Under the Curve (AUC) emanates from a branch of statistics and decision theory called Receiver Operator Characteristics (ROC) Analysis. The misinterpretation and misapplication of this statistical parameter is rife in SVP assessments, as is evidenced by Slobogin's unwarranted confidence in its primacy. He is not alone in his failure to comprehend to what, precisely, this parameter refers. Many psychologists also fail to comprehend the limitations of relying on this single parameter in SVP assessments, as has been robustly argued elsewhere.[37]

4.   A BRIEF OVERVIEW OF ROC ANALYSIS AND RISK ASSESSMENT

Suppose you are on a guided missile cruiser that is standing in harm's way and you are observing a radar screen. Your job is to determine whether any enemy aircraft are approaching, but it is made more difficult because, within the area covered by the radar, are civilian aircraft. As you turn up the gain (more or less equivalent to the volume on an amplifier), there is an increased chance of detecting enemy aircraft (the signal); but as the gain is increased there is also an increased chance of mistaking passenger aircraft for enemy aircraft (noise). On the radar screen is a signal that may, or may not, represent an enemy aircraft and you have to make decisions – quickly.

Based on your decision as to whether an enemy aircraft or a harmless civilian aircraft is approaching, a number of things can happen. First, you can correctly decide that an enemy aircraft is approaching (*True Positive* decision) and alert the captain with the result that an anti-aircraft missile is fired and the threat is neutralised. Second, you can incorrectly decide that an enemy aircraft is approaching (*False Positive* decision) and alert the captain with the result that an anti-aircraft missile is fired and a harmless civilian aircraft is destroyed. Third, you can correctly decide that the 'signal' on the radar screen is in fact 'noise', ie a harmless civilian aircraft (*True Negative* decision); you do not alert the captain, an anti-aircraft missile is not fired and civilian lives are spared. Fourth, you can incorrectly decide that an enemy aircraft is not approaching, merely a civilian aircraft (*False Negative* decision); you do not alert the captain with the result that an anti-aircraft missile is not fired and the ship may be destroyed.

What has this example to do with risk assessment of sexual and violent offenders? Quite a lot: consideration of the types of decisions individuals make in such circumstances was subject to considerable thought during and after World War

---

[37]   T W Campbell, 'Predictive Accuracy of Static-99R and Static 2002R' (2011) 3 *Open Access Journal of Forensic Psychology* 82–106.

II. Signal Detection Theory was thus derived: it is generalisable to any situation where a dichotomous decision has to be made, such as interpreting medical imaging results aimed at determining whether a patient does or does not have cancer and the results of actuarial tests aimed at predicting recidivism.[38] It has come to be referred to, in its more general applications, as Receiver Operating Characteristics (ROC) Analysis.

Returning to the example[39] of the radar operator, plotting the True Positives (ie hits) on the vertical (y) axis of a Cartesian Plane familiar to any school student and the False Positives (ie false alarms) on the horizontal (x) axis produces a ROC curve, which delineates the *area under* the plot or *curve* (AUC) depicting hits/false alarms. Perfect interpretation of what the blip on the radar screen represents would result in True Positives 100% of the time, and a plot of the decisions would therefore start at the x/y axes intersection (ie the origin in Cartesian terms) at 100% and then be plotted parallel to the x-axis. It would therefore describe a right angle. A perfectly inaccurate interpretation of what the blip on the radar screen represents[40] would result in False Positives 100% of the time and would also describe a right angle that is a mirror image to the former. Thus, these two extremes would describe plots that would form the left and right hand side and top and bottom of a rectangle respectively.[41] A radar/operator diagnostic system that performed at chance level would describe a diagonal line inclined at 45° to the x/y origin.

There are very few perfectly good or perfectly useless tests and, in practice, the relationship between True Positives and False Positives describes an irregular curve. Measuring the Area under these 'curves' (by convention they are referred to as curves even if they are straight lines) results in an AUC = 0.50 when no

---

[38] D M Green and J A Swets, *Signal Detection Theory and Psychophysics* (Wiley and Sons, 1966); J A Swets, 'Measuring the Accuracy of Diagnostic Systems' (1988) 240 *Science* 1285–93; D L Streiner and J Cairney, 'What's under the ROC? An Introduction to Receiver Operating Characteristics Curves' (2007) 52(2) *The Canadian Journal of Psychiatry* 121–8.

[39] In our example, we have only used one instance. However a ROC curve is the result of plotting a number of True Positive and False Positives and the AUC, delineated by this curve, represents the mean predictive value over a number of measurements/decisions or scores in the case of actuarial instruments. In our example, lower gain, with the resultant image interpreted by the radar operator, would result in more False Positives to True Positives and higher gain, with the resultant image interpreted by the radar operator, more True Positives to False Positives. In the case of the Static-99, there would be 15 such measurements corresponding to the range from the lowest to the highest score: -3 to 12.

[40] Clearly, the performance of the radar operator cannot be divorced from the functioning of the radar since the operator interprets the results of the radar signal presented on a VDU: the ROC curve represents this interpretation.

[41] It would, of course, be simpler to use a diagram to illustrate this. However, in Australia the use of such diagrams when giving expert evidence is frowned upon, in part, so the argument goes, since diagrams are not incorporated in judgments. Thus, we have attempted to describe the concepts without recourse to illustrations.

discrimination exists (that is, when the curve lies along the diagonal) and an AUC 1.0 for perfect discrimination (when the curve follows the left and top axes).[42]

It is critical to note that the statistical parameter AUC does not, *per se*, tell us anything about the probability of an event occurring: the fundamental issue the courts have to consider in terms of recidivism of SVP offenders. In the example of the radar operator trying to discriminate between possible hostile aircraft and harmless passenger planes, the radar signal and how it is interpreted says *nothing* whatsoever about the probability that hostile aircraft are there to be detected in the first place. That is, whether hostile aircraft are present is independent of the functioning of the radar screen and the skill of the radar operator. An AUC of 0.75, which may be referred to as the diagnostic accuracy of the system, tells us that the radar operator will 'get it right' based on multiple observations of radar images of aircraft in declaring that an enemy aircraft is approaching rather than a civilian aircraft 75% of the time *if enemy aircraft are, in fact, in the air*. In this example, information on this point may be derived from military intelligence, which is a notoriously imprecise art. Fortunately, there is somewhat better guidance available, when considering SVP offenders, that can militate against conflating diagnostic accuracy with the probability of an event occurring: the base rate of recidivism as is explicated in what follows.[43]

A relatively non-mathematical example explicates the problem of conflating the diagnostic accuracy of any particular test with the probability of an event occurring based on the results of the test. Suppose dichotomising high and low scorers on a reading test, such as the Wechsler Adult Reading Test (WART), enabled discrimination between those who have Foreign Accent Syndrome[44] from those who exhibit altered speech patterns as a result of methamphetamine-induced psychoses. Foreign Accent Syndrome is extremely rare (as of 1996 only 15 cases were reported worldwide): perhaps as few as 100 individuals currently suffer from this worldwide. It follows neurological insult, or, more rarely, some other psychogenic processes that are not understood. Whatever the cause, those afflicted start speaking with, say, a Finnish accent when they have only ever resided in, say, the remote Pilbara region of Western Australia and have had no contact with Finnish speaking individuals–nor have they even heard someone speak Finnish.

---

[42]   Technically an AUC of 0.5 cannot indicate a ROC curve since this is only a chance response and thus there is no response curve per se. However, for practical purposes in the context of the arguments espoused herein, this can be ignored and an AUC of 0.5 may be considered equivalent to a diagnostic accuracy of 50%.

[43]   This is properly defined as the relative frequency with which a particular circumstance occurs in a reference group (eg the proportion of left-handed people in the population).

[44]   K M Kurowski, S E Blumstein and M Alexander, 'The Foreign Accent Syndrome: A Reconsideration' (1996) 54 *Brain and Language* 1–25.

Methamphetamine-induced psychosis is considerably more common. It is difficult to determine how many individuals actually develop this condition since it can be conflated with other drug-induced psychoses, and methamphetamine abuse varies across countries and time. Nonetheless, it is certainly orders of magnitude greater than Foreign Accent Syndrome and it is beyond doubt that a very significant proportion of methamphetamine users develop psychosis: about 13% according to studies in the Australian context.[45] In such cases about 27% of individuals exhibit altered speech patterns during the acute withdrawal phase.[46]

For the purpose of this example, consider that the WART demonstrates an AUC of 0.90[47] in discriminating between those suffering from Foreign Accent Syndrome and altered speech patterns arising from methamphetamine-induced psychosis.[48] What is the probability that someone with altered speech patterns who scores high (in terms of errors) on the WART actually has Foreign Accent Syndrome? It is intuitively obvious that it is not 90% since only 100 individuals in the entire world (assuming that the current world population is 7 billion) have this syndrome. If you had to make a decision whether to recommend neurosurgery for an individual with altered speech patterns on the basis of the WART alone in this situation, your best bet would be to completely ignore the test results on the WART and determine that p=100/7,000,000,000 (p=0.0000000143).[49] This, for all practical purposes, equates to zero. Another way of looking at the problem is to ask how often administration of the WART would result in False Positives when attempting, by administration of this test alone, to diagnose Foreign Accent Syndrome. This is easy to calculate: it is 0.1 x 7,000,000,000 = 700,000,000. It would be outright lunacy to recommend neurosurgery solely based on a high score on the WART in this situation.

To be sure, the base rate of sexual recidivism is much higher than in this example: between 3% and 35% depending on the sample employed and the length of follow up, to name but two factors. Generally, it hovers around 6–10% except for those preselected as being 'high risk'.[50] Nonetheless, the underlying statistical principle

---

45 R McKetin et al, 'The Prevalence of Psychotic Symptoms among Methamphetamine Users' (2006) 101 *Addiction* 1473–8.

46 C C Cruickshank and K R Dyer, 'A Review of the Clinical Pharmacology of Methamphetamine' (2009) 104 *Addiction* 1085–99.

47 In considering this example, it is critical to note that no tests, of whatever type, have been reliably demonstrated to discriminate between recidivists and non-recidivists in SVP cases with an AUC >0.90: none.

48 It does not have any application to this as far as the authors are aware, although there is a certain amount of face validity in positing that it might, and is only used by way of example.

49 This is not precisely correct. Bayes Theory enables the exact probability to be calculated given the prior probability and the diagnostic accuracy of the test but in the interests of avoiding mathematical proofs and since the difference is utterly trivial in this example, it will suffice.

50 See, for example: L Helmus et al, *Variability in Static-99R and Static-2002R Recidivism Estimates: Absolute Recidivism Rates Predicted by Static-99R and Static-2002R Sex Offender Risk Assessment*

still pertains. The lower the occurrence, or base rate, of *any* phenomenon the higher the diagnostic accuracy of *any* test has to be before confidence can be placed on the predictions made. It is important to note that the AUC is insensitive to base rates, and relying on the AUC alone can give a rosier picture of accuracy than is warranted with low base rates. Thus, while the diagnostic accuracy of any test is not affected by the rate of occurrence of the disease or situation the test/procedure is designed to detect, whether it be enemy aircraft or recidivism, the end result in terms of the decision made *is* most certainly affected. In SVP cases, the problem is particularly chronic as, all other things being equal, low base rates effectively preclude the prospect of clearing the minimum legal bar of 'more than likely than not'.[51]

The problem of committing False Positive errors was most graphically demonstrated when, on 3 July 1988, the guided missile cruiser US Vincennes launched an anti-aircraft missile that shot down a harmless Iraqi passenger jet – with the loss of 290 lives. False Positive errors also have inimical consequences in SVP cases, as do False Negative errors, but in common law jurisdictions, the law is presumed to be biased against the latter. This presumption is best illustrated by reference to the oft-quoted phrase: 'It is better that ten guilty persons escape than that one innocent suffer.'

Expressed by the English jurist Sir William Blackstone in his Commentaries on the Laws of England, published in the 1760s, this is still considered good law.[52] Yet this doctrine is often vitiated in SVP cases with the result that False Positive errors are all too frequently committed. As Campbell[53] notes:

> When assessing the recidivism risk of sex offenders, base rates amount to an 'inconvenient truth.' Although we might want to wish them away via AUC values obtained via ROC methods, base rates are a persistent nuisance when attempting to predict infrequently occurring events. SVP evaluators who disregard the base rate problem too often commit false-positive errors.[54]

Tools Vary across Samples: A Meta-Analysis (12 January 2012) Static-99 Clearinghouse <http://www.static99.org/pdfdocs/Helmus_et_al_2012_ActuarialBaseRateVariabilityInPress.pdf>. A recent long-term study claims to have demonstrated recidivism rates of 47%–81%, but this is a statistical outlier and it seems likely that over sampling bias was an important factor in this study. See: R Langevin and S Curnoe, 'Lifetime Criminal History of Sex Offenders Seen for Assessment in Five Decades' (2012) 56(7) *International Journal of Offender Therapy and Comparative Criminology* 997–1021.

[51] R Wollert, 'Low Base Rates Limit Expert Certainty When Current Actuarials are Used to Identify Sexually Violent Predators: An Application of Bayes' Theorem' (2006) 12 *Psychology, Public Policy and Law* 56–85; Coyle, above n 12.

[52] W Blackstone, *Commentaries on the Laws of England 1765–1769* (Clarendon Press, 1766–1769).

[53] Campbell, above n 37, 104.

[54] This is somewhat simplistic. As Campbell, ibid, notes, a more comprehensive way of looking at the problem is to consider the relationship between the Positive Predictive Values (PPV) and Negative Predictive Values (NPV) and base rates. PPVs identify the accuracy with which

To put this slightly differently, the AUC provides an overall image of the diagnostic accuracy of a test or detection instrument but tells us nothing about the accuracy of a prediction at any given score and, as noted previously, it tells us nothing about the accuracy of the probability estimate.

The implications of this are profound and obvious. Recently, the developers and proponents of the Static-99R opined, in connection with variability between outcomes arising from base rate variability between different samples:

> Another approach to addressing base rate variability is to ignore it. In many contexts, precise estimates of absolute risk are not needed because decisions can be based on relative risk (which was found to be stable). For example, probation officers may have the resources to conduct home visits for only 20% of the highest risk offenders. In this context, other quantitative metrics for communicating risk (such as percentile ranks; Hanson et al., in press) may have more utility than absolute recidivism rate estimates.[55]

This is arrant, hypothesis-saving nonsense as is demonstrated later.

There are other important statistical and logical issues to consider before it can be concluded that the errors in Slobogin's thesis as to the primacy of actuarial instruments in terms of the evidence that the courts can receive can be fully exposed. It is convenient to do this by reference to the Static-99 in its various iterations, since it is the most widely used actuarial test employed to inform the courts as to the risk of sexual recidivism. In any event, the same arguments also apply to other actuarial instruments used to predict sexual and violent recidivism to one degree or another.

---

recidivism risk may be ruled in: they are calculated by dividing the number of true-positive predictions by the number of true-positive predictions plus the number of false-positive predictions. Thus, PPV = TP/TP + FP. NPVs identify the accuracy with which recidivism risk may be ruled out: they are calculated by dividing the number of true-negative predictions by the number of true-negative predictions plus the number of false-negative predictions. Thus, NPV = TN/TN + FN. PPVs and NPVs are base-rate sensitive. As the base rate of sex offender recidivism (or any other event for that matter) increases, PPVs also increase while NPVs decrease. Conversely, as the base rate of some event decreases, PPVs decrease and NPVs increase.

[55] Helmus et al, n 50.

5. PREDICTING RECIDIVISM OF GROUPS OF INDIVIDUALS WITH ACTUARIAL TESTS

The Static-99R is an empirically derived actuarial[56] instrument designed to predict recidivism in male sex offenders.[57] It consists of ten items (eg age of the offender at release, number of convictions, convictions for non-contact sex offences) with the total score ranging from -3 to 12. It can be used to place offenders into one of four risk categories low (-3–1), moderate–low (2–3), moderate to high (4–5) and high (6+). When risk estimates are associated with a particular score they are referred to as score-wise risk estimates.

From early in its development, the Static-99[58] in its various iterations has been the primary actuarial tool used by mental health professionals in their attempts to predict the risk of sex offense recidivism. The Static-99R (the latest version) yields score-wise estimates of risk in percentages. The authors of the Static-99 use the term 'absolute risk'[59] when referring to the actuarial score-wise estimate; it is the risk estimate for the sample (group) at each score (that is, the average risk for the individuals who made up the normative group). Given that the estimates are the product of proportions, the average or mean is the best measure of central tendency and, hence, the best risk estimate for individuals in the normative group.

Recently, the developers and proponents of the Static-99R, and another variant, Static-2002/R, have stated[60] that:

> [e]valuators cannot, in an unqualified way, associate a single reliable recidivism estimate with a single score on the Static-99/R or Static-2002/R risk scales. Evaluators interested in reporting absolute recidivism rate estimates must not only calculate a Static score but also make a separate professional judgment concerning which sample the offender most closely resembles.

While this is a *volte-face* from the position they have previously adopted, this acknowledgment does not go far enough. For one thing, making decisions as to which sample the offender 'most closely resembles' is pseudo-actuarial and enables

---

[56] The term 'nomothetic' is often used interchangeably with actuarial: for economy of language only actuarial is used herein.

[57] L Helmus et al, 'Improving the Predictive Accuracy of the Static-99 and Static-2002 with Older Sex Offenders: Revised Age Weights' (2012) 24 *Sexual Abuse: A Journal of Research and Treatment* 64–101.

[58] For the sake of convenience, the arguments advanced here deal with the later version, the Static-99R.

[59] Helmus et al, above n 50.

[60] Ibid.

confirmatory bias to parade as science.[61] Using only one's professional judgement with which to assign individuals to a sample group, without empirically-based justification, amounts to the *ipse dixit* of the expert.

Aside from this obvious problem, it is necessary to consider basic statistical and epistemological concepts to understand why there *cannot* be an absolute recidivism rate but only a probability statement. Similarly, for risk estimates based on a range of scores, such as when 'high' is equated to score of 6 or higher on the Static99/R,[62] the use of the descriptor 'high' can only connote a range of risk estimates.

In Science and Medicine, the examination of cause-effect relationships involves the analyses of data in the attempt to predict an outcome (eg, sex offense recidivism, diseases) from available data (eg, sex offense history of offenders and presence of certain 'risk' factors, virus and/or bacteria). In the context of SVP cases, we may consider the correlation between, say, age and sexual recidivism. By way of analogy, the association of viruses and bacteria with disease may be considered. Correlations range from -1 to + 1: the negative correlation meaning that the *absence* of something is predicative of something else. The proportion of total variance accounted for is called the *coefficient of determination*. It is the square of the correlation coefficient. All in all, the square of the correlation coefficient informs of the 'goodness' of prediction. Understanding and applying this fundamental statistical concept is vital in assessing the efficacy of various risk assessment tests as it is not unusual for the subtests, or even individual items within these tests, to be specifically relied upon in risk assessments.

Consider, for argument's sake, that one of the items scored on the Static-99R, such as age of the offender, correlated 0.13 with recidivism. This would mean that the amount of total variance *unaccounted* for by age is $1-0.13^2 = 1-0.2$ (rounded) or 98%. This example is not randomly chosen: age does correlate 0.13 with sexual recidivism but, as demonstrated, the amount of variance accounted for is miserable.[63] Since age is one of the factors most strongly associated with

---

61   See, generally: B R Abbott, 'Applicability of the New Static-99 Experience Tables in Sexually Violent Predator Risk Assessments' (2009) 4(1) *Sexual Offender Treatment* 1–28. Abbott also makes the critical point that 'clinical override', whereby actuarial scores are 'adjusted' based on 'clinical judgment', results in lower diagnostic accuracy.

62   For practical purposes, this equates to scores of 6–9 since scores higher than 9 are exceedingly rare: less than 0.1% of scores on the Static-99R fall into this category.

63   R K Hanson and M T Bussière, 'Predicting Relapse: a Meta-Analysis of Sexual Offender Recidivism Studies' (1998) 66 *Journal of Consulting and Clinical Psychology* 348–62; R K Hanson and K Morton-Bourgon, 'The Characteristics of Persistent Sexual Offenders: a Meta-Analysis of Recidivism Studies' (2005) 73 *Journal of Consulting and Clinical Psychology* 1154–63.

recidivism in SVP offenders, this is of some note and is referred to later in this chapter.

In no relationship, or correlation, is the actuarial estimate of the association between the cause and the effect equivalent to an accurate or absolute finding for an individual. To the contrary, there are a myriad of other variables that can and do affect the chance that the actuarial estimate will accurately reflect an individual's risks. Thus, not all *individuals* who come into contact with virus and bacteria will develop diseases associated with them and not all sex offenders, regardless of their Static-99 score, will recidivate. However, the problem also extends to *groups* of people who are exposed to, say, a virus and to groups of offenders who, based on their score-wise estimate of risk, may or may not be considered more likely than not to recidivate.

A common way of providing guidance on the latter is to employ Confidence Intervals (CIs). These are usually interpreted as the range of uncertainty about the risk estimate: the CI indicates a range of scores within which the true score can be said to lie with a defined probability. Usually this is expressed in terms of a 95% confidence interval whereby it is considered that there is a 95% probability that the true score lies within a defined range of scores.[64]

As Donaldson and colleagues[65] note when referring to Confidence Intervals:

> It is axiomatic that all sex offenders with the same score on a risk-prediction instrument do not have the same probability of reoffense. Despite this important fact, little or no information is available regarding the sources of variability in risk among offenders with identical scores, and there has been almost no discussion in the literature regarding the effects of variable probabilities of risk on reported CIs.

Having identified profound statistical errors[66] in the way in which the authors of the Static-99R analysed data from various samples to derive score wise risk estimates, Donaldson et al then dealt with statistical consideration that are relevant to a seminal question: do the group CIs meet the minimum legal test for accuracy?

---

[64]   Technically, a confidence interval is an estimated range of values with a given probability of covering the true population value or parameter. It is not possible to express a probability about a population value or parameter; it is either there or it is not.

[65]   Donaldson, Abbott and Michie, above n 17, 11.

[66]   These are complex and beyond the scope of this chapter. Simply put, the errors in the statistical analyses engaged in by the authors/proponents of the Static-99/R identified by Donaldson et al are withering. It is the authors' view that the arguments espoused by the authors and proponents of the Static-99, in its various iterations, on this score alone, may be fatal to the reception of evidence based on this instrument by the courts.

For score-wise estimates of risk derived from the Static-99R with the PHRN group, Donaldson and colleagues[67] paint a bleak picture for those who argue that this instrument enables an absolute level of risk to be determined that is congruent with the minimum legal test:

> Using corrected predicted estimates based on the slope parameter for the PHRN group data shows that a risk estimate of more likely than not, i.e., greater than 50%, *is almost never obtained when based on the actuarial information* (emphasis added).

In fact, it is only when a score of 9 or higher is obtained that there is any prospect of the actual recidivism rate exceeding 51%. For a score of 6, which it may be recalled is the cut-off score for 'high' risk according to the progenitors of the Static-99R, the mean risk of recidivism was 26%. By way of elaboration, a score of 6 on the Static-99R is equivalent to the 94th percentile. A score of 9 is equivalent to the 99.9th percentile.[68]

The problem does not end there: the 95% CI for the score-wise estimate of recidivism calculated by Donaldson and colleagues is 23%–30% for the PHRN group. For those who score within the range of 6–9, the 95% confidence interval is 23%–50%. Since the PHRN group represents the most extreme situation in terms of base rates, this conclusion is very, very, conservative. Even considering the group of individuals who are assigned a score of 6 on the Static-99R (which the reader will recall is the cut-off score for 'high' risk of recidivism), there is no absolute estimate of the risk of recidivism and such CIs as can be relied upon for the range of recidivism based on this score are so wide as to preclude relying upon them in many cases.

The basic reason why the estimates yielded by the actuarial instruments cannot, even at the group level, attain the level of predictive accuracy required to meet the minimum legal tests is that each of the individual items that make up the Static-99R are very poor predictors of sex offense recidivism. Review of the individual items that make up the Static-99 reveals poor predictive quality, that is, low correlations with sex offense recidivism.[69] To reiterate, age, which is considered one of the more powerful predictors of sex offense recidivism, accounts for less than 2% of the variance, leaving 98% unaccounted for. To amplify this point, it

[67] Donaldson, Abbott and Michie, above n 17, 16.
[68] R K Hanson et al, 'Developing Non-Arbitrary Metrics for Risk Communication: Percentile Ranks for the Static-99/R and Static-2002/R Sexual Offender Risk Tools' (2012) 11 *International Journal of Forensic Mental Health* 9–23.
[69] T S Donaldson and B Abbott, 'Prediction in the Individual Case: An Explanation and Application of Its Use with the Static-99/R in Sexually Violent Predator Risk Assessments' (2011) 29(1) *American Journal of Forensic Psychology* 5–35.

has been recently acknowledged by the proponents of the Static-99R that half of the individual items that go to make up the test do *not* consistently predict risk across samples.[70]

Although it is possible to combine risk factors to increase predictive validity[71] in practice, such procedures are rarely, if ever, followed. It is also necessary to note that use of multiple actuarial tests and/or 'other risk factors' in the attempt to improve confidence in the accuracy of the actuarial estimate can actually reduce the degree of confidence to be placed in the estimate.[72] Further, even if combining the results of various actuarial instruments did increase predictive accuracy such that the range of error as indicated by the CI was congruent with the legal tests,[73] there are compelling reasons why this would not overcome the problem in making risk predictions for any particular individual.

6.   PREDICTING RECIDIVISM OF INDIVIDUALS WITH ACTUARIAL TESTS

There is an analogous relationship to risk assessment in SVP cases when an actuarially based clinical/personality instrument, say, the Minnesota Multiphasic Personality Inventory (MMPI2), is used in the attempt to determine whether and to what degree an individual patient suffers a clinical or personality disorder. Even though the patient's own test-taking responses produce results (actuarial elevations) that suggest the presence of the very signs, symptoms, traits and characteristics associated with various clinical/personality scales, the elevations do not describe a sufficient level of confidence that would enable the clinician to make the diagnosis for an individual on the sole basis of the scale elevations.

The pivotal issue in the application of the score-wise estimate to an individual is not the score-wise risk estimate measured by its group confidence interval (CI) but the *accuracy* of that estimate when applied to an individual. The differences in the group versus individual confidence intervals, while well established, is a matter of much confusion in the application of risk predictions in SVP proceedings.[74]

---

[70]   L Helmus and R K Thornton, 'Performance of Individual Items of Static-99R and Static 2002R' (Paper presented at the Association for the Treatment of Sexual Abusers Conference, Denver, Colorado, USA, October 2012).

[71]   A Mokros et al, 'Assessment of Risk for Violent Recidivism through Multivariate Bayesian Classification' (2010) 16(4) *Psychology Public Policy and Law* 418–50.

[72]   S L Vrieze and W M Grove, 'Multidimensional Assessment of Criminal Recidivism: Problems, Pitfalls, and Proposed Solutions' (2010) 22(2) *Psychological Assessment* 382–95.

[73]   That is, reduce the CI. Somewhat counter-intuitively, as the correlation between the predictor and outcome increases, there is an inverse effect on the CI in that it narrows.

[74]   J Cohen and P Cohen, *Applied Multiple Regression/Correlation Analysis for the Behavioral Sciences* (Lawrence Erlbaum Associates, 1983); J Cohen, *Statistical Power Analysis for the Behavioral Sciences* (Psychology Press Publishers, 1988); D J Cooke and C Michie, 'Limitations

Apart from the group CI, it is also necessary to consider the confidence interval for the individual (CII),[75] which quantifies the predictive power of decisions based on group data for application to individuals. The statistical issues involved are complex and beyond the scope of this chapter, but the conclusions reached by the research on this topic can be summarised. When estimating the degree to which estimates of *group* risk applies to individuals, the result is always the same: the *group* confidence score-wise estimates are extremely narrow compared to those calculated for individuals.

From a practical viewpoint the result is that there will be overlap between those who are likely to recidivate and those who do not, to such an extent that little or no confidence can be placed in the estimate for the individual. Cooke and Michie[76] cite a CII of between 0–99%; that is, the estimate that any particular individual will recidivate ranges between 0% and 99%. This, it might be noted, does not trouble actuaries. Actuaries are not interested in any particular individual; they are only interested in groups of individuals. This is a distinctly different situation than obtains in risk assessment of dangerousness. In essence, Cooke and Michie demonstrated that, at the individual level, actuarial tests are essentially meaningless, a point that has been confirmed by others most recently.[77] It is, perhaps, necessary to reiterate that the problems of drawing inferences about individuals based on group data is completely well established,[78] although the application of this to actuarial assessment in SVP cases had escaped notice until recently.

Hanson and Howard have challenged the validity of individual confidence intervals (CII) in assessment of recidivism risk. They argued that the confidence interval for the individual will range between 0 and 1 due to the dichotomous nature of the outcome measures (ie recidivate or not recidivate) and, thus, has no utility in determining prediction accuracy.[79] Hence, their reasoning goes, a distinction between the group and individual estimates is a non-issue. The error in their line of thought is that the actuarial instruments do *not* predict an ultimate either/or outcome but only *estimates* of the *likelihood* of an outcome.

---

      of Diagnostic Precision and Predictive Utility in the Individual Case: a Challenge for Forensic Practice' (2009) 34(40) *Law and Human Behavior* 259–74; Donaldson and Abbott, above n 69.

[75]   Cooke and Michie, ibid.

[76]   Ibid.

[77]   Donaldson and Abbott, above n 69.

[78]   Cohen and Cohen, above n 74; Cohen, above n 74.

[79]   R K Hanson and P D Howard, 'Individual Confidence Intervals Do Not Inform Decision Makers about the Accuracy of Risk Assessment Evaluations' (2010) 34 Law and Human Behavior 275–81.

Their arguments are then fatally flawed from a logical and statistical viewpoint: indeed as has been commented, '[T]hey commit some devastating errors.'[80]

The problem with attempting to determine predictive accuracy at the individual level has been approached from a different perspective by Scurich and John.[81] Employing a Bayesian approach, they argue that the statistical methodology employed in calculating CIIs is flawed. The arguments are complex and detailed discussion is beyond the scope of this chapter, however their conclusions can be adequately addressed without recourse to statistical theorems. They argue that Bayesian Credible Intervals (BCI) can be used to calculate the probability of any particular individual recidivating. However, their exposition of this proposition reveals that this depends upon someone's estimate of the probability of an individual recidivating *before* considering the results of any actuarial test. This is referred to as the *subjective prior probability*. According to Scurich and John[82] it may be described as:

> [a] subjective or personalistic degree of belief in a proposition ...the prior can be influenced by a multitude of factors, including previous experiences, the perception of change, dynamic factors and even an objective base rate. An objective base rate can inform a prior but it would almost never be the sole determinant.

Aside from the logical, practical and prejudicial problems created by relying on a *subjective* estimate of probability as a basis on which to calculate a supposedly objective assessment of risk when considering the results of an actuarial test, it can be demonstrated that when the subjective prior probability is the same as that employed in calculating CIIs the results are the same.[83] Essentially, Scurich and John[84] determined the CIs for the group based on different estimates of the uncertainty on the base rate: in their example, the BCI and the CI were numerically the same. Their calculations of BCIs then were based on group data. As Donaldson and Abbott note: '[P]rior subjective probabilities have very little influence compared to the difference between the CI and the CII.'[85] That is, the probability of recidivism overlaps to such a degree that there is no meaningful way of discriminating between credible intervals of risk for the individual, as the

---

[80]   N Scurich and R S John, 'A Bayesian Approach to the Group versus Individual Prediction Controversy in Actuarial Risk Assessment' (2012) 36(3) *Law and Human Behavior* 237–46, 239.

[81]   Ibid.

[82]   N Scurich and R S John, 'Prescriptive Approaches to Communicating the Risk of Violence in Actuarial Risk Assessment' (2012) 16(1) *Psychology Public Policy and Law* 50–78, 56–7.

[83]   Personal communication with B Abbott, 2012.

[84]   Scurich and John, above n 80.

[85]   Personal communication with T Donaldson and B Abbott, 2012.

intervals are too wide and overlapping. Scurich and John[86] attempt to explain this inconvenient fact away by arguing that:

> [o]verlapping confidence intervals have implications for statistical hypothesis, but legal relevance does not depend on whether there is a 'statistical difference' between categories…relevance, not sufficiency, goes to admissibility and relevance, potentially unlike sufficiency, does not depend on whether the intervals are wide and overlapping.

This argument demonstrates a comprehensive misunderstanding of the legal tests of admissibility and the weight to be applied to evidence that is admitted. The cogency of such evidence that is adduced *most assuredly* rests on whether confidence intervals of risk assessment are wide and overlapping. Parenthetically it might be noted that in *R v T* the decision as to the inadmissibility of Bayes Theory was founded, *inter alia*, on the use of subjective prior probabilities. Since this decision is persuasive at law in both the USA and Australia, this is of some note. That said, it is hard to see why the most objective measure of prior probabilities, the base rate of recidivism, should not be used as the basis for determining BCIs – and this will achieve the same net result as calculating CIIs.

7. OTHER LIMITATIONS OF ACTUARIAL INSTRUMENTS

The limitations of the predictive power of the Static-99 can be considered in other ways. First, consider the overall amount of the variability (ie variance) in sexual recidivism accounted for by the test. In light of the miserable predictive power of the individual items that go to make up the test, it is intuitively obvious that the overall predictive power is likely to be low. This is the case: the Static-99 overall accounts for approximately 11% of the variance in outcome.[87] This is scarcely impressive. Second, as the developers and proponents of the Static have been forced to concede recently when comparing recidivism rates across various samples (eg PHRN):

> The range in absolute recidivism rates across studies was sufficiently large that values within the observed range could lead to meaningfully different conclusions concerning an offender's likelihood of recidivism.[88]

---

86   Scurich and John, above n 80, 244.
87   Donaldson and Abbott, above n 66, 28.
88   Helmus et al, above n 50, 1164.

Leaving aside the demonstrably incorrect presumption that score-wise estimates provide an absolute risk of recidivism, to the extent that the triers of fact rely on expert testimony based on this instrument, it is clear that an individual may or may not be preventively detained despite the variability in these so-called absolute recidivism rates. Third, considering the effects of inter-rater reliability when individuals are assigned to the various verbal categories encompassing ranges of scores, variations of as little as one point can make a world of difference in outcomes. As Boccaccini and colleagues[89] have observed:

> [T]he total scores assigned by pairs of evaluators differed for approximately 45% of offenders in each state. Because each individual Static-99 score has a unique interpretation, and a 1-point difference in a Static-99 score can have substantial practical implications for decision making, these findings suggest the need for administration procedures or interpretation methods that acknowledge and account for measurement error in Static-99 total scores.

8.   A REBUTTABLE PRESUMPTION

When considering the bases on which preventive detention may be warranted, Slobogin proposes, as noted previously in this chapter, that evidence based on actuarial tests may be rebutted with 'clinical risk assessments, even if they are not as provably reliable as actuarial prediction'. It is moot whether this encompasses Structured Professional Judgment procedures (SPJ).[90] However, these instruments used to inform SPJ (eg the Historical Clinical Risk 20 (HCR-20)), do not, by their nature, usually permit numerical scores to be derived; rather ordinal categories (eg low, medium, high) are assigned, which is not without its problems, as the triers of fact can interpret these adjectives very differently. Further, Cooke[91] has suggested that while SPJ might be of interest vis-à-vis risk assessment:

> [The] whole point of SPJ is not to allocate someone to a low, medium, or high risk group, rather it is to generate a coherent risk formulation and risk management plan…if SPJ techniques are being used effectively then predictive validity should be low, as effective intervention means that 'high' risk cases are managed so that they don't reoffend.

---

[89]   Boccaccini et al, 'Implications of Static-99 Field Reliability Findings for Score Use and Reporting' (2012) 39 *Criminal Justice and Behavior* 42–58.

[90]   M Yang, S Wong and J Coid, 'The Efficacy of Violence Prediction: A Meta-Analytic Comparison of Nine Risk Assessment Tools' (2010) 136 *Psychological Bulletin* 740–67.

[91]   Personal communication with D Cooke, 2012.

Commenting on the difficulties faced with development of SVP risk prediction tools Donaldson and Abbott[92] conclude:

> [T]here do not appear to be any likely solutions to overcome the effect of low correlations on predictive accuracy for the individual in the near future. This point is illustrated by Yang et al... who conclude: 'After almost five decades of developing risk prediction tools, the evidence increasingly suggests that the ceiling of predictive efficacy may have been reached with the available technology' ... This brings us to our final conclusion that statistical prediction of risk has little relevance to sexually violent predator procedures in the courtroom. It would seem that a more feasible argument for high risk would be based on the mental abnormality itself. That is, the individual currently suffers from some condition (usually, a paraphilia) that predisposes[93] him to sexual violence, and for which he currently has serious difficulty controlling acting on that condition. Given that one had valid and reliable evidence for that, it would seem that prediction is a moot issue. In the absence of such a condition, no degree of risk is relevant.

Winsman has amplified this argument most cogently.[94] Noting that, from a legal standpoint in the USA, a mental abnormality is understood to be a mental disorder with impaired behavioural self-control he comments:

> Ultimately, an idiographic approach is regarded as central to conducting a comprehensive evaluation. This approach does not abandon nomothetic components, but, rather, incorporates such data into a larger picture... In sum, each case must be understood idiographically, and the nomothetic data that the tests produce must be integrated into such an idiographic understanding of the person. That is, an individualized conceptualization of Volitional Impairment is created in each case. It is the ability to inhibit action by will that is the nub of the behavioral control conundrum. The ability to inhibit by will, examined idiographically, and with nomothetic components, is the heart of the scientific, psychological evaluation of behavioral control... This presents the best fit for opining about psychological questions in a forensic context where each individual must be examined in the light of the law.

These arguments as to volitional control doubtless apply in all Australian jurisdictions as they clearly go to the heart of the matter of an 'unacceptable level of risk'. Parenthetically, it might be noted that clinical judgment in situations where lack of volitional control is clearly related to circumscribed clinical conditions is often so demonstrably superior to actuarial predictions that the later are rendered

---

[92] Donaldson and Abbott, above n 69, 31.
[93] It should be noted that the diagnostic criteria for paraphilia is vague, at best. It is necessary to look elsewhere for evidence that a paraphiliac is also predisposed to acting out their fantasies and urges.
[94] F Winsmann, 'Assessing Volitional Impairment in Sexually Violent Predator Evaluations' (2012) 7(1) *Sexual Offender Treatment* 1–14, 8.

completely irrelevant. Coyle provides an example on this point.[95] This, of course, rebuts the conclusion that proceeds from Slobogin's assertion that 'clinical risk assessments… are not as provably reliable as actuarial prediction in all cases'.[96]

9.   LOGIC, MORALITY, RUSSIAN ROULETTE AND ESTIMATES OF RECIDIVISM

It has been argued[97] that, if the risk of recidivism of any particular individual is informed by the behaviour of the group to which they belong (eg those who have offended against multiple victims, those of a particular ethnic or racial group, or those of a certain age), it is logically and morally impermissible to use this as a criteria to inform the triers of fact as to the prospect of any particular individual recidivating. This argument is, of course, of critical import insofar as it applies to the application of actuarial instruments employed in risk assessment. Cooke and Michie[98] note that drawing a conclusion about an individual member of a group based on the collective properties of the group is subject to the logical fallacy of division: 'For example it is obviously fallacious to argue that if, in general intelligent people earn more that less intelligent people then Jules, with an IQ of 120 will earn more that Jim with an IQ of 100.'

In response to this, the oft-quoted reference as to the probability of playing Russian roulette with varying numbers of bullets in the chamber is trotted out to 'disprove' the problems of arguing from the group level to the individual when the outcome is dichotomous (ie recidivate or not recidivate). Scurich and John[99] put it thus:

> It is not incoherent to speak of what *probably* will occur, even when the event is dichotomous. The subscriber to this logic would, if forced to play a single game of Russian roulette, have to be indifferent to using a gun with five empty chambers or a gun with only one empty chamber on the basis that the outcome will either be devastating or not (Dawes, Faust, (sic) & Meehl 1989).

There is a subtle, illogical argument here that is not immediately apparent that goes as follows: even if we cannot specify what the probability of recidivism is for any particular individual based on actuarial tests, it must be higher for those who

---

[95]   Coyle, above n 12, 274–5.
[96]   As matter of logic, if Slobogin's evidentiary rule is accepted at face value then clinical evidence is always inferior to actuarial evidence.
[97]   G T Harris, 'Men in His Category Have a 50% Likelihood, but Which Half Is He in? Comments on Berlin, Galbreath, Geary, and McGlone' (2003) 15(4) *Sexual Abuse: A Journal of Research and Treatment* 389–92.
[98]   Cooke and Michie, above n 74, 271.
[99]   Scurich and John, above n 15, 238.

get scores of, say, 6 on the Static and so the logical problems of arguing from the group to the individual level can be discounted.

This sounds plausible, fair and even-handed. It is none of these things. The Russian roulette analogue is false for a number of reasons. First, the comparisons of score-wise estimates on the Static-99 are dependent on the reference group chosen, as has been explained. Thus, the base rate of recidivism, which affects the final result in terms of the probability of recidivism from scoring the Static-99, varies according the reference group chosen. This is not the same as the rotation of the cylinders of a fairly weighted pistol cylinder which is unaffected by any assessment of those stupid enough to play Russian roulette. Second, the probability of the next event occurring has, for all practical purposes, *no* variability in a well-maintained pistol when the cylinder is spun more or less immediately after the last player has had their turn. The number of bullets in the pistol's cylinder fixes the probability. If a bullet is in the cylinder when it is aligned with the firing pin then the player is dead. This is distinctly different to the situation that obtains vis-à-vis the Static-99 where the error of measurement at the group level is significant: at least 50%. This is analogous to the saying that there is at least a 50% probability that the pistol's cylinder will not rotate when the trigger is pulled. The probability of an event occurring in the case of Russian roulette (death) is considered in this analogy to be a defined percentage, determined by the number of bullets in the cylinder, *with no possible variability.* Third, at the *individual* level the error of measurement in the Static-99 is so wide that it equates to a probability of the cylinder rotating of something like 0% to 99% on any one occasion when it is spun. Fourth, the effects of playing Russian roulette are immediate. This is distinctly different to the application of nomothetic instruments to predict the future when many other variables can intervene. This may be conceptualised as, say, putting the gun down and coming back in ten years to finish the game – during which time the cylinder has frozen due to rust. The effects of increasing age on recidivism have been incorporated into the scoring of the Static-99, albeit that the scoring is confused vis-à-vis age of the last offense and age at release. This is analogous to considering the putative effects of rust on a well-maintained pistol when playing Russian roulette and ten years later. In essence, this analogue completely fails because, at least when the 'game' is underway, it is based on essentially fixed probabilities as compared to the conditional probabilities that apply when actuarial instruments are employed.

In the light of the arguments advanced here it is, perhaps, time to reconsider whether making legal decisions that are inextricably based on the group that an individual belongs to, as is the case by definition vis-à-vis actuarial instruments, is logically or legally permissible.

10. THE ELEPHANT IN THE ROOM

The elephant in the room is this: conflating assessment risk of recidivism with the consequences of recidivism. Put another way, this involves conflating the risk of recidivism with the consequences or gravity of harm that might flow from such recidivism. Either wittingly or unwittingly, the various state legislation in Australia encompasses this issue by reference to the concept of an unacceptable risk to the community should SVP offenders who are considered to pose a serious risk of dangerousness be released. It seems that exactly the same thing happens in individual cases in the USA as a result of the tendency of the triers of fact to err on the side of 'caution', although erring on the side of not making a False Negative decision is a better way of putting it. Certainly, the experience in Minnesota in the USA where only *one* SVP offender preventively detained has been released in the last 23 years speaks to this.[100]

For example, consider that an offender with advanced scientific training in toxicology is, by every scientific metric now available, considered to be at low risk compared to a comparable population of high-risk violent offenders. Then consider that one of the crimes of which he has been convicted involved attempting to poison the water supply of, say, Los Angeles. Then consider that there is no evidence that he suffers from any mental abnormality: he is a perfectly sane, thoroughly evil, jihadist. What is an acceptable level of risk for such an individual? Should this person be released if the chance that he will reoffend, according to expert opinion, is considered to be low? Any reasoned cost-benefit analysis would probably result in a clear answer: no. As to whether the same sort of cost-benefit analysis should be applied to SVP cases is another matter.

Yet the law is not concerned, according to standard concepts of jurisprudence in those jurisdictions that have embraced the common law, with cost-benefit analysis. It is not even *directly* concerned with justice; it is concerned with the application of legal principals and concepts that, in theory, will result in justice more often than not. It is hoped that justice will be delivered with a high degree of confidence, but nowhere, in any common law jurisdiction, is this quantified for any particular case. Nor can it be: the myriad facts that each case presents preclude that prospect.

The law guarantees that a decision will be made but it does not guarantee outcomes. Yet that is precisely what the law seeks to require of those engaging in the task of risk-analysis of dangerousness. It is time, once and for all, to acknowledge that estimates derived from actuarial tests cannot predict the future behaviour of individuals with anything approaching that implicit in the

---

[100] Personal communication with K Franklin, 2012.

minimum legal standards of proof. Estimates of 'absolute' and relative accuracy in risk assessments derived from actuarial tests give the impression of scientific accuracy that is simply not warranted. It is arrant nonsense to assert otherwise. Unless, like Humpty Dumpty, when we use a word it means what we want it to mean.

ASSESSING RISK FOR PREVENTIVE DETENTION OF SEX OFFENDERS: THE DICHOTOMY BETWEEN COMMUNITY PROTECTION AND OFFENDER RIGHTS IS WRONG-HEADED

Astrid BIRGDEN

1. INTRODUCTION

The debate regarding preventive detention of serious high-risk sex offenders is often played out as a dichotomy between proponents arguing for community protection *versus* opponents arguing for offender rights, as if the two positions are mutually exclusive. Advocates of community protection argue that serious high-risk offenders ought to be incapacitated and perhaps receive treatment as a risk management strategy (treatment-as-management). Advocates of offender rights argue that serious high-risk offenders should not be used as a means to an end and that they still possess human rights (treatment-as-rehabilitation). The role of mental health professionals currently influences court decision-making regarding preventive schemes, in terms of supervision or detention, based on their assessments of risk of re-offending.

Policy development in Canada, the United Kingdom and Australia has been heavily influenced by the risk management policy direction in the US, which relies upon risk management strategies such as community notification, sex offender registers, residency restrictions and civil commitment. Herzog-Evans noted that legal rules in the UK and Australia reflect the decline in the rehabilitative ideal while legal rules in France, Germany, and Spain support desistence from offending.[1] Petrunik and Deutschmann described this difference in terms of a continuum from sex offender exclusion (US risk management in response to populist pressure) to offender exclusion-inclusion (UK and Canadian

---

[1] M Herzog-Evans , 'Special Issue: "Judicial Rehabilitation" in Six Countries: Australia, England and Wales, France, Germany, The Netherlands, and Spain' (2011) 3(1) *European Journal of Probation*, 1–3.

rehabilitation programs) to sex offender inclusion (Canadian community-based restorative justice initiatives and European treatment models).[2] This continuum is also influenced by the independence of bureaucrats: in Continental Europe, bureaucrats are fiercely independent; in the US, bureaucrats are elected and so subject to lobbying regarding public policy; and in Canada and the UK (and presumably Australia), bureaucrats are located somewhere in the middle in being accountable to the elected government of the day.[3]

Public policy discourse around the topic of preventive detention tends to be based on an 'either/or' dichotomy between community protection and offender rights: for example, the balance between the rights of the community and potential victims versus the rights of offenders who have served a sentence[4] with an ensuing tension between community protection and legal principles,[5] the debate that all players in the criminal justice system ought to be concerned about 'making the best decisions about community safety, prevention, treatment, and the delivery of justice',[6] and the dilemma between punishment in the criminal justice system versus treatment in the mental health system.[7]

Preventive schemes are one public policy response to preventing future harm by serious high-risk sex offenders, purportedly to protect the community. This post-sentence strategy extends government control over sex offenders after they have served their prison sentences.[8] In particular, sex offenders are considered to be exceptionally risky, requiring special legislative control directly linked to punitive penal popularism.[9] Within this subgroup of sex offenders are those serious high-risk offenders who represent the pointy end of potential violations of offender rights and so require particular attention by practitioners regarding likely ethical problems. At 2013, such prevention schemes have been in Australia for a decade commencing with the *Dangerous Prisoners (Sexual Offenders) Act 2003* (QLD), followed by the *Dangerous Sexual Offenders Act 2006* (WA) and the *Crimes (Serious Sex Offenders) Act 2006* (NSW), and then followed by the *Serious*

---

2   M Petrunik and L Deutschmann, 'The Exclusion-Inclusion Spectrum in State and Community Response to Sex Offenders in Anglo-American and European Jurisdictions' (2008) 52(5) *International Journal of Offender Therapy and Comparative Criminology* 499–519.

3   Ibid.

4   B McSherry, 'High-Risk Offenders: Continued Detention and Supervision Options' (Community Issues Paper, Sentencing Advisory Council, Melbourne, 2006).

5   K Gelb, 'Recidivism of Sex Offenders' (Research Paper, Sentencing Advisory Council, Melbourne, 2007).

6   D A Andrews and J Bonta, *The Psychology of Criminal Conduct* (Anderson Publishing Co, 5th ed, 2010) 339.

7   A Birgden and F Vincent, 'Maximising Therapeutic Effects in Treating Sexual Offenders in an Australian Correctional System' (2000) 18(4) *Behavioural Sciences and Law* 479–88.

8   B McSherry and P Keyzer, *Sex Offenders and Preventive Detention: Politics, Policy and Practice* (Federation Press, 2009).

9   K Hannah-Moffat, 'Punishment and Risk' in J Simon and R Sparks (eds), *The SAGE Handbook of Punishment and Society* (Sage Publications, 2012) 129–51.

Sex Offenders (Detention and Supervision) Act 2009 (VIC). Preventive schemes restrict the liberty of serious sex offenders who *may* re-offend in the future and, as a consequence, subjects them to coerced treatment and management. Restricting liberty on the basis of what an individual may do undermines legal principles and core rights such as the presumption of innocence, finality of sentencing, the principle of proportionality and the principle against double punishment.[10] This significant departure from accepted criminal justice practices has implications for serious high-risk sex offenders in Australia. The following chapter will first consider the implications of assessing risk for preventive schemes in terms of science (does it work?) and ethics (is it the right thing to do?) and then recommend improvements to preventive schemes regarding procedures and roles of mental health professionals.

Craisatti has devised a useful structure for considering practical and policy implications in managing high-risk offenders in the community.[11] Adapted to preventive schemes, the following normative framework will be proposed. *Risk considerations* include offenders' risk of re-offending, the likely harm to the victims and what level of risk is posed in labelling offenders as serious high-risk. *Scientific considerations* require the risk of re-offending to be determined in order to predict risk, address dynamic risk factors and meet human needs. *Ethical considerations* include the sociopolitical risk management context, ethical principles that should be enacted by practitioners, regardless of the contemporary political environment, and the style of interaction with sex offenders that ethical practice therefore entails. At present, preventive schemes do not address the shaded areas (figure below) – risk considerations (risk to offender), scientific considerations (human needs), and the entirety of ethical considerations (the socio-political context, ethical principles and an ethic of care). If these areas were to be addressed in the procedures and roles of legal actors, then it is possible that offender rights would be met and community protection therefore enhanced.

---

10 Patrick Keyzer, Cathy Pereira and Stephen Southwood, 'Pre-emptive Imprisonment for Dangerousness in Queensland under the *Dangerous Prisoners (Sexual Offenders) Act 2003*: The Constitutional Issues' (2004) 11 *Psychiatry, Psychology and Law* 244–253; D J Doyle, J Ogloff, and S Thomas, 'Designated as Dangerous: Characteristics of Sex Offenders Subject to Post-Sentence Orders in Australia' (2011) 46 *Australian Psychologist* 41–8.

11 J Craisatti, *Managing High Risk Sex Offenders in the Community: A Psychological Approach* (Brunner-Rutledge, 2004).

Figure 1: A Preventive Scheme

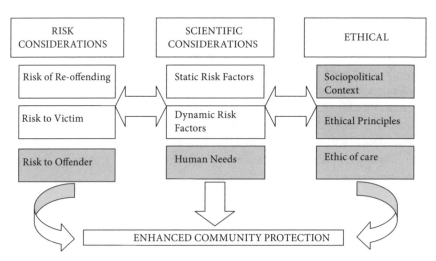

Adapted from Craisatti, 2004, 200.

Sentencing principles generally capture retribution, deterrence, incapacitation and rehabilitation.[12] In common, preventive schemes in Australia are designed to protect the community from the harm that sex offenders pose in re-offending. The emphasis here is on community protection by managing risk through detention or supervision, rather than emphasising rehabilitation. This is despite social science evidence based on meta-analyses of general offenders that lengthy detention actually increases the likelihood of re-offending, and intensive supervision alone does not reduce re-offending.[13] In current preventive legislation in the four Australian states, the primary objective is to ensure community protection and the secondary objective is to provide control, care, *or* treatment to facilitate rehabilitation (QLD), to merely provide control, care, *or* treatment (WA), or facilitate treatment *and* rehabilitation (VIC and NSW). Presumably Queensland considers that control alone can facilitate rehabilitation, and Western Australia is unconcerned about whether rehabilitation occurs. These objectives in legislation are applied whether sex offenders like it or not.

Within the objectives, conditions or directions are imposed upon offenders placed on supervision orders (there are no conditions for detention orders it seems). Under the *Serious Sex Offenders (Detention and Supervision) Act 2009* (VIC), the primary purpose of conditions imposed on offenders is to reduce the risk of re-offending and the secondary purpose is to consider the safety and

---

12   'Sentencing' (Discussion Paper No 33, NSW Law Reform Commission, 1996) <http://www.lawlink.nsw.gov.au/lrc.nsf/pages/DP33CHP3>.

13   See, eg, M W Lipsey and F T Cullen, 'The Effectiveness of Correctional Rehabilitation: A Review of Systematic Reviews' (2007) 3 *Annual Review of Law and Social Science* 297–320.

welfare of the victims (s 1). Regarding supervision orders, numerous conditions are listed and offenders may be ordered to reside in a residential facility if there is no other accommodation available (s 18). A residential facility is gazetted by the government and is designed to: case manage and supervise offenders; provide safe accommodation; protect the community; and support offenders to comply with the conditions on their orders (s 133). Eight core conditions that must be fulfilled are listed, and they are all focused on surveillance and management of the individual (s 16). Fifteen suggested conditions are listed that again focus on surveillance and management (s 17). Suggested condition (e) refers to treatment or rehabilitation programs or activities that the offender *must attend and participate in*. Provision is made for discretionary conditions that promote rehabilitation and treatment to reduce re-offending or provide for victims' safety and welfare such as restricted internet access or banned alcohol use (s 19). As a consequence, legislative intervention relies on surveillance and management to afford community protection rather than the state being obliged to meet identified offender needs that lead to an offending pathway in the first place.

As entry into preventive schemes turns on assessment, it is important to note the difference between a *serious* sex offender and a *high-risk* sex offender. Offender *seriousness* is determined in legislation. For example, 'serious offender offences' are defined in Schedule 1 of the *Sentencing Act 1991* (Vic) and include violent offences, serious violent offences, drug offences, arson offences and sexual offences (rape, indecent assault, and sexual penetration of a child under 16 years etc). Offender *risk* means the assessed risk of re-offending. However, the two constructs are often conflated in policy. The Victorian Attorney-General requested that the Sentencing Advisory Council provide 'advice about the merit of introducing a scheme that would allow for the continued detention of offenders who have reached the end of their custodial sentence but who are considered to pose a continued and serious danger to the community'.[14] This term of reference infers that repeat offenders are serious offenders. A more accurate descriptor is 'serious high-risk offenders'. Nevertheless, both risk and seriousness are normative judgements that try to resolve complex moral, social and ethical issues; they are not scientifically-based.[15] Judgements regarding seriousness are determined by legislative definitions (frequently driven by public opinion rather than science and ethics). Judgements regarding risk are often made by mental health professionals categorising 'low', 'medium' and 'high' risk (where cut-off levels of risk are driven by resource capacity rather than science and ethics). The normative nature of this issue raises scientific and ethical concerns regarding the assessment of risk and its consequences.

---

[14]   McSherry, above n 4, 1.
[15]   A Birgden, 'Offender Rehabilitation: A Normative Framework for Forensic Psychologists' (2008) 15(3) *Psychiatry, Psychology and Law* 1–19.

2. ISSUES: RISK, SCIENCE, AND ETHICS

At 2008, there were 82 sex offenders subject to preventive schemes in Australia,[16] and in the period 2010–11 there were 36 offenders subject to supervision orders in Victoria.[17] Despite the likely increase in numbers, there is no outcome data regarding the efficacy of prevention schemes since they emerged in the Australian context in 2003. The following section will raise scientific and ethical concerns regarding risk prediction and risk management.

2.1. RISK PREDICTION

Preventive strategies rely upon judgements regarding the risk of re-offending, and a finding of high-risk opens the gateway to preventive detention and supervision. In legislation, the risk of re-offending is ultimately determined by the court. The *Serious Sex Offenders (Detention and Supervision) Act 2009* (VIC) indicates that a detention or supervision order is to be imposed if the court is satisfied that there is an unacceptable risk (s 35), even if the likelihood that the offender will commit a relevant offence is less than a likelihood of more likely than not (s 35(4)). In regard to a supervision order specifically, the court must be satisfied by acceptable, cogent evidence and a high degree of probability that the evidence is of sufficient weight to justify the decision (s 9(2)). In making this determination, the court relies upon the opinion of mental health professionals. Briefly, there are three possible methods for mental health professionals to determine the likelihood of re-offending-clinical judgement, actuarial assessment and structured clinical judgement.[18] *Clinical judgement* involves predictions based upon the collection of information about offenders and their situations, relying on unstructured interview, files searches, psychological testing and so on. Monahan in a seminal review concluded that psychiatrists and psychologists who used clinical judgement were inaccurate in two out of three predictions of violence in mentally disordered clients released from institutions.[19] *Actuarial assessments* are based on empirical research and theories to develop a list of risk factors, empirically test them on

[16] D J Doyle and J Ogloff, 'Calling the Tune without the Music: A Psycho-Legal Analysis of Australia's Post-Sentence Legislation' (2009) 42(2) *Australian and New Zealand Journal of Criminology* 179–203.

[17] Victoria, Legislative Assembly, 26 October 2011.

[18] D A Andrews and J Bonta, *The Psychology of Criminal Conduct* (Anderson Publishing Co, 5th ed, 2010); R K Hanson, 'What Do We Know about Sex Offender Risk Assessment?' (1998) 4(1/2) *Psychology, Public Policy, and Law* 50–72; K Heilbrun, J R P Ogloff and K Picarello, 'Dangerous Offender Statutes in the United States and Canada: Implications for Risk Assessment. (1999) 22 *International Journal of Law and Psychiatry* 393–415; Krauss et al, 'Beyond Prediction to Explanation in Risk Assessment Research: A Comparison of Two Explanatory Theories of Criminality and Recidivism' (2000) 23(2) International Journal of Law and Psychiatry 91–112.

[19] J Monahan, *The Clinical Prediction of Violent Behaviour* (Government Printing Office, Washington DC, 1981).

various populations, and create a common set of questions applied to everyone and weighted to produce a score to categorise the person. *Structured clinical judgement* is a more comprehensive analysis of theoretically and empirically determined static and dynamic risk factors linked to re-offending with an overall opinion of re-offence risk provided rather than a probability estimate. It has been argued on the one hand, that actuarial methods should completely replace clinical judgement[20] and on the other hand, that clinicians should be able to revise actuarial risk estimates on the basis of clinical judgement.[21]

In assessing risk, psychiatrists tend to apply clinical judgement while psychologists tend to apply actuarial assessment and/or structured clinical judgement. Whether assessors are to be psychiatrists or psychologists varies between states. For example, assessors in Victoria may be medical experts (psychiatrist, psychologist or other health provider), assessors in New South Wales may be psychiatrists or psychologists, and assessors in Western Australia and Queensland must be psychiatrists. On the one hand, psychologists have argued that the profession is in a better position to conduct risk assessments as psychologists tend to conduct more research in the area and psychiatrists have not been shown to be any better at predicting risk.[22] On the other hand, psychiatrists have criticised psychologists for being too reliant on actuarial assessments at the expense of clinical judgement and diagnostic abilities.[23] At present, across three Australian states, psychiatrists conduct risk assessments for the courts regarding preventive schemes more often than psychologists at a 6:4 ratio.[24]

As stated, psychologists administer actuarial tools to determine the risk of re-offending. The Static-99 is the most utilised actuarial risk assessment tool applied in the courts in North America to assess recidivism in adult male sex offenders.[25] The Static-99 measures ten static (or unchangeable) risk factors that include previous sexual and non-sexual offences and unrelated/stranger/male victims.[26] In Victoria, the Static-99 is utilised to screen for risk, and those offenders who score greater than 6 (high-risk) are then referred to an independent

20   See, eg, Quinsey et al, *Violent Offenders: Assessing and Managing Risk* (American Psychological Association, 1998).
21   See, eg, Hanson, above n 19.
22   C C Mercado and J R P Ogloff, 'Risk and the Preventive Detention of Sex Offenders in Australia and the United States' (2007) 30 *International Journal of Law and Psychiatry* 49–59.
23   McSherry and Keyzer, above n 9.
24   D J Doyle, J Ogloff and S Thomas, 'Designated as Dangerous: Characteristics of Sex Offenders Subject to Post-Sentence Orders in Australia' (2011) 46 *Australian Psychologist* 41–8.
25   L Helmus et al, *Static-99R: Revised Age Weights* (5 October 2009) Static-99 Clearinghouse <http://www.static99.org/pdfdocs/static-99randage20091005.pdf>.
26   A Harris et al, *STATIC-99 Coding Rules Revised-2003* (2003) Public Safety Canada <http://www.publicsafety.gc.ca/res/cor/rep/_fl/2003-03-stc-cde-eng.pdf>.

psychologist for a full risk assessment.[27] As it is a popular tool, the scientific and ethical concerns regarding the Static-99 will be discussed in more detail.

The Static-99 has been empirically shown to provide explicit probability estimates of sexual re-offending, albeit at a moderate predictive accuracy.[28] However, the Static-99 has also been found to both over-estimate re-offending for those individuals who score above 4 (moderate- to high-risk) and under-estimate re-offending for a score of 0 or 1 (low-risk) with re-offending at twice the predicted rate.[29] This is of concern because if a screen on the Static-99 identifies that a person is high-risk then the psychologist conducting the more detailed clinical assessment may be influenced by that result. Additional versions of the tool, including the Static-99/R and the Static-2002/R, have been developed with updated age weights as it was found that older offenders are less likely to re-offend when released. Most recently, Helmus et al evaluated the absolute predictive accuracy of these two tools. They found that while there was stability in relative risk (comparing recidivists to non-recidivists) there was instability in absolute recidivism rates (eg, a ten-year predicted rate ranging between 3 per cent and 20 per cent in different samples of offenders). This means that such tools can lead to different conclusions regarding the same offender's predicted recidivism rate. The authors warned that the linking of scores to recidivism rates 'turned out to be a gross simplification [which] complicates the interpretation of these Static risk measures…evaluators cannot, in an unqualified way, associate a single reliable recidivism estimate with a single score on the Static-99/R or Static-2002/R risk scales'.[30] Structured clinical judgement was recommended as a consequence to supplement these tools. Moreover, in 2012 a United States judge in Wisconsin barred the result of a Static-99/R administered for a sexually violent predator case. According to Franklin, this was the result of the refusal of one of the expert witnesses- and developer of the tool- to provide the Static-99/R data requested by the defence as part of a *Daubert* challenge (to establish the scientific reliability and validity of expert testimony before the court).[31]

In response to these findings, Franklin warned that the Static-99 tools are normed on high-risk offender groups (who are more easily accessible for developing

---

27   J Vess and L Eccleston, 'Extended Supervision of Sex Offenders in Australia and New Zealand: Differences in Implementation across Jurisdictions' (2009) 16(2) *Psychiatry, Psychology and Law* 271–87.
28   Harris et al, above n 26.
29   L Helmus et al, *Variability in Static-99R and Static-2002R Recidivism Estimates: Absolute Recidivism Rates Predicted by Static-99R and Static-2002R Sex Offender Risk Assessment Tools Vary across Samples: A Meta-Analysis* (12 January 2012) Static-99 Clearinghouse <http://www.static99.org/pdfdocs/Helmus_et_al_2012_ActuarialBaseRateVariabilityInPress.pdf>.
30   Ibid 22–3.
31   K Franklin, 'Judge bars Static-99R risk tool from SVP trial' on Karen Franklin, *In the News: Forensic Psychology, Criminology, and Psychology-Law* (14 December 2013) <http://forensicpsychologist.blogspot.com/2012/12/judge-bars-static-99r-risk-tool-from.html>.

tests).[32] She provided the unethical scenario where a sex offender is referred in a biased manner (eg, based on race or sexual orientation) and is then subjected to a tool that has not been peer-reviewed regarding its validity and reliability and will undoubtedly elevate the risk level in comparison to 'ordinary' offenders. Franklin concluded that such tools are therefore inadequate for legal proceedings. Evidence regarding the use of the Static-99 in an internet chat room case in the United States discounted the psychologist's evidence. Upon appeal, the Seventh Circuit highlighted problems with the Static-99 such as moderate predictive accuracy, low base rates for sex offending and too limited a number of potentially relevant characteristics; the Court's view was that the judge was entitled to discount the prediction.[33]

Regardless, best practice in predicting risk of re-offending is considered to be the application of empirically validated actuarial measures combined with specific dynamic (ie, changeable or treatable) risk factors for sexual re-offending.[34] It would be expected that mental health professionals conducting risk assessments for the court in Australia are doing so in the context of structured clinical judgement that includes assessment of dynamic risk factors.[35] Andrews and Bonta have identified eight empirically-derived dynamic risk factors for general offenders.[36] However, they view less promising dynamic risk factors as: increasing self-esteem without addressing anti-social attitudes, associates, and groups; conventional ambition regarding education and employment without providing concrete assistance; focusing on vague emotional/personal complaints not linked to offending; improving neighbourhood conditions without targeting dynamic risk factors; and showing respect for anti-social thinking or attempting to turn the offender into a 'better person' when that standard is not linked to re-offending. Various static and dynamic risk factors have been identified in sex offenders. These include: the number and type of victims and offences (particularly diverse sexual offences, non-contact offense, extra-familial child victims, male child victims, and stranger victims); commencing sex offending at a young age; having never been married; conflict in intimate relationships; psychopathy and hostility; deviant sexual arousal; attitudes tolerant of sexual assault; emotional identification with children and negative emotional states, exacerbated by mood

---

[32]   K Franklin, 'Static-99R Risk Estimate Widely Unstable, Developers Admit' on Karen Franklin, *In the News: Forensic Psychology, Criminology, and Psychology-Law* (18 October 2012) <http://forensicpsychologist.blogspot.com/2012/10/static-99r-risk-estimates-wildly.html>.

[33]   C Miller, 'Static Cling?: Seventh Circuit Doubts Reliability of Static-99 Results in Recent Opinion' on Colin Miller, *EvidenceProf Blog* (20 January 2008). <http://www.lawprofessors.typepad.com/evidenceprof/2008/01/the-static-99-i.html>.

[34]   Vess and Eccleston, above n 27.

[35]   'Dynamic risk' and 'criminogenic need' are the same construct.

[36]   D A Andrews and J Bonta, *The Psychology of Criminal Conduct* (Anderson Publishing Co, 5th ed, 2010).

changes and substance use; poor interpersonal skills/self-management; poor social support; and treatment drop out.[37]

An example of a tool that utilises structured clinical judgement is the Sexual Violence Risk-20 (SVR-20).[38] The SVR-20 is a 20-item checklist identified from a literature review and includes the history of sex offending, psychosocial adjustment and future plans. Further, the SVR-20 considers some rare but contextualised risk factors such as relationship breakdown or job loss, frequent contact with potential victims and poor attitude toward treatment. On the one hand, Wood and Ogloff indicated that the SVR-20 has been found to have better predictive value than the Static-99 with the proviso that it still needs to be tested on a range of populations for use in court.[39] On the other hand, Singh et al, in comparing the Static-99 and the SVR-20, concluded that they were roughly equivalent using a ranking system for predictive validity.[40]

It is important to note that dynamic risk factors are correlational in that they do not 'cause' re-offending. Dynamic risk factors are also yet to be empirically derived and so are currently based on clinical experience, theoretical inference and common-sense.[41] As a consequence, the assessment criteria for the risk areas are vaguely defined as 'non-rewarding family relationships', 'attitudes supportive of crime', 'could make better use of time' and so on.[42] Therefore, such structured clinical judgement tools are still in their early stages of development and cannot yet be relied upon to identify treatment targets or likely changes in risky behaviour or determine changes in risk levels; they are better at making commitment than release decisions.[43] Dynamic factors include risk factors that increase risk and protective factors that decrease risk.[44] Protective factors and situational factors are less well articulated in the literature and ought to include social relationships that

---

[37]   R K Hanson and K Morton-Bourgon, 'Predictors of Sexual Recidivism: An Updated Meta-Analysis' (Report No 2004–02, Public Safety and Emergency Preparedness Canada, February 2004) <http://www.publicsafety.gc.ca/res/cor/rep/_fl/2004-02-pred-se-eng.pdf>; D Perkins et al, 'Review of Sex Offender Treatment Programmes' (Prepared for the High Security Psychiatric Services Commissioning Board (HSPSCB), November 1998) <http://www.ramas.co.uk/report4.pdf >.

[38]   D P Boer et al, *Manual for the Sexual Violence Risk – 20: Professional Guidelines for Assessing Risk of Sexual Violence* (The Mental Health, Law, and Policy Institute, Vancouver, 1997).

[39]   M Wood and J R P Ogloff, 'Victoria's *Serious Sex Offender Monitoring Act 2005*: Implications for Accuracy of Sex Offender Risk Assessment' (2006) 13(2) *Psychiatry, Psychology and Law* 182–98.

[40]   J P Singh, M Grann and S Fazel, 'A Comparative Study of Violence Risk Assessment Tools: A Systematic Review and Metaregression Analysis of 68 Studies Involving 25,980 Participants' (2011) 31 *Clinical Psychology Review* 500–12.

[41]   Andrews and Bonta, above n 36.

[42]   K Hannah-Moffat, P Maurutto and S Turnbull, 'Negotiated Risk: Actuarial Illusions and Discretion in Probation' (2009) 24(3) *Canadian Journal of Law and Society* 391–409.

[43]   Mercado and Ogloff, above n 22.

[44]   T W Campbell, 'Sex Offenders and Actuarial Risk Assessments: Ethical Considerations' (2003) 21 *Behavioural Sciences and the Law* 269–79.

may counteract risk factors and lower re-offending[45] and environmental factors such as unsupervised release environments.[46] Nonetheless, structured clinical judgement provides a shift from risk prediction to risk management in order to determine risk factors, type of harm, and likelihood that harm will occur.[47]

In general, all risk assessment tools pose scientific and ethical problems.[48] Szmukler has contrasted the 'numbers' in risk assessment (the statistical likelihood of re-offending within a particular timeline) and the 'values' in risk assessment (attaching a value to the risk assessment outcome and determining what to do about it).[49] The former is an evidence-based consideration, and the latter is an ethical consideration. First, risk assessment tools are wholly or partially based on static (ie, unchangeable or untreatable) risk factors, which means that although they may identify certain risk factors and predict risk, they do not provide guidance on how to manage future risk. Second, contrary to popular opinion, sex offenders have very low re-offending rates and tend to not have previous convictions.[50] This low base rate effects the accuracy of predicting risk. Accurate risk prediction can best be achieved when the base rates of re-offending are 30 to 60 per cent.[51] Most recently the sexual re-offending rate in 23 samples (N=8,106) was measured and was found to be between 4 and 12 per cent at five-year follow-up (most likely 7% or less) and between 6 and 22 per cent at ten-year follow-up.[52] In Australia, one study found that the sexual re-offending rate was also low for untreated adult rapists (4.5%) and untreated child sex offenders (5.6%) at up to seven-year follow-up.[53] Based on 17 Australian studies, Lievore concluded that most base rates for sexual re-offending were below 10 per cent. Third, actuarial risk assessment tools provide probability estimates as opposed to a certainty (eg, a 60% likelihood of re-offending) that compares an offender to a group of 'like' offenders but cannot determine whether the offender actually belongs to the group who is likely to offend (ie, 60% category) or is unlikely to offend (ie,

---

[45]   P Maurutto and K Hannah-Moffat, 'Assembling Risk and the Restructuring of Penal Control' (2006) 46(3) *British Journal of Criminology* 438–54.

[46]   Hanson, above n 18.

[47]   Heilbrun, Ogloff and Picarello, above n 18.

[48]   See A R Beech, D D Fisher and D Thornton, 'Risk Assessment of Sex Offenders' (2003) 34(4) *Professional Psychology, Research and Practice* 339–52; K Hannah-Moffat, P Maurutto and S Turnbull, above n 43; McSherry and Keyzer, above n 8.

[49]   G Szmukler, 'Risk Assessment: "Numbers" and "Values"' (2003) 27 *Psychiatric Bulletin* 205–207.

[50]   See Gelb, above n 5.

[51]   D A Andrews, J Bonta and R D Hoge, 'Classification for Effective Rehabilitation: Rediscovering Psychology' (1990) 17(1) *Criminal Justice and Behaviour* 19–52.

[52]   Helmus et al, above n 29.

[53]   D M Greenberg, J Da Silva and N Loh, *Evaluation of the Western Australian Sex Offender Treatment Unit (1987–1999)*: A Quantitative Analysis (Forensic Research Unit, Department of Psychiatry and Behavioural Sciences and the Crime Research Centre, The University of Western Australia, 2002) cited in D Lievore, *Recidivism of Sexual Assault Offenders: Rates, Risk Factors, and Treatment Efficacy* (Australian Institute of Criminology, 2004).

40% category). This problem raises issues for the court who consider each sex offender on a case-by-case basis. For example, in 1998 the Western Australian Parole Board determined that while sex offenders who refuse treatment may be moderate- to high-risk, 'the Board generally accepts these assessments, but in the end is obliged to deal with each prisoner individually'.[54] Fourth, risk assessment tools can result in 'false positives' (the detention of an ineligible sex offender) or 'false negatives' (the release of an eligible sex offender). Further, Fazel, Singh, Doll, and Grann conducted a thorough systematic review and meta-analysis of 24,827 offenders subject to risk assessments across 13 countries (1995–2011) and concluded that tools that predicted violent offending were more accurate than those that predicted sex offending, and all such tools identified low-risk offenders with more accuracy than high-risk offenders.[55] Of concern is that, of sex offenders judged to be moderate- or high-risk, only 23 per cent went on to re-offend; for every one offender correctly identified, three will be falsely identified as recidivists. The authors concluded that while risk assessment tools can be used to guide rehabilitation and management decisions in corrections, they should not be used as sole determinants of detention or discharge in courts. Put another way, they should 'only be used to roughly classify individuals at the group level, and not to safely determine criminal prognosis in an individual case',[56] although at least such tools can be used to rule out low-risk offenders being subject to preventive schemes.

Fifth, risk assessment tools are insensitive to sex offender types and individual characteristics. Different re-offending rates are found for different types of sex offenders, and sex offenders are not homogenous.[57] In terms of individual characteristics, cultural and gender insensitivity has been of concern. The authors of the Static-99 argued that, although the tool is mainly normed on a white sample, race is not a risk factor for re-offending and therefore the Static-99 is considered culturally neutral.[58] Meanwhile, Singh, Grann and Fazel compared numerous risk assessment tools, including the Static-99, in a meta-regression analysis of 25,980 offenders and concluded that predictive validity was better in those samples with white participants.[59] In discussing indigenous offenders in Canada in general, Rugge noted that there is over-representation regarding socioeconomic disadvantage such as unemployment, poor education, poor health, dysfunctional families, community police presence and so on which, while it does not mean that being indigenous causes offending, indigenous

---

[54] *Varney v Parole Board* (2000) 117 A Crim R 541, 518.
[55] S Fazel et al, 'Use of Risk Assessment Instruments to Predict Violence and Antisocial Behaviour in 73 Samples Involving 24827 People: Systematic Review and Meta-Analysis' (2012) 345 *British Medical Journal* 1–12.
[56] Ibid 5.
[57] See Gelb, above n 5.
[58] Harris et al, above n 26.
[59] Singh, Grann and Fazel above n 40.

peoples are over-represented on certain risk factors.[60] In Australia, Hsu, Caputi and Byrne[61] considered a generalist actuarial risk assessment tool – the Level of Service Inventory-Revised[62] – applied to 13,911 male and female indigenous offenders in New South Wales Corrective Services between 2004 and 2007. They found that indigenous offenders scored higher than non-indigenous offenders on every subscale and on the total score. Overall, Hsu et al found that indigenous offenders had lengthier criminal records, more violent crimes, lower education and employment status, more living arrangement issues, more anti-social peers, and offended at a younger age and re-offended more promptly. Note that these observations are in relation to general offending, not sex offending *per se*. Rugge supported the view that all these problem areas (not just those to be empirically found to be correlated with re-offending) ought to be included in the initial development of risk assessment tools.

Last, the statistical nature of actuarial tools masks the range of discretionary and value judgments that occur, informed by personal knowledge, experience and beliefs; Canadian practitioners reported that they would ensure a high-risk designation for sex offenders or, conversely, for more general offenders 'modify the strict interpretation of risk criteria and fill out scores by incorporating preconceived and non-actuarial knowledge of offenders [reducing] the overall risk by score by choosing to ignore various criminogenic factors or by scoring certain factors as relatively low'.[63] Overall, Fazel et al concluded that an important message has to be provided to bureaucrats, the media, the community (and presumably the judiciary): the view that risk assessment tools are accurate in most cases is not evidence-based.[64]

2.2. RISK MANAGEMENT

Once subjected to preventive detention, risk then needs to be managed. To reiterate, in the four Australian states the secondary objective in legislation is to provide control, care, treatment and/or rehabilitation. In practice, it is expected that strategies such as incapacitation, residence in identified facilities, intensive supervision and offender rehabilitation result. However, where incapacitation goes beyond the least restrictive means or utilises burdensome restrictions,

---

[60] T Rugge, 'Risk Assessment of Male Aboriginal Offenders: A 2006 Perspective' (Report No 2006–01, Corrections Research, Public Safety and Emergency Preparedness Canada, January 2006)<http://www.bpiepc-ocipep.gc.ca/res/cor/rep/_fl/abo-offen-eng.pdf>.
[61] C-I Hsu, P Caputi and M K Byrne, 'Level of Service Inventory-Revised: Assessing the Risk and Need Characteristics of Australian Indigenous Offenders' (2011) 17(3) *Psychiatry, Psychology, and Law* 355–67.
[62] D A Andrews and J Bonta, *The Level of Service Inventory-Revised* (Multihealth Systems, 1995).
[63] Hannah-Moffat, Maurutto and Turnbull, above n 42, 402.
[64] S Fazel et al, above n 55.

the treatment process becomes punishment.[65] What 'rehabilitation' means in legislation is undefined. Based on legislative objectives, it is assumed that the emphasis is on what has been described by Birgden and Cucolo[66] as treatment-as-management (ie, managing offender risk) rather than treatment-as-rehabilitation (ie, meeting offender need). Heseltine, Day and Sarre noted that, where relevant, Australian legislation only mentions rehabilitation as a legal requirement rather than to guide the value, purpose and structure of rehabilitation, allowing the government to avoid concrete commitment to the rehabilitative ideal.[67]

According to the North American Association for the Treatment of Sexual Abusers (ATSA), the treatment of male sex offenders is designed to: (1) assist offenders to identify and change thoughts, feelings, and behaviours that lead to re-offending; (2) develop strategies and plans to control, avoid, and productively address risk factors for re-offending (a risk management approach); and (3) develop offender strengths and competencies to address needs.[68] Addressing 'needs' can either be a risk management approach (if targeting dynamic risk factors and providing treatment-as-management) or an offender support approach (if supporting human needs and providing treatment-as-rehabilitation), but ATSA is silent on this distinction. Sex offender treatment and rehabilitation in Australia has been found to follow prescribed international standards based on the Risk-Need-Responsivity (RNR) model of offender rehabilitation.[69] The RNR model is the dominant approach in Canada, the United Kingdom, New Zealand and Australia. The RNR model is based on 'what works' empirical literature developed by Andrews and Bonta and their colleagues. The model is a science of criminal conduct which links risk prediction and classification (described above) with treatment targets and treatment intensity and directs service delivery to reduce the risk of re-offending by addressing identified dynamic risk factors.[70] Briefly, the model includes principles regarding risk (who should be targeted for treatment), need (what should be targeted for treatment), and responsivity (how treatment should be delivered). The problem with the RNR approach is that it emphasises risk management for community protection.[71]

---

[65]   E J Miller, 'Embracing Addiction: Drug Courts and the False Promises of Judicial Interventionism' (2004) 65 *Ohio State Law Journal* 1479–1576.

[66]   A Birgden and H Cucolo, 'The Treatment of Sex Offenders: Evidence, Ethics, and Human Rights' (2010) 23(3) *Sexual Abuse: A Journal of Research and Treatment* 295–313.

[67]   K Heseltine, A Day and R Sarre, 'Prison-Based Correctional Offender Programs: The 2009 National Picture in Australia' (AIC Reports: Research and Public Policy Series 112, Australian Institute of Criminology, 2011).

[68]   Association for the Treatment of Sexual Abusers, *Sex Offender Treatment for Adult Males* (2008)<http://www.atsa.com/sites/default/files/ppSOAdultMaleTx.pdf >.

[69]   Heseltine, Day and Sarre, above n 67.

[70]   A W Leschied, 'Implementation of Effective Correctional Programs' in L L Motiuk and R C Serin (eds), *Compendium 2000 on Effective Correctional Programming, Volume 1* (Canada: Ministry of Supply and Services, 2001).

[71]   See Birgden, above n 15.

Heseltine et al provided an updated audit of all sex offender programs in Australia, noting that legislative developments had increased the focus on rehabilitation of high-risk and dangerous sex offenders.[72] Of the four states with preventive schemes, Heseltine et al found that there were well-developed case management systems to identify, assess, and allocate sex offenders. Again, the Static-99 is used to identify the level of risk and then the level and type of need is determined through interview and further actuarial assessment with additional determination of treatment readiness or responsivity, the rehabilitation options available and extensive pre-post testing of change. As in other jurisdictions, the program content utilises cognitive-behavioural treatment and aims to develop insight into offending, increase understanding of the effects on the victims, challenge cognitive (or thinking) distortions that justify offending, modify deviant sexual arousal, explore the role of fantasy, develop appropriate intimacy and relationship skills, enhance problem solving, and develop an individualised relapse prevention plan with places and situations to avoid.

3.   IMPROVING PREVENTIVE SCHEMES

As previously indicated, the implementation of preventive schemes does not address the entirety of ethical considerations and only aspects of scientific or risk considerations. Current preventive schemes lack consideration of the impacts of the current sociopolitical context, applied ethical principles, the style of service delivery, meeting human needs, and determining the risk imposed upon offenders and what this all may mean for community protection; RNR is an inadequate model to address these issues.

Therapeutic jurisprudence (TJ) considers social science evidence regarding law, legal procedures and legal roles based on the value stance that the law ought to be therapeutic rather than anti-therapeutic.[73] As an inter-disciplinary endeavour, TJ produces scholarship that is particularly useful to law reform. However, in TJ terms, preventive schemes are unlikely to be reformed; the High Court of Australia, in reviewing the *Dangerous Prisoners (Sexual Offenders) Act 2003* (QLD), confirmed that preventive detention was constitutional in *Fardon v Attorney-General (Qld)*[74] and was a legitimate, preventative and non-punitive purpose in the public interest (ie, community rights). However, this does not mean that the procedures and roles of legal actors (in this case mental health professionals) cannot aim to be therapeutic rather than anti-therapeutic when implementing preventive schemes.

---

[72]   Heseltine, Day and Sarre, above n 67.
[73]   See www.therapeuticjurisprudence.org and D Wexler and B Winick, *Law in a Therapeutic Key: Developments in Therapeutic Jurisprudence* (Carolina Academic Press, 1996).
[74]   *Fardon v Attorney-General (Qld)* (2004) 223 CLR 575.

3.1. ETHICAL CONSIDERATIONS

Ethical considerations include the sociopolitical risk management context, ethical principles that should be enacted by practitioners regardless of the contemporary political environment, and the style of interaction with sex offenders that ethical practice therefore entails. While legislation does consider offender rights, it is questionable whether these rights are implemented in practice due to the sociopolitical environment. For example, the *Serious Sex Offenders (Detention and Supervision) Act 2009* (VIC) indicates that any conditions, other than the core conditions, must minimally interfere with the offender's liberty, privacy or freedom of movement and be reasonably related to the gravity of the risk of re-offending (s 15(6)). Most recently, the *Serious Sex Offenders (Detention and Supervision) Amendment Act 2011* (VIC) has allowed that the obligation to apply for periodic reviews is suspended if a renewal application is being made and to remove the obligation to apply for a periodic review for offenders held on remand. In *Fletcher v the Secretary to the Department of Justice 2006*, a child sex offender placed on an extended supervision order in the community under previous legislation – the Serious Sex Offenders Monitoring Act 2005 (VIC), which back then did not authorise preventive detention – argued that being directed by the Adult Parole Board to reside at the secure facility meant he was denied freedom of movement and was not able to leave the facility unless escorted by Corrections Victoria staff.[75] The facility was on a portion of land degazetted from Ararat Prison but within the prison walls. The Supreme Court acknowledged that Mr Fletcher's freedom of movement was severely impacted, concurred that this situation could not be described as 'residing in the community', found that the Adult Parole Board had engaged in improper and unlawful exercise of power in ordering him to reside there, and determined that the Department of Justice was responsible for providing appropriate residential accommodation (although the Court did not define what 'residing in the community' meant). The Court did support the Adult Parole Board imposing conditions regarding the level of supervision in the community. In response, the Victorian government amended the legislation to provide the Adult Parole Board with the power to direct an offender on a supervision order to reside within the perimeter of a prison, and later 'Corella Place' on the grounds of Ararat Prison but outside the wall of the prison was established as a residential facility under the *Serious Sex Offenders (Detention and Supervision) Act 2009* (VIC). In practice, there currently appears little distinction between community supervision and detention for some sex offenders.

While legislation may or may not support human rights, practitioners ought to regardless. As highlighted by Ward and Salmon, 'every aspect of practice [with sex offenders] is shot through with value commitments, and each of us

---

[75]   *Fletcher v Secretary to the Department of Justice* [2006] VSC 354.

is obligated to think deeply about our responsibilities to sex offenders, victims, the community and ourselves'.[76] Offender assessment and treatment necessarily involves moral values regarding community rights and offender rights. A community rights approach imposes rehabilitation for behaviour change upon the individual (treatment-as-management), while an offender rights approach engages the individual to consider rehabilitation to facilitate behaviour change (treatment-as-rehabilitation). There is no question that offenders as autonomous agents have enforceable human rights,[77] and if human rights are held by all humans then sex offenders also possess human rights.[78] The state should generally provide the offender with the same rights for a dignified life as it provides to non-offenders, and the violation of human rights occurs when individuals are treated as objects or as a means to other individuals' ends.[79] For example, subjecting serious but low-risk offenders or less serious but high-risk offenders to preventive detention in response to community outrage is a violation, and assessors ought not to provide recommendations that support preventive detention under those circumstances. As discussed, legislation in preventive schemes is clear that community protection overrides offender rights. However, from a human rights perspective, it is not morally acceptable for human beings to forfeit their human rights altogether, although they may be curtailed in some circumstances. In particular, preventive schemes cannot be justified if they do not provide access to ethical and effective rehabilitation. An individual's universal entitlement to lead a dignified life can be a *moral* right (ie, based on a moral theory or principle), a *social* right (ie, guaranteed by a social institution such a prison), and a *legal* right (ie, prescribed by particular laws).[80] Human rights reflect both social rights and legal rights (or policies and procedures) and moral rights (or principles).

Ward and Birgden have noted that there is a lack of theoretical and research attention paid to the application of human rights to offender rehabilitation, presumably as a result of popular punitivism.[81] In particular, Perlin argued that there is a significant and disturbing disconnect between psychology practice

---

[76]   T Ward and K Salmon, 'The Ethics of Care and Treatment of Sex Offenders' (2011) 23(3) *Sexual Abuse: A Journal of Research and Treatment* 397–413, 398.

[77]   See P Keyzer and S Blay, 'Double Punishment? Preventive Detention Schemes under Australian Legislation and Their Consistency with International Law: The *Fardon* Communication' (2006) 7 *Melbourne Journal of International Law* 407; A Birgden and M L Perlin '"Tolling for the Luckless, the Abandoned and Forsaked": Therapeutic Jurisprudence and International Human Rights Law as Applied to Prisoners and Detainees by Forensic Psychologists'(2008) 13 *Legal and Criminological Psychology* 231–43; T Ward and A Birgden, 'Human Rights and Clinical Correctional Practice' (2007) 12(6) *Aggression and Violent Behaviour* 628–43.

[78]   T Ward, T E Gannon and A Birgden, 'Human Rights and the Treatment of Sex Offenders' (2007) 19(3) *Sexual Abuse: A Journal of Research and Treatment* 195–204. See also Keyzer and Blay, ibid.

[79]   Ward and Birgden, above n 77.

[80]   Ibid.

[81]   Ibid.

and human rights norms.[82] Human rights violations arise because of abuse of power, the vulnerability of clients, blurred role boundaries and lack of respect for the individual's rights and dignity. Ward and Birgden argued that it is time for forensic psychologists to consider human rights to guide offender rehabilitation, and they subsequently proposed a human rights model. Briefly, the human rights model argues that the two core moral values of freedom (non-coerced situations and internal capabilities such as the capacity to formulate intentions, to imagine possible actions and to form and implement valued plans) and well-being (physical, social and psychological well-being as defined by offenders) should be ensured. Even if serious high-risk offenders are rights-violators, a human rights perspective would consider that they still possess well-being rights and some freedom rights which should not be overridden by community rights.[83] Understanding that human rights support autonomy and dignity assists practitioners to deliver ethical rehabilitation.

From a human rights perspective, offenders are simultaneously *rights-holders* (with a right to non-interference in personal affairs unless they infringe upon the rights of others), *duty-bearers* (in that they are able to pursue goals as long as they do not infringe upon the rights of others), and *rights-violators* (when they infringe upon the rights of others through offending behaviour).[84] Therefore, although rights-violators, sex offenders are also rights-holders and duty-bearers or carry both rights and responsibilities.[85] Sex offender programs based on a human rights model would treat sex offenders as rights-holders (addressing histories of neglect, abuse and inadequate socialisation that require support to achieve goals in socially acceptable ways) as well as duty-bearers (providing learning experiences and resources to develop due regard for the rights of others through increasing empathy skills, problem solving capacity, supportive social networks and intimacy skills or appropriate alternatives). If sex offenders are acknowledged as rights-holders and duty-bearers as well as rights-violators, then this will support 'rights and duties, duties and rights: the ethical foundations of a liberal and flourishing community and a fairer and more humane criminal justice system'.[86] Equipping sex offenders with the capabilities necessary to both secure their own rights and those of others ought to reduce the risk of re-offending.

---

[82] M L Perlin, '"With Faces Hidden while the Walls Were Tightening": Applying International Human Rights Standards to Forensic Psychology' (Paper presented at the 30th International Conference of the Society of Interamerican Psychologists, Buenos Aires, Argentina, June 2005).
[83] Ward and Birgden, above n 77.
[84] See ibid; Ward, Gannon and Birgden, above n 78.
[85] Ward, Gannon and Birgden, above n 78.
[86] Ward and Birgden, above n 77, 642.

Australian national standards for offender program delivery are currently being developed.[87] However, nowhere in the national audit of current programs is the issue of consent to rehabilitation, or coerced rehabilitation, addressed. Presumably sex offenders subject to preventive schemes are coerced to some extent to engage in treatment. Lack of treatment engagement while serving a sentence can lead to consideration for prevention schemes. Informed consent is made up of capacity, information and voluntariness. While the informed consent process may include the provision of adequate information and the capacity of the offender to understand, the voluntariness of the decision within corrections is vexed.[88] Coerced treatment interferes with offender autonomy. Autonomous individuals develop an integrated life (or a good life) by reviewing and shaping their projects, motives and conduct.[89] Autonomy may be restricted by lack of rights and capacity such as poor decision-making or by lack of rights and skill such as poor control of deviant arousal. Whether the criminal justice system should be concerned with autonomy is a normative question, but at present it is expected that individuals should be protected in this way; it is a basic moral obligation.[90] Threats to autonomy ought to be of concern to practitioners who need to consider the ethical complexities in working effectively with coerced sex offenders subject to preventive schemes.

This major ethical issue regarding coerced treatment and violating offender autonomy has not been explicitly acknowledged by the authors of RNR. For example, Birgden criticised Andrews and Dowden[91] for failing to address offender autonomy and argued that therefore RNR could not claim to be ethical, humane or respectful.[92] In response, Andrews and Dowden[93] acknowledged their inattention to respect for personal autonomy as a basic value and later stated, '[W]e think respect for personal autonomy should be underscored in a field of practice in which so much emphasis is placed upon structure, discipline, accountability and state-sanctioned imposition of restrictions and punishment'.[94] It is difficult to determine in what way autonomy is supported in sex offender programs at

---

[87]   Heseltine, Day and Sarre, above n 67.
[88]   See Birgden and Vincent, above n 7.
[89]   R F Schopp, 'Therapeutic Jurisprudence and Conflicts among Values in Mental Health Law' (1993) 31 *Behavioral Sciences and the Law* 31–45.
[90]   B J Winick, 'On Autonomy: Legal and Psychological Perspectives' (1992) 37 *Villanova Law Review* 1705–777.
[91]   D A Andrews and C Dowden, 'The Risk–Need–Responsivity Model of Assessment and Human Service in Prevention and Corrections: Crime-Prevention Jurisprudence' (2007) October *Canadian Journal of Criminology and Criminal Justice* 439–64.
[92]   A Birgden, 'Crime Prevention Jurisprudence? A Response to Andrews and Dowden' (2009) 51(1) *Canadian Journal of Criminology and Criminal Justice* 93–118.
[93]   D A Andrews and C Dowden, 'Keeping a Respectful Eye on Crime Prevention: A Response to Birgden' (2009) 51(1) *Canadian Journal of Criminology and Criminal Justice* 119–122.
[94]   Andrews and Bonta, above n 18, 7.

present.[95] In terms of program completion, Doyle et al conducted an analysis of 50 male sex offenders across three Australian states who had been subject to risk assessments for preventive schemes.[96] They found that 74 per cent had commenced sex offender treatment with 54 per cent completing a program. The remaining men had refused treatment (38%), had been removed from a program (18%), were deemed ineligible due to denial (8%), and one offender had dropped out of treatment. Overall, treatment amenability was considered by the authors to be poor. It is expected that coerced treatment within preventive schemes was not conducive to engaging 65 per cent of the targeted offenders. A practice that engages offenders in change attends to ethical principles and practices and delivers services within an ethic of care.

Codes of ethics exist to guide practitioners. For example, the International Union of Psychological Science provided a Universal Declaration of Ethical Principles for Psychologists which enumerates four principles: (1) respect for dignity; (2) competent caring for well-being; (3) integrity of psychologists; and (4) professional and scientific responsibilities to the community.[97] Glaser considered sex offender rehabilitation within the context of harsh and disproportionate punishment, denial of human rights, and practitioners serving both clients and the state, which undermines the rehabilitative ideal.[98] Glaser argued that in corrections, practitioners breach ethical codes such as confidentiality, beneficence and autonomy; sex offender treatment programs are currently 'a systematic sabotage of traditional ethics',[99] and 'this sort of control comes perilously close to brainwashing, with the aversive stimulus being the threat of further punishment if the offender does not comply'.[100] It is expected that this problem particularly arises for sex offenders subject to preventive schemes. When faced with ethical dilemmas in balancing offender rights and community rights, practitioners may override traditional ethical guidelines and weight their responses toward community rights. Ward and Salmon also argued that current ethics codes are actually insufficient in guiding ethical professional practice in that each

---

[95] For an example of how offender autonomy was supported in a compulsory drug treatment prison, see Birgden and Grant, 'Establishing a Compulsory Drug Treatment Prison: Therapeutic Policy, Principles, and Practices in Addressing Offender Rights and Rehabilitation' (2010) 33 *International Journal of Psychiatry and Law* 341–9.

[96] Doyle, Ogloff and Thomas, above n 24.

[97] International Union of Psychological Science, *Universal Declaration of Ethical Principles for Psychologists* (2008) <http://www.am.org/iupsys/resources/ethics/univdecl2008.html>.

[98] B Glaser, 'Therapeutic Jurisprudence: An Ethical Paradigm for Therapists in Sex Offender Treatment Programs' (2003) 4(2) *Western Criminology Review* 143–54. <http://wcr.sonoma.edu/v4n2/glaser.html>.

[99] Ibid 144.

[100] Ibid 146.

traditional ethical theory they may rely upon has its own area of applicability but then suffers limitations particularly when conflict between principles arise.[101]

In response to Glaser,[102] Levenson and D'Amora argued that sex offender treatment is consistent with ethical codes for various mental health professionals, citing programs combining punishment, rehabilitation and management such as civil commitment, community notification sex offender registration and coerced treatment.[103] They concluded the ethical guidelines provided by ATSA conform to the principles of autonomy (empowering offenders to take long-term behaviour change), non-maleficence (clinicians are trained to develop a therapeutic alliance), beneficence (balancing community rights and offender rights) and justice (community protection is enhanced and repercussions for the offender is diminished through collaborative risk management). However, problems with their response to Glaser are: the ATSA guidelines are weighted towards community rights anyway; 'approved and qualified providers' does not address choice of treatment or providers or that inadequately trained correctional staff may deliver treatment programs (including in Australia); stating that breaches in confidentiality do not occur because informed consent is obtained ignores the capacity to meet the 'voluntariness' element of informed decision-making in corrections; and often offenders who have pled not guilty are required to engage in treatment programs to obtain parole or avoid ongoing monitoring, which would be expected to be the same for sex offenders subject to preventive schemes who would 'need to be seen' to engage prior to a review.

From a TJ perspective, preventive schemes with their violation of autonomy rights would be considered anti-therapeutic. Treating a sex offender without dignity is likely to result in poor treatment compliance.[104] Ward and Salmon have articulated five categories of problematic approaches that arise in working with sex offenders: (1) a risk management approach – lacking attention to offender interests and well-being; (2) a 'one size fits all' approach – relying on inflexible manuals rather than responding to the offenders context in an individualised manner; (3) a technical approach – focusing on content rather than process in terms of therapist and relationship factors; (4) a community protection approach – failing to address the tension with offender interests; and (5) a poor therapeutic approach – failing to ensure therapist factors such as supporting self-care, addressing bias and dual roles, and avoiding conflicts of interest. The authors propose an alternative, feminist ethical position described as *an ethic of care*. An ethic of care builds a

---

[101]   T Ward and K Salmon, 'The Ethics of Care and Treatment of Sex Offenders' (2011) 23(3) *Sexual Abuse: A Journal of Research and Treatment* 397–413.
[102]   Glaser, above n 98.
[103]   J Levenson and D D'Amora, 'An Ethical Paradigm for Sex Offender Treatment: Response to Glaser' (2005) 6(1) *Western Criminology Review* 145–53.
[104]   Ward and Salmon, above n 101.

relationship based on trust and a strong therapeutic bond. An ethic of care views offenders through a lens of empathic concern that supports them as fellow human beings rather than over burdened by feelings of fear, dislike, anger or guilt.[105] TJ literature has also promoted an ethic of care. Brookbanks described TJ as a sea change in ethical thinking about the role of the law and proposed that an ethic of care could be incorporated to provide for ethical legal practice based trust, social relationships and 'grace' – a far cry from current legislative approaches to managing serious high-risk offenders.[106]

Utilising an ethic of care, Ward and Salmon addressed the problematic approaches outlined above: (1) a risk management approach – considering the offenders' true interests which may result in making recommendations that may be restrictive and with which offenders may not agree; (2) an individualised approach – delivering interventions that are attentive, responsive and respectful of offenders; (3) a therapeutic alliance – establishing a helping relationship with genuine interest and concern; (4) a community protection approach – focusing on offender needs, strengths and capabilities as well as risk management; and (5) a therapeutic approach – therapists caring for themselves as they are expected to care for others.[107] These statements are applicable to the assessment process in preventive schemes.

3.2. SCIENTIFIC CONSIDERATIONS

Scientific considerations include meeting human needs; court assessments need to address the human needs underpinning offending behaviour, not just the risk factors. With its focus on addressing empirically-derived risk factors, RNR is an inadequate model to address offenders needs as rights-holders and duty-bearers. In Australia, Doyle et al conducted an analysis of 50 male sex offenders across three Australian states who had been subject to risk assessments for prevention schemes.[108] They found that problem areas included: developmental history (50% familial instability, 72% physical and/or sexual abuse, 54% learning difficulties, and 24% learning difficulties and behavioural problems); substance use (in childhood/ adolescence 48% alcohol abuse and 36% illicit substance abuse, in adulthood 54% alcohol abuse and 46% illicit substance abuse); and diagnoses (in addition to

---

[105] T Ward and S Maruna, *Rehabilitation: Beyond the Risk Paradigm* (Routledge Taylor and Francis Group, 2007).

[106] W Brookbanks, 'Therapeutic Jurisprudence: Conceiving an Ethical Framework' (2001) 8 *Journal of Law and Medicine* 328–41.

[107] Ward and Salmon, above n 101. Concerning conflicting ethical norms regarding community rights versus offender rights and relational ethics, see also Ward 'Addressing the Dual Relationship Problem in Forensic and Correctional Practice' (in press) *Aggression and Violent Behaviour*.

[108] Doyle, Ogloff and Thomas, above n 24.

current diagnoses of 70% with paraphilia and 52% with antisocial personality disorder, 32% having lifetime diagnoses of depression, anxiety, paraphilia, and psychosis, 26% with a history of suicide attempts, and 28% with a history of self-harm). Clearly, these are complex clients with multiple problem areas who exhibit characteristics that may be viewed as immaterial in a risk management approach 'characterised by disrupted home environments, inconsistency of caregiving, self-reported exposure to physical and sexual abuse, poor education, learning difficulties, behavioural problems, and unstable employment histories … significant sexual deviance antisocial and maladaptive personalities, and moderate rates of mental illness'.[109] Of eight vulnerability factors identified by the authors, 50 per cent of the sex offenders experienced five or more of them. In response to these findings, Doyle et al concluded that these offenders needed to be more effectively engaged in utilising well-validated treatment programs and required a comprehensive treatment approach to address the vulnerability factors in addition to the dynamic risk factors.

The Good Lives Model (GLM)[110] is a psychological theory of offender rehabilitation that can serve to broaden the assessment in court and provide a comprehensive treatment approach that includes meeting human needs. The GLM acknowledges that offenders have human needs as all other individuals do. Humans seek physical well-being (healthy functioning of the body), social well-being (family life, social support, meaningful work opportunities and access to leisure activities), and psychological well-being (relatedness, competence and autonomy).[111] The GLM posits that sex offenders use anti-social means to meet their human needs, and while the identified dynamic risk factors in the RNR are problems in achieving human needs, they are merely 'red flags' of problem areas that need to be addressed.[112] By focusing on the offenders' needs and wants, offender rehabilitation motivates offenders to ask, 'How can I live my life differently?'[113] This humanistic approach directs rehabilitation programs to support offender capabilities so human needs are met in pro-social ways, which in turn improves quality of life and so reduce the likelihood of re-offending. That is, the primary goal is to support offenders through meeting needs, and the secondary goal is to control offenders through managing risk. Treatment therefore focuses on both avoidance goals to eliminate undesirable outcomes and approach goals to provide desirable outcomes.[114] The GLM is in a good position to address protective factors

109   Doyle, Ogloff and Thomas, above n 24, 45.
110   See www.goodlivesmodel.com.
111   T Ward, 'Good Lives and the Rehabilitation of Offenders: Promises and Problems' (2002) 7(5) *Aggression and Violent Behaviour* 513–28.
112   T Ward and M Brown, 'The Good Lives Model and Conceptual Issues in Offender Rehabilitation' (2004) 10(3) *Psychology, Crime, and Law* 243–57.
113   T Ward and C A Stewart, 'Criminogenic Needs and Human Needs: A Theoretical Model' (2003) 9 *Psychology, Crime and Law* 125–43, 143.
114   Ward and Maruna, above n 105.

and offender-environment interactions. Offender rehabilitation can serve to assist sex offenders to develop the internal capacities and external conditions necessary to achieve personal goals, and if the aim is to encourage them to appreciate the rights and interests of victims, then it is obviously counterproductive to violate their own rights and interests.[115]

In the national audit of sex offender programs in Australia, Heseltine et al did not mention the application of case formulation,[116] which is a natural extension of a GLM approach. A case formulation is a functional analysis using clinical interview and assessment results to develop a hypothesis about the offender's pathway to offending and allows for individual differences to be addressed in a rehabilitation plan.[117] To individualise the case formulation in complex cases, the psychologist can reconstruct vignettes that reveal themes, events, offender or contextual factors, or offender-context interactions.[118] The case formulation should be applied therapeutically by ensuring that offenders clearly understand the assessed likelihood of re-offending, which factors may place them at future risk of re-offending, the opportunities available to address identified dynamic risk factors and human needs, and what strategies may be put in place to increase treatment readiness.[119] Subsequent adjustments to the rehabilitation plan are to be made in collaboration with the offender throughout the detention or supervision order.

3.3.   RISK CONSIDERATIONS

Risk considerations determine what level of risk is posed to offenders by being labelled as serious high-risk. Sex offenders subject to prevention schemes are dehumanised and stigmatised by the community and, possibly, correctional staff. In Australia they have been subject to violence and vigilante activity. For example, community harassment of the now deceased Dennis Ferguson has been both fuelled and documented by the media.[120] The Supreme Court acknowledged this potential issue in *Fletcher v the Secretary to the Department of Justice 2006*, noting that:

---

[115]   Ibid.
[116]   Heseltine, Day and Sarre, above n 67.
[117]   See K Howells, 'Cognitive Behavioural Interventions for Anger, Aggression and Violence' in N Tarrier, A Wells and G Haddock (eds), *Treating Complex Cases: The Cognitive Behavioural Therapy Approach* (Wiley and Sons, 1998) 295–318; T Ward, F M Vertue and B D Haig, 'Abductive Method and Clinical Assessment in Practice' (1999) 16(1) *Behaviour Change* 49–63.
[118]   M Miller and N Morris, 'Predictions of Dangerousness: An Argument for Limited Use' (1988) 3 *Violence and Victims* 263–83.
[119]   See Birgden, above n 15.
[120]   See McSherry and Keyzer, above n 8.

> [He] must not overlook the fact that the purposes include not only a concern for the community, but also a concern for him. It should not be lost upon him that there may be sections of the community who find his views repugnant and his past deeds appalling, and who may seek to cause him harm. There has to be a balance.[121]

As a consequence, an assessment report to the court should include the likely anti-therapeutic impact of a prevention scheme upon offenders in terms of restrictions imposed and likely community responses.

4. CONCLUSION

Despite issues with ethics and evidence, prevention schemes are likely to remain in Australia. An offender-community balance acknowledges that punishment through incapacitation is not against human rights, as long as it is reasonable and for a finite period; preventive schemes break this rule. While the law may not be reformed, the procedures and the role of mental health professionals can be adjusted to deliver therapeutic rather than anti-therapeutic outcomes. These adjustments are supported by the humanistic approaches of TJ and the GLM. Indeed, in *Fletcher v the Secretary to the Department of Justice*, the Supreme Court noted that it is the Department of Justice and the Adult Parole Board who implement the supervision conditions in the community, not the Court. The following recommendations, at an individual and policy level, are based on the suggested improvements above.

At an individual level, the assessment report to the court needs to be broadened to include clear statements regarding: (1) whether the offender is both serious and high-risk; (2) the scientific and ethical problems with actuarial assessment tools and structured clinical judgement; (3) the risk of harm to the offender upon being labelled; (4) the human needs, determined through case formulation, that ought to be addressed in rehabilitation; and (5) the coerced nature of procedures and the likely impact on compliance with conditions. In this way, the assessment report counterbalances the current weighting toward community rights by considering offender rights. Both assessment and treatment ought to be delivered within an ethic of care.

At a policy level, ethical rehabilitation ordinarily requires that only those offenders who would benefit should be offered treatment, the offender ought to provide an informed decision to participate in treatment, and treatment needs to be rationally justified (ie, an explicit value-judgement). In order to salvage an

---

[121] *Fletcher v Secretary to the Department of Justice* [2006] VSC 354 [69].

unethical situation posed by prevention schemes, it is preferable that treatment is offered as an attractive alternative at the point where bureaucrats consider applying to the courts for detention or extended supervision. The offer for treatment should allow offenders to provide an *informed* decision to refuse, and then offender rights may be over-ridden in the interests of community rights (ie, coerced treatment is justified because the offender poses a high likelihood of harm to the community). In this instance, rehabilitation is quasi-coerced in offering a constrained choice – through an offer not a threat – that recognises some voluntary interests (eg, between rehabilitation and no preventive scheme or no rehabilitation and a preventive scheme). While quasi-coerced treatment can match individuals to treatment, it ultimately cannot coerce them to actively participate. If offenders are not willing to engage in rehabilitation then decision-making opportunities should again be emphasised with more stringent standards set for continued refusals, while emphasising an ethic of care. Alternatively, a motivational module that encourages the development of a plan for a fulfilling life and/or a focus on managing external conditions can be offered. Mediation by a nominated and independent third party may assist.

If the offender still continues to refuse treatment, then the outcome is supervision or detention. This approach should only be considered for serious high-risk sex offenders to avoid wider nets (increase in sex offenders being subject to prevention schemes), denser nets (increase in intensity of treatment) and different nets (new agencies and services supplementing existing control mechanisms).[122] This chapter proposes that procedures and roles can balance offender rights and community rights to enhance community protection – a 'rights and rights' or 'win-win' proposition not an 'either/or' or 'win-lose' proposition. To support this approach, bureaucrats need to acknowledge that, in the long-term, treatment-as-rehabilitation in meeting needs is likely to be more effective than treatment-as-management in managing risk.

---

[122]   Miller, above n 65.

THE PRISON:
ITS CONTRIBUTION TO PUNISHMENT, REHABILITATION AND PUBLIC SAFETY

Andrew COYLE

1. THE CONTEXT

This volume considers the increasing use of preventive detention in its varying forms in recent years and analyses the implications of this development from a number of perspectives. In order to place this topic in context, it is useful to understand some of the basic principles that underpin the use of imprisonment generally. What, for example, is the justification for the use of imprisonment, what is it intended to achieve and of what should it consist? This chapter seeks to answer some of these questions and, in so doing, to provide a theoretical basis for the issues raised in other chapters.

Almost 40 years ago, I first walked through the gates of Edinburgh Prison in Scotland and I found myself in a world of which I had no previous knowledge: a world that existed in parallel with but quite separate from the everyday world that I shared with millions of other fellow citizens. From that very first day, I found myself asking the question, 'What is the purpose of imprisonment?'[1]

Throughout the following 25 years I moved from prison to prison and in due course governed several of them, including two of the most iconic in the United Kingdom. In the late 1980s, I became Governor of Peterhead Prison in Scotland. At that time Peterhead held those prisoners who had been assessed as being the most disruptive and dangerous in the Scottish prison system. All of them had been involved in riots, in taking hostages or in escape attempts from other prisons. When I went there as Governor in 1988, I walked into a world where there was continual violent confrontation between staff and prisoners. The normal uniform for staff each day included a riot helmet, body armour and Perspex shields. Prisoners were locked up in isolation for 23 hours each day; a number of them wore only blankets and had covered themselves in their own excrement. Many

---

[1]   Andrew Coyle, *The Prisons We Deserve* (Harper Collins, 1994).

prison systems have one prison that is 'the end of the line'. It is frequently referred to as 'The Hate Factory'. Peterhead was that prison for Scotland in the late 1980s.

In 1991, I was appointed as Governor of Brixton Prison. Brixton was built in 1819 and is the oldest prison in London. I went there in the immediate aftermath of a violent incident in which two IRA prisoners shot their way out of the prison. Shortly before I went to Brixton, the European Committee for the Prevention of Torture had inspected the prison and had concluded that the conditions in which prisoners were held were 'inhuman and degrading'. I shall never forget the first day I walked into F Wing in Brixton Prison. The wing held 230 prisoners who had been remanded in custody by the court for psychiatric reports. The walls were painted bottle green. Permanent semi-darkness meant that artificial lighting had to be kept on all day. The all-pervading smell was overpowering: a combination of urine, faeces and stale food. There was an incessant barrage of noise, an unrelenting cacophony of keening, wailing, shouting and banging, which went on even during the night. Each cell had a large flap in its door. These were normally open. A face peered out from most of them, hungry for human contact. The last thing that these prisoners, many of whom were severely disturbed, needed was to be confined in such conditions. If a man was not unstable before admission to F Wing, he was likely soon to become so.

In both of these prisons, faced with quite different sets of prisoners, I continued to ask myself the original question, 'What is the purpose of imprisonment?' At one level, the question was easier to answer in Peterhead. All the prisoners there had been convicted of committing serious crimes for which they had been sentenced to deprivation of liberty for considerable periods of time. Their subsequent behaviour in custody confirmed that the public needed to be protected from them: in other words, that the possibility of their escape should be reduced to a minimum. My task was to ensure that they were treated in prison with decency and humanity and that, in so far as could be achieved, they passed their time in prison as positively as possible in a manner that might assist them to reintegrate into society when the time came eventually for their release. At a strategic level, the task of the prison staff was very straightforward, although at an operational level it was immensely complex. The task of the staff at Brixton was equally complex at an operational level. But this was compounded by an uncertainty as to the purpose of imprisonment for many of the men who were detained there. For a large number, particularly the mentally ill, the reality was that they were in prison simply because there was nowhere else for them to go. The health services did not want to become involved with them, there were no community services to care for them or they were in prison by default until the court system decided what to do with them. For many of them prison might have been a place of asylum, a place of safety, although in reality it was anything but that.

For a number of years now the main focus of my work has been in the international arena, and I have been a close observer of prisons and imprisonment in every region of the world. In the 1990s, I spent a lot of time in prisons in Eastern Europe and Central Asia, the countries of what had previously been the Soviet Union. Overcrowding in prisons in these countries did not mean three persons in a cell built for one, as it had done in Brixton. Instead it meant three prisoners allocated to each bed, sleeping in eight-hour shifts. Bunk beds were tiered to the ceilings, crammed into rooms with little air and virtually no natural light. These arrangements were breeding grounds for infectious diseases, such as tuberculosis, and later HIV and AIDS, to the extent that one senior Russian prison official described a prison sentence as equivalent to being sentenced to death.[2]

I have visited prisons in sub-Saharan Africa and South East Asia, prisons built in the 19th century by colonial powers to subdue local populations and still in use today. In some of these prisons, there was no running water and a drastic shortage of food. Prisoners might languish for years awaiting trial because the authorities had no transport to take them to court.

I have seen prisons in Western Europe housed in mediaeval castles, totally inappropriate for use in the 21st century. I have seen many prisons in Latin America where violence is endemic; staff do not go inside the prisoner areas, gang battles result in several murders each week and the staff's only response to is be equally violent in their dealings with prisoners. I have been in prisons in the United States of America where prisoners spend their entire day locked in complete isolation with no human contact and will do so for the rest of their lives.

So, after 40 years of being in and around prisons I still ask myself, 'What is the purpose of imprisonment?' And increasingly I have come to realise that if I, with all my experience of prisons, am unsure of the answer to that question, is it any surprise that the courts, politicians and the public are even more uncertain?

2. THE PURPOSES OF IMPRISONMENT

In the majority of countries, imprisonment is the most severe disposal available to the court. Yet its use is far from consistent or predictable, even within the confines of codified legal systems. Why is it that some persons who are accused or convicted of crimes are sent to prison and others are not? What does the court mean to achieve when it sends an offender to prison? This question of purpose is an important one because, unless there is some clarity about this key issue, it

---

[2] Quoted in V Stern (ed), *Sentenced To Die? The Problem of TB in Prisons in Eastern Europe and Central Asia* (International Centre for Prison Studies, 1999).

will be difficult to discover whether imprisonment is effective. If we wish to know whether prison achieves its purposes, we have to understand what those purposes are. Traditionally, at least four purposes have been suggested. Sometimes they have different titles, but in broad terms they are punishment, deterrence, reform and protection of the public.

2.1. PUNISHMENT

The first given purpose of imprisonment of convicted persons is to punish them for the crime they have committed. The argument in this case is that some crimes are so serious that the only appropriate disposal is to punish the offender by taking away his or her liberty. The sentence of imprisonment carries great symbolism in the eyes of the public. When the judge sentences someone to be 'taken down', very often the convicted person is seen to be taken directly from the dock downstairs to the cells underneath the court. In high profile cases, the press will photograph the prison van swinging out of the yard of the courthouse and later turning into the forbidding walls of the prison. The 'clang of the prison gate' carries a resonance in the mind of both the public and of the prisoner which is different from any other punishment.

Throughout most of the 20th century in the United Kingdom there was broad acceptance of the principle that the punishment intended by the court when it passed a prison sentence was deprivation of liberty alone. Being required to stay behind the walls of a prison for the period specified by the court, not permitted to go out from the prison other than in exceptional circumstances, was in itself a heavy punishment. In the words of Alexander Paterson, a famous English Prison Commissioner in the early part of the 20th century:

> It must be clear from the outset to all concerned that it is the sentence of imprisonment, and not the treatment accorded in prison, that constitutes the punishment. Men come to prison as a punishment, not *for* punishment.[3]

That principle does not apply in all jurisdictions. The law in the former Soviet Union, for example, required the court to specify as part of the sentence the type of regime under which prisoners were to be held and the severity with which they were to be treated, and this provision remains in a number of countries in the region.

---

[3]   S K Ruck (ed), *Paterson on Prisons: Being the Collected Papers of Sir Alexander Paterson* (Frederick Muller, 1951).

In the United Kingdom, a House of Lords judgement in 1982, often referred to as the Wilberforce judgement, confirmed that the punishment involved in imprisonment is not absolute but is restricted in its nature:

> Under English law a convicted prisoner, in spite of his imprisonment, retains all civil rights which are not taken away expressly or by necessary implication.[4]

While this is all very well as a principle, there is room for a great deal of interpretation about which civil rights are 'expressly or by necessary implication' taken away by the fact of imprisonment. That is a worthy sentiment, but what does it mean in practice?

What does it mean, for example, in respect of the right that all human beings have to family life? In the United Kingdom, this right is severely limited when a person goes to prison. Direct family contact will be relatively infrequent, with short visits taking place in a very public environment and with minimal physical contact. In many other countries, the situation is quite different. The best arrangements are to be found in countries where families are allowed to spend extended periods, often of several days, in special flats or units, living together as parents, spouses or children. This is, as yet, unthinkable in the United Kingdom, where the press and the public would regard such arrangements merely as an opportunity for prisoners to have sexual relations – and what would be left of the pain of imprisonment if that were to be allowed? In other countries, the focus in these matters is not only on the prisoner but also on the rights of her or his children, partner or parents to have a family relationship that is more than minimal.

When a person is sent to prison, does he or she forfeit all civil rights, or is it the case that some civil rights have been suspended? A topical example of this matter in the United Kingdom is that of voting in elections. In the majority of European countries, either all prisoners have the right to vote or the limitation is applied on an individual basis. Yet in the United Kingdom, the Prime Minister has said that even to contemplate allowing a convicted prisoner the vote in elections, never mind to introduce such an arrangement, would make him 'physically ill'.[5] This is the reality, despite the fact that the European Court of Human Rights has found that such a blanket ban on voting is in breach of the European Convention on Human Rights.[6] In some states of the United States of America, the ban on voting is extended to persons after release from prison.

---

[4]   *Raymond v Honey* [1983] 1 AC 1.
[5]   House of Commons, Hansard (3 November 2010) Column 922.
[6]   *Hirst v United Kingdom* (No 2) [2005] ECHR 681.

In more general terms, the coercive nature of the prison environment means that the punitive element of imprisonment extends into many features of daily life in prison. Even within the prison walls, prisoners do not have freedom to circulate at will. In most circumstances, they are told what they must do and where they must be at every moment of the day. Their personal possessions are limited. They and their cells are subject to regular inspection and search. They are told how much money they may have and what they may spend it on. Their opportunities for activities such as work and education are severely limited.

The point being made by Alexander Paterson one hundred years ago was that it is not the task of the prison system to impose punitive regimes on prisoners as part of their sentence. The truth is that imprisonment is a blunt instrument of punishment, and it affects individuals in different ways. For some, the pains of deprivation of liberty and separation from family are almost unbearable. This punishment affects not only the prisoners but also other members of their families, parents, children, partners and siblings, whose contact with the imprisoned family member are severely restricted. For some people, especially those who usually live at the margins of society, the prison may be a haven, a place of safety from the pressures and severity of external life. Whatever the personal reaction, there is little dispute that punishment is invariably a major element of imprisonment.

2.2. DETERRENCE

The second given purpose of imprisonment is deterrence. The choices most of us make in our daily lives are affected by what we foresee as the likely consequences of our actions. That means that we are sometimes deterred from doing a particular thing because we think the adverse consequences would outweigh the benefit of what we propose to do. We may decide not to smoke because of the danger that we might get cancer. We may decide to cut down alcohol consumption because of the damage being caused to our liver. Sometimes the adverse consequences are legally imposed rather than a direct consequence of our actions. For example, driving at high speed in a built up area might well cause an accident, but the likelihood of that happening may not in itself be sufficient to deter every driver from speeding. So, there is a law that determines that everyone who is caught speeding will be fined or suffer penalty points on their licence. The possibility of that happening is enough to deter most drivers from speeding most of the time.

A similar argument is applied to the deterrent effect of imprisonment. If a person who is tempted to commit a crime knows that the result is likely to be a period of imprisonment, then that may well be enough to deter that person from committing a crime, and the greater the punishment, the greater the deterrent.

It can be argued, for example, that the prospect of one month in prison might be enough to deter someone from stealing $200 but not from stealing $200,000. To deter someone from stealing that amount of money, the prospect might have to be several years in prison. The same principle of deterrence can be applied to other crimes, such as violence against the person.

There are two main forms of deterrence: individual and general. Individual deterrence is when the prospect of being sent to prison deters an individual from committing a specific crime or when the fact of having been sent to prison makes one decide never to commit crime again. General deterrence exists when we see someone else being sent to prison for an offence and that makes us decide that we had better not commit a similar offence for fear that happens to us.

The principle of deterrence is based on an important premise, that of detection. If I know that no one is likely to check the speed at which I am driving then a law against speeding is not likely to be much of a deterrent. Even when speed cameras were first introduced, I might have known that a large percentage of them had no film and would not record any passing car. The likelihood of escaping detection was high and, therefore, deterrence was low. With the introduction of digital cameras, the likelihood of detection increased and, with it, the power of deterrence. That, at least, is the theory, but there is evidence that even a high probability of detection is not sufficient to deter all speeding drivers.

The threat of prison as a means of crime control, let alone crime prevention, is even more problematic than that of cameras for the speeding driver. In terms of deterrence, the statistics speak for themselves. Research some years ago by the UK government found that, of every hundred offences committed in England and Wales, only three resulted in a criminal conviction or police caution and one resulted in a custodial sentence.[7] In the unlikely event that a potential criminal will apply actuarial considerations, these are pretty good odds and hardly an argument that the possibility of being sent to prison will act as a form of general deterrence. The value of imprisonment as an instrument of individual deterrence is equally questionable. It is true that we cannot calculate how many crimes are avoided because potential criminals are deterred by the prospect of imprisonment, but in terms of deterring those convicted from future offending, the statistics do not give a great deal of cause for optimism. In many jurisdictions, a majority of all prisoners are reconvicted of a further offence within two years of their discharge. These figures do not inspire confidence in the deterrent effect of imprisonment.

---

[7] Home Office Research and Statistics Department, Digest 4: Information on the Criminal Justice System in England and Wales (1999).

2.3. REFORM

The concept of prison as a place of reform grew from the 19th century onwards, often encouraged by the claims of those who worked within the prison system. The notion that prison can be a place where individuals can be taught to change their behaviour is appealing on a number of counts. In the first place, it provides a positive justification for what would be otherwise a purely negative form of punishment. The notion of prison as a place where personal reform can be engineered and encouraged is also attractive to those public spirited men and women who work in prisons and who wish to do more professionally than merely deprive prisoners of their liberty.

This idea of using the prison as a place of reform is particularly appealing if it is linked to the notion that most crime can be traced to a specific group of individuals. If crime is seen as a series of acts committed by a relatively small, identifiable group of people who are different from the majority of law-abiding citizens, then the objective of changing their behaviour as a result of their experience in prison should lead to a reduction in the amount of crime they commit after they are released. If one holds that this small group of people are responsible for a disproportionate amount of crime, then any reduction in their rate of committing crime will lead to an overall reduction in crime. This argument has proved attractive to politicians who need to find a way of responding to public fear of crime.

The general principle that human beings can be encouraged to change their patterns of behaviour for the better is a sound one, but whether this can be achieved in conditions of captivity is very problematic. Personal change comes as a result of a personal decision; it is not something which can be imposed against an individual's will. In the constrained environment of the prison, it is very difficult for an individual to make a truly free decision. Even when prisoners have a degree of personal choice, they have to weigh carefully the consequences of any decisions they make. Agreement to take part in a particular course or programme or refusal to do so may mean that they will be given more or less privileges, be transferred from one prison to another or that their date of release may be affected. In the words of an oft-quoted aphorism, people cannot be trained for freedom while in conditions of captivity.

The reality is that the prison is essentially a world set apart from normality. The prisoner's links with the social structures the rest of us take for granted are at best tenuous. It would be wrong to create the impression that someone who has had problems at home, problems at school, problems in the workplace and problems in social relationships (as many prisoners have had throughout their lives) can be changed by a few months in a prison and then sent back to the world from which he or she came as a reformed individual. It is true that, in many prisons, some staff carry out sterling work in attempting to provide prisoners with opportunities to change themselves and their behaviour. A few individuals may be changed for the better by their experiences in prison, but they will always be a small minority and it can be argued that such change comes about despite the prison environment rather than because of it.

There is an additional danger in regarding the prison as a place of reform rather than of punishment and that is that this will be used as a justification for using it to detain those whom society finds 'difficult': people who have mental health problems; people who have substance abuse problems; people who are homeless or, in this globalised world of ours, are stateless; people who in one way or other are considered by those in authority to be a danger to the law abiding majority; or people who quite simply can defined as 'the other'. This is an issue dealt with in more detail elsewhere in this book.

2.4. PUBLIC PROTECTION

Another stated purpose of imprisonment is to protect the public from those who commit crime, particularly in a persistent way. 'Prison works', so the argument goes, because during the time offenders are in prison they are prevented from committing other crimes. The argument is known as incapacitation. In some respects, this argument is valid, particularly in respect of specific neighbourhoods where a significant proportion of crime is being committed by identifiable individuals. However, this type of crime tends to be low level, attracting relatively short prison sentences. The person concerned may be taken out of their community for a short period of time, but they are likely soon to return. This is not a new problem. In the first half of the 20th century in the United Kingdom the problem was resolved by a form of preventive detention, which involved persistent offenders being given additional sentences because of the repeat nature of their offending. The legal provision for this was eventually rescinded because it was seen to be unjust and also ineffective in the long term. An added problem is that many of the crimes which destabilise communities are not resolved by removing one or two individuals. For example, when drug dealers are removed from a local neighbourhood it will often be a matter of days, if not hours, before they are replaced by new drug dealers.

There is also an issue of public protection in respect of those people whose behaviour is such that it presents a continuing and serious threat to the safety of society. Some of them may already be in prison, convicted of serious crimes, particularly of violence against the person, and still give every indication that, if they were to be released, they would continue to present a real threat to the public.

Thankfully, there are very few of these people, and in most countries, they will have a high public profile, which means they are easily identifiable. It may well be necessary that these people should be in prison for as long as they continue to present a threat to the public. However, it is essential that decisions in these cases be made in an independent judicial forum, based on rigorous evidence.

Persons who have been charged with a crime but have not yet been tried or sentenced can be detained in prison on grounds of public protection in the broad sense. These grounds can include the likelihood that the person may abscond, that the person may interfere with the course of justice by putting pressure on potential witnesses or in other ways, or that the offence with which the person is charged is so serious that detention is deemed to be necessary. There is a raft of international law and standards, as well as domestic law, dealing with the treatment of persons who are detained prior to trial. We need to bear in mind that in respect of these prisoners, the sole purpose of detention is that of public safety in the broad sense described above. None of the other purposes of imprisonment for convicted prisoners, that is to say, punishment, deterrence or personal reformation, can apply to these prisoners.

Finally, there is a problematic group, which includes those who have not committed a serious crime but who have been identified by experts as likely to do so. This is a matter of topical concern in a number of jurisdictions, with experts expressing concern about the basis on which decisions affecting such person might be made. Other contributors to this book deal with this matter in detail. In this contextual chapter, the principle to be highlighted is that all persons who are held in prison for what might be described as administrative reasons are, by definition, not convicted of any offence or crime. Such persons must be treated in the same manner as other prisoners who have not been convicted. This will affect the conditions in which they are held and also the access which they have to legal representatives and other official persons. This provision is referred to in the United Nations Standard Minimum Rules for the Treatment of Prisoners:[8]

> Rule 94
>
> In countries where the law permits imprisonment for debt or by order of a court under any other non-criminal process, persons so imprisoned shall not be subjected to any greater restriction or severity than is necessary to ensure safe custody and good order. Their treatment shall not be less favourable than that of untried prisoners, with the reservation, however, that they may possibly be required to work.

---

[8] *Standard Minimum Rules for the Treatment of Prisoners*, First United Nations Congress on the Prevention of Crime and the Treatment of Offenders, UN Doc A/CONF/611, annex I, ESC Res 663C 24 UN ESCOR Supp No 3, 11, UN Doc E/3048 (1957) amended ESC Res 2076, 62 UN ESCOR Supp No 1, 35, UN Doc E/5988 (1977, adopted 30 Aug 1955).

2.5.   CONCLUDING REMARKS

In any jurisdiction, decisions about the use of prison are not purely a matter of criminal justice priorities. They are also affected by views about social justice and about the nature of society.

Prisons do not exist within a vacuum nor is their use determined in an entirely dispassionate manner by the courts of justice. They are symbolic institutions. The level at which they are used and the sort of people who are sent there has much to say about the attitude which a society has towards the acceptable limits of punishment, about punishment as a social phenomenon, about approaches to the treatment of people while they are being punished and the international legal framework within which prisons should operate.

What is clear is that the deprivation of liberty at the core of imprisonment is *per se* a punishment. To talk of imprisonment which is not punitive is an oxymoron, a contradiction in terms.

PREVENTIVE DETENTION BEYOND THE LAW: THE NEED TO ASK SOCIO-POLITICAL QUESTIONS

Arlie Loughnan and Sabine Selchow

The proliferation of preventive detention regimes over recent decades demands ever-vigilant attention. Although preventive detention is typically understood via its legal profile – according to which it is measured in terms of procedural fairness, fidelity to legal principles and against human rights norms – or in relation to its effectiveness, the significance of preventive detention stretches beyond its identity as a particular set of practices located within the legal realm. Given its three main ingredients – the logic of 'prevention', the technology of 'risk' and the practice of 'security' – preventive detention is both implicated in and implicates large socio-political concerns relating to the very constitution of society. Consequently, policy debates must go beyond traditional legal concerns and concern with effectiveness, to ask what preventive detention does to society. This larger question represents an essential but oft neglected aspect of any legislative proposals regarding preventive detention. The aim of this chapter is to invite policy makers to appreciate the complexity of preventive detention – in its socio-political as well as legal nature – in order that such an appreciation might inform debate about and development of policy into the future.

1. INTRODUCTION

Under the heading 'Fear of Violence Could Keep Offenders in Jail', ABC News recently reported a New South Wales (NSW) government announcement to provide for the preventive detention of individuals convicted of serious violent offences.[1] This announcement followed the publication of a report by the NSW Sentencing Council recommending that the government introduce continuing detention and extended supervision for 'high-risk violent offenders'.[2] According to the government's media release, the legislation will provide that a Supreme

---

[1]   'Fear of Violence Could Keep Offenders in Jail', ABC News, 24 September 2012 <http://www. abc.net.au/news/2012-09-24/fear-of-violence-could-keep-offenders-in-jail/4276938>.
[2]   *High-Risk Violent Offenders: Sentencing and Post-Custody Management Options*, NSW Sentencing Council, May 2012, para 5.89. It is interesting to note that the Sentencing Council

Court judge can make an order to keep a person in jail who is a serious risk to the community, or to release him or her on strict conditions.[3] The Attorney-General Greg Smith compared the proposed legislation to that which exists for serious sex offenders and justified it by stating that the government is 'just looking out how do we best protect the community'.[4] If the proposed legislation is drafted and enacted, it represents another move in the expansion of the regime of preventive detention experienced in Australia (and elsewhere) over the past decades. As the announcement of the proposed legislative development itself suggests, preventive detention is increasingly regarded as part of the criminal justice mainstream – it is no longer restricted to the margins of the field, applied only to those offenders who are mentally ill and thus non-responsible, as well as dangerous, or who have been found unfit to plead. Rather, various preventive detention regimes may now be found across the criminal justice field, including those regimes which apply to potential terrorists and those convicted of serious sexual violence offences.[5] More broadly, other preventive measures, including control orders, consorting offences, youth conduct orders and serious crime prevention orders, have also proliferated.[6] In addition, preventive detention regimes may also be found beyond the criminal justice field, including, for instance, in migration.[7]

The public and political debate about preventive detention regimes, such as the newly proposed one in NSW, circles broadly around two main concerns. First, there is an abiding concern with *effectiveness*. This is apparent in the response of NSW Opposition Leader John Robertson to Attorney-General Smith's announcement. According to the ABC News report, Robertson is concerned that '[t]his proposed legislation would only impact on fourteen inmates over the next three years. [...] So I'm not sure how significant this change would be anyway.'[8] Robertson's reaction reveals a principle concern with the impact and effectiveness of the regime in the broader fight against crime. His main concern

---

had difficulty pinning down the boundaries of this category of offenders [2.39]–[2.46] and was not unanimous in putting forward this recommendation [5.82]-[5.89].

[3]   Department of Attorney-General and Justice, 'Violent Offenders to Stay in Jail' (Media Release, 24 September 2012). <http://www.lawlink.nsw.gov.au/Lawlink/Corporate/ll_corporate.nsf/pages/LL_Homepage_news2012#vo>.

[4]   'Fear of Violence Could Keep Offenders in Jail', above n 1.

[5]   In relation to sex offenders, see *Crimes (Serious Sex Offenders) Act* 2006 (NSW). For discussion, Bernadette McSherry and Patrick Keyzer, *Sex Offenders and Preventive Detention: Politics, Policy and Practice* (Federation Press, 2009).

[6]   See, for example, *Terrorism (Police Powers) Act* 2002 (NSW); *Crimes Amendment (Consorting and Organised Crime) Act* 2012 (NSW); *Children (Criminal Proceedings) Act* 1987 (NSW); *Serious and Organised Crime (Control) Act* 2008 (SA).

[7]   In relation to migration, see *Al-Kateb v Godwin* (2004) 219 CLR 562; *Minister for Immigration & Citizenship v Haneef* [2007] FCAFC 203; *Plaintiff M47-2012 v Director General of Security* [2012] HCA 46 (5 October 2012). See also Ben Saul, 'Trapped in the Puzzle of Security', *Sydney Morning Herald*, 5 October 2012 <http://www.smh.com.au/opinion/politics/trapped-in-the-puzzle-of-security-20121004-2725q.html>.

[8]   'Fear of Violence Could Keep Offenders in Jail', above n 1.

regarding the proposed preventive detention regime seems to be whether it will make a measurable difference to improve security against crime in NSW. The terms of reference of the 2012 Council of Australian Governments' (COAG) Review of Counter-Terrorism Legislation provides an additional illustration of this point.[9] An express aim of the COAG initiative is to evaluate and make recommendations regarding 'whether the laws: […] are effective against terrorism – that is, they provide law enforcement, intelligence and security agencies with adequate tools to prevent, detect and respond to acts of terrorism'.[10] Second, there is concern with and debate about the *adequacy* and *proportionality* of practices of preventive detention. (Narrow) legal questions concerning how to balance the protection of the community with the rights of the 'dangerous' person are addressed and debated. Again, the terms of reference of the 2012 Council of Australian Governments' (COAG) Review of Counter-Terrorism Legislation illustrates this concern as it set out to determine 'whether the laws: are necessary and proportionate[;] […] are being exercised in a way that is evidence-based, intelligence-led and proportionate[;] contain appropriate safeguards against abuse'.[11] It is these legal issues that also dominate the extant legal scholarship.[12]

Yet, there is more to preventive detention – understood broadly as a practice that detains individuals on the basis of the need to protect the community – than its effectiveness and its legal dimension. As evident in Greg Smith's public defence of the proposed NSW legislation it is, for instance, linked to broad and complex socio-political issues and collective perceptions of fear and dangerousness. In a press release Smith stated, '[s]ome inmates are like ticking time bombs, just waiting to go off and cause untold damage. We cannot stand by and let that happen if we have been warned of the risk.'[13] In a radio interview, he stressed, '[t]he fact is that there are some prisoners who are so dangerous that we feel that the community needs to be safeguarded by having this procedure in place'.[14] Further, preventive detention is linked to the notion of 'security', which constitutes a powerful determinate in modern politics. Over and above the traditional legal concerns and those relating to effectiveness, the main ingredients of preventive detention – the rationality of 'prevention', the technology of 'risk' and the practice of 'security' – make it a highly complex practice. Hence, preventive detention or, more precisely, any kind of legislative moves regarding it, must be debated in much broader terms. Discussions need to go beyond the bounds of legal and effectiveness concerns. Of course, there is no question about the need to tackle

---

[9] COAG Review of Counter-Terrorism Legislation, commencing 6 August 2012 (the Hon Anthony Whealy QC, Chair) <http://www.coagctreview.gov.au/Pages/default.aspx>.

[10] Ibid.

[11] Ibid.

[12] See for instance Christopher Slobogin in this volume.

[13] Department of Attorney-General and Justice, above n 3.

[14] 'AM with Tony Eastley' ABC Local Radio, 24 September 2012 <http://www.abc.net.au/news/2012-09-24/violent-offenders-could-have-sentences-extended/4276976>.

legal questions to ensure that preventive detention is 'subject to sensible judicial oversight' and demonstrates a government's 'commitment to due process, fairness and the presumption of innocence for all', as former NSW Premier Kristina Keneally emphasises.[15] Yet, in addition to asking questions about these issues, we also need to give consideration to the larger question: 'what does preventive detention do to society?'

Aimed at policy makers, our chapter argues that, given both its expansion over time and its specific nature as a measure within the broader field of preventive action, any debate about legislative moves regarding preventive detention must be understood as a debate about the nature of the respective society and must be conducted as such. So, while existing debates typically relate to (a range of) legal concerns and concerns regarding the effectiveness of preventive detention, there is another important set of concerns to be discussed that is wider and deeper. These concerns are more foundational in that they relate to the vision(s) about the future configuration of the respective society. Putting it slightly differently, our chapter aims to make policy makers aware of the further consequences for the (future) constitution of the respective society which must be taken into account in evaluating legislative proposals regarding preventive detention in particular and preventive measures more generally. These consequences are currently less prominent in public and political discussion. They are not universal or fixed but need to be identified and discussed in wide, genuinely public but localised debates about the (envisioned and entailed) foundations of society. Consequently, a debate about a vision for the future of society must become an explicit dimension of debate about preventive detention, alongside those issues that are already the subject of debate.

In particular, our chapter makes the reader aware of the socio-political complexity of preventive detention that goes beyond its legal profile or, in the words of the title of this chapter, beyond the law. There is a comprehensive set of mainly criminological material which deals with the politics of preventive control. Drawing on some of this material, as well as on insights from across the social and political sciences more broadly, we proceed in two steps. In Part II, we provide an overview over the rise of preventive detention, which reveals that it has undergone both quantitative and qualitative change over time. In Part III of this chapter, we turn to a deep examination of the practice of preventive detention. In order to do this we will zoom in on key aspects of the three constitutive ingredients of preventive detention: the rationality of 'prevention', the technology

---

15   New South Wales, *Parliamentary Debates*, Legislative Assembly, 23 June 2010, 24651 (Kristina Keneally) <http://www.parliament.nsw.gov.au/prod/parlment/hansart.nsf/V3Key/LA20100623021>.

of 'risk' and the practice of 'security'.[16] We identify three relevant aspects of the rationality of prevention, several key aspects of the technology of 'risk' and the essential dimensions of the practice of security. This discussion reveals that each of these main ingredients of preventive detention are social products, neither ahistorical nor value- or power-free. This in turn exposes the socio-political complexity of preventive detention and the need for policy-makers to ask socio-political questions.

2. THE RISE TO PROMINENCE OF PREVENTIVE DETENTION

Prevention is a familiar aspect of the criminal justice terrain. Indeed, prevention of harm may be taken to be one of the rationales for criminal law.[17] Understood broadly, prevention aims to prevent, or to reduce, harm occurring at some future point in time. In this sense, it is forward-looking aim and may be contrasted with retribution, which is backward looking. Prevention makes itself felt on the criminal justice terrain in a number of ways, and it has been cited as a rationale for, for instance, bail laws, endangerment offences, and sentencing.[18] As a result, it is difficult to capture the history of preventive detention because of the nebulous and widespread concern with prevention suffusing the criminal justice terrain. What is easier to capture is the preventive turn in law more generally, that is, the move to 'pre-crime' societies,[19] which we discuss below. In relation to preventive detention, while this term might be given different meanings, we approach it broadly and take it to denote the detention, as opposed to punishment, of an individual in order to protect the community.[20] In this section of the chapter, we trace the rise to prominence of preventive detention in common law countries, with a focus on England and Wales and Australia. Through this examination we demonstrate that, over recent decades, preventive detention has undergone a qualitative as well as quantitative change.

In tracing the development of preventive detention, a good place to start lies in the informal practices relating to those who were considered a danger to others

---

[16]   Support for our approach in identifying the relevance of these ingredients of preventive detention is provided by McSherry and Keyzer who identify the development of actuarial justice, the rise of the risk society and the shift to protection against unknown threats as the main themes emerging from the criminological literature to explain the shift towards use of coercive measures to prevent harm: see McSherry and Keyzer, above n 5, 20–3.

[17]   See, for discussion, Andrew Ashworth and Lucia Zedner, 'Just Prevention: Preventative Rationales and the Limits of the Criminal Law' in R A Duff and S Green (eds), *Philosophical Foundations of Criminal Law* (Oxford, 2011) 279.

[18]   See ibid. See also *Veen v The Queen* (No. 2) (1988) 164 CLR 465 regarding sentencing principles.

[19]   Lucia Zedner, 'Pre-Crime and Post-Criminology?' (2007) 11(2) *Theoretical Criminology* 261–81, 262.

[20]   The NSW Sentencing Council recently adopted a similar approach. See above n 2, [2.4].

and themselves.[21] Preventive detention regimes grew up around a population of suspect individuals – vagrants, inebriates and habitual criminals, as well as the mentally ill – who comprised the so-called 'dangerous classes'.[22] In the common law world, the origins of what are now formal rules and procedures governing preventive detention lie in informal and discretionary detention practices. They date from a time when local magistrates and others exercised a range of powers without a clear enunciation of aims or purposes. It is worth noting that such powers were originally exercised by the monarch (in granting mercy, for instance) and later expressly in the name of the monarch (captured by the reference indefinite detention at His or Her Majesty's 'pleasure'), reflecting the idea that, ultimately, clemency resided in the sovereign, the embodiment of the executive.[23] It is also important to note that these practices were generally regarded as beneficent, as the exercise of state power contrasted favourably with leaving the individual to destitution or, alternatively, the imposition of capital punishment.

Prevention was a key driver in the formalisation of these discretionary and informal processes. For instance, the first step in the formalisation of practices relating to insane individuals charged with offences in the English context, the *Criminal Lunatics Act* 1800,[24] was prompted by the perceived need to be able to detain such individuals on the basis that they were dangerous. Although it had been possible to detain insane defendants before 1800, the Act introduced a 'more systematic means of containing them within a voluntarist legal system'.[25] As Martin Wiener argues, this procedure offered a 'middle path' between humanity and security: it was an alternative to conviction and punishment and also provided 'new legal means to incarcerate an offender'.[26] While in theory individuals could be released if they were no longer a danger to themselves or others, in practice, the period of confinement was life.[27] While precise formulation of detention regimes

---

[21] As Christopher Slobogin points out, under traditional legal theory, the detention of the mentally ill is 'pure' preventative detention: see 'The Jurisprudence of Dangerousness' (2003–04) 96 *Northwestern University Law Review* 1, 2. See also Christopher Slobogin, *Minding Justice: Laws That Deprive People with Mental Disability of Life and Liberty* (Harvard UP, 2006) 104.

[22] Martin J Wiener, *Reconstructing the Criminal: Culture, Law and Policy in England, 1830–1914* (CUP, 2009); see also Andrew McLeod 'A History of Consorting Laws' unpublished paper, on file with authors, regarding the development of laws in Australian jurisdictions.

[23] See Nigel Walker, *Crime and Insanity in England (Vol. 1: The Historical Perspective)* (Edinburgh University Press, 1968) 25–6 on the history of executive discretion regarding mentally incapacitated offenders.

[24] *Criminal Lunatics Act 1800*, 39 & 40 Geo 3, c 94.

[25] Wiener, above n 22, 85.

[26] Ibid.

[27] Richard Moran 'The Origin of Insanity as a Special Verdict: The Trial for Treason of James Hadfield' (1985) 19(3) *Law and Society Review* 487–521,515. The effect of the passage of the 1800 Act was that an individual did not have to be convicted of a crime in order to be confined under the criminal law (Moran at 517). See further Arlie Loughnan, *Manifest Madness: Mental Incapacity in Criminal Law* (OUP, 2012).

varied, these sorts of regimes shared a preventive (as opposed to punitive) ethos and were open-ended.[28] Thus, while we may now distinguish between indefinite detention and preventive detention,[29] this distinction has not always been sharply drawn, and the history of the latter implicates the former.

Legacies of this early period remain. Arguably the most long-lived of this type of preventive practice, habitual criminals legislation, still exists in several jurisdictions. In NSW, the *Habitual Criminals Act* 1957 allows a judge to declare certain individuals habitual offenders and impose an additional 5–14 years on top of the sentence imposed on those individuals.[30] The key aspect of habitual criminals legislation is that the sentence imposed exceeds the deserved punishment.[31] The basis for such an extension is the dangerousness of the individual. As Jonathan Simon argues, the priority of the individual in penality in this early period meant that 'knowledge produced at the level of the person was crucial to the truth of crime'.[32] This approach to the sort of knowledge that is crucial to the 'truth of crime' has changed in the move to the more recent era – where knowledge at the level of population and group has become crucial – and we discuss this below.

More recently, preventive detention has been deployed in relation to new groups such as serious violent offenders and sex offenders. As Willem de Lint argues, these groups represent 'worthy targets', groups that have become staples of public policy.[33] Sex offenders feature prominently among these 'worthy targets'. As a result of widespread public concern with sexual violence (and particularly with offences committed against children), sex offenders now comprise the highest profile of those subject to preventive detention (alongside suspected terrorists).

---

[28] For instance, after the *Pritchard* criteria for unfitness to plead were outlined in 1836, and the *M'Naghten Rules* governing insanity formulated in 1843, disposal of unfit and insane individuals remained indefinite. This changed in England and Wales only in the 1990s with the *Criminal Procedure (Insanity and Unfitness to Plead) Act* 1991.

[29] See Bernadette McSherry, 'Indefinite and Preventive Detention Legislation: From Caution to an Open Door' (2005) 29 *Criminal Law Journal* 94, who distinguishes between an order made at the time of the sentence to detain an offender indefinitely (indefinite detention) and an order that the offender be detained after the expiry of their sentence in order to prevent harm to the community (preventive detention).

[30] This law is rarely used and in its report, *High-Risk Violent Offenders*, the NSW Sentencing Council recently recommended that it be repealed: see above n 2, [5.115].

[31] See Paul H Robinson, 'Punishing Dangerousness: Cloaking Preventive Detention as Criminal Justice (2001) *Harvard Law Review* 114(5), 1429–56, 1435.

[32] Jonathan Simon, 'Managing the Monstrous: Sex Offenders and the New Penology' (1998) 4 *Psychology, Public Policy and Law* 452–67, 452. See also Bernard E Harcourt, 'From the Ne-er-Do-Well to the Criminal History Category: The Refinement of the Actuarial Model in Criminal Law' (2003) 66(3) *Law and Contemporary Problems* 99–151.

[33] Willem de Lint, 'Risking Precaution in Two South Australian Serious Offender Initiatives' (2012) 24(2) *Current Issues in Criminal Justice* 145–165, 145. De Lint argues that the 'combination of a proliferation of decision-making instruments that convert legal questions into risk measures and the common purpose in public policy to manage crime has contributed to producing a politics of worthy targets'.

Laws enacted in the USA, which have been repeatedly copied around the world, permit the civil commitment of sexually violent predators and uphold the constitutionality of mandating a system of registration and selective community notification of convicted sex offenders.[34] As Bernadette McSherry and Patrick Keyzer point out, such regimes are usually justified on the basis that sex offenders have a high rate of reoffending, although this is not borne out by the empirical research.[35] Simon argues that such laws are premised on the futility of effort with sex offenders, reflecting a pervasive scepticism about the power of the state to fundamentally change offenders.[36] As Simon argues, sex offenders used to be seen as exemplifying the psychopathological basis for crime; now they are seen as a lesson about the intransience of evil, where crime has become a problem of managing high-risk categories and subpopulations, not normalising individuals to community norms.[37]

The creation of preventive detention regimes received a significant boost in the wake of the 9/11 attacks on the USA. In the period since the attacks, we have witnessed an explosion in the number of preventive detention regimes in operation in Australian jurisdictions and elsewhere. In Australia, at Federal level, a raft of anti-terrorism legislation was passed in the first half of 2002.[38] More recently, the Commonwealth Government enacted the *Anti-Terrorism Act* (No. 2) 2005, which was designed to strengthen existing anti-terrorism laws and which encompasses a preventive detention scheme. According to this scheme, persons suspected of involvement with terrorism can be detained for up to 48 hours where there is insufficient evidence to support a formal charge.[39] Several states have also amended their anti-terrorism legislation to encompass preventive detention in the years since 9/11. For instance, Section 2A of the NSW *Terrorism (Police Powers) Act 2002* provides for preventive detention,[40] but as the Ombudsman noted in his

---

[34] For a discussion of the US laws, see Simon, above n 33. In the Australian context see Patrick Keyzer, Stephen Southwood QC and Cathy Pereira, 'Pre-emptive Imprisonment for Dangerousness in Queensland', (2004) 11 *Psychology, Psychiatry and Law* 244; Anthony Gray, 'Detaining Future Dangerous Offenders: Dangerous Law', (2004) 9 *Deakin Law Review* 243–60 assessing the *Dangerous Prisoners (Sexual Offenders)* Act 2003 (Qld). Most recently, WA announced the introduction of a publically-accessible Community Protection Register naming those who have been convicted of child sexual offences: see <http://www.news.com.au/national/wa-police-community-protection-register-tells-parents-where-padedophiles-are-lurking/story-fndo4eg9-1226496344985>.

[35] See McSherry and Keyzer, above n 5, 23–5.

[36] Simon, above n 32.

[37] Ibid.

[38] See for discussion, Paul Fairall and Wendy Lacey, 'Preventative Detention and Control Orders under Federal Law: The Case for a Bill of Rights' 31(3) *Melbourne University Law Review* 1072–98.

[39] See *Criminal Code* s 105.9 (Commonwealth). For critical assessment, see Fairall and Lacey, above n 38.

[40] Under section 26D, the police can apply to the Supreme Court for a preventative detention order to prevent an imminent terrorist act or to preserve evidence of terrorist acts that have occurred. The Supreme Court can take into account any evidence or information that the

review of that Act, such powers have not been used since the commencement of the Act.[41]

As this overview suggests, in the recent era, preventive detention has changed – both qualitatively and quantitatively. Regarding quantitative change, it is clear that preventive detention regimes have burgeoned in recent decades.[42] Several of these regimes are premised on the provision of treatment to those detained, as treatment seems to figure prominently in the rationalisation and justification of preventive detention.[43] As a number of commentators have pointed out, the expansion of preventive detention is not confined to the criminal law. Rather, civil law mechanisms have been harnessed to the task of preventively dealing with the mentally ill, the anti-social, the 'sexual predator' and the dangerous.[44] In addition to a quantitative change in preventive detention, it has undergone a qualitative change. Different commentators have attempted to capture this qualitative change under various labels. One useful term in this respect is 'radical prevention', coined by Eric Janus. According to Janus, and by contrast with 'routine prevention', 'radical prevention' denotes intervention where there is some sort of risk of future harm, as opposed to actual or attempted harm.[45] The use of preventive detention in anti-terrorism laws, and laws relating to 'sexual predators', fall into the category of 'radical prevention', with the absence of safeguards paving the way for 'an expansive, and liberty-constricting, preventive state'.[46] As Richard

---

Court considers *credible or trustworthy in the circumstances*' and, in that regard, is not bound by the principles or rules governing the admission of evidence (s 26O). The NSW scheme permits an initial preventative detention order to be made by the Supreme Court without notice to the person and in his or her absence for up to 48 hours (ss 26H and 26L(1)). Within this 48-hour period another hearing to confirm the order must be held. At this hearing, the detained person can be represented and heard. The New South Wales scheme operates so that a person can be detained without charge for up to 14 days (s 26K).

[41] NSW Ombudsman Review of Parts 2A and 3 of the *Terrorism (Police Powers) Act 2002* August 2011, Recommendation 13, 33.

[42] McSherry points to the 1990s as the start of the increasing use of preventive and indefinite detention in Australia: see McSherry, above n 29.

[43] See *M v Germany* [2010] ECHR No. 19359/04 and *Kansas v Hendricks* 521 US 346 (1997), discussed by C Slobogin in this volume.

[44] For critique of this use of the civil law, see Robinson, above n 32. There is some question about the novelty of such developments, see eg Carol Steiker, 'Punishment and Procedure: Punishment Theory and the Criminal-Civil Procedural Divide' (1996–97) 85 *Georgetown Law Journal* 775–819. Steiker argues that the civil/criminal distinction has been blurred by a number of factors, including the unstable distinction between remedial and retributive justice and the collapsed distinction between preventative and retributive punishment with the rise of dangerousness (as opposed to mad or bad binary) through cognitive and behavioural sciences.

[45] Eric Janus, 'The Preventive State, Terrorists and Sexual Predators: Countering the Threat of a New Outsider Jurisprudence' (2004) 40(3) *Criminal Law Bulletin* 576.

[46] Ibid. See also Filip Gelev, '"Risk Society" and the Precautionary Approach in Recent Australian, Canadian and UK Judicial Decision Making' (2009) 5(1) *Comparative Research in Law & Political Economy Research Paper Series* 22–4 < http://www.comparativeresearch.net/papers.jsp?order=Title>.

Lippke points out in a separate analysis, the provision of treatment does not seem appropriate in this sort of context.[47]

It is in this period that the legal legitimacy of preventive detention has been seriously challenged. In the legal literature, rule of law issues, proportionality, the principle against double punishment and fairness to those subject to preventive detention represent the chief concerns.[48] Here, particular issues include the rules of evidence, standards of proof, and the availability of review of decision-making, but, also increasingly, concerns with compatibility with constitutional protections and human rights norms loom large.[49] Part of the debate about preventive detention revolves around the contrast between preventive detention and criminal punishment. As the NSW Sentencing Council notes, preventive detention involves decisions that may be based on a lower standard of proof than the criminal standard ('beyond reasonable doubt'), elevates protection of the public above other rationales, incapacitates an offender without a fresh offence, and detains him or her in a custodial environment, although there is no additional conviction.[50] Criticism of preventive detention is not restricted to commentary but may also be found in appellate level decisions. Beginning with the decision of *Kable*, Australian appellate courts have critically reviewed preventive detention regimes, giving careful consideration to the precise conditions under which the detention of offenders beyond the expiry of their sentences will be acceptable,[51] although, as McSherry argues, the strength of opposition shown by courts to preventive detention has been diluted in recent years.[52] As is clear in the legal

---

[47]   Richard L Lippke, 'No Easy Way Out: Dangerous Offenders and Preventive Detention' (2008) 27(4) *Law & Philosophy* 383–414, 412.

[48]   See, for example, David Cole, 'Out of the Shadows: Preventive Detention, Suspected Terrorists and War' (2009) 97 *California Law Review* 693; A Goldsmith, 'Preparation for Terrorism: Catastrophic Risk and Precautionary Criminal Law' in Andrew Lynch et al (eds), Law and Liberty in the War on Terror (Federation Press, 2007) 59–74; R L Lippke, above n 48; Patrick Keyzer and Sam Blay, 'Double Punishment? Preventive Detention Schemes under Australian Legislation and their Consistency with International Law' (2006) 7 *Melbourne Journal of International Law* 407-22; Philip Montague, 'Justifying Preventive Detention' (1999) 18(2) *Law & Philosophy* 173–85.

[49]   See for example, Fairall and Lacey, above n 39. For an illustration of judicial engagement with human rights norms, in the context of anti-terrorism, see *Thomas v Mowbray* (2007) 233 CLR 307.

[50]   See above n 2, [2.5].

[51]   See *Kable v Director of Public Prosecutions* (NSW) (1996) 189 CLR 51 and *Fardon v A-G (Qld)* (2004) 210 ALR 50; see also *A-G (Qld) v Francis* (2005) QSC 381; *A-G(Qld) v Fardon* (unreported, QSC No 416, September 2003); *A-G (NSW) v Gallagher* (2006) NSWSC 340; *A-G (NSW) v Tillman* (2007) NSWSC 605; *A-G (NSW) v Quinn* (2007) NSWSC 87; *A-G (NSW) Winters* (2007) NSWSC 1071; *Cornwall v A-G* (NSW) [2007] NSWSC 374; *Director of Public Prosecutions (WA) v GTR* [2008] (Unreported); *Director of Public Prosecutions (WA) v Mangolamara* (2007) WASC (27 March 2007); *TSL v Secretary to the Department of Justice* (2006) VSCA 199. For critical discussion, see M Brown, 'Prevention and the Security State: Observations on an Emerging Jurisprudence of Risk' (2011) VIII *Champ pénal/Penal Field* XX <http://champpenal.revues.org/8016>.

[52]   McSherry, above n 29.

literature, preventive detention is something that does not necessarily sit easily with traditional legal precepts.

Alongside legal concerns, an additional site of criticism concerns the effectiveness of preventive detention regimes. Here, issues include legal use and understanding of psychiatric tests, the reliability of predictions of dangerousness, profiling and the likelihood of reducing reoffending.[53] For instance, in the context of a discussion of preventive detention of sex offenders, Cynthia Mercado and James Ogloff argue that risk assessment instruments should be utilised by courts because, while no one instrument has superior predictive capability, their reliability 'far exceeds' clinical judgment.[54] But, as the NSW Sentencing Council points out, systems of preventive detention do not reduce recidivism if predictions of risk are not infallible because any offender who is incorrectly assessed as not dangerous will be at large in the community.[55] Further, as Heather Douglas argues in the context of preventive detention of sex offenders, the claim that preventive detention is rehabilitative is seriously strained by the inadequacy of therapeutic resources in prison settings.[56] As this brief discussion suggests, concerns about the effectiveness of preventive detention trespass onto the territory of risk, a broader issue that is intimately related to the practice of preventive detention, and which we discuss in Part III below.

The qualitative and quantitative change in preventive detention is part of broader changes across the criminal justice field. Garland has understood this newly configured criminal justice terrain as a 'culture of control'.[57] Garland identifies 12 characteristics of penality in the current era, including the expansion of crime prevention, the privileging of public protection against crime and a perpetual sense of crisis about crime.[58] In relation to prisons, for instance, broad shifts in penal strategies – towards neo-liberalism, 'penal populism' and risk management – have played out since the post-war era. As part of the shift from modernity to late modernity, by the end of the 1980s, prison was seen 'less as a place for treating

---

53   See for example, McSherry and Keyzer, above n 5. In relation to sex offenders, McSherry and Keyzer argue that regimes that aim to remove offenders from their communities and restrict their movements are expensive and may not reduce rates of reoffending.
54   Cynthia Calkins Mercado and James R P Ogloff, 'Risk and the Preventive Detention of Sex Offenders in Australia and the United States' (2007) 30(1) *International Journal of Law and Psychiatry* 49, 54.
55   Above n 2, [2.92].
56   Heather Douglas, 'Post-Sentence Preventive Detention: Dangerous and Risky' [2008] 11 *Criminal Law Review* 854–73, 873.
57   David Garland *Culture of Control* (OUP, 2001). Garland argues that the main features of contemporary criminal law and justice systems in many Western industrialised countries are the products of global or shared trends toward increasingly punitive and populist penal policies.
58   Ibid.

offenders and more as a place for containing them'.[59] Augmenting this approach to prisoners was the rise of a managerial ethos and an increasing emphasis on the administration of risk. As Simon suggests, 'master narratives of penology' have changed subjects formerly defined as aberrant and in need of transformation into high-risk subjects in need of management. Managing risk has become the primary and an explicit focus of penology. According to Simon, 'latent in this managerialism is a growing sense that little or nothing can be done to change offenders'.[60]

An alternative account for the changes in the criminal justice field, including those relating to preventive detention, has been developed by Lucia Zedner. As Zedner points out, crime is conventionally regarded as a harm or wrong, but is increasingly conceived of as essentially risk or potential loss. Zedner has argued that we are on the cusp of a shift from a post- to a pre-crime society: the post-crime orientation of criminal justice is increasingly overshadowed by the pre-crime logic of security. Other legal scholars have also taken up the issue of security.[61] According to Zedner, this is a temporal (but also sectorial) shift.[62] As Zedner writes:

In a post-crime society there are crimes, offenders and victims, crime control, policing, investigation, trial and punishment, all of which are staples of present criminological enquiry. Pre-crimes, by contrast, shifts the temporal perspective to anticipate and forestall that which has not occurred and may never do so. In a pre-crime society, there is calculation, risk and uncertainty, surveillance, precaution, prudentialism, moral hazard, prevention and, arching over all of these, there is the pursuit of security.[63]

The result of the shift to 'pre-crime' is that, rather than focusing on wrongdoing, criminal legal rules and practices, criminal justice institutions aim to pre-empt,

---

[59]   Tony Seddon, *Punishment and Madness: Governing Prisoners with Mental Health Problems* (GlassHouse Press, 2007) 55.

[60]   Simon, above n 32, 454.

[61]   See eg Victor Tadros, 'Crimes and Security' (2008) 71(6) *Modern Law Review* 940–70. Tadros argues that discussion of criminalisation in the legal literature has not taken the concept of security sufficiently seriously and thus failed to see one of the central drivers behind recent developments in criminal law and justice. For Tadros, a legitimate concern with security is driving the creation of inappropriate criminal offences (most notably, in the area of terrorism). Tadros argues that security has not been appropriately counterbalanced with other values and that this value can be eroded by 'badly thought out, under-researched, poorly designed and hastily enacted criminal offences' (970). The idea of balancing security and liberty has been subject to critique: see Lucia Zedner, 'Securing Liberty in the Face of Terror: Reflections from Criminal Justice' (2005) 32(4) *Journal of Law and Society* 507–33.

[62]   Zedner, above n 19, 262. According to Zedner, this temporal shift is also evident in profiling, offender registers, surveillance, CCTV, situational crime prevention and community safety initiatives.

[63]   Ibid.

minimise and displace loss. This means that a key issue is the protection provided as a public good. It is in this broad context that we have seen the qualitative change in preventive detention.

As these accounts of the criminal justice field suggest, preventive detention regimes are increasingly likely to be part of a suite of preventive measures. Ashworth and Zedner define preventive measures as those that restrict individual liberty in order to prevent harm or risk of harm and which are backed by the threat of coercive sanctions.[64] As Ashworth and Zedner point out, preventive measures have been promoted for multiple reasons – including to provide an avenue for state intervention without resort to criminalisation, and without criminal rules of evidence and procedure; and to deal with types of behaviour with which criminal law and procedure have been ill-equipped to deal (such as a course of conduct or a series of omissions).[65] Preventive detention takes on an even greater prominence when it is set against a background of the increasing popularity of preventive measures more generally.

Reliance on preventive detention is increasing. Recent examples include the preventive detention legislation enacted in the Northern Territory, under which a number of indigenous people with disabilities or mental impairment are being held indefinitely although they have not been convicted of a new offence.[66] The proliferation of forms of preventive detention, and its qualitative change, indicates that it is more than just a legal practice; it is a complex socio-political issue. Like all techniques of social control, preventive detention is not ahistorical: it is a product of its society, that is, of the social horizon – the shared meanings and understandings which constitute the basis for daily encounters with others, within the respective society. Hence, policy makers need to acknowledge that the policy and practice of preventive detention stretches beyond its identity as a particular set of practices located within the legal realm. The deep and expansive roots of preventive detention emerges clearly when we zoom in and identify the three main 'ingredients' of the practice of preventive detention – the rationality of 'prevention', the technology of 'risk' and the practice of 'security'.

---

[64]   Andrew Ashworth and Lucia Zedner, 'Preventative Orders: A Problem of Undercriminalization?' in R A Duff et al (eds) *The Boundaries of the Criminal Law* (Oxford, 2010) 59–87, 61. Ashworth and Zedner categorise preventative measures into nine families, including civil preventative hybrid orders aimed at preventing risk, pre-trial orders aimed at preventing risk and offences having the prevention of harm as a primary explicit rationale (63–5).

[65]   Ibid 65–7.

[66]   A constitutional challenge is being considered. See ABC Radio, Law Report, 24 July 2012 <http://www.abc.net.au/radionational/programs/lawreport/nt-indefinite-detention-hca-challenge/4151268>. See also the chapter by Ian Freckelton SC in this volume.

Arlie Loughnan and Sabine Selchow

3. THE RATIONALITY OF 'PREVENTION', THE TECHNOLOGY OF 'RISK' AND THE PRACTICE OF 'SECURITY'

In this section, we examine the three ingredients that constitute and shape the practice of preventive detention: the rationality of 'prevention', the technology of 'risk' and the practice of 'security'. Although these three ingredients are closely interlinked in the practice of preventive detention, it is worth looking at each of them separately. Of course, each is complex and their contours change depending on the (disciplinary) vantage point adopted to examine them. Hence, it would be a formidable challenge to capture them in their totality, and this is not our aim. We do not attempt to provide a full account of the rationality of 'prevention', the technology of 'risk' and the practice of 'security': rather, we aim to make policy makers aware of the complexity of each of these ingredients and, consequently, of what is at stake in legislative moves regarding preventive detention by highlighting relevant aspects of each.

3.1. THE RATIONALITY OF PREVENTION

Prevention is a complex rationality, and, as we suggested above, it extends beyond but encompasses preventive detention. For our purposes in this chapter, three aspects of it are worth noting because they bear on the practice of preventive detention. We discuss each in turn.

The first aspect of note relates to the 'productiveness' of the rationality of prevention. The rationality of prevention is captured by the maxim that 'prevention is better than cure'. That is, prevention is about avoiding undesired events that may take place, before they take place, be they criminal offences, diseases that may break out or accidents that may occur. So, it appears as if the rationality of 'prevention' is about reducing and/or eradicating the probability of these events taking place. On this basis, the rationality of prevention is about the absence of something; that is, security is taken to be the absence of crime, peace is taken to be the absence of war, health is taken to be the absence of disease etc.[67] Yet, despite the fact that avoidance is at the core of the rationality of prevention, we need to understand that it is also 'productive'. By this, we mean that the rationality of prevention 'produces' conduct, in that it is manifest and is played out in measures that reward, punish, encourage, survey, threaten etc. It is through these measures that both specific subjects and normalized ways of conduct are 'actively' produced.

---

[67] See further Ulrich Broeckling, 'Praevention' in U Broeckling, S Krassmann and T Lemke (eds), *Glossar der Gegenwart* (Suhrkamp, 2004) 210–15, 210.

The second noteworthy aspect of the rationality of prevention relates to the nature of the events that are to be avoided by preventive action. As mentioned above, the rationality of prevention is about avoiding in advance an undesired event occurring: preventive action takes place before an event happens that is to be avoided. This is why every action that follows the rationality of prevention takes place in the field of the imagined: it is the idea of a (possible) event to take place that motivates and shapes preventive action. In other words, preventive action is motivated by the anticipation of an undesired event. This means that preventive action is not simply a form of pro-action (although that is how it is usually perceived). Rather, it can just as accurately be understood as a re-action – not a reaction to an actuality, but a reaction to an idea of a potential event that could happen, that is, to an imagined event. To be clear, the fact that the events to which preventive action reacts are imagined does not mean that they are random or amorphous, or that they can be simply 'made up'. They are not random and they cannot be simply made up – they are solid social products, the result of complex processes of social ratification. It is this social nature of imagined events, to which preventive action reacts, that reveals that action drawing on the rationality of prevention is never value-free. On the one hand, it inevitably builds on and implicates complex assumptions about the social world, such as a specific understanding of human agency, ideas about how to govern behaviour and, perhaps most significantly, notions about the very constitution of society. On the other hand, the image of the undesired event to be avoided is a product of complex socio-political and socio-cultural processes coming from within and being shaped by the given social horizon, that is, the shared meanings and understandings that constitute the basis for daily encounters with others within the respective society.

The third and final aspect to note regarding the rationality of prevention is that it implies the idea of expansion. Prevention has a two-fold expansive nature. First, as highlighted above, preventive action can be seen as a reaction to an imagined event that may happen in the future and that is undesired and, hence, to be avoided. Given it is directed at an imagined event, there is something open about preventive action. It is not 'tamed' or limited by a distinct, tangible actuality that occurs in a specific moment of time. Consequently, we need to acknowledge that, by nature, the rationality of prevention is expansive: since everything could be imagined as constituting an undesired event to be avoided, the rationality of prevention could be applied to everything. Hence, it is potentially expansive in regard to the fields – the kinds of imagined events – to which it is applied. Indeed, over recent decades, we have witnessed an expansion of the rationality of prevention in general and, as sketched out in the previous section of this chapter, in regard to preventive detention in particular. But, as Ulrich Broeckling points out, the rationality of prevention also implies an idea of expansion in another respect.[68] Prevention requires knowledge: knowledge to identify and distil certain relevant 'factors' for consideration; knowledge about the environment which brings out certain 'factors'; and knowledge about the relationship between certain 'factors' and the probability that their coming together leads to an undesired event that should be avoided. Yet, it is often impossible to determine clear causal relations when it comes to human behaviour and social phenomena. In general, in those cases in which it is possible to determine a plausible causal relation, its plausibility refers to the past, not to the future, that is, not to the possible event that may occur and is to be avoided.[69] Consequently, preventive knowledge is essentially incomplete: it is always partial, with the need to gain more knowledge ever-present. In Broeckling's words, '[t]hose who aim to prevent, never know enough';[70] in other words, the hunger for preventive knowledge is insatiable. This point about knowledge, within the rationality of prevention, is closely interlinked with the second main ingredient that underlies the practice of preventive detention: the technology of 'risk'. It is to this we now turn.

3.2.   THE TECHNOLOGY OF 'RISK'

The second main ingredient that forms the basis of the practice of preventive detention is the technology of 'risk'. As stated in the preceding subsection, it is the purpose of preventive action to attempt to ensure that an undesired event does not take place. The undesired event is something that may take place in the future; it is something that is anticipated. There is the potentiality of it taking place; in other words, there is a risk that the undesired future event will take place.

'Risk' is a complex phenomenon that is not easy to grasp. This is not because the issue of 'risk' is an untouched scholarly site. Indeed, the opposite is the case. 'Risk' is not only an explicit or, more often, implicit, but persistent companion in everyday life, but over the past few decades, it has also attracted an extensive body of scholarship. This body of scholarship is not only growing in size but also diversifying in terms of the array of disciplinary traditions on which it builds. While 'risk' used to be at home in the domains of scientists, economists and managers, as Garland observes, 'Today's accounts of risk are remarkable for their multiplicity and for the variety of senses they give to the term. [...] Whatever one makes of these claims, it seems clear that risk and its management have outgrown the domain of the technical specialists and are becoming increasingly pervasive features of the contemporary world.'[71] In this subsection of Part III, we identify

---

[68]   Ibid 211.
[69]   Ibid.
[70]   Ibid.
[71]   David Garland, 'The Rise of Risk' in R V Ericson and A Doyle (eds), *Risk and Morality* (University of Toronto Press, 2003) 50.

five distinct aspects of the technology of 'risk', in order to make the reader aware of its complex socio-political nature and, crucially, the socio-political dimension that is implied in the practice of 'risk assessment', which we mentioned above.

The first significant aspect of 'risk' is that it concerns agency and, as implied in this, responsibility. Across the various conceptualisations of 'risk', one thing is readily apparent: 'risk' is a child of modernity – it builds on and presupposes the idea of an open and contingent future which is understood to be able to be shaped by human agents through their actions and decisions. As Anthony Giddens puts it, 'risk' is 'the mobilising dynamic of a society bent on change, that wants to determine its own future rather than leaving it to religion, tradition, or the vagaries of nature'.[72] As such, 'risk' is inextricably linked to agency and human action – more precisely, it is linked to agency and human action in an uncertain world. Hence, 'risk' can be understood as a specific technology that is applied to deal with the state of uncertainty. 'Risk' can be understood as a kind of 'tool' that enables (or, equally, restricts) human action in the face of an uncertain future. In providing us with an idea of the likelihood of an undesired event taking place, it constitutes a guide in our decision making. Of course, this does not mean that the assessment of 'risk' makes the future fully predictable, let alone that it erases uncertainty. Rather, '[i]ndependently of success or failure, it provides a justifiable guide for behaviour. Although it cannot make the future predictable or the world certain, it can create the means for *acting as though it were*.'[73] 'Risk' is then a technology that provides the basis for responsible behaviour and decisions or, more precisely, for what is perceived as responsible behaviour and decisions. Yet, it does this not in regard to an actuality, but through calculable assessments of potential future happenings, based on past experiences and, when undertaken within a formal context, following set procedures. This means that the technology of 'risk' can easily lead to paradoxical situations in which a 'wrong decision is right',[74] that is, 'right' in accordance with risk assessment rules and procedures. 'If the impossible happens, one can defend oneself with the argument that one decided correctly, namely in risk-rational manner.'[75] Thus, as Gerda Reith states, quoting Niklas Luhmann, the technology of 'risk' 'immunize[s] decision-making against failure'.[76] And it must be noted that the assessment that something constitutes a 'risk' is not about (normative) categories of 'right' and 'wrong,' but builds on and measures whether something is 'adequate' or 'inadequate' in

---

[72] Antony Giddens, *Runaway World: How Globalisation Is Reshaping Our Lives* (Profile Books, 2002) 24.

[73] Gerda Reith, 'Uncertain Times: The Notion of 'Risk' and the Development of Modernity' (2004) 13(2/3) *Time & Society* 383–402, 396.

[74] Niklas Luhmann, cited in ibid 399.

[75] Ibid 396.

[76] Ibid.

following the imperatives of health, security or success in the respective socio-political context.[77]

The second noteworthy aspect of the technology of 'risk' is implicit in the above, but it is worth express identification. This aspect of 'risk' relates to the fact that, contrary to the general tenor of the public and political debates, 'risk' does not exist *per se*. In general, 'risk' 'exists as a feature of knowing, not as an aspect of being'.[78] Again, drawing on Luhmann, Gerda Reith succinctly communicates this point when she argues that 'as long as human actors who perceive and think and respond are involved in the probability equation, there can be no such thing as "objective" risk. As Luhmann [...] puts it: "The outside world itself knows no risks, for it knows neither distinctions, nor expectations, nor evaluations, nor probabilities."'[79] In particular, 'risk' has a *relational* meaning', as Garland stresses, in that it 'defines a perceived relationship between ourselves and our world. [It] involves a vision of what might happen and how it might affect us.'[80] This means that 'the social' is inevitably inscribed in the technology of 'risk'. There are no risks without someone identifying various relevant factors and putting them into relation to each other and to some kind of subject. '[R]isk is not a first order "thing" existing in the world. It is rather a specific way of assessing and categorizing the (hazardous) relationship that these things have to us, to our plans, our interests, and our well-being.'[81] So, the technology of 'risk' is about categorization; things are brought 'into a calculable form'.[82]

It is this nature of the technology of 'risk' and risk assessment that accounts for the fact that the increasing application of the technology of 'risk' in various social fields impacts so profoundly on the character of these fields. There are many sophisticated studies that highlight the change of various social fields through the concept of 'risk', which is most apparent in the replacement of 'the individual' with 'groups', 'categories' and 'classes'.[83] For instance, as Simon points out in relation to the field of criminal justice, when compared with the 'dangerous classes' of the nineteenth or twentieth centuries, periods in which the 'truth of crime was thought to lie in the personality and social conditions of the offender', the current dominance of 'statistical as opposed to characterological concepts of group boundaries' means that justice is becoming increasingly actuarial.[84] In general,

[77] See Henning Schmidt-Semisch, 'Risiko' in U Broeckling, S Krassmann and T Lemke (eds), *Glossar der Gegenwart* (Suhrkamp, 2004) 222–7.
[78] Reith above n 73, 387.
[79] Ibid 385–6.
[80] Garland, above n 71, 50.
[81] Ibid 52.
[82] Mitchell Dean, 'Risk, Calculable and Incalculable' in D Lupton (ed), *Risk and Sociocultural Theory: New Directions and Perspectives* (Cambridge University Press, 1999) 131–59, 131.
[83] See for discussion Harcourt, above n 32.
[84] Simon, above n 32, 453.

this entails 'a swing away from the individualized category of dangerousness towards the collectivized logic of risk'.[85] For instance, specifically addressing the production of psychiatric knowledge, Niklas Rose observes that harnessing it to the task of addressing risk implies that the 'logic of diagnosis' is replaced with the 'logic of prediction'.[86]

The third aspect of the technology of 'risk' that we wish to identify here is a point about the categories on which risk assessments build – they are never value-free. Again, this aspect is implicit in the above discussion but is worth noting expressly. This point is nicely illustrated by the topic of anti-terrorism measures. As part of their reflection on US risk-based security measures in place since the terrorist actions of 11 September 2001, Louise Amoore and Marieke de Goede state that 'risk-based screening [at airports] is offered to civil liberties groups as being more objective, neutral and expert led than the potentially discriminating and prejudicial decisions taken by airport security personnel and border guards,'[87] but the process of selecting and establishing data that constitute categories for screening is of course neither ahistorical nor value-neutral. As Amoore and de Goede conclude in relation to the US screening practice, '[I]nside these data, designations of exception and exemption are always already made on grounds that are absolutely racialized and prejudicial.'[88]

The fourth and fifth aspects of the technology of 'risk' we wish to mention relate to its expansive and productive nature, respectively. As stated above, in the context of the rationality of prevention, logics that are not naturally 'tamed' or limited by actualities are potentially expansive. The case of preventive security measures applied by the US anti-terrorism measures makes this readily apparent. As Amoore and de Goede point out, in this context, risk technologies are applied with the aim to 'identify terrorists who are not (yet) terrorists[;]'[89] in this way, these technologies expand in time to an extreme pre-crime state, one in which the categorized subjects themselves might not even know that they are at risk of becoming terrorists. Furthermore, the technology of risk is productive in that it produces conduct and 'risk'-subjects but also in that it inevitably produces other 'risks' and insecurity. As Richard Ericson and Kevin Hoggarty observe, 'The yearning for security drives the insatiable quest for more and better knowledge of risk. However, in the search for inexhaustibly detailed and continuous risk

---

[85] Gabe Mythen and Sandra Walklate, 'Criminology and Terrorism: Which Thesis? Risk Society or Governmentality?' (2006) 46 *British Journal of Criminology* 379–98, 385.

[86] Nikolas Rose *Powers of Freedom: Reframing Political Thought* (CUP, 1999) 261 and 260–3 more generally.

[87] Louise Amoore and Marieke de Goede, 'Introduction' in L Amoore and M de Goede (eds), *Risk and the War on Terror* (Routledge, 2008) 5–19, 8.

[88] Ibid.

[89] Ibid.

management knowledge, each new form of knowledge and the measure of protection it makes visible gives rise to new knowledge about insecurity.'[90]

3.3.   THE PRACTICE OF 'SECURITY'

We now turn to a brief reflection on the last of the three ingredients of preventive detention, the practice of 'security'. Like the logic of prevention, and the technology of 'risk', an appreciation of the practice of security is crucial for understanding preventive detention. 'Security' is constitutive of (the idea of) the state – in fact, it is 'security' that legitimises the state.[91] Consequently, providing security is not only a fundamental role of the state but also something that constitutes it.[92] Yet, as a growing body of literature in critical security studies tells us,[93] and by contrast with the way it is typically conceptualized in public and political discourses, 'security' cannot be simply understood as a distinct good which must be provided, or as a state of being which must achieved. Rather, it must be understood and treated as a (political) *practice*. In this section, we discuss the idea of security as a (political) practice and provide an overview of recent developments in security discourses worldwide.

What does it mean to approach security as a (political) practice? This means that 'security' is not a distinct good that could be easily provided by the state or a state of being to be realised once and for all. This is an insight that has been developed by scholars in critical security studies, most explicitly in the seminal work *Security: A New Framework for Analysis* by Buzan, Wæver and de Wilde, who provided the foundation of the so-called *Copenhagen School* in International Relations.[94] Rather than taking security as something objectively measurable, these scholars argue that 'security is a particular type of politics applicable to a wide range of issues';[95] 'security' is manifest in what they label 'securitization' (speech) acts. Accordingly, '[s]ecurity is [...] a self-referential practice, because it is in this practice that the issue becomes a security issue – not necessarily because a real existential threat exists but because the issue is presented as such a threat.'[96] The central and powerful claim of this take on security is that, through this

---

[90]   Richard V Ericson and Kevin D Haggerty, *Policing the Risk Society* (University of Toronto Press, 1997) 85.

[91]   See Thomas Hobbes, *Leviathan* (Penguin, 1968) and J Locke, *Two Treaties of Government* (CUP, 1960). See also Lucia Zedner, *Security* (Routledge, 2009).

[92]   As Michael Dillon eloquently points out, security is even more than that: it sits at the heart of Western thinking. See Michael Dillon, *The Politics of Security* (Routledge, 1996).

[93]   Prominently Barry Buzan, Ole Wæver and Jaap de Wilde, *Security: A New Framework for Analysis*. (Lynne Rienner Publishers, 1998); L Hansen, *Security as Practice: Discourse Analysis and the Bosnian War* (Routledge, 2006).

[94]   Buzan, Wæver and de Wilde, ibid.

[95]   Ibid vii.

[96]   Ibid 24.

practice of security, issues are lifted beyond the sphere of 'normal politics' into the sphere of 'security'. 'Traditionally, by saying "security," a state representative declares an emergency condition, thus claiming a right to use whatever means necessary to block a threatening development.'[97] Hence, by framing something as a security issue it gets transformed into something 'posing an existential threat'.[98] Buzan, Wæver and de Wilde describe this 'securitization' move as an 'extreme form of politicization'[99] because it enables political actors to break rules of political conduct and procedures, that is, for instance, it legitimizes the use of force or the prohibition of debates about a 'securitized' issue in public or academic discourses. The acknowledgment that empirical reality, more precisely, security threats are not objectively 'out there' – in other words, that they are not just innocently perceived and reacted to by political actors – but that political actors are actively involved in creating them through the symbolic framing of issues highlights 'the responsibility of talking security, the responsibility of actors, as well as of analysts, who choose to frame an issue as a security issue. They cannot hide behind the claim that anything in itself constitutes a security issue.'[100] This reveals that the use of 'the security label', as Ole Wæver puts it, is a 'political choice';[101] hence, it highlights the necessity to continually reflect on and ask 'with some force whether it is a good idea to make [an] issue a security issue – to transfer it to the agenda of panic politics'.[102]

The second noteworthy aspect of security as a (political) practice is that the drive for more security inevitably leads to more insecurity. This is implicit in what some International Relations scholars – who are concerned with national security – have called the 'security dilemma'.[103] The security dilemma exists because 'many of the means by which a state tries to increase its security decrease the security of others',[104] which, in turn, motivates others to increase their security measures, which decreases the security of others *ad infinitum*. Frank P Harvey points to another, slightly different 'security dilemma' which he considers that governments (in his case study, the US government) are facing. In *The Homeland Security*

---

[97]   Ibid 21.
[98]   Ibid. Through this (symbolic) 'transformation', called 'securitization'-speech act, the issue gets pushed to the far end of a spectrum, which, as the *Copenhagen School* scholars explain, consists of the following three main stages: 'nonpoliticized (meaning the state does not deal with it and it is not in any way made an issue of public debate and decision)[,] politicized (meaning the issue is part of public policy, requiring government decision and resource allocations or, more rarely, some other form of communal governance) [and] securitized' (24).
[99]   Ibid 23.
[100] Ibid 34.
[101] Ole Wæver 'Securitization and Desecuritization.' in R Lipschitz (ed), *On Security* (Columbia University Press, 1995) 65.
[102] Buzan, Wæver and de Wilde, above n 93, 34.
[103] Prominently, Robert Jervis, 'Cooperation under the Security Dilemma' (1978) 30(2) *World Politics* 167–214.
[104] Ibid 169.

Dilemma Harvey argues that '[t]he more security you have, the more security you will need'.[105] Statistical evidence suggests decreasing public satisfaction with and trust in the US administration's efforts to secure the US homeland over the past years.[106] Contrasting this finding with the (arguably) high amount of public spending associated with the Department of Homeland Security and its percental increase, on the one hand, and a post-9/11 'perfect record of success (so far) with respect to preventing other attacks on US territory' on the other,[107] Harvey highlights the dilemma: the more the US administration invests in 'security' the more the public expectation rises and the more dissatisfied people are about security measures. So, what we see here is that, in different ways, security produces insecurity and, with that, produces dilemmas for policy makers.

This brings us to the final noteworthy aspect about the practice of 'security': the nature of contemporary security discourses. There has been a remarkable development over the past decades in regard to security discourses worldwide. Broadly speaking, security discourses worldwide are shaped by three interacting developments. First, there has been an increasing significance of 'security' for and within public and political discourses. We saw at the beginning of this subsection that 'security' is at the very heart of modern politics; i.e. it is an omnipresent and foundational ingredient of modern politics. Yet, during the past decades, 'security' has also come to be an ever more *explicit* point of reference within political discourses. As Christopher Daase points out, security has become the 'gold standard' of national and international politics today, having outplayed the concept of 'peace' in strategy debates and political programmes.[108] It has come to be an explicit and ineluctable discursive and rhetorical device in political practice, which is brought into play through the above mentioned acts of 'securitization'. As Zedner suggests, 'security' has come to dominate the criminal justice field.[109] Second, there has been a gradual widening of the notion of 'security' since the middle of the 20th century and especially after the end of the Cold War. This means that a greater number of issues, increasingly broadly defined, have come to be grasped as *'security'* issues and, with that, shaped by the security-logic; the criminal justice field is of course a prime example.[110] So, in short, concerning the concept of 'security' we have seen that the concept has both spread in its application and deepened in its implications. The third development that shapes

---

[105] Frank P Harvey, *The Homeland Security Dilemma: Fear, Failure and the Future of American Insecurity* (Routledge, 2008) 1.

[106] Ibid 7–10.

[107] Ibid 13 and 7, respectively.

[108] Christopher Daase, 'Der erweiterte Sicherheitsbegriff' (2010) Sicherheitskultur im Wandel, Working Paper 1.

[109] See Zedner, above n 91.

[110] See Zedner above n 91; see also Wolfgang Bonss, '(Un)Sicherheit in der Moderne' in Peter Zocher, S Kaufmann and R Haverkamp (eds) *Zivile Sicherheit: Gesellschaftliche Dimensionen gegenwaertiger Sicherheitspolitiken* (Transcript, 2011), 43–69.

contemporary security discourses is the increasing significance of the technology of 'risk', which we discussed above. In sum, the impact of 'risk' is that a powerful technology is brought together with a powerful practice that is nothing less than constitutive of modern politics and the state.

In this Part of our chapter, we zoomed in on the practice of preventive detention and looked at its three main ingredients: the rationality of 'prevention', the technology of 'risk' and the practice of 'security'. The aim of this exercise was to reveal the complexity of each of these ingredients in order to expose the complexity of preventive detention. Each of these components is a social product; that is, they are neither ahistorical, value- or power-free. This is true for 'risks', which are often taken as objective measures. In regard to the rationality of 'prevention' and the technology of 'risk', we have seen that they do not simply avoid but actively produce. In regard to the practice of 'security', we have become aware that 'security' is not only fundamental to modern politics, but also that it is a powerful political move and that it produces insecurity. Now, we can appreciate the complexity/power of all these three components coming together. We can thus come back to our main aim in this chapter. Currently, preventive detention is usually 'tamed' or limited through the legal considerations; it is also 'tamed' by concerns about its effectiveness. Yet, the above unveiling of the complex, dynamic and essentially expansive nature of its ingredients makes us aware that there needs to be another, third way in which we 'tame' or reign in the naturally expanding nature of preventive detention. This expansion cannot be 'tamed' alone by legal or effectiveness considerations but needs to be 'tamed' by the vision that a society has for its own future. This vision needs to come out of genuinely public debates about the consequences that preventive detention has specifically and preventive measures in general have for the constitution of society.

4. CONCLUSION

On 24 July 2011, Norwegian Prime Minister Jens Stoltenberg addressed the Norwegian public at the memorial for those who, two days before, were killed by Anders Behring Breivik. Breivik had killed 77 people in the streets of central Oslo and on the island of Utøya in shooting rampages and bomb attacks. At the time of Stoltenberg's address, it was not yet clear what motivated Breivik, nor what would be the most appropriate response. It was not clear then if the conduct was a terrorist attack, the act of a right wing extremist, or the act of an insane person.

The key message of Stoltenberg's address was: 'We are still shocked by what has happened, but we will never give up our values. Our response is more democracy, more openness, and more humanity.'[111] The message in Stoltenberg's address echoed the general sentiment in the Norwegian public. The reaction of one of the young women who survived the massacre on Utøya – '[i]f one man can create that much hate, you can only imagine how much love we as a togetherness can create' – was repeated over and over (and included in Stoltenberg's address).[112] This unified national/public reaction was notable for its calm and measured tenor. As Norwegian minister of foreign affairs Jonas Gahr Store recently explained: 'The public reacted with grief but did not call for extraordinary measures.'[113] At that time, the event, which was perceived as 'the worst atrocity [Norway] has seen since the Second World War',[114] was not (mis)used for political purposes, nor was the public discourse co-opted by security questions. On the contrary, the reactions made clear that the public was aware that what was at stake in any security debate was the very DNA of its (open) democratic society, which was under threat by the potential use of 'exceptional powers'.[115] This reaction contrasts starkly with the public and political reactions to the terrorist attacks of 9/11 in the US and 7/7 in the UK, which were marked by demands for revenge and a cry for heightened security measures.

The Norwegian debate in the aftermath of Breivik's actions was a wide and genuinely public debate about security, risk and prevention, and it captures the point of this chapter. We have argued that, in addition to the significant questions to be asked concerning the legal aspects of preventive detention and about its effectiveness, the question of what it does to society needs to be realised and considered as a constitutive aspect of future debates and decisions as well. Consequently, this chapter aimed to make policy makers aware of this less explicitly considered dimension. To be clear, there is no singular or unified answer to the question of what the regime of preventive detention does to society. Any concrete answer depends on the historical context. Yet, our chapter provided a picture of the various complex ingredients that constitute the societal considerations of the issue in order to make policy makers aware of their significance. In addition to the imagination of what terrible harm could possibly happen (that naturally underlies any security steps), we also need to imagine how (different) our society will look with every legislative change utilising the preventive logic.

[111] Address by Prime Minister Jens Stoltenberg, Oslo Cathedral, 24 July 2011 <http://www.regjeringen.no/en/dep/smk/Whats-new/Speeches-and-articles/statsministeren/statsminister_jens_stoltenberg/2011/address-by-prime-minister-in-oslo-cathed.html?id=651789>.
[112] Ibid.
[113] Jonas Gahr Store, 'Learning from Norway's Tragedy' The New York Times, 19 July 2012, <http://www.nytimes.com/2012/07/20/opinion/jonas-gahr-store-learning-from-norways-tragedy.html?_r=0>.
[114] Above n 112.
[115] Gahr Store, above n 113.

As McSherry and Keyzer point out, preventive detention is politically attractive – it is 'an ostensible demonstration to the electorate that the government is taking serious measures to protect the community against crime' – but it is a step that should not be taken lightly.[116] Given the nature of preventive detention, any policy discussion about it needs to extend further than just the legal and effectiveness considerations. Discussion must be embedded in a public debate about the future of society: the nature of preventive detention – with its basis in the rationality of prevention, the technology of risk and the practice of security – is an outcome of, and plays back into, the foundation of a society, and this needs to be clear to the public. Thus it is not necessary to accept claims made about prevention – such as that those preventive orders dealing with terrorism are 'necessary to protect national security and public order' and are 'in no way arbitrary'[117] – at face value. Rather, such claims should be part of a wide and genuinely public debate about the kind of society imagined by its members. Such debate represents a safeguard against the overreach of the law and is just as important a limit as any legal or effectiveness considerations.

---

[116]   McSherry and Keyzer, above n 5, 104.
[117]   Graham McDonald, 'Control Orders and Preventive Detention – Why Alarm Is Misguided' in A Lynch et al (eds), *Law and Liberty in the War on Terror* (Federation Press, 2007) 106–15, 115.

CASES

AUSTRALIA

A-G (Cth) v R (1957) 95 CLR 529 (Wel)

Azzopardi v R (2001) 205 CLR 50 (Gog)

Al-Kateb v Godwin (2004) 219 CLR 562 (Fr, Lo)

Baker v R (2004) 223 CLR 513 (Wel)

Briginshaw v Briginshaw (1938) 60 CLR 336 (C&H)

Buckley v R (2006) 224 ALR 416 (Gog)

Chu Kheng Lim v Minister for Immigration (1992) 176 CLR 1 (Gog, Wel, Fr)

Dietrich v R (1992) 177 CLR 292 (Gog)

Ex parte Walsh and Johnson (1925) 37 CLR 36 (Fr)

Fardon v A-G (Qld) (2004) 223 CLR 575 (Gog, Slo, Birg, Stern,Wel, Lo, Gl , Int, Kz)

Forge v Australian Securities and Investments Commission (2006) 228 CLR 45(Wel)

Green v R (1971) 126 CLR 28 (C&H)

Grollo v Palmer (1995) 184 CLR 348 (Wel)

Gypsy Jokers Motorcycle Club Inc v Commissioner of Police (2008) 234 CLR 532 (Gog) (Wel)

Ha v New South Wales (1997) 189 CLR 465 (Wel)

Hicks v Ruddock (2007) 239 ALR 344 (Fr)

Huddart, Parker & Co Pty Ltd v Moorehead (1909) 8 CLR 330 (Wel)

International Finance Trust Co Ltd v New South Wales Crime Commission (2009) 240 CLR 319 (Wel)

Kable v DPP (NSW) (1996) 189 CLR 51 (Gog, Wel, Lo)

K-Generation Pty Ltd v Liquor Licensing Court (2009) 237 CLR 501 (Wel)

Kirk v Industrial Relations Commission (NSW) (2010) 239 CLR 531 (Wel)

The King v Carter; Ex parte Kisch [1934] HCA 50; (1934) 52 CLR 221 (Fr)

Minister for Immigration & Citizenship v Haneef [2007] FCAFC 203 (Lo)

Naumovska v Minister for Immigration and Ethnic Affairs (1982) 60 FLR 267 (Fr)

Nicholas v R (1998) 193 CLR 173 (Wel)

North Australian Aboriginal Legal Aid Service Inc v Bradley (2004) 218 CLR 146 (Wel)

Officer in Charge of Cells, ACT Supreme Court, Re; Ex parte Eastman (1994) 123 ALR 478 (Fr)

Plaintiff M47-2012 v Director General of Security (2012) 292 ALR 243 (Lo)

Precision Data Holdings Ltd v Willis (1991) 173 CLR 167 (Wel)

Re C (Mental Patient: Contact) [1993] 1 FLR 940 (Fr)

RPS v R (2000) 199 CLR 620 (Gog)

Ruddock v Vadarlis (2001) 110 FCR 491 (Fr)

R v Bolton; Ex parte Beane (1987) 162 CLR 514 (Fr)

R v Carter; Ex parte Kisch [1934] HCA 50; (1934) 52 CLR 221 (Fr)

R v Davey; Ex parte Freer (1936) 56 CLR 381 (Fr)

R v Joske; ex parte Australian Building Construction Employees and Builders Labourers Federation (1974) 130 CLR 87 (Wel)

R v Kirby; Ex parte Boilermakers' Society of Australia (1956) 94 CLR 254 (Wel)

R v Trade Practices Tribunal; Ex parte Tasmanian Breweries Pty Ltd (1970) 123 CLR 361(Wel)

South Australia v Totani (2010) 242 CLR 1 (Wel)

Thomas v Mowbray (2007) 233 CLR 307 (Wel, Lo)

Veen v R (1979) 143 CLR 458 (Gl)

Veen v R (No 2) (1988) 164 CLR 465 (Lo, Gl, Int)

Victorian Council for Civil Liberties Incorporated v Minister for Immigration & Multicultural Affairs (2001) 182 ALR 617 (Fr)

Wainohu v New South Wales (2011) 243 CLR 181 (Wel)

Williams, In re (1934) 51 CLR 545 (Fr)

Wilson v Minister for Aboriginal and Torres Strait Islander Affairs (1996) 189 CLR 1 (Gog, Wel)

Australian Capital Territory

J by his litigation guardian Vardanega v Australian Capital Territory [2009] ACTSC 170 (Fr)

R v the Superintendent of the Belconnen Remand Centre; Ex Parte Jack Victor Diamond Also Known As Victor Grzeszkiewicz [1986] ACTSC 76 (Fr)

New South Wales

A-G (NSW) v Gallagher (2006) NSWSC 340 (Lo)

A-G (NSW) v Quinn (2007) NSWSC 87 (Lo)

A-G (NSW) v Tillman (2007) NSWSC 605 (Lo)

A-G (NSW) Winters (2007) NSWSC 1071(Lo)

Cornwall v A-G (NSW) [2007] NSWSC 374 (Lo)

Ex parte Lo Pak (1888) 9 NSWR 221 (Fr)

In re Canney [1831] NSWSupC 22 (Fr)

Prisoners A to XX Inclusive v New South Wales (1994) 75 A Crim R 205; (1995) 38 NSWLR 622 (Fr, Int)

Storey v Storey [1832] NSWSupC 62 (Fr)

Queensland

A-G (Qld) v ADJ [2010] QSC 221 (Kz)

A-G (Qld) v AJD [2010] QSC 294 (Kz)

A-G (Qld) v Bridson [2007] QSC 307 (Kz)

A-G (Qld) v Currie [2009] QSC 112 (Kz)

A-G (Qld) v Downs [2005] QSC 16 (Gog)

A-G (Qld) v Downs [2008] QSC 87 (Kz)

A-G (Qld) v Dugdale [2009] QSC 358 (Kz)

A-G (Qld) v Eades [2011] QSC 408 (Kz)

A-G (Qld) v Edwards [2007] QSC 396 (Kz)

A-G (Qld) v Ellis [2011] QCA 377 (Kz)

A-G (Qld) v Fardon [2003] QCA 416 (Lo)

A-G (Qld) v Fardon [2003] QSC 331 (Gog)

A-G (Qld) v Fardon [2003] QSC 379 (Kz)

A-G (Qld) v Fardon [2005] QSC 137; [2006] QSC 275; [2006] QCA 512]; [2007] QSC 299
    (Kz)

A-G (Qld) v Fardon [2011] QCA 155 (Kz)

A-G (Qld) v Fisher [2010] QSC 117 (Kz)

A-G (Qld) v Francis (2005) QSC 381 (Lo, Kz)

A-G (Qld) v Friend [2011] QCA 357 (Kz)

A-G (Qld) v Friend [2012] QSC 108 (Kz)

A-G (Qld) v Gilchrist [2012] QSC 287 (Kz)

A-G (Qld) v Hansen [2006] QSC 35 (Kz)

A-G (Qld) v HTR [2007] QSC 19 (Kz)

 A-G (Qld) v Hynds [2009] QSC 355 (Gog)

A-G v Hynds & Anor (No 3) [2012] QSC 318 (Kz)

A-G (Qld) v Kynuna (No 2) [2011] QSC 376 (Kz)

A-G (Qld) v Lawrence [2008] QSC 230 (Gog, Kz)

A-G (Qld) v Levack [2007] QSC 275 (Kz)

A-G (Qld) v LSS [2007] QSC 202 (Kz)

A-G (Qld) v McLean [2006] QSC 37 (Gl)

A-G (Qld) v O'Rourke [2009] QSC 362 (Kz)

A-G (Qld) v Perkins [2009] QSC 53 (Kz)

A-G (Qld) v Robinson [2007] QCA 111 (Kz)

A-G (Qld) v Smith [2009] QSC 381 (Kz)

A-G (Qld) v Sybenga [2009] QSC 161 (Kz)

A-G (Qld) v Sybenga [2009] QCA 382 (Kz)

A-G (Qld) v Sybenga [2010] QSC 348 (Kz)

A-G (Qld) v Tiltman [2012] QSC 159 (Kz)

A-G (Qld) v Toms (2007) 176 A Crim R 401; [2007] QSC 290 (Kz)

A-G (Qld) v Toms [2008] QSC 131 (Kz)

A-G (Qld) v Twigge [2006] QSC 107 (Kz)

A-G (Qld) v Voois [2008] QSC 168 (Kz)

A-G (Qld) v Yeo [2007] QSC 274 (Kz)

DPP v Ferguson (unreported, Qld Sup Ct, No 001, Mackenzie J, 8 January 2003) (Kz)

LAB v A-G (Qld) [2011] QCA 230 (Kz)

Tasmania

Re T [1993] TASSC 17 (Fr)

Victoria

Antunovic v Dawson [2010] VSC 377 (Fr)
Fletcher v Secretary to the Department of Justice [2006] VSC 354 (Birg)
In re Gregory (1899) 25 VLR 539 (Fr)
Kracke v Mental Health Review Board [2009] VCAT 646 (Fr)
*Murray v Director-General, Health and Community Services and Superintendent, Larundel
    Psychiatric Hospital* Unreported, Supreme Court of Victoria, 23 June 1995 (Fr)
PR v Department of Human Services [2007] VSC 338 (Fr)
Rich v The Secretary to the Department of Justice [2011] VSC 413 (Fr)
R v Cavkic, Ahtanasi & Clarke [2005] VSCA 182 (C&H)
R v Governor of Metropolitan Gaol; Ex parte Di Nardo [1963] VR 61 (Fr)
TSL v Secretary to the Department of Justice (2006) VSCA 199 (Lo)
Zwillinger v Schulof [1963] VR 407 (Fr)

Western Australia

DPP (WA) v GTR (2008) 38 WAR 307 (Lo)
DPP (WA) v Mangolamara (2007) 169 A Crim R 379 (Lo)
DPP (WA) v Moolarvie [2008] WASC 37 (Gl)
Re Writ of Habeas Corpus Ad Subjiciendum; Ex Parte Hooker [2005] WASC 29 (Fr)
Varney v Parole Board [2000] 117 A Crim R 541 (Birg)

CANADA

May v Ferndale Institution, 2005 SCC 82, [2005] 3 SCR 809 (Fr)
Re Brooks' Detention (1962) 38 WWR 51 (Fr)
Re McCann (1982) 67 CCC (2d) 180 (Fr)
R v Lyons, 2 SCR 309 (1987) (Slo)
R v LM, 2 SCR 163 (2008) (Slo)
R v Miller (1985) 24 DLR (4th) 9 (Fr)
R v Sarson [1996] 2 SCR 223 (Fr)
R v Storgoff, [1945] SCR 526 (Fr)
Ex parte Nichols [1839] SCC 123 (Fr)

EUROPEAN COURT OF HUMAN RIGHTS

Amuur v France, (European Court of Human Rights, Application No 17/1995/523/609,
    25 June 1996) (Gog)

AS v Poland (European Court of Human Rights, Application No 39510/98, 20 June 2006) (Gog)

A v United Kingdom (European Court of Human Rights, Application No 100/1997/884/1096, 23 September 1998) (Gl)

Bouamar v Belgium (1988) Eur Court HR (ser A) (Gog)

Bromiley v United Kingdom (European Court of Human Rights, Application No 33747/96, 23 November 1999) (Gl)

B v Germany (European Court of Human Rights, Grand Chamber, Application No 61261/09, 19 April 2012) (Slo)

Calvelli and Ciglio v Italy (European Court of Human Rights, Application No 32967/96, 17 January 2002) (Gl)

Ciulla v Italy (1989) Eur Court HR (ser A) (Gog)

Edwards v United Kingdom (European Court of Human Rights, Application No 46477/99, 14 March 2002) (Gl)

Engel and Others v the Netherlands (1976) Eur Court HR (ser A) (Gog, Gl)

Guzzardi v Italy (1980) Eur Court HR (ser A) (Gog)

Haidn v Germany (European Court of Human Rights, Grand Chamber, Application No 6587/04, 13 January 2011) (Slo)

Hirst v United Kingdom (No 2) [2005] Eur Court HR 681 (Coyle)

HL v United Kingdom (European Court of Human Rights, Application No 45508/99, 5 October 2004) (Fr, Gl)

HM v Switzerland (European Court of Human Rights, Application No 39187/98, 26 February 2002) (Fr)

Ireland v the United Kingdom (1978) Eur Court HR (ser A) (Gog)

James, Wells and Lee v UK, (European Court of Human Rights, Application Nos 25119/09, 57715/09, 57877/09, 18 September 2012) (Slo, Birg, Brk, Gl)

Jendrowiak v Germany (European Court of Human Rights, Application No 30060/04, 14 April 2011) (Stern)

Kafkaris v Cyprus (European Court of Human Rights, Grand Chamber, Application No 21906/04, 12 February 2008) (Slo)

Keenan v United Kingdom (European Court of Human Rights, Application No 27229/95, 3 April 2001) (Gl)

K-F v Germany (European Court of Human Rights, 27 November 1997) (Gl)

Kudla v Poland (European Court of Human Rights, Grand Chamber, Application No 30210/96, 26 October 2000) (Fr)

Kurt v Turkey (European Court of Human Rights, Application No 15/1997/799/1002, 25 May 1998) (Gog)

LCB v United Kingdom (European Court of Human Rights, Application No 14/1997/798/1001, 9 June 1998) (Gl)

Litwa v Poland (European Court of Human Rights, Application No 26629/95, 4 April 2000) (Gl)

Mastromatteo v Italy (European Court of Human Rights, Application No 37703/97, 24 October 2002) (Gl)

Mork v Deutschland (European Court of Human Rights, Application Nos 31047/04, 43386/08, 9 June 2011) (Brk)

M v Germany (European Court of Human Rights, Application No 19359/04, 17 December 2009) (Gog, Slo, Lo)

Nasrulloyev v Russia (European Court of Human Rights, Application No 656/06, 11 October 2007) (Gog)

Öneryildiz v Turkey (European Court of Human Rights, Application No 48939/99, 18 June 2002) (Gl)

Opuz v Turkey (European Court of Human Rights, Application No 33401/02, 9 June 2009) (Gl)

Osman v United Kingdom (European Court of Human Rights, Application No 87/1997/871/1083, 28 October 1998) (Gl)

Powell v United Kingdom (European Court of Human Rights, Application No 45305/99, 4 May 2000) (Gl)

Schmitz v Deutschland (European Court of Human Rights, Application No 30493/04, 9 June 2011) (Brk)

Soering v United Kingdom (European Court of Human Rights, Application No 14038/88, 07 July 1989) (Fr)

Steel and Others v the United Kingdom, (European Court of Human Rights, Application No 67/1997/851/1058, 23 September 1998) (Gog)

Tomašić and Others v Croatia (European Court of Human Rights, Application No 4762/05, 15 January 2009) (Gl)

Tyrer v United Kingdom (European Court of Human Rights, Application No 5856/72, 25 April 1978) (Fr)

Van Droogenbroeck v Belgium (1982) 4 EHRR 443 (Gog, Slo)

Winterwerp v The Netherlands (1979) Eur Court HR (ser A) (Gog, Gl)

Z and Others v United Kingdom (European Court of Human Rights, Application No 29392/95, 10 May 2001) (Gl)

GERMANY

Bundesverfassungsgericht [German Constitutional Court], 2 BvR 2029/01 , 5 February 2004 (Gog)

Bundesverfassungsgericht [German Constitutional Court], 2 BvR 2365/09, 4 May 2011 (Gog, Slo)

INDIA

Vishaka v State of Rajasthan (1997) 6 SCC 241 (Fr)

INTER-AMERICAN COURT OF HUMAN RIGHTS

I-A Court HR, Gangaram Panday Case v Suriname, judgment of January 21, 1994, in OAS doc. OAS/Ser.L/V/III.31, doc. 9, *Annual Report of the Inter-American Court of Human Rights 1994* (Gog)

Velasquez Rodriguez v Honduras, Judgment of the Inter-American Court of Human Rights (29 July 1988) (Gog)

IRELAND

The People v O'Callaghan [1966] IR 501 (Gog)

Ryan v DPP [1989] IR 399 (Gog)

NEW ZEALAND

Belcher v Chief Executive of the Department of Corrections [2007] 1 NZLR 507 (Brk)

Chief Executive of the Department of Corrections v J HC Wellington CRI-2009-485-100, 9 November 2009 (Brk)

Chief Executive of the Dept of Corrections v McDonnell HC Auckland CRI-2005-404-239, 19 May 2008 (Brk)

Chief Executive of the Department of Corrections v McIntosh HC Christchurch CRI 2004-409-162, 8 December 2004 (Brk)

Grieve v Chief Executive of the Dept of Corrections (2005) 22 CRNZ 20 (CA) (Brk)

McDonnell v Chief Executive of the Department of Corrections [2009] NZCA 352; (2009) 8 HRNZ 770 (Brk)

R v Exley CA279/06 [2007] NZCA 393 (Brk)

R v Johnson [2004] 3 NZLR 29 (Brk)

R v Leitch [1998] 1 NZLR 420 (Brk)

R v Mist [2005] 2 NZLR 791 (Brk)

R v Rameka [1997] NZCA 178 (Brk)

R v Kale (1993) 9 CRNZ 575 (CA) (Brk)

R v Pairama CA216/97, 8 September 1997(Brk)

R v Parahi [2005] 23 NZLR 356 (Brk)

R v Puaga[1992] 3 NZLR 241 (Brk)

R v Peta [2007] 2 NZLR 62 (Brk)

Taunoa v Attorney-General [2008] 1 NZLR 429 (Fr)

SOUTH AFRICA

Dodo v The State [2001] 3 SA 382 (Fr)

State v Coetzee [1997] 2 LRC 593 (Gog)

UNITED KINGDOM

Abbasi v Secretary of State [2002] EWCA Civ 1598(Fr)

AG's Ref No 32 of 1996 (Whittaker) [1997] 1 Cr App R(S) 261 (Gl)

A Local Authority v MA [2005] EWHC 2942 (Fam) (Fr)

Ashley v Chief Constable of Sussex [2008] UKHL 25; [2008] 1 AC 962 (Fr)

Attorney General of Trinidad and Tobago v Ramanoop (Trinidad and Tobago) [2005] UKPC 15 (Fr)

A v Secretary of State for the Home Department [2004] UKHL 56; [2005] 2 AC 68 (Gog, Stern)

Barnardo v Ford [1892] AC 326 (Fr)

Case of Titus Oates [1685] KB 1316 (Fr)

CD v Secretary of State for the Home Department [2011] EWHC 1273 (Stern)

Cox v Hakes (1890) 15 App Cas 506 (Fr)

Fraser v Judicial and Legal Services Commission [2008] UKPC 25 (Fr)

Greene v Secretary of State for Home Affairs [1942] AC 284 (Fr)

Inniss v Attorney General [2008] UKPC 42 (Fr)

Johnson v Secretary of State for the Home Department [2008] 1 WLR 74 (Brk)

Jones v Isleworth Crown Court [2005] EWHC 662 (Admin), [2005] MHLR 93 (Gl)

Liversidge v Anderson [1941] UKHL 1; [1942] AC 206 (Fr)

Lumba (WL) v Secretary of State for the Home Department [2011] UKSC 12 (Fr)

Lyons v Blenkin (1821) 1 Jac 245 (Fr)

Merson v Cartwright and Attorney General [2005] UKPC 38 (Fr)

Raymond v Honey [1983] 1 AC 1 (Coyle)

R (D) v Home Secretary and National Assembly for Wales [2004] EWHC 2857 (Admin), [2005] MHLR 17 (Gl)

R (DK) v Secretary of State [2010] EWHC 82 (Admin), [2010] MHLR 64 (Gl)

Re S-C (Mental Patient: Habeas Corpus) [1996] QB 599 (Fr)

Re SK (Proposed Plaintiff) (An Adult by way of her Litigation Friend) [2004] EWHC 3202 (Fam), [2005] 2 FLR 230 (Fr)

R (F) v Secretary of State for Justice [2008] EWCA Civ 1457, [2008] MHLR 370 (Gl)

R (James, Lee and Wells) v Secretary of State for Justice [2009] UKHL 22, [2009] 2 WLR 1149, [2009] Prison LR 371 (Gl)

R (Middleton) v West Somerset Coroner [2004] UKHL 10, [2004] 2 AC 182 (Gl)

R (on the application of Munjaz) v Mersey Care NHS Trust [2003] EWCA Civ 1036, [2004] QB 395 (Fr)

R (on the application of Wells) v Parole Board; R (on the application of Walker) v Secretary of State for the Home Department [2008] 1 All ER 138 (Stern, Brk)

R (SP) v Secretary of State for Justice [2010] EWCA Civ 1590, [2011] MHLR 65 (Gl)

R (T) v Home Secretary [2003] EWHC 538, [2003] MHLR 239 (Gl)

R v Adams (No 2) [1998] 1 Cr App R 377 (C&H)

R v Birch (1990) 90 Cr App R 78 (Gl)

R v Board of Control; Ex parte Rutty [1956] 2 QB 109 (Fr)

R v Boswell [2007] EWCA Crim 1587 (Gl)

R v Bournewood Community and Mental Health NHS Trust, ex parte L [1998] 2 WLR 764 (CA) (Fr)

R v Bournewood Community and Mental Health NHS Trust, ex parte L [1999] AC 458 (HL) (Fr)

R v Chapman [2000] 1 Cr App R 77 (Gl)

R v Clarkson (1722) 1 Stra 445; (1722) 93 ER 625 (Fr)

R v Delaval (1763) 3 Burr 1434, 97 ER 913 (Fr)

R v Deputy Governor of Parkhurst Prison; Ex parte Hague [1992] 1 AC 58 (Fr)

R v Denis Adams [1996] 2 Cr App R 467 (C&H)

R v Doney [1997] 1 Cr App R 369) (C&H)

R v Drew [2003] UKHL 25, [2003] 1 WLR 1213, [2003] MHLR 282 (Gl)

R v East London and the City Mental Health NHS Trust [2003] UKHL 58; [2004] 2 AC 280 (Fr)

R v Golding [2006] EWCA Crim 1965, [2006] MHLR 272 (Gl)

R v Governor of Brixton Prison; Ex parte Ashan (1969) 2 QB 222 (Fr)

R v Hodgson (1968) 52 Cr App R 113 (Gl)

R v Home Department State Secretary; Ex parte Khawaja; Ex parte Khera [1984] AC 74; [1983] 1 All ER 765; [1983] 2 WLR 321 (Fr)

R v Johnson [2006] EWCA Crim 2486, [2007] 1 WLR 585, [2006] 2 Prison LR 159 (Gl)

R v Kamara [2000] MHLR 9 (Gl)

R v Lambert [2001] 3 WLR 206 (Gog)

R v Nafei [2004] EWCA Crim 3238, [2006] MHLR 176 (Gl)

R v Newnham [2000] 2 Cr App R(S) 407 (Gl)

R v Offen and others [2000] EWCA Crim 96, [2001] 1 WLR 253, [2001] Prison LR 283 (Gl)

R v Paul Lee Smith [2001] EWCA Crim 743, [2001] MHLR 46 (Gl)

R v S and Others [2005] EWCA Crim 3616, [2006] 2 Prison LR 119 (Gl)

R v Secretary of State for Home Affairs ex parte O'Brien [1923] 2 KB 361 (Fr)

R v Secretary of State for the Home Department ex parte Gilkes [1999] MHLR 6 (Gl)

R v Simmonds [2001] EWCA Crim 167, [2001] MHLR 54 (Gl)

R v Steele [2010] EWCA Crim 605, [2010] MHLR 107 (Gl)

R v T (2010) EWCA Crim 2439 (C&H)

Secretary of State for Home Affairs v O'Brien [1923] AC 603 (Fr)

Secretary of State for Justice v Walker and James [2008] EWCA Civ 30 (Stern, Gl, Int)

Secretary of State for the Home Department v E [2007] UKHL 47 (Stern)

Secretary of State for the Home Department v JJ [2007] UKHL 45 (Stern)

Secretary of State for the Home Department v MB (FC) (Appellant) [2007] UKHL 46 (Stern)

SW London and St George's Mental Health NHS Trust v 'W' [2002] EWHC 1770 Admin, [2002] MHLR 392 (Gl)

UNITED NATIONS HUMAN RIGHTS COMMITTEE

Human Rights Committee, *Communication No 560/1993*, UN Doc CCPR/C/59/D/560/1993 (30 April 1997) ('*A v Australia*') (Gog, Kz)

Human Rights Committee, *Views: Communication No 702/1996*, UN Doc GAOR/ A/52/40 (18 July 1997) ('*C McLawrence v Jamaica*') (Gog)

Human Rights Committee, *Communication No 900/1999*, UN Doc CCPR/C/76/D/ 900/1999 (25 December 1991) ('*C v Australia*') (Gog)

Human Rights Committee, *Communication No 66/1980*, UN Doc CCPR/C/OP/2 (15 March 1980) para 18.1 ('*David Alberto Campora Schweizer v Uruguay*') (Gog)

Human Rights Committee, *Communication No 1629/2007*, UN Doc CCPR/ C/98/D/1629/2007 (10 May 2010) ('*Fardon v Australia*') (Gog, Slo, Gl, Int, Kz)

Human Rights Committee, *Communication No 488/1992*, UN Doc CCPR/C/50/D/488/1992 (25 December 1991) ('*Nicholas Toonen v Australia*') (Gog)

Human Rights Committee, *Communication No 1128/2002*, UN Doc CCPR/C/83/D/1128 (18 April 2005) ('*Rafael Marques de Morais v Angola*') (Gog)

Human Rights Committee, *Communication No 1090/2002*, UN Doc CCPR/ C/79/D/1090/2002 (6 November 2003) ('*Rameka v New Zealand*') (Gog)

Human Rights Committee, *Communication No 1635/2007*, UN Doc CCPR/ C/98/D/1635/2007 (10 May 2010) ('*Tillman v Australia*') (Gog, Brk, Gl, Int, Kz)

Human Rights Committee, *Communication No 305/88*, UN Doc CCPR/C/39/D/305/1988 (23 July 1990) ('*Van Alphen v The Netherlands*') (Gog, Kz)

UNITED STATES (including individual state cases)

Addington v Texas, 441 US 418 (1979) (C&H)

Baxstrom v Herold, (1966) 383 US 107 (Gl, Int)

Brown v Plata, US Slip Opinion No 09-1233, 23 May 2011 (Fr, Int)

Coker v Georgia, 433 US 584 (1977) (Fr)

Coleman v Brown, 912 F Supp 1282 (ED Cal) (Fr)

Cunningham v California, 549 US 270 (2007) (Slo)

Dixon v A-G (Pennsylvania), (1971) 325 F Supp 966 (Gl)

Estelle v Gamble, 429 US 97 103 (1976) (Fr)

Ewing v California, 538 US 11 (2003) (Slo)

Farmer v Brennan, 511 US 825 (1994) (Fr)

Fay v Moia, 372 US 391 (1963) (Fr)

Furman v Georgia, 408 US 238 (1972) (Fr)

Gagnon v Scarpelli, 411 US 778 (1973) (Slo)

Gregg v Georgia, 428 US 153 (1976) (Fr)

Hamdi v Rumsfeld, 542 US 507 (2004) (Slo)

In re Blodgett, 510 NW 2d 910, 913 (Minn, 1994) (Slo)

In re Commitment of W Z, 801 A 2d 205, 216–8 (NJ, 2002) (Slo)

In re Kemmler, 136 US 436 447 (1890) (Fr)

Jacobsen v Massachusetts, 197 US 11 (1905) (Slo)

Jones v Cunningham 371 US 236 (1963) (Fr)

Jurek v Texas, 428 US 262 (1976) (Slo, Gl)

Kansas v Crane, 534 US 407 (2002) (Slo, C&H)

Kansas v Hendricks, 521 US 346 (1997) (Slo, C&H, Lo, Gl, Int)

Kennedy v Louisiana, 554 US 407 (2008) (Fr)

Millard v Harris, 406 F 2d 964 (DC Cir 1968) (Slo)

Morrissey v Brewer, 408 US 471 (1972) (Slo)

Penn ex rel Sullivan v Ashe, 302 US 51 (1937) (Slo)

Plata v Schwarzenegger, USDC ND, Cal No C01-1351 THE (Fr)

Presider v Rodriguez, 411 US 475 (1973) (Fr)

Robinson v California, 370 US 660 (1962) (Fr)

Seling v Young, 541 US 250 (2001) (Slo)

Specht v Patterson, 386 US 605 (1967) (Slo)

State ex rel Pearson v Probate Court, 287 NW 297, 302 (1939) affd 309 US 270 (1940) (Slo)

Tapia v US, 131 US 2382 (2011) (Slo)

Thomas v State, 74 SW 3d 789, 791–2 (Mo, 2002) (Slo)

Trop v Dulles, 356 US 86 (1958) (Fr)

United States v DiFrancesco 449 US 117 (1980) (Slo)

Wilkerson v Utah, 99 US 130 (1878) (Fr)

Wilson v Seiter, 501 US 294 (1991) (Fr)

LEGISLATION

AUSTRALIA

Commonwealth

Administrative Appeals Tribunal Act 1975 (Wel)
Anti-Terrorism Act (No 2) 2005 (Lo)
Australian Security Intelligence Organisation Act 1979 ('*ASIO Act*') (Wel)
Criminal Code Act 1995 ('*Criminal Code*') (Wel)
National Security Information (Criminal and Civil Proceedings) Act 2004 ('*NSIA*') (Wel)

Australian Capital Territory

Human Rights Act 2008 (Fr)

New South Wales

Children (Criminal Proceedings) Act 1987 (Lo)
Community Protection Act 1994 (Gog)
Crimes Amendment (Consorting and Organised Crime) Act 2012 (Lo)
Crimes (Criminal Organisations Control) Act 2009 (Wel)
Crimes (Serious Sex Offenders) Act 2006 ('*CSSOA*') (Birg, Brk, C&H, Lo, Int, Kz)
Habitual Criminals Act 1957 (Lo)
Terrorism (Police Powers) Act 2002 (Lo)

Northern Territory

Sentencing Act 1995 (Gog, Int)
Serious Crime Control Act 2009 (Wel)

Queensland

Criminal Organisation Act 2009 (Wel, Int)
Dangerous Prisoners (Sexual Offenders) Act 2003 (Gog, Birg, C&H, Gl , Int, Kz)
Penalties and Sentences Act 1992 (Gog, Int)

South Australia

Criminal Law (Sentencing) Act 1988 (Gog, Int)
Serious and Organised Crime (Control) Act 2008 (Wel, Lo)

Tasmania

Sentencing Act 1997 (Gog, Int)

Victoria

Charter of Human Rights and Responsibilities Act 2006 ('The Charter') (Fr)
Community Protection Act 1990 (Gog)
Mental Health Act 1986 (Fr)
Sentencing Act 1991 (Gog, Birg, Int)
Serious Sex Offenders (Detention and Supervision) Act 2009 (Birg, C&H, Int)
Supreme Court (General Civil Procedure) Rules 2005 (Fr)

Western Australia

Dangerous Prisoners Act 2005 (Int)
Dangerous Sexual Offenders Act 2006 (Birg, C&H)
Sentencing Act 1995 (Gog, Int)

GERMANY

Grundgesetz fur die Bundesrepublik Deutschland [Basic Law of the Federal Republic of Germany] (Slo)
Strafgesetzbuch (StGB) [Criminal Code] (Gog, Slo)
Violent Offenders (Custodial Therapy) Act 2010 (Slo)

NEW ZEALAND

Crimes Act 1908 (Brk)
Crimes Act 1961 (Brk)
Criminal Justice Amendment Act 1967 (Brk)
Criminal Justice Amendment Act (No 2) 1987 (Brk)
Criminal Justice Amendment Act 1993 (Brk)
Criminal Justice Act 1954 (Brk)
Criminal Justice Act 1985 (Brk)
Criminal Procedure (Mentally Impaired Persons) Act 2003 ('CP (MIP) Act') (Brk)
Habitual Criminals and Offenders Act 1906 (Brk)
Intellectual Disability (Compulsory Care and Rehabilitation) Act 2003 ('IDCCR') (Brk)

Judicature Act 1908 (Gl)

Mental Health (Compulsory Assessment and Treatment) Act 1992 (Brk)

New Zealand Bill of Rights Act 1990 ('NZBORA') (Brk)

Parole Act 2002 (Brk)

Parole (Extended Supervision) Amendment Act 2004 (Brk)

Public Safety (Public Protection Orders) Bill 2012 (Brk)

Sentencing Act 2002 (Brk)

Sentencing and Parole Reform Act 2010 (Brk)

UNITED KINGDOM

Anti-terrorism, Crime and Security Act 2001 (Stern)

Bill of Rights 1689 (Fr)

Crime and Disorder Act 1998 (Gl)

Crime (Sentences) Act 1997 (Gl)

Criminal Lunatics Act 1800 (Lo)

Criminal Justice Act 2003 (Stern, Gl)

Criminal Justice Act 2005 (Brk)

Criminal Justice and Court Services Act 2000 (Gl)

Criminal Justice and Immigration Act 2008 (Stern, Gl)

Criminal Justice and Police Act 2001 (Gl)

Criminal Procedure (Insanity) Act 1964 (Gl)

Criminal Procedure (Insanity and Unfitness to Plead) Act 1991 (Gl)

Firearms Act 1968 (Gl)

Football Spectators Act 1989 (Gl)

Habeas Corpus Act 1679 (Fr)

Habeas Corpus Act 1816 (Fr)

Human Rights Act 1998 (Stern, Fr)

Legal Aid, Sentencing and Punishment of Offenders Act 2012 (Stern, Brk, Gl)

Mental Health Act 1983 (Gl)

Mental Health Act 2007 (Gl)

Murder (Abolition of Death Penalty) Act 1965 (Gl)

Offences Against the Person Act 1861 (Gl)

Prevention of Terrorism Act 2005 (Stern, Wel)

Serious Crime Act 2007 (Gl)

Serious Organised Crime and Police Act 2005 (Gl)

Sexual Offences Act 1956 (Gl)

Terrorism Prevention and Investigative Measures Act 2011 (Stern)

Violent Crime Reduction Act 2006 (Gl)

UNITED STATES

Prison Litigation Reform Act 1995 (Fr)
United States Bill of Rights 1791 (Fr)
United States Constitution (Fr)

LIST OF CONTRIBUTORS

Benedict Bartl developed an interest in preventive detention whilst living in Germany between 2009 and 2012. During his time in Germany he volunteered for the European Center for Constitutional and Human Rights representing suspected terrorists in their attempts to be removed from the United Nations 'black list'. Whilst in Germany Benedict undertook a Masters in Law at the Free University, Germany of which preventive detention was one of his areas of interest. Benedict is now working as a solicitor at a community legal centre in Hobart, Tasmania.

Dr Astrid Birgden has worked for 25 years developing policy and managing services to coerced clients in disability services and corrections – primarily serious/high risk offenders. Between 2006 and 2011 she established and managed the Compulsory Drug Treatment Correctional Centre in Sydney. Recently she has joined a European Union funded Torture Prevention Research Project and will be developing a training package to be delivered by a military expert to police/military personnel in Sri Lanka and Nepal. She is published in offender rehabilitation, therapeutic jurisprudence and human rights.

Professor Warren Brookbanks is a professor of law at the University of Auckland Law School. His principal research areas are criminal law, mental health law and therapeutic jurisprudence. He has published widely in these and related areas. In his writing he has also surveyed the challenges of "anticipatory containment" and sexual predator legislation, measures imposed after the expiry of a penal sentence. More recent writing has dealt with issues around unfitness to stand trial.

Professor Andrew Coyle is Emeritus Professor of Prison Studies in the University of London and Visiting Professor in the University of Essex. He was Director of the International Centre for Prison Studies between 1997 and 2005 and again from 2010 until 2011. He previously worked at a senior level in the prison services of the United Kingdom. He is an adviser on prison issues to a number of intergovernmental bodies, including the United Nations, the Inter American Commission on Human Rights and the Council of Europe. Professor Coyle was one of the main drafters of the European Prison Rules (2006) and of the Council of Europe Code of Ethics for Prison Staff (2011). His books include *A Human Rights Approach to Prison Management, Managing Prisons in a Time of Change* and *The Prisons We Deserve*.

Professor Ian Coyle has a PhD in psychopharmacology from La Trobe University in Victoria, and has been giving expert evidence in Australian superior courts for thirty years. He has researched and published widely in the fields of human factors engineering, psychology and psychopharmacology. He is an accredited expert in Medico-Legal Psychology to the International Criminal Court and a Professorial Associate in the Centre of Law Governance and Public Policy.

Professor Ian Freckelton SC is a Senior Counsel in Victoria and a Professor of Law, Forensic Medicine and Forensic Psychology at Monash University. Ian has written extensively about habeas corpus, involuntary detention and false imprisonment. As counsel, he has appeared in many high profile cases in relation to inappropriate deprivation of liberty. Ian is Editor-in-Chief of Psychiatry, *Psychology and Law*.

Kris Gledhill developed an appellate criminal and public law practice as a barrister in England, which included numerous appearances in precedent setting cases in the European Court of Human Rights, the House of Lords and the Court of Appeal; he also sat as a Tribunal Judge on mental health cases. Kris taught extensively on continuing professional education courses in the UK; he had in the past been engaged as a tutor at SOAS, UCL and University College Oxford and as a part-time lecturer at the London School of Law and had been involved in an online mental health law course with the New York Law School. Kris came to New Zealand in 2006, initially to take a PhD; he accepted a lectureship at Auckland University Law School from the start of 2007. As of 1 January 2012, Kris is the inaugural Director of the New Zealand Centre for Human Rights Law, Policy and Practice.

Dr Brendan Gogarty is a public lawyer and lecturer at the University of Tasmania where he teaches constitutional law, privacy and technology law. Brendan has a particular research interest in judicial independence. In 2010 he was a visiting scholar at the Minerva Research Group on Judicial Independence, Max Planck Institute for Comparative Public Law and International Law in Heidelberg where he undertook comparative work on judicial independence in the European Union and Australia. His recent work with co-author Ben Bartl explores the tension between judicial independence and preventive detention.

Dr Robert Halon is an independent clinical and forensic psychologist in practice on the Central Coast of California. He has written about, consulted and/or testified in most areas related to the interaction of psychology and criminal, civil and domestic/family Law, from the impact of interview techniques on the reliability of children's responses and narratives to sentencing issues in capital murder. He is a fellow and advisory board member of the American College of Forensic Psychology and regularly presents on issues related to the integration of Psychology and Law; a primary focus of all his work. He is co-author (M. B. First,

M.D.), of "The Use of DSM Paraphilia Diagnosis in Sexually Violent Predator Commitment Cases", the first publication (2008) to identify and fully explain the error "or behaviors" in the diagnostic criteria for the paraphilias that made its first appearance in version IV of the DSM (1994). His research on the use of the MCMI-III in child custody cases led to description and explanation (2001) of how the internal structure of the inventory and its scoring combined to create significant problems related to over-pathologizing.

Professor Patrick Keyzer is Director of the Centre for Law, Governance and Public Policy at Bond University in Queensland, Australia. Patrick holds a PhD in Law from the University of Sydney and is a lawyer with 20 years experience, particularly in the provision of advice to prisoners, people with disabilities and indigenous Australians. He prepared two communications to the United Nations Human Rights Committee that settled international standards relating to post-sentence preventive detention (*Fardon v Australia* and *Tillman v Australia*). Keyzer's books that consider the topic of preventive detention include Offshore *Processing of Asylum Seekers: The Search for Legitimate Parameters* (2007, with Sam Blay and Jennifer Burn), *Sex Offenders and Preventive Detention: Politics, Policy and Practice* (2009, with Bernadette McSherry), and *Dangerous People* (2011, also with Bernadette McSherry).

Dr Arlie Loughnan is ARC Postdoctoral Research Fellow in the Faculty of Law, University of Sydney. She is the author of *Manifest Madness: Mental Incapacity in Criminal Law* (OUP, 2012), which provides a socio-historical study of the relationship between legal doctrines, practices and knowledge about mental incapacity in criminal law. Her interest in preventative detention relates to the treatment of mentally disordered offenders, and the legal and social construction of ideas of 'dangerousness' and 'abnormality'.

Dr Sabine Selchow is London School of Economics Fellow in the Civil Society and Human Security Research Unit at the Department of International Development at the London School of Economics and Political Science (LSE). She is core researcher in the 5-year-research-programmes "Security in Transition" (grant holder: Professor Mary Kaldor) and "Methodological Cosmopolitanism – In the Laboratory of Climate Change" (grant holder: Professor Ulrich Beck). Both programmes are funded by the European Research Council (ERC).

Professor Christopher Slobogin has authored more than 100 articles, books and chapters on topics relating to criminal procedure, mental health law and evidence. Named Director of Vanderbilt Law School's Criminal Justice Program in 2009, Professor Slobogin is one of the 10 most cited criminal law and procedure law professors in the nation, according to the Leiter Report. The book Psychological Evaluations for the Courts, which he co-authored with another lawyer and two psychologists, is considered the standard-bearer in forensic mental health; in recognition for his work in that field, he was named an honorary distinguished member of the American Psychology-Law Society in 2008. Professor Slobogin has also served as reporter for the American Bar Association's Task Force on Law Enforcement and Technology and its Task Force on the Insanity Defense, chair of the Florida Assessment Team for the ABA's Death Penalty Moratorium Implementation Project, and co-reporter for standards dealing with mental disability and the death penalty that have been adopted by the ABA, the American Psychiatric Association and the American Psychological Association. Professor Slobogin holds a secondary appointment as a professor in the Vanderbilt School of Medicine's Department of Psychiatry.

Baroness Vivien Stern has been a Crossbench (independent) member of the House of Lords since 1999 and was a member of the Parliamentary Joint Committee on Human Rights from 2004 to 2008. From 1999 to 2003 she was a member of the House of Lords European Select Committee. In 2010 she became a member of the Joint Committee on Statutory Instruments. She chairs the All Party Parliamentary Group on the Abolition of the Death Penalty. In September 2009 she was appointed by the UK Government to lead a review of how rape complaints are handled from when a rape is first disclosed until the court reaches a verdict and the Review was published in March 2010. She is a Visiting Professor at the University of Essex and has Honorary degrees from Bristol, Oxford Brookes, Stirling, Glasgow and Edinburgh Universities and is an Honorary Fellow of the London School of Economics. She is a Trustee of the Civil Liberties Trust and the International Centre for Prison Studies, and a member of the Advisory Council of the International Legal Foundation in New York, and the Advisory Council of the Legal Policy Research Centre in Kazakhstan. She is also Honorary President of Penal Reform International (PRI), a non-governmental organisation promoting penal reform throughout the world which she founded with others in 1989. From 2003 to 2009 she was the Convenor of the Scottish Consortium on Crime and Criminal Justice. She is Patron of the Alternatives to Violence Project, the Venture Trust, Clean Break (the theatre company set up by, and for, women prisoners), Amicus (assisting lawyers for Justice on Death Row in the United States), the Alternatives to Violence Project, the Havens (London's Sexual Assault Referral Centres) and the United Kingdom Network of Sex Worker Projects.

Rebecca Welsh is a doctoral candidate, sessional lecturer and research associate at the University of New South Wales Faculty of Law Sydney, where she is a member of the Australian Research Council Laureate Project: 'Anti-Terror Laws and the Democratic Challenge'. Rebecca's doctoral research concerns the challenge to judicial independence posed by control orders and preventive detention under Australia's anti-terror laws. Rebecca has spoken at conferences in Australia, Europe and the Americas on anti-terror and constitutional law topics, and has been published in a number of academic journals. Prior to commencing her doctorate Rebecca held positions as a litigator and with the Federal Attorney-General's Department.